For Margaret Busby CBE,
pathfinder publisher and inspirational friend

*'It's astonishing what you can do,
when you don't mind who gets the credit.'*

**Margaret Busby quoting Harry S. Truman
on *Desert Island Discs*, BBC Radio 4, January 2022**

Witness in a Time of Turmoil

About the Author

Ian Mayes was the Guardian's first readers' editor and during his decade in the role became president of the international Organization of News Ombudsmen. The wry humour which marked many of his Guardian corrections gained him a cult following; the serious side of the role had a wide-ranging influence at home and abroad.

He first wrote for the Guardian's arts pages as a freelance in 1962. He joined the staff of the paper in 1987 after working in regional journalism and then for BBC radio news. He returned to print journalism for the brief life of Robert Maxwell's London Daily News.

At the Guardian he was involved with Alan Rusbridger in the launching of Guardian Weekend and G2, subsequently becoming arts editor and obituaries editor. He concluded his full-time career with the paper as an associate editor.

While readers' editor he was instrumental in the restoration of William Hazlitt's grave in Soho, and the founding of the Hazlitt Society. He began work on the history in 2007.

Witness in a Time of Turmoil

Inside the Guardian's Global Revolution

Volume One: 1986–1995

Ian Mayes

guardianbooks

Published by Guardian Books 2025

2 4 6 8 10 9 7 5 3 1

First published in Great Britain in 2025 by
Guardian Books
Kings Place, 90 York Way
London N1 9GU

A CIP catalogue record for this book is available from the British Library

ISBN 978-1-916204-76-8

Cover design by Guardian News & Media Ltd
Typeset by seagulls.net

Printed and bound in Great Britain by
CPI Group (UK) Ltd, Croydon CR0 4YY

Printed and bound in the UK on FSC© certified paper
in line with our continuing commitment to ethical
business practices, sustainability and the environment.

Our authorised representative in the EEA is
eucomply OÜ, Pärnu mnt 139b-14, 11317 Tallinn, Estonia
hello@eucompliancepartner.com

The **Contents**

Introduction   1

1. Sedimentary: The Making of the Modern Guardian   5
2. Preston's Paper: From Insouciance to Mortal Combat   20
3. A Great Editor in His Element   40
4. Turmoil in the Newsroom and a Shock Departure   51
5. The Radical Redesign of 1988   68
6. The Changing Agenda   79
7. The New Look Guardian and the Birth of Weekend   90
8. A Beeline to Beijing   103
9. The Shock of the New   110
10. Ethical Issues as the Correspondent Dies   124
11. Europe and Journalism Without Borders   139
12. A Post-prandial Nap and a Rude Awakening   155
13. Comment, Cartoons and a Touch of Poetry   166
14. A Tale of Two Exiles in a Time of Turmoil   176
15. War over Kuwait: A Lion Among the Gazelles   185
16. Order, Disorder and the Message from Mesopotamia   199
17. The Guide: A Little Thing That Meant a Lot and Led to More   214
18. 'Small but Perfectly Informed': The Birth of G2   225
19. Witnesses to War in Europe   236
20. The Price of Journalism   250
21. The Observer: A Marriage, but No Honeymoon   259
22. Teething Troubles – And a Painful Extraction   269
23. A Direct Hit on the Guardian's 'Agent Ron'   284
24. Heat, Dust and Death on the Books Pages   293
25. Changing of the Guard   300

Notes   313
Select Bibliography   327
Acknowledgements   329
Picture Credits   332
Index   333

Introduction

'There is no period so remote as the recent past.'

Alan Bennett[1]

In the relatively short span of Volumes 1 and 2 of this book, roughly three decades, the Guardian, in what at first may have seemed to be extravagant ambition, laid convincing claim to the title 'the world's leading liberal voice'. In an act of transformation - a word that was actually written into the job description of at least one senior editorial executive - what in 1986 was still a one-section black and white newspaper that ritually inked the fingers of its readers became a Pulitzer-prize-winning global media organisation reaching many millions daily through a website frequently judged the best of its kind in the world. By the end of the main period covered here, the Guardian had substantial editorial and commercial web operations based not only in Britain, but also in the United States and Australia, and it had an eye on similar developments elsewhere. But the speed with which a bleak new global economic context for the industry challenged the Guardian's aspirations would provide a shocking reminder of the volatility of the market.

The paper, let us call it, lived through the period covered here in a state of continuous and sometimes hair-raising revolution, unprecedented in its long history. Change, someone quipped, had become the new status quo.

The period of the two volumes of this book falls entirely within the editorships of two modernising but very different editors, Peter Preston and Alan Rusbridger. The first, the consummate newspaperman, was to be the last person to edit the Guardian simply as a printed paper, the circulation of which peaked at record levels under his innovatory regime. Near the point of handover, Preston was twice voted the editors' editor in successive polls of his peers. The other, a visionary editor with a particularly quick apprehension of the new world opened out by the internet and the development of digital technology, seized the opportunity to develop a huge global following for the Guardian's brand of public service journalism. He did that at a time when the long-term survival of printed newspapers was increasingly being called into question. The sensational way in which he did this would add to the Guardian's great many prizes during his tenure, culminating uniquely in a Pulitzer Prize in the most prestigious of its forms for journalism for its 'disinterested' and meritorious 'public service' – words that would have warmed the cockles of its Unitarian founders' hearts.

The book opens with the Guardian, like the rest of Fleet Street, already in the midst of the greatest technological revolution in print since Gutenberg introduced moveable type in the 15th century. The end of hot metal and its replacement with computerised methods of typesetting and printing were clearly just a beginning. In the years that followed, covered within this volume, both the character and the ambition of the Guardian were tested. In the success with which it faced these challenges it sometimes seemed to have surprised itself. It fought off competition from the new Independent (launched in 1986); it went through the most radical redesign in its history up to that point (1988); it acquired the Observer, the world's oldest Sunday newspaper (1993), saving it from almost certain extinction; and, as it grappled with the considerable difficulties that followed the purchase of a great but ailing Sunday paper, it stood firm for several years against a vicious price war (instigated in 1993) in an important statement of principle.

In the second volume, we take up the story from the beginning of Rusbridger's editorship in 1995 to the Guardian's move to Kings Place 13 years later, a period that coincided with several enormous upheavals: a bold – and controversially costly – format change for the printed paper set against a backdrop of plummeting newspaper circulation; a revolutionary shift towards digitisation; and a series of labyrinthine libel actions that were brought against the paper in the 1990s, to name just three.

Both volumes of this book will seek to show that, as change followed change, the Guardian amply justified its purpose. Its journalism continued to be pursued in print and online with great courage and conviction, exploiting all the new means that digital technology provided as they became available. In a sense it was independent of them. It continued to speak truth to power, and it is the tacit argument of this book that it continued to be true to itself, 'to carry on as heretofore', in the words of the only instruction traditionally given to Guardian editors.

The present book is the successor to two previous 'official' volumes of Guardian history, the first by David Ayerst and the second by Geoffrey Taylor (although the excellent 1921 centenary essay by William Haslam Mills is not to be overlooked).[2] This book is primarily an account of the recent years of the Guardian, told wherever possible in the words of its protagonists. But there is necessarily a great deal here about the Observer and the travails in its recent history, by no means all of which developed after 1993 when it was 'rescued' by the Guardian Media Group, although it is with this later period that the book is mainly concerned. The Observer is an older paper than the Guardian. They both have radical roots and proud histories. They were both born in revolutionary times. They are both bastions of liberal journalism. It was supposed to be, in the words of one of the Observer's champions, Anthony Sampson, 'a marriage made in heaven'. Instead, what the two volumes of this book relates is the story of, put mildly, a difficult and sometimes dysfunctional relationship, which eventually reached a workable accommodation.

If the realities of the Guardian and Observer relationship proved more difficult than anticipated, the stresses to which the Guardian alone was exposed as it faced an uncertain future, for most of the time accompanied by alarmingly mounting losses, should also be borne in mind as individual conflicts are recounted. Various attempts were made to illustrate the task that the Guardian faced during these years: it was like the manoeuvre to turn round a giant tanker in heavy seas; it was like an attempt to sustain an ocean liner in an age of jet travel. They are both inadequate to describe the reality of a task undertaken amid continuously and unpredictably changing circumstances.

There remains nothing passive about the Guardian's journalism nor about the reaction that it prompts. It has made a virtue of being open to criticism: since 1997 the paper has had what the author Giles Foden described as 'the revolutionary presence' of an independent readers' editor[3] to deal publicly with specific complaints and comments, a system that it became the present author's task to inaugurate. The open relationship with readers that this betokens, something also reflected in the development of the membership scheme for readers promoted with passion and urgency under the current editor Katharine Viner, is a product of the freedom and independence that those inside the Guardian have continued to enjoy.

There is no attempt here at a comprehensive summary of the entire history of the Guardian. The paper's last historian, Geoffrey Taylor (who died as the present book was nearing completion), brought the story of the Guardian nominally up to 1988, the year of the radical redesign at the hands of David Hillman and Pentagram. In dealing with the great developments of that time, Taylor was handicapped, so to speak, by proximity. The starting point here, therefore, is 1986, the year of Rupert Murdoch's strategic flight to Wapping and the birth of the Independent; the end of the second volume takes us up to 2008, the point at which the Guardian finally vacated the Farringdon Road offices it had inhabited for over 30 years.

By the end of the period covered by both volumes, it appeared that the Guardian had broken through into what at last promised to be a period of financial stability - a hope that was punctured just a few years later when changes in the pattern of internet advertising again appeared to threaten its very foundations. As all new editors-in-chief of the Guardian have discovered, one thing that can be guaranteed, it seems, is a bumpy ride.

Chapter 1

Sedimentary: The Making of the Modern Guardian

'Character ... is the slow deposit of past actions and ideals.'

CP Scott[1]

Roughly once a month for many years, a remarkable gathering of Guardian alumni - the word is derived from the Latin *to nourish* - would meet in the drab conviviality of an upper room at the Gay Hussar in Greek Street, Soho, and tuck into a robust Hungarian lunch.[2] There, working steadily through the smoked sausage, the chilled wild cherry soup, the veal goulash with galuska, might be found on average 20 or so journalists who, from the middle of the 20th century to the very recent past, covered the world for readers of the Guardian, reporting riots, revolutions, famines, wars and natural disasters, recording, and now and again contributing to, great social changes. Well into the second decade of the 21st century, these gatherings were organised by the Guardian's former literary editor, WL (Bill) Webb, a sometimes-quixotic standard-bearer for the word, and himself an engaging writer. He had believed so passionately in the value of world literature, especially from the censored sources of eastern Europe during the Cold War, that he had been known to reduce the type-size of a review progressively rather than cut it.[3]

The Guardian was and remained at core a 'writer's paper'. Journalists entering the Guardian of its great editor Charles Prestwich 'CP' Scott, 100 to 150 years ago, did not have to 'surrender all individuality' as they supposedly did when joining the Times. Many would maintain that Alistair Cooke's assertion of more than 50 years ago remains essentially true today: 'Within the severe limits of the modern, snappy daily, the

5

Guardian has recruited and encouraged more "personal journalists" who feel with less triteness, think with more clarity, and so write better than the staff of any other daily I know.'[4] How far that still stands as a description of the Guardian is best left for the reader to judge.

But if the Guardian is still a writer's paper it has become much more. Today, it is also a photographer's paper, a graphic artist's paper, a film-maker's paper, a broadcaster's paper, and it is a gatherer, processor and elucidator of great masses of data.[5] In the relatively short period with which this book mainly deals several of those functions have come to describe the same person, as the definition of journalist has changed to accommodate all the new means now available. In 2013, when the Guardian decided to invite six aspiring 'digital journalists' to join it for a year, the editor-in-chief's announcement said, 'Applicants must have proven experience in digital journalism (which might include blogging, social media, multimedia or coding) and a passion for pursuing a digital media career.' Nowhere was the word 'paper' mentioned.[6]

In this shifting context, the Guardian's journalism has thrived in a quite extraordinary way. Its journalism ranges wider in style and content than ever before, and it has become a reader's 'paper' in a participatory and collaborative sense and with a global readership on a scale beyond imagining when the older members of the Gay Hussar fraternity were fresh and avid in the 1950s. Some of them started when the paper, still under newsprint rationing introduced in the Second World War, was a mere four or six pages with a rising circulation striving to reach 100,000. It was still a one-section black and white broadsheet paper in 1986, the beginning of the period covered by this book.

The Gay Hussar was an appropriate meeting place. It had become a haunt of leftwing politicians and journalists almost as soon as its doors opened in the early 1950s, with Aneurin Bevan and Michael Foot among the regulars. It was particularly favoured by the Guardian, becoming almost an extension of the office for the political staff, led by John Cole and Ian Aitken. Aitken began using it while the bloom was still on the décor, in 1954, when working for Tribune a decade before he joined the Guardian. By the time he began his 15 years as political editor of the paper in 1975, the Gay Hussar had long been the favoured venue for the senior staff meetings of Alastair Hetherington, an editor of inspirational frugality: no gravy train ran in his province.

The Gay Hussar was the natural choice of venue when Bill Webb came to organise his lunches. With due respect to its kitchen, the principal reason for these meetings was always the nourishment to be derived from each other's company rather than the plate. But although nostalgia was practically an item on the menu, current news was always a part of the diet for a group so long concerned with what one Guardian historian had called the commotion of human affairs.[7] Very few of those assembled ever seemed to have fully retired in any conventional sense. Books, fiction and non-fiction, articles, lectures, blogs, continued to flow in abundance: pensions were augmented by numerous consultancies. An octogenarian among them, a former motorcycling news editor, would occasionally share her terse thoughts about the paper's current performance on Twitter[8] even before the paper itself had seriously explored its potential as an essential tool of the trade. Much might be concluded about the vitality of an organisation from the activity of its staff after they have retired from it.

Typically, the members of the Gay Hussar crowd were among the most keenly critical and proprietorial readers of the Guardian in a generally proprietorial readership, always hungry for the latest intelligence from colleagues who had recently left. 'What news on the Regent's Canal?', the muddy channel on which the present Guardian stands, was an ever-present question in the years immediately following the move to Kings Place in 2008, asked with an extra anxiety as the global financial crisis quickly claimed more than 200 redundancies among the Guardian and Observer and indeed put the Observer's existence in question. Still more voluntary redundancies were sought in 2011 and 2012 and the paper entered 2013 with conflict looming over the possibility of compulsory redundancies, narrowly avoided. Whether the Guardian, like Antonio's ships, would weather the storm and 'richly come to harbour' seemed uncertain to say the least. But in March 2014 when the Guardian Media Group's 51% share in the Trader Media Group was sold for £609m it did begin to look at last as though the Guardian's ships were indeed coming home. Dame Elizabeth (Liz) Forgan, the chair of the Scott Trust, felt able to announce, 'The unique contribution made by the Guardian to national and international debate is now secure for generations to come.' Within two years this confident assertion seemed more than a little optimistic.

Like all newspapers of any age, the Guardian had survived a succession of life-threatening crises: an early one followed the death in

7

1905 of John Edward Taylor the second, the son of the founder, who became possibly the wealthiest person ever directly associated with the Guardian. His death prompted an ownership crisis eventually resolved with the purchase of the paper by his cousin CP Scott (who had by then been editing it for almost 34 years). The acquisition was helped by other members of the Scott family, including CP Scott's extraordinary elder philanthropic sisters, Catherine and Isabella. Had it not been for what Ayerst called 'the solidarity of this Victorian family', the Guardian would have passed into other hands.[9] It was this Taylor who in his will expressed the desire that successive editors should conduct the paper 'on the same lines and in the same spirit as heretofore'. 'In other words,' said CP's grandson Richard Scott, 'he hoped that its radical views and its independence and integrity would be maintained and that this would be regarded as the paramount concern of those who controlled it.' By the time of Taylor's death it was Scott more than anyone who had given the paper the qualities Taylor wished to see perpetuated. These 'sacred words', said David Ayerst, came to mean that the Guardian should be continued 'at the same level as in CP's time', as an independent, progressive paper of international standing.[10]

To understand this crisis of succession that followed Taylor's death is to make more understandable another event, even more remarkable and still unique in the history of newspapers in Britain - the creation of the Scott Trust in 1936, an act of extraordinary generosity and commitment. In creating the Trust the members of the Scott family divested themselves of all 'beneficial interest' in the paper, that is all personal financial interest except for the relatively modest salaries of those family members employed in it. In doing that they recognised and endorsed Scott's higher purpose for the Manchester Guardian as a public service. Death duties, magnified by an extraordinary sequence of events, had threatened the Guardian's existence on this occasion. CP Scott, having handed the reins to his son Edward (Ted) in 1929 - although whether he ever let go completely is an arguable point - finally died in January 1932. In the spring of the same year, Ted Scott was drowned while trying to swim ashore after a sudden squall upset the boat in which he was sailing on Windermere with his son Richard, who was then 17. Richard was able to clamber on to the upturned boat and survive to become the saviour of the Guardian in a later crisis in the 1960s, this one well within the memory of many of the Gay Hussar diners.

These two deaths left CP Scott's surviving son, Ted's elder brother, John Russell Scott, as the sole proprietor of the paper. He is one of the undersung heroes of the Guardian. He worked for the Guardian from 1902 for more than four decades, a servant of the paper. As the senior manager he had been adept at guiding the Manchester Guardian through rough weather. On his death in 1949 one of his former Guardian colleagues, Sir William Haley, by that time director general of the BBC, and later to become editor of the Times, recalled, 'If you expressed your pleasure in working for him he would quietly correct it to the fact that you worked *with* him and *for* the papers' (plural: the other one at that time being the Manchester Evening News).[11]

In this light it becomes less surprising that the Trust was John Scott's creation. It was his declining health that prompted the replacement of the 1936 Trust with a new one in 1948. There was a significant difference between the two. Under the first, John Scott had retained the right to appoint the trustees, and therefore the absolute control he had had as the sole proprietor. Under the new trust of 1948 he ceded the right to appoint trustees to the trustees themselves and with it, inevitably, the ultimate control of the company. From that point on the Guardian really did have no proprietor in the conventional sense, or rather it had a genuinely collective one in the shape of the self-perpetuating trust. As Ayerst explained: 'The Scotts had secured the life of their paper by disinheriting themselves. The paper really did come first ... The Scott Trust is a personal gift to the public comparable with other great benefactions.'[12]

Here again, CP Scott had pointed the way. As one commentator has put it, 'Scott was not interested in making money.'[13] An often-overlooked point in Scott's famous centenary essay is the revelation that first and foremost he regarded himself as 'a member of the working-staff'. The Manchester Guardian as Scott had developed it, although he wanted it to pay its way - an ambition that in modern times has seldom been realised - was meant to be a public service. But beyond that, Scott encouraged his staff to think of it as 'an organ of civilisation'.[14] Few editors would use such a phrase today without any touch of irony or self-consciousness. But, deep down, Scott's successors as editor of the Guardian have probably all believed it to be true.

In the end it was the thought of losing the liberal identity that owed so much to Scott, and to his Unitarian forebears, that pulled the paper back from the brink of disaster in the mid-1960s. It led the Trust, under the chairmanship of CP's grandson, Richard Scott, the survivor of Windermere, to reject the idea of merging with the Times at a time when the heavy losses that had accompanied the Guardian's phased move from Manchester to London threatened to sink the ship.[15] The bold decision to reject the merger and weather the storm was one of the fine achievements of Alastair Hetherington's editorship. Perhaps the words of CP Scott, spoken 40 years earlier, expressing concern about the loss of independent newspapers to larger commercial groups, came to mind. 'There are newspapers which will never be sold, which would rather suffer extinction.'[16] Many of those latterly gathered at the Gay Hussar could vividly recall that particular crisis, among them Hetherington's successor Peter Preston, who had been on the Guardian for only three years when it happened. The experience of that time was a formative one for him.

No existing newspaper in Britain has a history more relevant to its present than the Guardian. There is a very strong sense of continuity that has become more important as the pace of change has accelerated. In recent years you might have met at table at the Gay Hussar a journalist or two who had joined the Guardian when the front page was still entirely taken up by advertisements, which did not give way to news until 1952. That was when the Gothic 'Black Letter' masthead, variations of which had served since the beginning in 1821, was finally abandoned and the words Manchester Guardian appeared in all the modern clear elegance of Eric Gill's Perpetua. The reader's letter chosen to lead a page of responses to those changes had a condemnatory and now familiar ring: 'It is a great pity to see the Guardian trying to follow in the footsteps of the sensational press.'

The editor then was Alfred Powell Wadsworth – Waddy to Hetherington and the rest of his colleagues (but more often AP) – who had joined the Manchester Guardian in 1917 to become a significant figure on CP Scott's staff. This most scholarly of Guardian editors is the only modern editor of the paper not to have gone to university, his trajectory having been checked by an inebriate father. He left school at 14 with what Scott would have called an 'untrained intelligence', and came to the Manchester Guardian via his hometown paper, the Rochdale Observer. At that time Scott himself, born in 1846, had been editor for a mere 45 years – and still had 12 years to run, a record unlikely ever to be broken. Before editing the paper himself, from 1944 to 1956, Wadsworth served under two more editors - CP's son Ted, the one who was drowned on Windermere after only a brief tenure, and William Crozier, a classicist, who had been on the paper for 28 years before he became editor. Crozier edited the paper with selfless distinction from 1932 to 1944, the last of those years through a long period of illness. He deserves a better press than he has sometimes received. He had been a schoolmaster and a certain pedantry under-pinned his journalism. As news editor he had been a fastidious scourge of writers and sub-editors. As editor he brought a modern logic to the organisation of pages according to categories; he began to separate home and foreign news, for example.

John Douglas Pringle, who served as a leader writer under both Crozier and Wadsworth, remembered him thus: 'In some ways Crozier was not an easy man to know or to like. There was something chilling, particularly for young men, in his Puritanism - he never drank himself and thought that we should not drink either - his intellectual austerity, his apparent lack of human passions and human sympathies. Yet I grew to admire both the firm grip of his mind on the great political issues of those years and the enviable lucidity with which he wrote about them ... If the Manchester Guardian was in those years the leading anti-Nazi paper in Britain, both in its news and in its policies, this was mainly due to Crozier.'[17]

Pringle thought him perhaps a better writer than either CP Scott or Crozier's successor, AP Wadsworth,[18] 'the immortal Wadsworth',[19] as Alistair Cooke called him. Pringle and a colleague, Teddy (EC) Hodgkin, used to amuse themselves penning portraits of senior staff in the style of Balliol rhymes. Thus Crozier: 'I am the editor: come in./ I hope that bottle isn't gin./ Let us give credit where it's due/ To everyone except to you.' And on Wadsworth: 'I am little APW;/ I don't really want to trouble you./ But will you please just alter that,/ And that, and that, and that and that?'

The historian AJP Taylor was in no doubt about Crozier's qualities: he called him 'a great editor'.[20] No paper paid closer attention to the rise of Fascism in Italy, the ascent of Nazism in Germany and the accom-panying persecution of Jews, than Crozier's Guardian, which in this respect, according to an Israeli historian, 'stood in a class by itself'.[21] In fact, both Crozier and JR Scott were on Hitler's death-list, so that when a German invasion threatened, an escape plan had been devised for both of them. Almost unbelievably – but it is true – an emerald necklace had been purchased to finance their escape, and JR Scott and Haley, as the senior management figures, took it in turns to carry it with them.[22]

Change was accelerating. It was under Wadsworth, by then a respected historian of the Lancashire cotton trade,[23] that the great Manchester paper employed its last cotton correspondent in Harry Whewell who joined the Guardian in 1950, by which time the trade had long dwindled to a mere shadow of its former self. The paper was then gaunt with post-war news-print rationing, which still had several years to run. Whewell recalled, 'Everything you wrote was cut to the bone. We had a word for it – tersid, a combination of terse and lucid.' As the paper shortage continued, '[Wadsworth] had to make the hard choice of giving up the Guardian's position as a great provincial paper or of abandoning its role as a national and international reporter – there was simply not enough paper to do both. He rightly decided to sacrifice his beloved Lancashire'.[24]

Matthew Engel, writing in the 175th anniversary issue of the Guardian, while welcoming the expansion of the Guardian's universe – *Urbi et Orbi*, he pronounced – that had enabled it to compete with the London papers, deplored the price that it had had to pay. 'One of its characteristics over the past quarter-century has been to pay more atten-tion to its branches than its roots, and the decline of its northern base has been one of its failures.'[25] Alan Rusbridger, the new editor of the Guardian at that time, may have taken Engel's message to heart. Several years later he made a brave, if not wholly successful, attempt to relieve the paper's beleaguered northern outpost, with the launch of a dedicated edition, Guardian North. But Rusbridger probably expressed the true legacy the Guardian derived from its northern origins when he wrote in December that year, 'The paper started as The Manchester Guardian – an outsider to the sometimes cosy world of Fleet Street. Though it has long since dropped "Manchester" from its masthead, its mentality is still that of the outsider.'[26] In fact the Guardian has been an outsider since birth: the Unitarians who founded it were regarded as outsiders, not only by the Anglican church and the great universities, but even by members of the other dissenting denominations.

Those members of the Gay Hussar fraternity who started their careers under Wadsworth or in the very early years of Hetherington's editorship worked with people who had worked with CP Scott. Three of

Scott's grandsons were employed by the Guardian when Hetherington took over. A newcomer to the gathering at the Gay Hussar in, say 2008, the year the Guardian moved to Kings Place, was still therefore only two handshakes away from CP Scott, if that is not too fanciful an idea. There might be present several who had joined before the umbilical word Manchester was cut from the title in 1959 - it had been the Manchester Guardian since the first issue, having come out on the day Napoleon died in 1821.

It was not uncommon for there to be a majority who had served under the editorship of Alastair Hetherington (1956-1975), an editor who became immediately famous for his forthright condemnation of the invasion of Suez, a statement of the paper's controversial belief that criticism of a war in which British forces were involved should not necessarily be stifled once a conflict was in progress. Hetherington took over as Wadsworth lay dying and there were bedside conferences until his last days. Hetherington's leader condemning the 'folly' of Eden's adventure represented at that point the vanguard of liberal opinion and his words still have a powerful resonance: '[The government's] action in attacking Egypt is a disaster of the first magnitude. It is wrong on every count - moral, military and political.'[27] His stand on Suez may have cost the paper some readers, and some advertisers,[28] although on nothing like the scale inflicted in response to CP Scott's opposition to the Boer War, when the paper lost one-seventh of its readers.

It was the Manchester Guardian's opposition to the South African war, more than any other event up to the end of the 19th century, that had confirmed its standing abroad, enabling devotees to call it the provincial paper with an international reputation. But it was the move of its headquarters from Manchester to London under Hetherington that extended its reach in Britain and enabled it to strengthen its status as a national paper. It remains the only regional paper to have made that journey, from the provinces to the metropolis (a word banned by CP Scott) and nationwide sales.

It was also Hetherington who had, with just a twinge of guilt, confirmed the Gay Hussar as an annexe of the Guardian when he began to use it regularly for his senior staff meetings. In 1963, in an attempt to recreate something of the 'collegiate atmosphere' of the Guardian's Manchester home in Cross Street, he had introduced regular open meetings in the new offices in Gray's Inn Road. They were held in Hetherington's office, sometimes with 35 or more people crammed in to discuss a wide range of topics over 'a woefully inadequate sandwich lunch'. Hetherington found them 'entertaining but diffuse' and usually inconclusive. 'I therefore devised a tighter gathering, with never more than 12 present and a proper lunch - usually in a top-floor room at the Gay Hussar, in Soho, where no more than 12 could sit round the table. These were the real policy seminars of the senior staff between 1970 and 1975, and invaluable to me.' And then the twinge of guilt: 'The proper lunch, let it be said, was in recognition that some of us would afterwards be working right through to 1am or later without leaving the office, and it was a blessed relief after those dreadful sandwiches.'[29]

Several of those at lunch in the Gay Hussar had in fact previously worked in Cross Street, the Manchester home of the paper from 1886 until it was usurped, although not totally, by the transfer of the head office to London in 1964. Some editorial operations lingered on in Manchester - the features and foreign departments and the office of the literary editor - long after the building was finally vacated on the move to nearby Deansgate in 1970.

After the Guardian's move to London, Cross Street remained a pungent memory for all who had worked there. For Nicholas Dallman, crossing the Pennines from Yorkshire in 1959 to join the subs' table, the contrast was striking: 'If the Sheffield Telegraph was a bawdy house, the subs room at Cross Street was a cathedral side chapel where prayerful silence reigned. Wearing the Archbishop's purple was the chief sub-editor John Putz, who called everybody by his surname and was addressed respectfully as Mr Putz in return.' Mr Putz was a character of exceptional significance. He had joined the Manchester Guardian when CP Scott was editing and coal fires heated the editorial offices in Cross Street. He had become, first, chief sub-editor in Manchester and then night editor in London, a man of indefatigable energy and authority during the move to London, 'remaining unshaken amid the nightly chaos that was all about him.'[30] Perhaps not quite unshaken. According to Alastair Hetherington, 'Muriel Putz said John, getting home [to bed] at 2am, had thrown off the top sheet at 6am and said, "There's another page gone to press at last."'[31]

For Christopher Dodd, the deputy features editor, it was not a cathedral, but a different analogy that would come to mind: 'This was a real block-floored, mahogany-lined newspaper building which smelt of ink and paper, each night running like a majestic liner leaving port, the lights twinkling in the canteen on the top floor, the whine of the basement presses starting up and tuning to a distant rumble, and the yellow vans flitting about the loading bays like tenders.'[32] Still there, practically unchanged, was the famous 'Corridor' that had been home to CP Scott's elite band of leader writers. Scott's own office, where he worked at a desk lit by a green lamp[33] beneath an engraved portrait of Charles James Fox, was at one end of the Corridor, behind a door with a letterbox in it.

It changed very little and very slowly, as is clear from Malcolm Muggeridge's recollection of Cross Street in the early 1930s: 'I recognised at once my native habitat in the Guardian office: in the tang of printer's ink, the yeasty aroma of newsprint: curious aged figures carrying copy, or battered trays with dregs of strong tea and the debris of chops or fried fish: the clatter of typeprinters and typewriters and the odd zones of silence somehow existing amidst the noise, like cloisters in a railway station.'[34] Nothing much had changed by the time Hetherington arrived in 1950: 'There were no telephones either in the editorial "Corridor" or in the reporters' room ... If you were wanted on the telephone, a messenger asked you to take the call in one of the booths off the reporters' room or at the end of the "Corridor".'[35] Whewell, remembering the early 1950s in Cross Street, wrote, 'Most of the older reporters wrote their copy in longhand with fountain pens so they had no need of machinery; the rest agreed that the clatter spoiled conversation and interrupted trains of thought.'[36]

In Dodd's time there, the mid-1960s, the offices off the Corridor might still 'sport the oak' if the leader writers within did not want to be disturbed; that is, in jargon imported from Oxford and Cambridge, whence nearly all of them had been recruited, the door was closed. Hetherington by then was the editor and valued the 'rational thought, good writing, and the peace to concentrate'.[37] At Cross Street the editorial offices, as Dodd noted, shared the building with the printing presses. The Cross Street journalists would hear the klaxon blare and feel the building vibrate as the great rotary presses rushed them into print (or misprint).

The move from Cross Street, the home of the Guardian since 1841, to Deansgate was a big event. It was duly marked by a commemorative run of pages in the Guardian of 31 August 1970 - the first day of publication from the new Manchester home - recording the journey over 'the long half-mile' from Cross Street to Deansgate. David Ayerst, one of the last leader writers to be engaged by Scott, in an article in that issue, has provided possibly the best description of the old home. Even though the editorial headquarters had moved to London six years earlier, and London printing had begun almost a decade before, Cross Street was still synonymous with the Guardian, he argued. 'We have inevitably left behind all the trappings of the paper's history, the dusty corners where books have lain for generations, the room where [CE] Montague wrote, the view of a back street that CP Scott endured, the doors with black numerals behind which old-time leader writers passed their judgment on the world with no small effect, the empty Chambertin bottle that has been left for long enough in the bottom of a filing cabinet.'

When the time had come to move, a huge hole was knocked through an exterior wall so that machinery and furniture could be lowered on to lorries. The hallowed and perhaps haunted Corridor was torn down and the panelling stored with the idea that it might one day be resurrected in a later building. That is what has happened to some of it. A series of door frames has been installed near the editor's office in the modern building at Kings Place – doorways symbolic, perhaps, of the long journey from the Guardian of the early Manchester days to the digital global Guardian of today.

The move to Deansgate had guaranteed Cross Street the status of myth. In Cross Street, John Cole wrote, reposed the Guardian's 'soul' and it had still seemed, on his arrival in 1956, to be stalked by the ghosts of Scott and the great men of his staff.[38] Deansgate, a cooperative endeavour with the Daily Mail to cut costs and share printing presses, was in all respects otherwise. On the first day in the building, Cole, now in London, rang the northern editor, Geoffrey Taylor, and asked him brightly what his new office in Deansgate was like. Taylor replied, 'I have been removed from an office formerly occupied by CP Scott, and placed in one which a decent building society would give to its North-Western district manager.'[39] Someone made the frivolous suggestion that a canary and an aspidistra might make it more homely and the next day the deputy news editor did indeed turn up with a canary. During the three-day break over Christmas Harry Whewell volunteered to take it home with him. On his way out of the building, swinging the bird in its cage, he passed some Daily Mail compositors going on shift in the shared building. '"What are you doing with that?" said one. "I'm taking it home for Christmas," said I. "Bloody hell," said the comp, "I knew the Guardian was hard up, but that's ridiculous. Come to our house, we are having a goose."'[40]

Journalists, it is true to say, are not easily moved. In fact, Hetherington knew that the significant change had come much earlier in the frantic period around the partial move to London in 1961. 'The old Corridor with its collegiate atmosphere disintegrated: some of its writers were in the capital and some in the North and nobody had enough time to talk or think,' he wrote.[41] But at the same time he recognised that the special atmosphere that had grown up inside the Guardian did not depend on location, even one as redolent of Scott as Cross Street. 'The staff are that "friendly company" of which CP Scott spoke, and they create the paper.'

Peter Preston made more or less the same point when he reflected on the move from Farringdon Road - where his entire editorship had been spent - to Kings Place. He drew a contrast: 'The most stunning newspaper office in the world? That's easy: the Miami Herald, pink, low and luscious, with huge picture windows looking out over the blue waters of Biscayne Bay. Pity about the paper! And the lousiest? Some harsh Guardian voices, poised to head for Kings Place and a canal view that, on a sunny day, may just remind them of Florida, would say 119 Farringdon Road. But, in truth, bricks and mortar don't have much to do with good journalism.'[42]

And Kings Place? A mallard or two, but no pelicans, might pass by the editor's windows on the canal - but Rusbridger had his eyes on the future. In an article in the paper on 15 December 2008, the first publication day from the new building, he outlined the rationale behind the move. The first reason for leaving Farringdon Road, he said, was that the paper had physically outgrown it and the assorted warehouses and office blocks that had been 'colonised' in the surrounding area. Secondly, the buildings were showing their age. The main building, 119 Farringdon Road, had twice been pulled about to be rewired for the advancing technology. It was hot, sweaty and overcrowded and lately plagued by incontinence in the form of burst pipes. Thirdly, it was not cut out for the digital age. 'Over the years, we have managed to carve out meagre shoebox spaces where you could take photographs or record audio in conditions of extreme discomfort and with the low rumble of traffic ever forcing its way in through the leaking window frames. It just wouldn't do any longer ...' And fourthly, 'We really couldn't concentrate on a 24/7 digital future with journalists scattered around 10 or more floors of four or five buildings. There was not enough communication between papers and website, nor coordination of resources across seven days and four or five different media.'[43]

It will be a sub-theme of this book that Scott's legacy is a genuinely living one that has been a benefit and challenge to all Guardian journalists past and present, to those who raised a glass of Hungarian red in the Gay Hussar and to those who, as the bicentenary approached, projected the paper's journalism by means Scott could not have dreamed of, but with an aim he might well have imagined, of making the Guardian the world's leading liberal voice.

If CP Scott did not entirely originate the liberal values that define the Guardian - as we have already seen, they owed a great deal to the Unitarian culture - he did develop them and articulate them with great persuasive force. Those values still resonate. At the end of 2008, shortly before the move to Kings Cross, staff arrived one day to find on their desks an olive-green booklet from Liz Forgan, the chair of the Scott Trust. It contained in a timely reprint the text of the essay that Scott wrote to mark the centenary of the Manchester Guardian in 1921. Known for Scott's famous declaration 'Comment is free, but facts are sacred', it set out the liberal values of 'honesty, cleanness [integrity], courage, fairness, [and] a sense of duty to the reader and the community' by which his own long tenure of 57 years as editor had been guided.

Almost half a century of the Scott epoch had passed by 1921 when the venerable but still vigorous Unitarian, then in his mid-70s and for several years sightless in his right eye, wrote that enormously influential essay. Liz Forgan, in circulating it once more, was making the point that what he had to say was just as relevant, possibly more relevant, in the turmoil of the 21st century than at any time in the paper's history. In an unprecedented period of great change and stress it was offered as a rallying call. Alan Rusbridger, speaking in Australia in 2010, pointed to a another passage from Scott in which he found inspiration for the Guardian that he was navigating through uncharted waters: 'As with the early 16th century,' Rusbridger said, 'it's our privilege, as a generation, not only to imagine the future of information, but to take the first steps on the road to re-crafting the ways in which it is created and spread. As the great editor, CP Scott, wrote about the technological changes in the air when the Guardian celebrated its first 100 years in 1921: 'What a change for the world! What a chance for the newspaper!'[44] As Katharine Viner took the helm in the summer of 2015, the Guardian was reaching a daily average of more than 8 million people worldwide, with the monthly average of unique browsers in excess of 130 million. Most of those were experiencing Guardian journalism through their mobile devices.[45] What a chance and what a challenge for a newspaper!

Chapter 2
Preston's Paper: From Insouciance to Mortal Combat

'I don't think an editor should come in with an election manifesto because no newspaper – certainly not this one – is a representative of any political party.'

Peter Preston on his appointment as editor in 1975[1]

Peter Preston was well over halfway through his tenure of almost 20 years as editor of the Guardian, well tempered and honed by experience, when the paper faced the challenges of the late 1980s. For the Guardian, and for Preston personally, it had been the best and worst of decades. It brought the highest circulation figures in the Guardian's history, frequently over 500,000. It also brought the most testing crisis of Preston's editorship, taking him to within a whisker of resignation. In one way he overcame it, leading the paper into and through the greatest technological revolution it had so far undergone. In another way, he carried it with him, a kind of hair shirt, for the rest of his career. It did not detract in any lasting way from the esteem in which he was held by the vast majority of his peers. He was and remained an editors' editor, the consummate newspaperman.[2]

It might be argued that the credit due to Preston for a decade of generally buoyant circulation should be shared with Margaret Thatcher. Her dominance as prime minister and her strident Conservatism through these years helped to make the paper a refuge and rallying point for a kind of non-Tory to aggressively anti-Tory, or more particularly anti-Thatcher, coalition. Her onslaught on the trade unions also emphasised the Guardian's position as the only quality daily favoured by the left, its left-leaning tendency moderated to some extent by significant support (*within* the paper, rather than *by* the paper) for the Social Democratic Party, the SDP.

The Guardian historian of the period, Geoffrey Taylor, thought this explained the paper's rise in circulation in the early part of the decade. 'The chief reason for the Guardian's success in the early 1980s was that the Social Democratic Party was founded in its pages and the battle for the soul of the Labour Party fought out there.'[3] Four prominent Guardian journalists stood for parliament as SDP candidates in the 1983 general election: Malcolm Dean, Chris Huhne, John Torode and Polly Toynbee. None of them got in. As Preston recalled with some vehemence a quarter of a century later, the Guardian's SDP aspirants accounted for 'the entire bloody leader-writing staff',[4] leaving for long periods just him and his deputy David McKie to write all the political editorials. In 1986, shortly after Rupert Murdoch had decamped to Wapping, Preston was interviewing Paul Webster, a Sunday Times employee who had refused to make the move and was now seeking a job. Webster recalled, 'I thought the interview was going quite well when he suddenly said, "I must ask you one question: what level of political engagement do you have?" I thought, oh well, that's it. There's no way I'm going to get the job ... So I said, "I worked on the Morning Star and my great passion is Marxism Today, which you know about." And at that point he seemed quite relieved and said, "Well the only reason I ask is because an awful lot of my staff are members of the SDP and they've all buggered off [again] to stand in the next election."'[5]

In fact, in the 1987 election - the nadir of the SDP in its unhappy association with the Liberal party in the Alliance - Malcolm Dean and Chris Huhne stood again, both coming a fairly close second in their respective constituencies. Of the trajectory of the SDP in its fairly brief history, it has been remarked, 'It went up like a rocket and came down like the stick.'[6] David McKie suspected Preston of having harboured SDP sympathies; when Preston talked politics with McKie he would refer to Labour accusingly as '*Your* party'. McKie defined his own position and what he thought should always be the paper's when the SDP leader David Owen accosted him at a party conference, and denounced the Guardian for what he saw as its vacillation: 'Say what you like about the Daily Mail,' Owen said, 'at least it knows what side it's on.' McKie replied: 'We know what side we're on; we're on our side.'[7]

Preston's politics appeared to have varied in non-Conservative areas, although Richard Gott, then features editor, was convinced that Preston was a progressive Tory. Some people may have gained that impression from a series of leaders Preston wrote from the early 1980s to the end of his editorship - no more than 20 or so in all - in the guise of J Arthur Composite, 'our occasional correspondent on the Conservative back benches'. In these Preston lent his familiar informal prose to the purported wetter-than-wet MP for Barchester West. This was 'the sort of seat you could sleep in for years', had it not been penetrated and disturbed by all the agonies and ecstasies of the Thatcher years. It was never quite clear what Preston was up to beyond demonstrating, in a mildly satirical way, an ability to see things from the other person's point of view. The perception of the Guardian, which grew through the 1980s, as the paper of the left, had progressively excluded Tory readers, who at an earlier stage had amounted to roughly a third of its circulation.

But few would have agreed with Gott's diagnosis of Preston's own deep-down position. Michael White, for a long time the paper's political editor, claimed, 'He's certainly not a Tory - Richard is wrong. His default position is Lib-Lab.'[8]

The confusion over Preston's personal politics supported the correct view that he was not a party animal. It did not support the incorrect view, sometimes voiced, that he had no real interest in politics. His J Arthur Composite editorials are, whatever else, the product of close and acute, if wry, observation of Preston's propensity to watch without direct involvement, which some saw as a characteristic of the daily editorial conferences he chaired. Hugh Hebert, in a piece in the Guardian when Preston's appointment as editor was first announced, wrote, 'Peter Preston began as a political reporter, and in essence that is very much what he remains.'[9] Later in Hebert's article, Preston made his view even clearer: 'You concentrate on what's happening and what's making it happen rather than moving in from a dogma, a dogmatic position. That's what the Guardian has done, is doing and should do. I don't think an editor should come in with an election manifesto because no newspaper - certainly not this one - is a representative of any political party.'

Above all, Preston wanted a paper that was politically independent, fair and rational. He recognised that the Guardian had 'gained substantially by being in many ways *the* paper of opposition' to Margaret Thatcher. Nevertheless, on an occasion when the paper seemed to be more than usually flooded by a visceral loathing of her he had exclaimed, banging a table for emphasis, 'Has she never done anything right?'

This view of the Guardian was the one that Jonathan Fenby brought to the paper when he joined as Preston's deputy in the early autumn of 1988, lured away from a key role on the Independent. Fenby was probably foremost among Preston's 'counter signings', as he called them. It was practically unknown for anyone to be recruited at such a high level from outside the hallowed walls. Preston explained, 'I just thought we'd all been together too long and we needed to give ourselves some clue as to how other papers actually went about things and to sort of change the mix'. In this case, of course, whether or not it was the primary motive, the Independent was wounded in the process. 'There's always an upside and an upside,' Preston quipped.

Preston's occasional bursts of exasperation did not stop factional tension from developing among his staff. The Labour Party was always well represented, not least by the Guardian's political editor, Ian Aitken, who served the Guardian for almost three decades; but also by others, ranging in sympathy from Labour's left, for example Seumas Milne, to its centre-right, for example Martin Kettle, two journalists who joined the paper in the mid-1980s and were to remain influential on it through-out the main period covered by this book.[10] A number of journalists belonged to the Socialist Workers Party, Trotskyists of a kind; this was more common among the sub-editors, who sometimes colluded in truculent knots, but also included one or two high-profile columnists, correspondents and editors.

The only real sin towards the end of the 1980s, Preston's view notwithstanding, appears to have been to have no detectable political commitment, or to believe, as the Guardian's star political interviewer Terry Coleman believed, in a kind of professional neutrality: 'Some on the editorial staff wanted to be politicians rather than reporters, never a good thing ... As for me, a fair number of staff thought me much too far to the right and would have shot me. I agreed with that old Guardian man Alistair Cooke - and he and I talked about this - that if you wanted to change the world you should become a missionary, and that a report-er's business was to report.'[11]

Such neutrality, in turn, aroused rage or contempt among some of those at the extremities of Guardian opinion, who saw it not as a matter of moderation but of abdication. However, the exodus of readers to the Independent at the time lent strength to the argument that the Guardian letters page presented an image of a readership much farther to the left than was the case in reality.

Martin Woollacott, one of the paper's most experienced foreign correspondents and an almost revered foreign editor, took a 'balanced view' of the Guardian's internal ideological struggles. 'One of the defining characteristics of the Guardian in my view is that it is a conversation between the left and the liberal centre.' It is, he explained, 'an inbuilt conflict, which in itself has value'.[12]

And Preston's politics? He kept them to himself. He emerged only partially from his silence on the subject in an interview for this book. Asked about party allegiance, he replied, 'I'm not in that sense anything.' And when pressed on the point, he said: 'I mostly vote Labour, occasionally Liberal, once Tory in a local election.'[13]

Paradoxically, the Guardian management, and many of the printers, who tended to play golf and cricket together, were fairly solidly Tory. After a management reshuffle announced in September 1987 it was even more unlikely that a board meeting would open with a singing of the 'Internationale'. The new group chairman, Harry Roche, was a Tory; Jim Markwick, who followed Roche as managing director of the Guardian early in 1988, had been a member of the Tory party since the age of 17; Caroline Marland, appointed deputy managing director, was married to the Conservative MP Paul Marland; and Michael Jack, the circulation director, was a Tory. 'We were in a clear majority on the [Guardian] board,' said Markwick, 'not that we ever talked politics' - nor, it might be added, did they ever try to influence editorial policy politically. The occasional eruption of hostility towards the unions was sometimes suspected to be a reversion to type.

Preston took pride in presiding over this 'broad church', by which he meant an organisation that both internally and in its published persona was an expression of liberal toleration. Many shared Terry Coleman's admiration 'for the way he kept the impossibly disparate elements of the Guardian together'. No one quite knew how he did it. One way, perhaps, was to be present in as many relevant forums of discussion as possible. He sometimes seemed to take the whole weight of it almost happily on his shoulders.

He had been part of the reshuffle announced in the autumn of 1987 when the intention had been declared to appoint a non-executive chairman of the Guardian board to succeed Harry Roche. It was Roche who suggested to Preston that he should put himself forward. Preston was appointed chairman with effect from March 1988 in the absence of any other candidate on whom the Scott Trust, of which Preston was also a member, were able to agree. But he was an eminently worthy candidate. By then he had seen the virtual completion of the Guardian's transition to full computer technology, and had shaken himself and the paper pretty well free from any trace of what he had called 'insouciance' in the face of the Independent, and he had brought about what, up to that time, was the most radical redesign in the Guardian's history. It was intended to be a provisional appointment, to be reviewed in two or three years. In fact Preston remained chairman of the Guardian board even after he had handed over the editorship to his successor, and he stayed in the post until 1996.

For Preston, amid the unprecedented success of his paper for most of the 1980s - a paper finally flourishing after its near disappearance in a merger with the Times - the decade also brought the disastrous diversion of the Tisdall affair. It is Preston's personal elephant in the room and perhaps best noted at the outset, although it is covered in more detail in Geoffrey Taylor's volume of the Guardian history. Preston described the experience as walking into an elephant trap.[14]

The train of events began when Sarah Tisdall, a 23-year-old Foreign Office clerk, anonymously delivered to the Guardian office two classified Ministry of Defence documents relating to the deployment of nuclear weapons in October 1983. The Guardian duly reported on the story, prompting Mrs Thatcher to call for an immediate inquiry into how it had been leaked. In retrospect the documents should have been immediately destroyed after publication but by now it was too late. A High Court writ demanding the return of the papers was issued and Preston, with great reluctance, handed them over. The result was the swift discovery of the whistleblower: not the highly placed person it had generally been assumed to be, but a grade 10 clerical officer in the Foreign Office. Sarah Tisdall was charged under the Official Secrets Act and on 23 March 1984 sentenced to six months' imprisonment.

Preston chastised himself, occasionally in published articles, for years afterwards. His harshest critics believed he should have martyred himself in the sacred cause of protecting a source. He did offer his resignation, and at least two senior colleagues - McKie and Peter Cole, the news editor – told him that if he insisted on going through with it they would go too. Had the Guardian journalists censured him in the union meeting they held when Tisdall was sentenced, he would have felt it was the only course left to him. But they didn't, unhappy though they were.

What restrained them? Partly perhaps they stopped short of censure because of Preston's visible anguish. Even so, what few of them were to know was the degree of personal devastation Preston felt. On the evening of the sentence he drove up to Holloway Prison, the women's jail in north London, where Tisdall was initially held, and kept a miserable vigil there. He later visited her after she had been transferred to a prison in Kent. He was not thought likely to be good at such encounters, although one colleague praised his gift for what he called communicative silence. (At times he could be disconcertingly quiet. The blind politician David Blunkett, some considerable time into a meeting with Preston and others, asked whether the editor was still with them.)

But there was more than sympathy or simple loyalty at work in his colleagues' restraint over Tisdall. Martin Woollacott, who joined the Guardian five years after Preston, said, 'For a variety of reasons Peter had in hand quite a capital of loyalty and affection among staff, quite a capital, because, despite some aspects of his personality he is essentially a person who responds warmly to people's problems and to people's professional needs, and that was widely known. And we could sense his pain.' Many, like Woollacott, had worked alongside Preston for a long time, both before and after he became editor in 1975. They admired his professionalism and utter dedication, and now they stood by him. This was to prove fortunate as he soon had a revolution to contend with, and to turn to the Guardian's purpose.

The most significant development for the newspaper industry in the 1980s was Rupert Murdoch's 'audacious' – the adjective often applied – move to Wapping at the end of January 1986, breaking the power of the print unions and changing 'everything, for good, for ever, in one weekend', as Maggie Brown rightly anticipated in the Guardian.[15] It was a ruthless stroke, liberating even those who condemned it. That he managed to keep his real intentions secret up to the last moment, telling the world he was planning to launch a new evening paper to rival the London Evening Standard, was itself an achievement in such a leaky and still bibulous industry. The drama of the move was captured for Guardian readers by Alan Rusbridger, soon to embark on his brief round trip, first to the Observer, then to the Washington office of the London Daily News, and then back to the Guardian in time to play a leading part in its own revolution. He felt a twinge of sympathy for the Murdoch journalists: 'What a world awaited them. When they left work on Friday night they had left behind them a slightly seedy office, paper strewn, dog-eared desks with ageing typewriters and half-drunk cups of coffee. And there on Monday morning was a gleaming, dust-free open-plan room. A clinic more than an office. The whole of it was bathed in soothing computer-compatible light. For there in front of them stood row upon row of gleaming dust-free computers.'[16] As Rusbridger noted, the vast majority of them had a complete lack of familiarity with the technology they were now called upon to operate.

With his coup, Murdoch was thought to have cut the production costs of his titles by so much - perhaps by £60 million - that a cut in the cover price of the Times, or a cut in advertising rates, or both, might quickly follow, 'to the destruction of the Telegraph and the Guardian', a writer in the *Spectator* gleefully predicted.[17] Not all perceived the severity of the threat. After all, the Guardian had its reassuringly high sales figures, a secure position in command of the left's most prestigious platform in the daily press, plus the unusual circumstance that it had money to spend - some of it still derived from the unexpected bonanza of its shares in Reuters.

The Guardian did occasionally make a modest profit on its own account - in 1986/87 it amounted to just under half a million pounds - which reduced its call on group profits. These were mainly generated by the Manchester Evening News, by some of the group's smaller provincial newspapers, and increasingly by the Auto Trader cluster of used-car sales magazines, which were to prove such a shrewd investment. Against this there was the frustrating cost in lost circulation caused by frequent disputes and stoppages due to wildcat strikes or the mechanical breakdown of its increasingly inadequate presses. Throughout 1985 the Guardian had run second to the quality market leader, the Daily Telegraph, and ahead of the Times for all but a couple of months in the summer, when it lost a million copies in disputes with the printers' union, the National Graphical Association (NGA). Unofficial strikes in the year up to Wapping had cost the Guardian £750,000. Frustration was palpable.

'The Guardian, in editorial and advertising, was experiencing considerable success,' Preston was to tell his staff, 'but its production was under the terrible strain of what we used to call "working without enthusiasm".' The Guardian had as strong an incentive as anyone to modernise and eliminate the troublesome printers by bringing in direct computerised input by journalists. But it was not just the printers. In the months before Wapping, there were unofficial stoppages by the stereo workers - the men who cast the plates from which the paper would be printed - and the editorial messengers, who took or fetched copy and pictures to or from wherever needed. Their strikes took the paper off the streets for several costly days. 'Nobody, I know, felt angrier about that than the journalists,' said Preston.[18]

Three months after the coup, with violent scenes still surrounding 'Fortress Wapping', where Murdoch's four titles - the Times, the Sunday Times, the Sun and the News of the World - were under permanent siege, Eddy Shah, as predicted, launched his mid-market daily, Today, making use of many of the hard-won technical advances. The paper was the fruit of his own earlier struggle with the print unions in 1983, where he sought to use his printing plant in Warrington to produce his local newspapers using non-union labour. Under siege himself, he successfully challenged the print unions in the courts through Mrs Thatcher's new employment laws. It was the first major assault on printers, whose restrictive practices had made the approaching calamity inevitable. Shah's experiences at Warrington were an important precursor to Wapping, and helped fire his resolution to produce his own national daily paper. Today's first editor, Brian MacArthur - a former Guardian journalist - was subsequently able to claim with some justification, 'We were the national pioneer of the electronic newspaper.' Shah's Today was fully computerised, albeit with a system that proved far from trouble-free, but which went one stage further than that brought into use at Wapping, where copy was set and edited electronically but then cut and pasted by hand onto the pages to be photographed and sent to the presses. At Today, there was no cut-and-paste: page make-up was done electronically too. The paper was also well in advance of others at that time in its extensive use of editorial colour, although that too was beset by teething troubles: the murky picture reproduction due to poor colour registration in the early weeks earned it the slur 'Shah vision'.[19]

Very soon the Guardian, struggling with its own poor-quality black and white hot-metal printing, never mind colour, had a much more threatening competitor to worry about in the Independent. Picture reproduction in the Guardian by now had become so dire that the use of single-column pictures was discouraged, particularly, it has to be said, if the subject was black, because they were likely to fill up with ink. Pictures in the Independent were displayed with startling clarity.

The new paper arrived in October, like Venus rising from the foam, perfectly formed, a beautifully designed, if conservative, upmarket broadsheet. And although it enlarged the market by about 10%, it was quickly robbing its rivals of both staff and circulation. It was no secret that its main target was to have been the flabby quality market leader, the Daily Telegraph, whence its three founders, Andreas Whittam Smith, Stephen Glover, and Matthew Symonds, had all recently absconded. All its initial planning had taken place while the founders were still employed by the Telegraph. 'I felt uncomfortable,' said Glover with an apparent spasm of guilt. 'We were, after all, planning to launch a newspaper which we saw as the Daily Telegraph's main competitor.'[20] That was the expectation in the wider industry too. As Peter Preston noted, 'All the drum beats were that it was intended to take on the Daily Telegraph, which was where the founders all came from, and so you didn't see them as people directly parking their tanks on your lawn.'

Wapping, and the disillusionment among some Murdoch employees with the way the move had been handled, with staff now corralled behind barbed wire and police cordons, had made it easier for the Independent to recruit experienced national newspaper journalists. A third of the original staff of the paper were recruited from the Times and Sunday Times,[21] both of which before Wapping had been housed in Gray's Inn Road, where the Guardian was still printed. (By contrast, almost three-quarters of the initial editorial staff of Today had had no previous Fleet Street experience.[22]) The Independent had also been recruiting in a limited way from the Guardian.

For six months before its launch the Independent conducted guerrilla raids on the Guardian, and not just on its journalists. Carolyn McCall, who had joined the paper as an ad planner not long before the appearance of the Independent, saw a fairly steady stream of classified sales staff being tempted away and she recalled that something like a siege mentality developed in the commercial departments of the Guardian. In their contacts with advertisers they were constantly being confronted with negative comparisons, only partly stemming from the stark contrast in print quality. The new employees of the Independent were experiencing a particularly energising sensation – the exhilaration of creating something new.

There appears to have been a stronger scent of danger on the commercial side of the Guardian than in the editorial departments, although they were also subject to poaching raids. David Hencke, a feverishly intense and brilliant reporter, had received a phone call from Andreas Whittam Smith, months before the new paper came out. Hencke had been one of Preston's first appointments very soon after he became editor in 1975. Now he chose not to go. In the time-honoured manner, he informed Preston about the Independent offer as soon as he had put down the phone to Whittam Smith. It produced a quick result. In June 1986, still four months before the Independent appeared, Hencke, with a modest increase in salary (all Guardian increases were 'modest'), began his long career as the Guardian's Westminster correspondent. He had a great gift as a journalist, a shambling presence that half suggested he wanted to play when what he really intended to do was bite. He more than justified Preston's decision to indulge him, not least in his exposure of parliamentary sleaze leading to the resignation of the Tory minister Neil Hamilton in 1994. Alan Travis was another who, having declined a pre-launch offer from the Independent, was given a loyalty award: he became the paper's long-serving and scoop-laden home affairs editor.

Poaching raids on the Guardian, while often unsuccessful, had generally been fairly frequent, partly because all knew that the paper tended to pay much less than the rest of Fleet Street. Now, over the next couple of years the Guardian lost some of its stars to the Independent. Peter Jenkins, its chief political columnist, was perhaps the greatest loss, although he went first to the Sunday Times, piqued and displaced, it was said, by the arrival at the Guardian of Hugo Young from the same place.

Polly Toynbee also found her way to the Independent, in her case much later via the BBC. Terry Coleman, after 25 years on the Guardian, left when Andreas Whittam Smith offered him roughly twice what he was then earning. By then, 1989, his departure was regarded by Preston as a serious defection: the Independent had replaced the Times as the Guardian's principal enemy.

After the shock of Wapping, the Guardian (and almost everyone else) was scorned by the Murdoch camp for only initiating its modernising reforms as a panicky response. The Times historian Graham Stewart wrote, '... after years of timid inertia, the speed with which the various proprietors shot out of their respective blocks was remarkable ... A week after the Times' move to Wapping, the Guardian rushed through an announcement that it would move to Docklands, switch from hot metal to computer typesetting and introduce direct input by 1987.'[23] This was not exactly true: in November 1984, more than a year before Murdoch moved his papers to Wapping, the Guardian had signed a contract with Wimpey to build a printing plant to house new presses that were at last to expose the Guardian's pages, and especially its pictures, in a more competitive clarity. The paper had told its readers about this a couple of months later, still a year ahead of Wapping. The final cost would be £25 million. It was long overdue.

There were two important decisions among the many that had to be made. The first involved a choice between letterpress printing – essentially the method that the Guardian was already using, not much changed since Gutenberg 500 years earlier – and web offset printing that was rapidly replacing letterpress throughout the modern industry, especially where the union grip had been loosened. Offset presses produced a better-quality print, and they required much smaller manning levels. They were what Murdoch was to introduce at Wapping. The manufacturer chosen to build the Guardian's new presses, Koenig & Bauer, could have produced machines of either kind. A team from the Guardian headed by Jim Markwick went to Zurich, where both methods could be observed at work on different newspapers.

It was the modern letterpress printing of the prestigious Neue Zürcher Zeitung, and the access to full-colour 'on-the-run' printing that its presses afforded that in part determined the Guardian's choice. But there was also a negative consideration. The choice of letterpress meant that the printing process would be essentially unchanged: it was an easy option. Committing then in 1984 to a change to web offset would have meant, in Jim Markwick's words, the retraining of the workforce and a massive round of union negotiations. 'If we could satisfy ourselves that the work being done in Zurich on letterpress machines met all our requirements then this was going to be a lot easier for us. And it did so we bought.'

The other important decision to be made was where the new presses would be housed. Still a major consideration in 1984 was easy access to key railway stations. It came to a choice between two locations. One was a site near a renowned public house, the Skinners Arms off the Old Kent Road in south-east London, which was favoured by Preston. The other was a site on the Isle of Dogs, favoured by Markwick. Access to Paddington station was tested, with each man setting off from his favoured site by car at midnight one night to see who would arrive at the station first. Inconclusively, they both arrived at the same time. The Isle of Dogs was chosen in the end because the site lay within the bounds of the development corporation created three years earlier and a press hall there would start off with a long period exempt from paying rates. The building firm Wimpey, who already owned the land, agreed to sell it to the Guardian for £199,000 provided they were awarded the contract to build the press hall.

For the time being the Guardian was still being printed on the creaking presses in Gray's Inn Road. It had hired these presses - housed in a building by now abandoned by Murdoch - for about £1 million a year. But it directly employed the people who worked on the presses, so retaining final production of the paper in its own hands. Now, at a time of maximum pressure, all was not going well. 'We were struggling with our own absolutely endless internal problems, including union problems,' recalled Preston. 'The presses kept breaking down. Michael Jack, our circulation director, would troop in and say, "You lost 30,000 in north London today" or "We didn't get any papers to Birmingham last night".'

If there was a high urgency to install the presses, there was by Guardian standards an almost relaxed approach to the expenditure involved. The Guardian had found itself the beneficiary of a £70-million windfall[24] from its shares in Reuters news agency, which during the early 1980s had become suddenly and unexpectedly profitable. It would be nice to be able to claim that the Guardian benefited from this as the result of great foresight and planning, but that was not the case. The millions descended like manna on the whole industry. Reuters was at the time effectively owned jointly by the Press Association, which was sustained by, and served, the provincial press, and the Newspaper Publishers Association, to which all the national newspapers belonged. Between them these two organisations owned 82% of Reuters. The Guardian group had a double interest: the Manchester Evening News was a shareholder in the PA, and the Guardian was a member of the NPA, which it had had to join on its move to London in the 1960s. In those difficult times, the Guardian chairman Laurence Scott, when he signed the cheque for £3,600 to take up obligatory membership of the publishers' association, had remarked, 'Do they think I'm made of money?' Now, two decades later, in June 1984 when Reuters was floated on the stock exchange, the Guardian group's 5% holding was worth about £50 million and rising. The signal to the rest of the industry was a strong one: Reuters' fantastic success stemmed from the lead it had taken in information and communications technology. According to Geoffrey Taylor, the flotation of Reuters released about £1 billion into 'Fleet Street' that year, stimulating its modernisation and evacuation from central London, and probably prolonging the life of the newspapers by several decades.

The Reuters windfall was not the only positive factor in these years. Overall there was an exceptionally good relationship between editorial and the management and commercial sides of the Guardian. At the head of the paper for a decade and more was the triumvirate of Peter Preston, Peter Gibbings, the chairman of the company, and Gerry Taylor, the managing director. Gibbings had been persuaded to join the Guardian from the Observer in 1967 by Preston's predecessor, Alastair Hetherington. 'Looking back,' Hetherington wrote, 'I believe that I never did a better day's work for the Guardian than on the afternoon when I put the case to Peter [Gibbings] for joining us.'[25] He joined as managing director of the Guardian, now with its own board separate from that of the Manchester Evening News. He became chairman in 1973, and held office until his retirement in 1988. Gibbings in turn recruited his friend Gerry Taylor from a leading advertising agency. He joined in 1967, in the first place as advertisement director, becoming managing director in 1973. He was responsible for giving fresh impetus to the development of classified advertising, building a team that produced crucial income for the company for the next two decades and providing new career opportunities, especially for women: it was on this Taylor escalator that Caroline Marland (who joined in 1976) rose to the top of the management structure, followed by her protégée, Carolyn McCall (recruited in 1986). Together, Taylor, Preston and Marland were able to create dedicated editorial sections that became huge revenue earners, helping to reduce the Guardian's reliance on the profitable Manchester Evening News.

Caroline Marland later claimed that sudden illumination came to her in 1979 when, examining some trade statistics, she realised that 74% of Daily Telegraph readers were too old for the jobs advertised in their paper.[26] The Guardian's share of the recruitment market at that time was 8%. The revelation led to an ad campaign showing a decrepit Telegraph reader in a bath chair being pushed by a sprightly young Guardian reader. 'We started running these ads and the Telegraph advertising director rang me up and said, "I'm going to sue you." I said, "What for?" He said, "I don't know, but I'm going to think of something." And that was the beginning of the change in everything. And we went on through the eighties and little by little we built up all the [classified] markets.'

It became one of the British newspaper industry's outstanding commercial success stories of the 1980s. By 1985 the Guardian share of the recruitment market had built up to 21% and the following year it overtook the Telegraph as the market leader.

In fact there were reasons to be optimistic on all fronts. Until the birth of the Independent, the Times was the Guardian's main competitor. Immediately after Wapping, the Guardian actually widened its lead over its rival: in February 1986, with the News International journalists and technicians besieged by pickets, and unfamiliarity with the new systems causing delays, not to mention disapproval in the wider world of the manner in which the move to Wapping had been handled, the Guardian's circulation went up to over 530,000 while the Wappingised Times fell back to just under 446,000.

Any complacency that the situation created was transient, however. It would be nearly two years before the Guardian's new printing plant would be fully operational: the printing contract with the Times on the presses in Gray's Inn Road was not due to expire until the end of 1987. On the lower ground level at the back of the Farringdon Road building about a dozen Harris Intertype automatic Monarch typesetting machines had been installed after the paper moved from Gray's Inn Road and were now being phased out. They had no keyboards. The typesetting was done remotely by compositors, members of the NGA, operating keyboards at green screens (slime, they called them) on the floor above. Before agreement on direct input by journalists was reached, initially in May 1986, all copy produced by journalists was tapped out again by these compositors. Much of it continued to be re-entered in that way long after the journalists had been provided with the means to do it themselves. The printers' computers translated the copy into punched tape and this was then fed into the Monarchs on the floor below, and these in turn automatically disgorged lines of hot metal type. The system had seemed quite advanced when it was introduced.

Change was taking place, but not without considerable difficulty, as one of the early Guardian computer pioneers, Harry Jackson, recalled. 'Technically the paper was still at the mercy of the printing unions. Though it had a small Atex system for phototypesetting, its use was subject to the standard rigid demarcation rules imposed by the compositors. The poor training given the supervisors (again because of union restrictions) meant the system was appallingly maintained and subject to frequent breakdowns which required the repeated attendance of Atex engineers at horrendous cost.'

When it came to page make-up, two systems operated side by side. One set of pages was made up in the traditional way by locking the metal lines of type into a frame or chase and taking an impression under pressure, from which the stereo workers would then cast a curved metal plate to be transported the short distance to Gray's Inn Road and clamped on the presses. This method was progressively giving way to the cut-and-paste pages made up not on the flat surface, or 'stone', used for hot metal, but on angled boards, somewhat like those that architectural draughtsmen employed. The compositors, now armed with scalpels, would cut up the photographic bromides that the computer had printed out, and stick them on a page template according to a plan provided by editorial. Standing by would be the make-up journalist, still referred to as the stone sub, upon whose relationship with the 'comp' the finesse of the completed page might depend. Harry Jackson again: 'The paste-up of pages was carried out under the same constraints as had existed with hot metal - make-up subs could point but never touch.' The pasted-up page went to be photographed as a whole and then again converted into a plate to be bolted to the press.

At the time of Wapping, some Guardian features pages and advertisement pages were already being pasted up, but all other pages, including the main news pages, were still set by hot metal. After Wapping the latter seemed more than a little old-fashioned.

Harry Roche, in a letter circulated to all staff in February 1986 - a version of which appeared in the paper a couple of days later - set out four essential priorities: to bring into use as soon as possible the new technology in Farringdon Road and at the Isle of Dogs; to establish 'sensible and appropriate manning levels, which inevitably means a reduction in staffing'; to introduce direct input in both editorial and advertising as soon as possible; and to guarantee continuous production through 'the kind of binding dispute and arbitration procedure already offered by the unions to Mr Murdoch'.

The letter concluded with a commitment to achieve all the necessary changes through negotiation - where possible. 'I do not need, I hope, to contrast the approach we have decided on with that adopted elsewhere.' But, he added, 'We are determined to bring about change.' In NUJ circles Roche was regarded as something of a hard man. He had arrived from the Manchester Evening News to become managing director of the Guardian, at the end of 1984, pursued, so to speak, by lawyers. The NUJ chapel of the Manchester Evening News were taking the paper's management, which had been led by Roche, to court in a pension dispute. In May 1985, five months into Roche's new post at the Guardian, the NUJ lost the case in the High Court and were stuck with costs running into six figures.[27]

Remarkably, in the month that Roche won the court case, he also achieved most of what he wanted in his negotiations in Farringdon Road. It was a month of major violence around the News International plant at Wapping, scenes that prompted the Guardian to announce with some emphasis that its deal on direct input had been achieved 'through negotiation not coup'. All the unions had agreed to it 'in principle'. There were to be 'job reductions' of 20%, compulsory retirement at 65, and a 3½% pay rise had been accepted. Appearances notwithstanding, the extensive and rapid programme of change left plenty of room for possible dispute, as time was to prove.

There was another indicator of change, perhaps not obvious at the time. It took the unpromising external form of a four-page report, 'Investing in Canada'. It had been a revenue-raising idea dreamed up by the advertising department, but someone had neglected to order any editorial material. Harold Jackson, who had not long returned to Farringdon Road after several years as Washington correspondent, was dispatched to provide some copy. Jackson had introduced new technology to the Guardian's Washington office, first of all in the form of an on-screen feed of Associated Press and then with the use of a portable computer, the Tandy 100. He acquired it in 1983 shortly after it became available, for $999 - he always remembered the shocked reaction when he told the paper's managing editor, Ian Wright. Soon both Jackson and his Guardian colleague Alex Brummer were using it to transmit their copy from Washington back to Farringdon Road, where it rattled out on a teleprinter at the Guardian at a steady 66 words a minute. By the time Jackson was dispatched to Canada on his rescue mission, early in 1986, copy could be transmitted directly down a telephone line: 'You dialled the number, reversed the charges, made the attachment using little cups that fitted over a standard telephone receiver, then just pressed a key to send.' Jackson had interviews across Canada. 'I was lurching from Ottawa to Montreal to Saskatoon with my Tandy 100, churning out the copy as I went. Every time I produced the Tandy in an airport lounge I would get great crowds of people round me saying, "Gee, what's that?"'

From Vancouver an exhausted Jackson rang Ian Wright to say he was coming back. Wright had some news for him. The planned computerisation of the Guardian was to be pushed ahead, post-Wapping, 'and we've just appointed a chief systems editor.' When Jackson asked 'Who?', he was told, 'You.'

So Jackson now became responsible for recommending the computer system that the first generation of fully computerised journalists at the Guardian would use to input their copy. Rather more than that, he became, as he put it, 'part of the small team deputed to change the habits of a lifetime'.[28]

Interest in computer technology generally had grown considerably from 1983, when Jackson obtained his first Tandy. A page called MicroGuardian had been added to a section about science and technology that had been running for four years under the banner Futures. The new 'regular page for the personal computer user - or people who just want to know a bit more', first appeared on 20 October 1983 and ran for a decade. In it, Guardian readers were introduced to someone who was to become the paper's resident computer guru for the next three decades, Jack Schofield, then the editor of the magazine Practical Computing. He joined the staff of the Guardian two years later as the editor of a new eight-page section, Computer Guardian, which successfully targeted the developing IT sector for classified job ads. Schofield recalled that at that time, 1985, there were only two computers in use in the Guardian: one was an IBM System 38, employed in Manchester to run the payroll, and the other was a Spectrum, used in Farringdon Road by the marketing director, John Gordon. Harry Jackson, more or less alone, was responsible for promoting the battery-powered Tandy 100 that was gradually to render the portable typewriter redundant among reporters.

Jackson was sent off on a fact-finding mission to newspaper publishers employing some of the most advanced editorial systems in the United States, far in advance of anything then being used in Britain. His first call was on the Minneapolis Star Tribune, which since 1977 had operated one of the first newspaper systems ever ordered from Atex. There was a degree of familiarity: as already noted, Atex had supplied the small system that was in use by the printers in Farringdon Road for photo-typesetting. One of the things that impressed Jackson was the way in which the newspaper had been able to develop its system jointly with Atex – necessarily at first, because the Atex headquarters were 1,300 miles away and in 1977 the company could not guarantee servicing. But now the result of their cooperative relationship meant that Atex, a subsidiary of Kodak, was an estimated two to five years ahead of the competition, and the Star Tribune had an editorial system for which it could write software itself. Most impressively, the system was being used for direct input by journalists and for onscreen page make-up.

There were other Guardian expeditions to Amsterdam, Paris and Madrid. By the autumn, Atex had been chosen as the editorial publishing system for the Guardian, and it proved to be a good choice that was to serve the paper well for the next decade. Within just two years an Atex system tailored to the Guardian's requirements was fully installed in Farringdon Road. 'In a hundred different ways,' Jackson said, 'we have had to tune the system to our particular needs – and are still doing so.'[29]

The final testing of the Atex system in Massachusetts more or less coincided with the first appearance on the streets of the Independent, an event that emphasised, more than Wapping, more than the arrival of Eddy Shah's Today, the urgency of the Guardian's situation.

When the Independent appeared, the last hot metal edition of the Guardian was still six months away, the new presses wouldn't be ready for another year, the great redesign of the Guardian by David Hillman of Pentagram was not yet conceived. And it was only then, at the beginning of 1988, that Harry Jackson would concede that the computerisation of the Guardian was complete.

Before that point could be reached, the building in Farringdon Road would have to be ripped apart so the place could be wired up to receive the new system, and more than 200 journalists and other editorial staff would have to be trained to use it. On the way there would also be protracted union disputes as the journalists, in particular, sought the best possible terms for working the new technology. By the early summer of 1987, negotiations between the management and the NUJ over direct input had been going on for almost six months. The journalists had had an all-round 'final offer' of £3,500 increase of pay, to cover direct input. In Preston's view it was an excellent offer, producing a starting rate for young journalists of £21,000 - 'The highest by miles anywhere in Fleet Street,' he told Guardian journalists in a long personal letter. Ironically, the real sticking point now was the proposed disputes procedure. Agreement was eventually reached on that too.

By now everyone belatedly perceived the seriousness of the threat posed by the Independent. Or did they? The new arrival had already, in Preston's words, 'wiped about £1 million off circulation revenue'. In the first few months of the Independent's existence the Guardian had maintained a gap of about 200,000 ahead of it, but its own circulation was soon struggling to stay above the magical mark of half a million that it had exceeded for most of the decade.

Despite the early warnings from Harry Roche and others, Preston, through a crucial period, had continued to feel that the general attitude towards the Independent inside the Guardian had been 'insouciant'. 'There was - from the word go - an assumption that we were in our own untouchable cocoon, and this gave the Indie a head start,' he said. Now things had to change; and most of Preston's senior colleagues believed the Guardian had the right man in the right place. 'Peter is a terrific fighter,' said his deputy and managing editor, Ian Wright.[30] He and others said anyone who knew of Preston's background and earlier career would share that view of him.

Chapter 3
A Great Editor in His Element

'Quality journalism has a serious purpose. It aims to inform and sometimes educate the reader ... We know, instinctively, that we should be poorer without it.'

Peter Preston, 2012[1]

Preston had not been long on the paper when, in the 1960s, it almost disappeared in a merger with the Times. With the paper teetering on the edge of disaster, the crisis awakened the Scott Trust to its responsibilities as the custodian and protector of the paper's core values and standards, and it led to lasting changes in the way the company was run. The drama being played out through Preston's early years on the paper had a profound effect on him. He needed no further demonstration that the welfare of the enterprise as a whole depended on its financial security: he had felt the foundations shake. For most of his career as editor he worked under the tightest economic constraints, capped by an implacable head count. As Martin Woollacott expressed it, 'The terrible head count, the impossibility of hiring somebody without letting somebody else go, or hoping that somebody else would leave. The difficulty of paying somebody extra money without going through all sorts of bureaucratic hoops ... of course it was to do with wage restraints in Britain as a whole. But all these things, I think, made running a paper like the Guardian rather like playing chess in three dimensions. You have to think about everything. He was very good at thinking about everything.' He had earned a reputation as a ferociously hard worker, always paying close attention to detail and yet rarely giving a sense of interference. Victoria Brittain, who was an assistant editor on the foreign desk at the end of the 1980s, recalled, 'Quite often early in the morning, when you were anxious to get your lists [of stories to be covered] done and your head clear before the editor's conference, you might find him hovering over your shoulder with a helpful suggestion, and his suggestions were always genuinely helpful.'[2] It was also typically tactful - a cynic would say wily - of him to make agenda suggestions of this kind before conference so that the recipients could present them as their own when they gathered with their peers.

It is doubtful whether any editor of the Guardian since its earliest days had been seen more around the shop, his presence usually announced by a whiff of pipe smoke, that is until his final years as editor when the pipe was replaced by chewing gum. In this phase he also chewed the tops of ballpoint pens, not always free from ink, and the added effect of this was to give him the appearance of a bizarre Petrushka. Some believed that the apparition could be summoned, not by rubbing a lamp, but merely by producing an expenses sheet and a pile of receipts.

To notice Preston's ubiquity left unanswered the question is he a 'hands-on' or a 'hands-off' editor? Neither is quite descriptive of Preston's style. His successor Alan Rusbridger described him as totally hands-off. In fact, his style was more a development of the collegiate approach of his predecessor Alastair Hetherington, in which senior staff and heads of departments were given ample freedom to confirm, or not, the wisdom of their appointments. Will Hutton, who as economics editor was a vigorous participant in Preston's morning conferences for the last five years of his editorship, used to say, 'Peter doesn't edit the paper, he chairs it.'[3]

Most of the time this approach worked well and helped to create within the paper a spirit that was considered to be unique to it. There was - on Preston's part at least - none of the ranting and raving, none of the peremptory firing, that supposedly went on in other Fleet Street papers, although it should be said that staff on the Guardian tended to have much less experience of life elsewhere in the industry than was the case among journalists on other newspapers. That was changing somewhat in the upheaval following Wapping, with the proliferation of new titles - both magazines and newspapers - that it stimulated. From Wapping onwards there were waves of new arrivals in Farringdon Road, as the Guardian added new sections and put on pagination.

The Wapping refuseniks were in a way pioneers. More came over the next two or three years from the failed enterprises of the time - the Sunday Correspondent, the News on Sunday, the London Daily News, and from weeklies such as City Limits. Many were still on the Guardian 20 or even 30 years later. Journalists would come to the Guardian and stay more or less for life.

Colleagues who worked closely with Preston in those years and earlier would speak of him admiringly both on a personal level and as a brilliantly innovative journalist, the consummate newspaperman (to use a recurring phrase) and a man in his element. They might sometimes speculate whether those qualities were transferable or depended upon the Guardian in some mutually exclusive contract: Preston sometimes seemed to permeate the Guardian rather than edit it in any conventional sense. Colleagues routinely use the words 'complex' or 'enigmatic' to describe his character when they began to explain the factors that, in their view, worked to produce such a clearly dynamic but apparently complicated individual.

Apart from the Sarah Tisdall debacle, which receives an obligatory mention in any account of his career, there were two factors commonly cited. One was the influence of his family background, and particularly the death of his father and the damage to his own health in a polio epidemic, and the other was the parsimony of Guardian life, both enforced and then carried on by habit, as the paper set out from Manchester to make its way in the world. It left Preston with a deeply ingrained habit of frugality or prudence, a kind of permanent anxiety. The paper's lack of financial resources in effect acted as a brake on innovation: how do you circumvent such economic constraints to do what you want to do and make the Guardian a truly competitive national newspaper, taken seriously by its rivals in Fleet Street? This is what Preston sought to do and what to a remarkable extent he managed to achieve.

His father was only recently demobbed from the Royal Air Force when he was swiftly killed by polio. He was 37. Preston may have reflected on this when, at the same age, he became editor of the Guardian. The epidemic left Preston himself with a permanent degree of disability, although he would grimace at that description since he dedicated himself to trying to ensure that his physical restriction was almost the last thing anyone noticed about him. He remembered Martin Woollacott, several years after they had begun working together at the Guardian, suddenly perceiving a difficulty and asking, 'Is there something wrong?' 'He didn't appear to have noticed that there were some things I couldn't do. I was very, very cheerful because Martin is an extremely bright and perceptive person.'[4] Cheerful and cheery are characteristically positive words in Preston's vocabulary.

Preston had been a very active boy, playing in goal for his form football team at Loughborough Grammar School, which he had entered only months before the polio outbreak. The family background was neither affluent nor intellectual but there was a very positive attitude towards education: there was no argument about finding the fees then necessary for Peter to enter the preparatory department of the grammar school. Preston's father, John Whittle Preston, was the son of a primary school head teacher and worked in the wholesale greengrocery business before and after military service. Preston's mother was the daughter of a builder. Peter, with his younger brother and sister, had grown up through the Second World War and seen the flicker of bombing raids in the night sky over Midlands cities.

When polio struck at the end of the 1940s he spent a couple of years in and out of hospital, with a long period in an iron lung, a life-saving ventilator in which the whole body except for the head was enclosed. 'I don't know whether they quite expected me to make it or not. It was a very dramatic time because you were clearly on the edge of dying.' On one of the very rare occasions, nearly half a century later, that Preston wrote about the experience, he described it as 'drifting back and forth across the edge of survival in a dreaming, fevered, but curiously peaceful way that, ever since, has made me feel a little less bad about dying itself'.[5] He had to spend several months flat on his back immobilised in a bed of plaster of Paris, which was used to manipulate, straighten and set limbs. His recovery was punctuated by a series of surgical operations designed to improve mobility, particularly in his arms, which had suffered severe muscle loss. One operation involved the grafting of bone from a leg to provide a shoulder joint, a peg, on which the worse-affected arm could pivot. Years later he would say, 'My left arm isn't much good. My right arm is pretty non-existent.'[6]

Surveying his 'long road back' to recovery at Harlow Wood, the orthopaedic hospital near Mansfield in Nottinghamshire, to which he was transferred after his operations, Preston recalled, 'The feared excursions to the hot baths where, if you slipped, there seemed to be no way of not sinking into oblivion. The tottery challenge of walking again. The stairs you had to inch down on your bottom. The simple, natural struggle to become passably mobile.'[7]

Ian Wright believed this period of illness and the struggle to survive it, to transcend it, set a pattern from which he never really deviated. The gritting of teeth was characteristic. As Wright said, 'Peter was and is a terrific fighter. You don't lie on your back for a year without character coming out.' David McKie, Preston's first deputy editor, shared that view. 'There's a lot of struggle in Peter and that's one reason why he was a good editor. He had surmounted so many obstacles that he was not deterred by them in the way that most people would have been.'[8] He pointed out too that Preston read prodigiously at this time.

Early in his long rehabilitation he was introduced to magic and found that, despite his restricted arm movements, he could perform conjuring tricks with great benefit to his self-confidence. He found that as well as tricks he was quite good at the distracting accompaniment of patter and jokes (almost a recipe for a newspaper diarist), so within a year or two he had started to do children's parties and school concerts. (For some later colleagues this was the part of Preston's story that required the hardest imagining.) The adult Preston often gave the impression he had something up his sleeve.

At the age of about 14 he became a junior member of Leicester Magic Circle, and a little later began contributing a column about magic programmes on television to the Circle's duplicated monthly newsletter. He was sacked for being too critical, but by then, through a friend at school whose father edited the Loughborough Monitor, he was contributing odds and ends to that. These were the first pieces of his to appear in a newspaper. However, it was not clear to all that a new direction was being determined.

His mother had remarried and Peter's headmaster, after discussion with his stepfather's father, suggested - ludicrously, says Preston - that he should leave at 16 to become a jewel cutter. That was resisted and happily he began to forge ahead at school, making it less of a surprise when he got to Oxford, where he read English at St John's. There he contributed to and finally edited the university newspaper Cherwell. By the time Preston came down he knew what he wanted to do.

Preston had come to Hetherington's Guardian in 1963 as a young married man with a recently arrived son, after a stint on the Liverpool Post where his real training, like that of several of his Guardian colleagues, took place. He had joined an office that was in mid-upheaval. Only a year later the editorial headquarters were transferred to the capital, where, from 1964, the Guardian shared a building with the Sunday Times in Gray's Inn Road. The Prestons moved to London the following year. For his first years on the paper the foreign desk remained in the old Manchester Guardian building in Cross Street, built in 1886. After the move, Alastair Hetherington commuted, generally spending three weeks in London and one in Manchester. A northern features and arts desk was maintained there into the 1990s. It was as though the paper could not or did not want to tear itself away from its native soil. Inter-city conferences were held by a two-way loudspeaker telephone known as a squawk box, with Manchester represented at editorial conferences in London by a disembodied and sometimes strangulated voice.

The move to London was always going to be a wrench. It was seen as a means to secure the long-term future of the Guardian, which in the end it appeared to have done. But initially it came close to disaster. An indication was the inordinate amount of time Hetherington was spending on the sleeper between Manchester and London - no fewer than 68 nights on the train in 1963, the year Preston joined the paper. Circulation did not make the predicted gains and budgets were tight: Hetherington considered that the worst mistake the Guardian made in the post-war years was to start printing in London on what he called 'an austerity basis'. The managerial structure was also inadequate - the Guardian had no separate management at this time. 'Editorially, too, we made the error of trying to run a two-headed operation, without one decisive centre of control.'[9]

Laurence Scott, the chairman and chief executive of the company and CP Scott's grandson, was the strongest advocate of a merger between the Times and the Guardian, believing the market could not sustain both titles. Failing that, he introduced the idea, on more than one occasion, of withdrawing from London and reverting to the title Manchester Guardian. This led to increasing friction between Hetherington and Laurence Scott, and finally to a standoff between Laurence and his cousin Richard Scott. Richard opened the decisive meeting of the Scott Trust on 21 November 1966 with quite a heroic and fundamental statement, asserting: '... ours is the chief responsibility for ensuring that actions are not taken which might jeopardise the essential character of the Guardian. If we fail in this, we are out of business.'

This was the background to Preston's early years on the paper. The proposed merger was ditched. Preston saw in the fate of his old paper the

Liverpool Post a final vindication of the Guardian's decision to go on alone. Like several other once-great provincial papers, it dwindled and died (its last issue was in December 2013). Preston thought that had the Guardian returned to Manchester, the same fate might eventually have overcome it too. The Scott Trust, in not turning back, had discovered its core role.

The decision to struggle on in London brought the need for redundancies throughout the organisation, but particularly in the editorial department, where 35 jobs were lost. The entire editorial staff of the paper at this time numbered fewer than 200. Ian Wright emphasised the influence on Preston: 'Peter lived through that period and he was absolutely shaped by that period.' For Preston, when the time came, there would be no standoff between editorial and commercial departments.

For now, Preston was making his mark writing the paper's diary, under the revived title of Miscellany. In his first three years on the Guardian he had already built up experience as a political reporter, a war reporter covering the civil war in Cyprus and the India–Pakistan war from Pakistan, and as an education correspondent. His Miscellany was distinguished by its humour, informality, breezy lack of deference and wide-ranging curiosity. It was unsigned but had what was already becoming known as Preston's inimitable style: the style was like the man and did not stand on ceremony. David McKie, a couple of years older than Preston, recalled being thrilled when nominated to stand in for him, then frustrated as he wondered whether Preston would ever take a break. 'Finally, he went away and I wrote a Miscellany column and took it through to Christopher Driver, the features editor, who in his lordly manner held it up by the scruff of its neck and said, "Tell me, did you self-consciously set out to parody Peter Preston?" And I said, "Yes of course I did."' McKie believed he could do no better than to continue seamlessly in the Preston manner. 'I plagiarised him really. He was just outstanding.'

How outstanding he was became apparent to all when in 1968 he succeeded Driver as features editor. The contrast could not have been more marked. Innovation was not the hallmark of Driver's pages; the department was, in Christopher Dodd's words, 'like a mausoleum'. Preston's arrival was a door opening. McKie, who postponed his transfer to the parliamentary staff to become Preston's deputy, recalled it as one of the great moments of his journalistic life. 'Peter and I had been a little ginger group in Alastair Hetherington's 10.30 conference constantly saying, "Why are features not doing that?" Christopher would say, "Well we'll be doing it some day next week." We'd say, "This is supposed to be a newspaper and we need to do it tomorrow." Then Peter suddenly got command of the area of which he'd been so critical and he absolutely transformed it. The day that he came in he took the feature writers, of whom there were a very small number, across to that awful pub [the Blue Lion in Gray's Inn Road] and they came out absolutely floating on air because his ideas were so exhilarating.'

Preston was certainly industrious, and inspirational, as features editor. He adopted the suggestion of his colleague Michael McNay to simplify or rationalise the layout of the feature pages, doing away with the design emanating from Manchester that had been typified by artfully deployed white space and bastard, that is non-standard, column measures, beautiful when it worked but difficult to coordinate among sub editors working in two centres. He cleared classified entertainments ads off the features page that he had inherited – a page dominated by a general feature with arts reviews below or around it – and created the Guardian's first all-arts page, making McNay, who had been the northern art critic, the arts editor. Under Preston, McNay, the most vociferous and talented, even belligerent, advocate of newspaper design, was to become assistant editor in charge of design ahead of the radical redesign of 1988.

Preston was features editor for four years and then became production editor, a position in which he was able to extend his knowledge of all the processes that go into the making and distribution of a paper, driving home the importance of meeting edition times whatever difficulties might stand in the way. A missed train meant a cut in circulation. According to colleagues, he was clearly Hetherington's preferred successor long before the change actually took place. In the event, the closest runner was John Cole – who subsequently left the Guardian to join the Observer – but he could not match Preston's range of experience, and so Preston, at the age of 37, became editor. Looking back, Preston said, 'I hadn't really expected it. I felt quite young as a matter of fact and pretty inexperienced in the sense that I hadn't been deputy editor, not even duty editor of the paper for more than a few Sundays.'

He took over at a time of international recession. Inflation in Britain had not long passed a peak of 27%. The price of the paper almost doubled in his first two years, rising from 8p when he took over in March 1975 to

15p in May 1977, hampering efforts to increase circulation or even maintain it at the 330,000 or so he had inherited. In addition, the Manchester office was being greatly reduced in size, and there were not comparable jobs available for everyone in London, where the move from Gray's Inn Road to Farringdon Road was little more than a year away. Eighteen years later, when Preston was addressing the staff of the newly acquired Observer for the first time, he referred to the virtual closure of the Manchester office as 'one of the most difficult things I have had to do in life'.

The building at 119 Farringdon Road was new but had not been custom-built to house a newspaper, or indeed to provide any aesthetic uplift to the area. It was in an advanced state of construction as a carpet warehouse when the Guardian stepped in and took it on a 15-year lease. One advantage of its originally designated purpose was that all the floors were reinforced to carry the unusual weight that massed carpets would have required. Peter Preston's Guardian moved into its new home in 1976. Shortly afterwards, Ratners, the jewellers, took over the whole of the fifth floor and used it as its distribution warehouse for the next nine years, during which time the Guardian on the lower floors was growing to bursting point. (Not long after Ratners moved out the Guardian bought the entire building on a 125-year lease for £3.2 million; it was sold on the move to Kings Place in 2008 for £37 million). Printing continued to be done in Gray's Inn Road, but the composing room with its Intertype typesetting machines had to be relocated in the basement of the new building over one weekend, so that no copies would be lost. Hot metal still had more than a decade to run. 'So, if you ask did I start with a set of fantastic aspirations and so forth, the answer is probably, yes, but I was so busy bailing north and south that it got a bit hairy.' You would call it a nightmare, except that Preston appears to speak of it - retrospectively, anyway - with a certain zest.

There is no zest associated with the Sarah Tisdall affair of 1983. Several things were brought home to Preston by the whole experience of the case, apart from the need to make sure that documents received in similar circumstances were destroyed and that the protection of sources, anonymous or not, did not rely upon inadequate legal safeguards. One was the total unpredictability of the flow of events, something that in normal circumstances was the main attraction of journalism. 'We'd had a pretty tumultuous first few years - moving office, almost going bust as it seemed to me, coping when the Times went out, starting to get some momentum and feeling pretty much that things had finally begun to move in a very good direction and then bang, all of this came and certainly produced a period of distraction and gloom and angst. And as you can possibly see it's still a bit raw. I was always and am always aware very acutely that there are human lives involved in all of this.'

The Tisdall affair was a good part of the reason for his joining the International Press Institute (IPI) in the mid-1980s. 'After Tisdall, which had been one of the most bruising and desultory times of my life, I re-realised what a very lonely job editing can be, and how isolated I could feel. I also ... became more concerned about editors and journalists in difficult situations.'[10]

The epigraph at the head of this chapter is an expression of the same thing. He wrote it to promote the European Press Prize, a kind of European equivalent to the American Pulitzer. It is a joint effort by a number of charitable foundations, which, like the Scott Trust, are dedicated to the promotion of quality journalism. The specific idea of the prize was Preston's.

Preston's will to communicate with Guardian journalists person to person was always strong. His stream-of-consciousness, informal style was generally appreciated, even though it sometimes resulted in puzzlement or amusement. A close colleague recalled, 'People would come to you and say, "What does the editor really mean?"' At times his language could become quite surreal. When an aspiring Jonathan Freedland, writing from Washington, applied for a reporter's job, Preston replied, 'The vibrant point is that Peter [Murtagh, then the home news editor] and I are extremely impressed with you and your potential. My solo vibrant point is that, unless you are going to throw cream buns at us, I would very much like to be kept informed of your movements over the next few months.' Freedland became the Guardian's Washington correspondent shortly after this. But nearly two decades later he was still wondering about the cream buns. Journalists sometimes left meetings with Preston genuinely puzzled as to what had transpired: Seumas Milne was among those who recalled being left in limbo after an inconclusive interview. 'We had a completely Prestonian-type discussion that was incredibly oblique. And at the end of it I said, "So that's all very interesting but are there any jobs coming up here?" And he said, "Oh I thought I just offered you one."'[11]

Preston's communiqués, posted on noticeboards for more general consumption, were apt to draw clusters of journalists offering contending interpretations. This was particularly so when the subject involved expenditure or the saving of money, when the language was likely to writhe uncomfortably.

He sometimes failed to share important information with the other members of the cabal that occupied his bunker. He had more than a touch of the conspiratorial loner, if that is not a contradiction in terms. When David McKie, closer to Preston than almost anyone - Michael White called him 'Preston's ambassador to the world'[12] - commiserated with Edward Pearce at losing his column on the Sunday Times, Pearce replied cheerily that he had been offered one at the Guardian. When McKie complained to Preston that he hadn't been told about it, he received the enigmatic response, 'There are things I try to shield you from.' It was never quite decided among students of Preston to what extent his obfuscation was a deliberately wielded tool of management. But a humorous irony was part of Preston's conversational style, and sometimes, yes, with a touch of mischief.

So Preston was just over halfway through his editorship of the Guardian when he faced the challenges at the end of the 1980s. But as we have seen, he had by then faced many challenges, both personal and professional, and dealt with them in his usual way, by carrying on.

In the middle of all the changes, there was an important and evocative marker. It was not Mrs Thatcher's confirmation of 11 June as polling day, noted in a leader in the Guardian under the heading: 'The lady may last forever'. Preston, for the moment, had other priorities. On the eve of poll in June he sent out a message calling all his heads of department to an awayday to plan strategy in the Guardian's battle against the Independent. But no, it was not that either.

The landmark event was the publication on Tuesday 12 May 1987 of the last edition of the Guardian in which hot metal type had played any part. By the end of the year the transition to fully computerised direct input and printing in the Isle of Dogs would be complete. Monday night, when the last hot metal front page was being prepared in Farringdon Road, was, as Christopher Dodd recorded, 'a night of wet-eyed sentiment'.[13]

But there was no time to mourn.

Chapter 4

Turmoil in the Newsroom and a Shock Departure

'I shall not run away. I shall not be pushed into a ghetto.
But I shall not deny myself to myself.'

Harriet Goldsmith, a character in *Traitors*,
a play by Melanie Phillips, 1986

There were significant changes on the news desk to accompany all the technological innovations of the late eighties and the most notable of these was the replacement of Melanie Phillips as news editor, with Paul Johnson, who had been recalled from Northern Ireland to work in effect as her deputy, or deputy-elect. Between them they ran the Guardian's coverage of the 1987 election, the first with a computerised results service, and the first in which reporters used mobile phones, if the term could be applied to the huge brick-like things with their long aerials that they were required to wield. Several of the Guardian's election staff had them, including David Gow and Alan Travis who were out on the stump with the two Alliance Davids, Gow with David Owen and Travis with David Steel. They were thus able to communicate with each other and record nuances of difference between the two Alliance leaders. (Gow, to the occasional annoyance of others, found the best place from which to dictate his copy was the lavatory closet on Owen's battle-bus).

There were only two daily newspapers favouring a Labour victory. They were Robert Maxwell's Daily Mirror, still with a circulation of over 3 million, and the Guardian with its half a million. The increasingly loss-making Today, by then owned by Tiny Rowland's Lonrho group and soon to be sold to Murdoch, wanted to see a coalition with the Alliance holding the balance as a moderating influence on Thatcherite

Conservatism. The new Independent loftily rose above the battle and endorsed no party at all. The rest, commanding between them a circulation of more than 10 million, were all for the Conservatives.

On the eve of the poll the Guardian set out its position in a long leader, not altogether clearly, perhaps. One analyst, Martin Harrop,[1] acknowledged that the Guardian's strength lay in the variety of viewpoints expressed in its columns. But he declared that on the basis of this particular leader the paper's own view could only be described as obscure. He compared the 'tortured ramblings' of the Guardian leader writers unfavourably with the accurate, thoughtful and detailed tone of the Independent's editorials. And, to rub it in, he made the obvious point that the Independent's photographs were 'quite the best of any paper'.

The Guardian leader writers were affronted to find themselves thus chastised, since on this occasion the leader had been written by the editor himself, a practice he followed on the eve of all general elections. To students of Prestonian language it is a rich study, but as Harrop tacitly conceded was certainly not impenetrable. It was broadly in favour of Labour, except when a tactical vote for the Alliance might keep out the Tories.

The internal politics of the newsroom were no less convoluted. Melanie Phillips recalled, '[Paul and I] worked very well together, I think to our mutual surprise because we hadn't been close, but I respected him a great deal, and I thought we'd both done a very good job. And then,' she declared, 'I was taken out and fired.' That was something of an overstatement. Almost immediately after the election Preston invited Phillips to lunch at the Kolossi, a Greek restaurant favoured by Guardian journalists (who knew it unappetisingly as the Kolostomy), not to fire her in any definitive sense, but to move her off the news desk. In fact, he offered her the position of policy editor, with a weekly column and the editorship of the social policy section, Society. This was not lightly done. The section had grown from a column begun in 1979 called Society Tomorrow and was soon attracting some £50 million a year in advertising. The quality of the editorial was crucial and not to be entrusted to any but the most capable. If that was being fired it would be difficult to imagine a less painful way of accomplishing it.

Paul Johnson was to become, for most of the next 30 years or so, probably the most important single individual in the daily production of the Guardian, a lynchpin amid all the changes of that time. He had a lust for and a grasp of news, a feeling for the nuances of the important stories of the day and, progressively, an encyclopaedic knowledge of the main players. He had been Peter Cole's preferred successor as news editor when Cole himself had been promoted to deputy editor after David McKie stepped down in 1984. 'I said to Preston there was only one person he could make news editor to succeed me and that was Paul Johnson. And he said, "Well yes Paul's very good but," etc, etc. He thought Melanie Phillips should have a crack at it. So Melanie became news editor and it was ... Well, it didn't work terribly well and she didn't like it, she wasn't happy doing it. And to his credit Peter came to me afterwards and he said, "I'm afraid I have to say you were right," and immediately appointed Paul.'

It was an untidy affair. Johnson was introduced on to the desk without any consultation with Phillips, 'without my say-so', as she put it. Few could have failed to notice that after Johnson's arrival on the desk, both Preston and Cole, when they needed to confer, bypassed Phillips and her nominal deputy John Gardner and went straight to Johnson. 'She did get bypassed both from below and above, with people preferring to deal with someone else,' Gardner agreed.[2] 'An appalling allegation that seems to have a kernel of truth,' Cole admitted.[3] Nikki Knewstub, who was the night news editor during this transitional period, suggested it went a little further than that, and that it was generally accepted by the reporters that, until Paul Johnson took over, John Gardner was the news editor.[4] It is perhaps a compliment to both Melanie Phillips and Paul Johnson that between them they supervised the transmission of a marginally greater volume of election coverage than any other paper without any falling-out between them. Several months after the election, Gardner resigned and left to work in New Zealand. His departure cleared the way for the Johnson news desk.

Phillips, then in her mid-30s, was by general consensus exceptionally bright with an incisive intelligence. She had joined the Guardian ten years earlier from Paul Barker's New Society, after Oxford and training on the Evening Echo, Hemel Hempstead. She had only just arrived at New Society when she heard that she had won the young journalist of the year award for a series she had written on hospitals for the Evening Echo; and only a couple of years after her arrival at the Guardian she won another award, reporter of the year, for her exposure of the use of virginity tests on immigrants from India arriving at Heathrow. Phillips had quickly become the Guardian's social policy correspondent and social policy leader writer in a newsroom run at that time by Jean Stead.

For many, particularly among her female colleagues, Phillips came not only to represent the advance of women in journalism, but also to epitomise the liberal values of the Guardian, being committed and passionate in her concerns and, although she identified herself as a leftie, apolitical or disinterested in the application of her reporting skills. It was a view that increased the shock caused by later developments. By the early 1980s she was being spoken of by senior colleagues as a possible future editor. Preston in an interview had referred to her as 'a corporal with a field marshal's baton in her knapsack' - 'corporal' rather than the usual 'private' presumably to signify that she already had a foot on a lower rung of the ladder.

It was the leader conferences that led to the realisation that some colleagues were consciously or unconsciously inclined to define her in a 'different' way. Her period as a leader writer coincided with the final stages of the Falklands war and the Israeli invasion of southern Lebanon. She was struck by a disparity in the attitude of her fellow leader writers towards Israel and towards other participants in the conflict, Syria in particular, and openly questioned the 'double standard'. She might have lobbed in a grenade. This was the first significant occasion on which she felt isolated among her Guardian colleagues. 'It was the first time it had been "you" and "us" ... "We do you the great honour of assuming that you are like us, that Israel is like us. You and the Israelis have the same value of human life so we judge you by our standards. And furthermore you tell us that you are superior to us, morally superior as Jews, so we are entitled to judge you by a higher standard."' Third world countries (as they were still called) did not share 'western' values and therefore were not judged by them. She insisted that this was no loose paraphrase. The second shock was the realisation that she was being seen first as a Jew, with the result that only that could account for her support for Israel in the present turmoil. This was brought home to her when one of the senior leader writers, leaving aside the major preoccupation with the Falklands, turned to her and said, 'Melanie, what are we going to say about *your* war?'

Three years as a leader writer ended when she was made news editor in 1984, and it was only then that she attempted to purge some of the anger and indignation she felt, not only at what she saw as the double standards of the Guardian's liberal intelligentsia, but also at its unconscious - mostly unconscious, she was prepared to say - anti-Semitism. The vehicle she chose was a play called *Traitors*, directed by Julia Pascal at the Drill Hall in London in 1986 (a lesbian theatre at the time, Phillips later recalled)[5] and reviewed by Michael Billington in the paper that it was fairly obviously castigating.[6] He found it overloaded with themes and often defying probability, but nevertheless confronting a number of important ideas, among them British anti-Semitism, the polite cruelties of liberalism and the divided loyalties of an assimilated English Jew. It is clearly based very closely indeed on Phillips's experience at the Guardian. Phillips summed up, 'It included the stuff I'd been told at the Guardian. And people from the Guardian came and saw the play. And those people who'd [actually] said these things to me said, "What kind of people would say this kind of thing to you?"'

Phillips has sometimes been called a north London bluestocking, but 'No, I was born and bred in Hammersmith. "North London" is code, it's just a way of saying I'm a Jew.' Her parents were observant, up to a point. 'They kept a kosher home. They did not observe the Sabbath. My parents worked in a shop on Saturday and it was their busiest day.' Her own household - she is married to the journalist Joshua Rozenberg - has been more observant, and her religion is an aspect of her life that has become increasingly important.

In some senses it was a sheltered life that did not prepare her for the ordinary insults of journalism. Then and throughout her career, strong motivation was always necessary to overcome a natural shyness, which she conceded was not a characteristic that many would attribute to her, least of all those who found her readiness to express forthright opinions 'aggressive', a term almost always applied to women rather than men.

From the beginning of her career at the Guardian, Preston had her marked as a rising star and may have been looking to broaden her experience. Phillips was aware that her name was being connected with the job of news editor. 'I thought it was all pretty unrealistic, and then Peter called me in and said, "I want to make you the news editor." I thought this is a really bad idea. And I remember saying to him, "Do you think this is quite me? Shouldn't I be doing features?" He said, "No, you are news." He was correct. I am absolutely a news person ... You have to recall that I thought I wouldn't be suited to journalism and I'd managed so far quite well. I had won two awards. So I thought, well, maybe I'm wrong again. Maybe it will be fine. I remember saying to him, "I'm a bit nervous." He said, "No, you'll be fine. You really will be fine." But I wasn't fine. It was a bad mistake.'

She became the Guardian's third female news editor, after Nesta Roberts (1961 to 1963) and Jean Stead (1969 to 1979). Stead had had the advantage of being for several years deputy to her predecessor John Cole (no relation to Peter) before she succeeded him. Phillips's experience might have been different had she had a similar period as deputy, but alas she hadn't. Phillips felt that being suddenly plucked from the newsroom (where she had chosen to remain rather than to move into the leader writers' room) attracted a degree of resentment. She had been one of the toilers in the field. Now she was in charge of the farm.

She had never encountered raw unsubbed copy before and the shock of that first sight of it stayed with her. She had also never come across anything like the strongly prevailing macho culture on the 'back bench' – the senior journalists who had the final decision on what would go into the paper. They were a formidable law unto themselves. Phillips would find that a story she had been developing with a reporter with a view to a place on page one was often rejected by the back bench. Not surprisingly, repetition of this kind of thing affected her standing in the newsroom. There were other problems. There were people in the newsroom who were regarded by the bunker and senior colleagues as not usefully productive and she was expected to do something about that too, although no one said exactly what.

The prevailing culture was totally alien to her. The back bench was all male (although both night *news* editors at that time were female). 'I was expected to go to the pub. I'd never been to a pub in London in my life. They [her news desk colleagues] would all stand there with their shiny, baggy trousers, jingling their coins in their pockets, sinking pints, and I would be gasping for breath because I couldn't bear the cigarette smoke. It was just hideous. And they all spoke a language I couldn't speak. They talked in elliptical phrases, many of them sporting metaphors, and I had absolutely no idea what they meant.'

The night editor was Philip Osborne, a post he held throughout Preston's entire editorship of practically 20 years. Osborne was habitually the last person of authority to see the paper off to press. Like Phillips, Osborne had read English at Oxford. He had come away with a passion for PG Wodehouse, a wry humour perhaps necessary to mitigate the stresses of late-night newspaper production. Despite the heavy burden of his own job, Osborne sympathised with Phillips's plight. 'He said, "It's no good. You've got to learn cricket, otherwise you can't cope."' He took her to Lord's, her first cricket match. 'That's how bad it was. They [the back bench] regarded me quite clearly with absolute contempt.'

The two female night news editors during her time as news editor, first Nikki Knewstub and then Anne McHardy, tried to help. McHardy, who had joined the night desk in 1981, in particular became friends with Phillips, and they bonded over their first children, who were both born in 1980. But there was little that could be done to help someone who, it became apparent, was fundamentally the wrong person for the job of news editor.

Phillips had set out with conflicting advice. On the one hand, she needed to change the copy flow system to one in which the news editor saw a story through from development to placement on a page and publication. On the other, 'I was told, "Don't try and change anything, manage it."' She felt there was a lack of support from Preston. 'To be fair to him, he expected me just to have the wit and the savvy to work out how to do it and then to do it. Had I been a different character I might have been more successful at this. I'm sure I made many mistakes.'

At one stage Peter Cole, to whom she frequently turned for advice, proposed she should visit Paul Johnson in Belfast. It was her first visit to Northern Ireland. From her point of view there were at least two good reasons for the trip. Northern Ireland was one of the most important parts of her constituency. 'But secondly I was aware that Paul was Peter Cole's protégé, and I needed to know him because he was someone who was going places.'

Johnson was the first person that Peter Cole had hired on becoming news editor in 1979 (the second was Alan Rusbridger). He was employed in the new role of Midlands correspondent, hired from the Western Mail in Cardiff, where he had been a leader writer. He had taken an economics degree at Cardiff University, then stayed on for a postgraduate diploma in journalism. He impressed Cole at the interview, mainly through his news sense, and because he was affable, highly intelligent and politically sharp.

His reporting from Birmingham quickly justified his appointment. In 1984 he was transferred to Belfast, becoming the latest in a long line of Northern Ireland correspondents whose close reporting of the Troubles had won the Guardian respect and trust. Johnson followed the Guardian practice of working close to his material. He took a flat in the Stranmillis area, close to the city centre, where he was quite often woken by the boom of one more bomb exploding.

Typical of Johnson's reporting was his coverage of events in mid-August 1984, not long after he had arrived there, when the RUC killed a man and injured many more in their failed attempt to capture the banned Noraid leader Martin Galvin at a rally. The man who was killed was only a few yards from Johnson when he was fatally struck by a plastic bullet. 'It was one of those times when you are caught up in things, and a little bit of emotion can take over. If you are in a situation where an unarmed man – he was brandishing a bit of a stick – can be shot dead only three, four, five yards away from you I think you are entitled to some personal emotion.' In 1985 Johnson was runner-up to the reporter of the year for his work in Northern Ireland (the winner of the top award that year was David Leigh).

When Melanie Phillips arrived in Belfast, Johnson took her to the Sinn Fein headquarters on the Falls Road, and after that he introduced her to the general secretary of the Official Unionist Party. Whether she had an idea that Johnson would eventually take over from her, indeed whether Johnson had any idea, is not clear. Certainly Peter Cole had not given up on the notion. More or less from the time he had hired Johnson he had thought him 'a born news editor'.

There were successes. She had hired Peter Murtagh, one of the Wapping refuseniks, from his gloomy exile in Gray's Inn Road. Before the Sunday Times he had worked for the Irish Times in Dublin. Partly because of his knowledge of the complexities of Ireland, Phillips put him to work on the Stalker Inquiry – the inquiry carried out by John Stalker, the deputy chief constable of Greater Manchester, into the alleged shoot-to-kill policy operated by the RUC against the Provisional IRA in 1983. In particular Murtagh exposed the false allegations that had led to Stalker's temporary suspension and removal from the inquiry in 1986. He won the reporter of the year award for his persistent coverage of the affair.

Phillips also claimed credit for signing up Ed Vulliamy, who was to become a great asset to both the Guardian and, after its acquisition in 1993, the Observer. He had already appeared in the Guardian. His first piece, published on 31 May 1985, was written jointly with his old school friend, Patrick Wintour, who had already been on the Guardian for

18 months. With another school chum, Roger Cohen (later of the New York Times), they had made an annual reunion of the European Cup Final. That year it was the fateful match between Liverpool and Juventus at the Heysel stadium in Brussels. Rioting English fans caused a panic and crush in which 39 people were killed. But Vulliamy's real entry into the Guardian was on New Year's Day 1986 – he remembered that New Year's Eve as a particularly abstemious one, as he didn't want to appear dishevelled when he presented himself for work the following day in the new job, taken at about half the salary he had been earning in his previous role at Granada Television. He entered a newsroom in which all was not well.

Phillips's achievements, weighed in the balance of newsroom opinion, were insufficient to tip the scales in her favour. Grumbling around the shop found a focus at the bar of the City Pride, across the road from the office, where half a dozen or so disgruntled colleagues calling themselves the '1789 Group' met to plot her removal from the job. In the subculture of Fleet Street, there was nothing unusual or, by prevailing standards, even particularly malicious in this. Such cabals, if not common in the Guardian, were not unknown to it either. As the crisis passed so did the 1789 group. But very soon another had taken its place: the Gulshan group, meeting occasionally over an Indian meal (actually Bangladeshi) in the Gulshan restaurant, in Exmouth Market, a five-minute walk from the office. A leading light was Seumas Milne, its organiser, and the group included, from time to time, Victoria Brittain, Richard Gott, John Gittings, Martin Kettle, Richard Norton-Taylor, David Pallister and others. Gittings remembered it as really little more than a talking shop of no political significance, but that is to understate it. As the changes over the next year or two determined the path the paper was taking with increasing clarity - that is towards a broadly left-of-centre but essentially independent mainstream paper, now adding diverse consumer matters to its range of interests - so the Gulshan group came to be seen even more clearly as a gathering of dissidents. They did not want the core of news and political coverage to be submerged in all this other stuff, or in popular and celebrity culture, in what Melanie Phillips - who was never a member of the group - dismissed as froth. They were anti-froth. The group was made up of two overlapping elements: those who were concerned that the changes were taking the paper downmarket, and those who believed the paper was drifting to the right, squeezing the radical element. They were not issues that would remain for long simply matters of internal debate.

In the circumstances it was greatly to her credit that Phillips quickly embarked upon a new phase of her career, as a columnist, and very soon an extremely controversial one. In her experience of the past few years she appeared to have discovered a steely resilience, something similar perhaps to that of her character Harriet Goldsmith in *Traitors*: 'I shall not run away. I shall not be pushed into a ghetto. But I shall not deny myself to myself.' After her first column Peter Cole had offered some advice. 'He took me aside and said, "This is a perfectly good piece but it's not a column. In a column you have to have passion, you have to release what you think. So write about something that really matters to you. Why don't you write about education for example? You've been going on and on about education for years." I had two little children. In 1987 they were seven and five. So I was preoccupied by the difficulty of finding schools for them and I could see that something had gone badly wrong with education. It couldn't be explained by the left's favourite bogey woman Mrs Thatcher. It wasn't explained by cuts to public spending. Something had gone wrong with what teachers were thinking and how they were teaching. He said, "Write about that. Write from your own experience. Write with passion."' That is what she did. 'The balloon went up overnight. My colleagues at the Guardian said, "Have you gone mad? This is Daily Mail." The left, the teaching profession, went ballistic.'

The balloon, having gone up, never came down. Her trenchant views challenged certain core Guardian constituencies and brought down upon her opprobrium expressed in terms that later internet monitors routinely cut from comment threads. Stephen Bates, hired as education editor in 1990 - from the Daily Mail, as it happened - sat next to her in 'B Block' (as part of the newsroom was known, in borrowed prison terminology) and found her a brave and beleaguered figure. They became friends and mutually supportive. 'She got a torrent of abuse from the readership. They were basically saying we think you're great, you write wonderful stuff about social deprivation and disadvantage, and then you get to education and your skull explodes and you're horrible about us teachers and it's not our fault and you ought to be boiled in oil.'[7]

Phillips had ranged ever wider, not hesitating to prod politically tender spots: care in the community, multiculturalism, family breakdown ... 'People in the office stopped sending me invitations, all the sort of little things that make office life bearable, you know, come out to lunch, little messages, it all stopped.' She became, with a kind of condescending affection, 'Mad Mel'.

There was a crucial divergence of opinion over the environment. The Guardian's environmental coverage increased throughout the 1980s, with John Ardill becoming the paper's first environment correspondent in 1985. Even earlier than that Paul Brown had become involved in environmental reporting. He had joined the Guardian in 1982 from the Sun - possibly the only reporter ever to arrive by that particular route - before which he had been news editor of the Evening Echo in Hemel Hempstead (where he supervised a young leftwing trainee, Melanie Phillips). In 1985, Brown spent a month aboard the Greenpeace vessel, the *Rainbow Warrior*, and had just returned to England when it was blown up by French intelligence operatives, killing the photographer with whom he had shared a cabin. There were other significant events: the discovery by British scientists of the hole in the Antarctic ozone layer, also in 1985; the Chernobyl nuclear accident of 1986; and the success of the Green Party in gaining 15% of the vote in the 1989 European Parliament elections.

John Vidal, an indefatigable environmental reporter, said: 'Coverage of all these events suggested that the environment was rising up the political and social agendas and becoming a multidisciplined issue that needed more reflection in the paper.'[8] Over the winter of 1988 Paul Brown spent three months in Antarctica as a crew member of another Greenpeace ship, the *Gondwana*, becoming the first journalist to report live from Antarctica via a new satellite link.

By then Preston had taken a number of significant steps to improve the Guardian's coverage. One of them was to replace John Ardill as environment correspondent with Paul Brown, a disappointment for Ardill, whose co-authored book, *The Greenhouse Effect*, had just come out. More dramatically, Preston raised the profile of environmental coverage in the paper. Two years earlier, in July 1987, Vidal, then a sub-editor, had suggested to him that the paper should have a weekly section dedicated to the environment, something no other newspaper had. The time now seemed right. Preston came back to him, saying, 'Your idea - you do it.' He gave him two weeks to prepare the first edition. Environment Guardian was launched in September 1989 to command the second broadsheet section on Fridays. The editor chosen for the job was Melanie Phillips.

A clash between the editor of the new section and the science and environment staff of the Guardian was inevitable. From the very start, according to Vidal, Phillips contested the validity of the emerging science. 'She could not accept that the world's climate could be changed by man.' Things came to a head at Preston's morning conference when she openly challenged a front-page lead by Brown. 'It was an exclusive. I had been given a draft of a report of the United Nations Intergovernmental Panel on Climate Change.' It was sensational stuff. 'It warned among other things that the south of England would be warm enough for malaria and other tropical diseases to invade. It was this that Melanie particularly objected to and said could not possibly be correct and accused me of going over the top.' John Vidal took over as environment editor in 1992. Melanie Phillips continues at the time of writing to propound the view that man-made global warming is a global fraud.

Meanwhile, in the newsroom, Paul Johnson had set about his new role in a way that gathered consensus round Peter Cole's declaration that he was 'a born news editor'. The newsroom that he inherited was riven. There were those who had supported Melanie Phillips and those who had not. There were those on the left, and those - in the way these things were defined at that time - who were on the right of the left. And there were defensive demarcation lines round other departments. Johnson recalled, 'It struck me that between some of the departments on the Guardian there existed a state of semi civil war. One of my colleagues walked down to the City department at one point in my early days on the news desk and somebody stood out into the corridor, blocked their way and said, "Can I help you?" It was an extraordinary set-up.' He decided that a start on breaking down these barriers could be made in the network of Clerkenwell pubs where journalists drank after (or in those days sometimes during) work. He inaugurated a peripatetic Thursday night drink, usually in the City Pride, sometimes in the Crown, where Karl Marx had occasionally had a tipple, or the Horseshoe, where the newsroom drank with other departments as well. The core always consisted of the reporters, home subs, news desk and parliamentary staff who came up from Westminster for the occasion - largely if not exclusively male gatherings.

Preston referred to it as 'the Thursday swill'. Fifteen or twenty people, sometimes more, raised their glasses together on these evenings. Those who stayed the course finished up drinking lager over a curry in the Gulshan. It became a ritual that lasted well into the 1990s.

Johnson saw the divisions within the newsroom as a diversion of energy from the real task. 'I was much more interested that people should concentrate their efforts on their reporting ... There was a bit too much ideology around news itself.'

He made what proved to be two very good appointments to his desk. One was Michael Ellison, a Northern Irelander who had eschewed the bigotry amid which he had grown up in favour of a sardonic scepticism; he was never quite ready to admit success in anything or anyone, including perhaps himself. He was taken from the home subs benches, which he had joined from the Irish Times a year or two earlier. He eventually conceded that better times had come upon him with his promotion to the news desk and bought a suit of Donegal tweed, to be worn with or without cowboy boots, in which he impersonated a misanthropic character from a John Huston movie. If he considered a story to be 'crap', then he would say, 'This is crap.' He was considered an excellent judge.

The other appointment was Duncan Campbell, whom Johnson thought 'absolutely terrific, calm, experienced, eclectic, witty and wise'. He arrived at the Guardian bathed in the aura of his association with Julie Christie, his partner, already the star of more than 20 films. For a while Campbell and Ellison were left in the Guardian manner to wonder which of them, if either, was deputy news editor, and then, as Ellison put it, '"They" made up their minds not to make up their minds and Duncan and I became joint deputy news editors.'[9]

Johnson, by now known around the newsroom simply as PJ, had created with his two deputies what Campbell, not given to overstatement, called 'a terrific camaraderie'. He said, 'I think it helped that the three of us got on well together. I can remember we all went down to watch second-division Plymouth Argyle play Oldham Athletic, eating meat pies on the terraces.'[10]

By now revolutions were under way in the two biggest sections of the paper: news, on the first floor at Farringdon Road, and features, on the floor above, with the Weekend Guardian making its first appearance on a Saturday at the end of 1988 (see Chapter 7). In the newsroom, the progressive changes had already been considerable. Ellison recalled, 'No one was told that things were not going to continue as they had done. It simply became apparent over time that just because you presented a piece of copy, that did not mean that it would appear; that it may well not appear as written; and that, horror of horrors, you might actually be told once in a while what to do and how to do it. Paul was very good at this but I'm sure it was resented in many quarters.'

Duncan Campbell spent three years working on Johnson's desk and developed a great admiration for him. At the end of his term he became crime correspondent, following the publication of his survey of the current crime scene, *That Was Business, This is Personal*,[11] a series of interviews with criminals, lawyers, policemen and the like. It was launched with a publisher's party attended by a selection of interviewees. 'A detective sergeant in the drug squad kept asking me, "Which ones are the bank robbers?" And I said, "I don't think they're here yet." Then he tapped me on the shoulder and said, "I've seen your bank robbers." And I looked round and there was Paul Johnson and Mike Ellison.'

Campbell's admiration for Johnson easily survived their three years of storm and stress together. 'PJ had a terrific news sense, great energy, made quick decisions, and was very good at seeing a line in a story that perhaps the reporter or correspondent had not spotted. He was always primarily a news man, and I think he and Peter Cole, who backed him up, were responsible for making the Guardian much more proactive as a news paper (I use the gap between the words advisedly) and not as an organ that followed things up slowly.' It was Peter Cole who had said - repeating an occasional slur - 'The Guardian's a fine paper, but you have to read something else as well if you want to know what's going on.' Now this was starting to change.

Then an offer out of the blue forced Cole to consider his own future. Should he go or stay? He was 42. Preston seemed totally secure in his bunker despite the inroads of the Independent. The word was that if it overtook the Guardian's circulation then that would be the end of him. It was not at all certain that Cole would inherit the throne. Melanie Phillips was still considered by some to be a possible candidate: she had at the very least the courage of her convictions. There were others in the running. Martin Kettle would have been a candidate. Martin Walker, perhaps: he was already seen as an outstanding correspondent and commentator. Even at this time Cole maintains he had put his own money on Rusbridger as the next editor. In the autumn of 1988 when Cole was offered the chance to edit what became the Sunday Correspondent, the launch of which was still a year away, he seized it.

Cole's departure came as a 'complete bombshell' (Cole's words) to Preston, and he tried to dissuade Cole from going. In Cole's account, Preston said, 'Look, I wouldn't stop you going off to edit [the new Sunday newspaper] but can I just advise you as a friend: do not do it, it will not work.' The seriousness of the situation was emphasised by the adjournment of their discussion to a lugubrious bar off Farringdon Road – 'a terrible place that no one ever went into,' said Cole – where they talked for two to three hours.

The decision to offer the Correspondent job to Cole seems to have been made on the spur of the moment. He was telephoned by Gavyn Davies, an economist with Goldman Sachs – later chairman of the BBC – and a former five-a-side football teammate of Cole's from the 1970s. Davies asked him to drop by his house in Lloyd Square, ten minutes' walk away from the Guardian office. Cole arrived to find a dinner party in progress. 'Gavyn broke away from that, took me into a back room and showed me what turned out to be a draft prospectus for the Sunday Correspondent and said, "Have a read of that and I'll come back after the main course." So I sat there and skimmed through it. When he returned he said, "I just wondered if you were remotely interested because we'd like to have you as editor-designate," but he quickly added, "I should say we haven't raised the money yet. We would have three or four months to do that and if we raised it you would be editor and if we didn't you wouldn't and there wouldn't be a Correspondent." So it was a risky strategy.'

Cole was briefed about the task ahead: 'They had an initial million pounds, seed-corn money, from Prudential, and the deal was that, having appointed me and Nick Shott [an investment banker who was to be chief executive], we would make a series of presentations to venture capitalists and try to raise the £18 million needed to launch.' Cole decided to take the risk.

He left the Guardian in September, to prepare for the planned birth of the new paper the following year. In quite a remarkable way Preston, helped by Ian Wright and Jim Markwick, turned Cole's departure and the impending arrival of the Sunday Correspondent into an advantage. Before the year was out, Jonathan Fenby, the home editor of the Independent, and said to be one of the main figures driving its success, responded to an approach from Ian Wright, jumped ship and joined the Guardian as Cole's replacement. Fenby's Independent colleague Peter Wilby signed his farewell card with the memorable advice, 'Beware of the Trots!' Fenby didn't feel too bad about his departure. He had gone into the office on his day off for the chat with Andreas Whittam Smith, the editor of the Independent, that might have persuaded him to change his mind and been kept waiting for three hours. There is no doubt that his transfer to the Guardian was a coup for Preston, the first major signing against a tide that was running in the Independent's favour.

There was something else that could be done. In October it was revealed that the Independent was preparing costings for a Sunday newspaper. An indirect blow might be struck against the Independent by investing in the Sunday Correspondent. Peter Cole was told he could count on a couple of million pounds from the Guardian, a sum agreed between Guardian chairman Harry Roche and Douglas Long, the chairman-designate of the Correspondent. What Cole wasn't told was that the investment had yet to receive the guarantee of full Guardian group board approval.

These were crucial months in the competition between the Guardian and the Independent. Just before Fenby took the call from Ian Wright, the Independent had launched its Saturday magazine under the editor-ship of Alexander Chancellor. It was an immediate success. Alarmingly, by November the Independent was selling more than the Guardian on Saturdays, although overall the Guardian was still ahead. But Preston was able to tell the Scott Trust that plans were well advanced for the Guardian's own Saturday magazine. Two days before the Guardian launched its Weekend tabloid, Andreas Whittam Smith sent a memo round to all Independent staff, which rapidly found its way to the press: there would be no Sunday Independent in 1989. The daily Independent was at last becoming profitable and extra resources were to be put into that – not good news for the Guardian, but music to the ears of the group committed to the Correspondent.

Cole was involved in a hectic round of money-raising with his new colleagues at the embryonic Sunday broadsheet. With Nick Shott he embarked on the task of raising the £18 million needed for the launch. By the end of the year they had made 86 presentations to venture capitalists - the precise number stuck in Cole's mind. They had a good response but were still some £4 million short. Then, early in January, a fairly exhausted Cole took a midnight phone call from Peter Preston. 'Preston said, "I think I'd better tell you that it's all a bit awkward and there will be contacts tomorrow officially, but I thought the least I could do after everything was to tip you off - the Guardian has decided to pull out its two million." This was completely devastating, because one moment we were four million short and now it was six million. I said, "Thank you for telling me, this is extremely bad news," and I was on the phone most of the night, obviously with the new colleagues.'

The next morning Cole phoned Preston and spoke to his secretary, Moira Gutteridge, and told her he had to see Preston on a 'seriously urgent' matter. 'Peter sent a message back through Moira saying it would be impossible because he was completely tied up all day. Meanwhile Harry Roche had been in touch with Douglas Long to formalise what I had been told, that the Guardian was pulling out. So I asked Moira where Peter was lunching and she told me he was due to have lunch with Roy Jenkins at some restaurant in Pimlico. I knew his pattern of life exactly, that the taxi would be sitting outside 119 Farringdon Road, and I said, "Just so that he's not surprised, tell him that when he comes out to go off to lunch I will be sitting in the taxi."'

It must have been an extremely uncomfortable taxi ride. Cole wasted no time. 'I'd rehearsed this speech in my mind numerous times, I said, "All right, you can't stop the money being pulled out but the reason I wanted to see you face to face was for you to be absolutely certain and in no doubt about it that it was the Guardian that killed the Sunday Correspondent" ... You could see that if the taxi hadn't been in motion he would have jumped out. He hated it. And I just hammered away because obviously I was highly emotional. He couldn't wait to get there but unfortunately the traffic was heavy so the journey took a long time. When we eventually got to the restaurant he said, "I've got to go. I've got Roy Jenkins waiting in there." So I said, "Well, before you get out, Peter, I just want you to know as you walk into your lunch with Roy Jenkins that you've killed the Correspondent. OK?"'

It was to prove a (somewhat) premature declaration of death. Meanwhile, the Guardian was busy exploring other ways to beat off its increasingly troublesome competition.

Chapter 5
The Radical Redesign of 1988

'Sir, I understand that next February you are introducing a new modern typeface. May I be the first to say I don't like it.

Yours faithfully, Robert Breckman'[1]

Part of what Preston had called the 'insouciance' that afflicted the Guardian in the face of the upstart Independent probably came from the reassuring presence of its core of loyal readers, or from an assumption that it was larger and more loyal than was perhaps the case. It was true that the paper had a strong bond with its readers - the arrival of three or four hundred letters in every day's post intended for publication as 'Letters to the Editor' said as much. In times of crisis there could be twice as many: and 'crisis' might mean anything from war in the Middle East to moving the crossword from its usual position. The Guardian reader was thought to be a type. There was a plaintive letter, 6 July 1987, from Robert Moore of Aberdeen. 'Sir, - I recently asked a smoker not to smoke in a small, non-smoking departure lounge at Heathrow. "What are you, a Guardian reader, or something?" he replied ... How common is "Guardian reader" becoming as a term of abuse?' The answer was quite common; and the image of the Guardian reader as someone ready to argue or complain has persisted. Guardian readers, annoying or otherwise, were jealously proprietorial. It was their paper and the question was whether the journalists were to be trusted with it.

How much more of a shock it was then, when those readers started hotfooting it to the Independent in droves. David McKie, in a memo to Preston, was forthright about the cause. 'I am struck by the drift to the Independent among friends of 30 years, people as old and boring as myself and therefore perhaps of declining significance, often because they find our political conditioning too aggressive. We claim we are the true independents but it lacks credibility when the paper is full of reporting which says "I know which side *I'm* on."' Looking back to this time, he put it bluntly, 'The Independent was in a way a rebuke to the Guardian. It pointed out to the Guardian its faults, which Peter immediately began to worry about and think about and decide how to redeem.'[2] Discussion of the Independent often seemed to dominate the morning conference to the point where on one occasion Peter Cole remarked, 'Shall we perhaps spend a couple of minutes on the Guardian?'[3]

The early inauguration of the new computerised Koenig & Bauer presses in their custom-built hall on the Isle of Dogs was the urgent goal. Two months after hot metal setting was finally phased out in Farringdon Road, and with the new presses still not ready, it was decided that the presses in Gray's Inn Road had definitely had their day. The quality of the papers they were producing was considered to be now so poor that the Guardian would have to look for some interim measure until the Isle of Dogs presses came into operation towards the end of the year.

Satellite printing provided the solution. From the beginning of July the Guardian was printed in five separate centres: Uxbridge, Manchester, Portsmouth, Northampton and Guildford. There was one advantage in the arrangement, apart from the general improvement in print quality. The end of printing in Gray's Inn Road released the Guardian's employees there and enabled them to become familiar with the new presses nearing readiness in the Isle of Dogs. But the coordination of five-centre satellite printing was a testing experience. The pages were transmitted by facsimile, but in Guildford the local branch of the typesetter's union, the NGA, unilaterally refused to print them. Urgent legal action was required to bring about an eleventh-hour change of mind. Jim Markwick, the managing director, summoned the Guardian's lawyers and together they roused the duty judge, Mr Justice Beldam, in his flat off Fleet Street. Clad in a dressing gown befitting the late hour, he granted an order that was soon being waved in front of the NGA pickets at Guildford. Markwick told the local NGA leader, 'I have no personal malice against you, but this is a judge's order allowing us to use these presses tonight and if you prevent us from doing so I shall sue you for your home, your car, your wife and your dog.' The reply came back, 'I haven't got a dog.' The paper was printed there for the rest of the interim.

Throughout 1987 the Farringdon Road building - the would-be carpet warehouse - was being torn apart and patched under the anxious eyes of Ian Wright and his assistant Philippa King. 'This was not only to house the eight new computers in almost surgical cleanliness,' said Harry Jackson, 'but to accommodate the vast amount of cabling needed to hook up nearly 200 terminals ... typesetters, line printers and all the other iron-mongery of newspaper production.'

In June the general election - the first with a computerised results service - took place with the news editor Melanie Phillips and her newly appointed assistant Paul Johnson sometimes working in a cloud of builders' dust. It provided one more difficulty to add to the others described in the preceding chapter. 'Amazingly, we met all our produc-tion deadlines,' said Jackson. He devised an ingenious plan to roll out the new computer system. 'I think it was probably the most unpopular thing I have ever done. I took over the canteen and had that wired up and equipped with terminals.' One department after another was then moved in and trained on the Atex system while the journalists' vacated home was being wired up for their return.

In September, the first press at the Isle of Dogs was started, and declared a success, although for several weeks Koenig & Bauer engineers continued to run it. Negotiations were well advanced for the Observer (not yet owned by the Guardian, of course) to be printed on them, and that contract would bring the Guardian a useful annual income of £500,000. By November, amid all the distracting necessities, the Guardian's circu-lation had slipped to 470,000, still holding off the Times at 455,000, but with the Independent at 370,000 continuing to narrow the gap. There were still eight weeks to go, Preston told the Guardian board - of which he was now chairman - before completion of the presses. That and the simultaneous completion of the final phase of direct input by journalists would 'enable us to do what we should have been doing 18 months ago to counter the Independent'. Preston also had an ace that he had not yet played: in characteristic manner, he had been keeping his cards very close to his chest.

In the meantime, a further posse of journalists arrived from two conspicuous failed enterprises, Robert Maxwell's London Daily News - 'For the city that never sleeps, the paper that never stops' - which survived just the five months from February to July, and the slightly longer-lived leftwing tabloid News on Sunday – 'No tits, but a lot of balls'[4] – which launched disastrously in April and closed in November. Rather nobly, it had been based in Manchester. Failed or not, the journalists involved in these entrepreneurial essays had gained first-hand experience of the revolution sweeping through Fleet Street. The collapse of the London Daily News brought back to the Guardian the person who would become its next editor, Alan Rusbridger. Magnus Linklater, the editor of the London Daily News, had recruited Rusbridger from the Observer, where he had been working, not altogether happily, as television critic, and led him in to see Maxwell in his glass tower at Holborn Circus so that the latter could confirm his appointment as Washington correspondent. Maxwell was less than impressed and made it clear that he was bowing to Linklater's unfathomable whim. After asking Rusbridger whether he took drugs, and if he was a communist, he told him he would have to interview his wife, Lindsay Mackie. 'I can't imagine why you've been offered this job, you appear to know nothing about America and there's nothing in your CV to suggest that you do.' He then surprised Rusbridger by insisting that he should sign a contract for three years, only reducing it to two when the interviewee demurred. Five months later when Maxwell suddenly closed the paper, the redundancy money, thanks to the proprietor's insistence on a long contract, was sufficient to pay for central heating to be installed in the Rusbridgers' home in Highbury, north London. By then Maxwell had fallen in love with his Washington correspondent and asked him to be his biographer and to write speeches for him. The offers were declined.

Rusbridger was not the only refugee from Maxwell's paper. Among others were Murray Armstrong, Desmond Christy, Ian Mayes (myself) and Richard Bates, who all came to work in Richard Gott's features department. Bates had been at the Guardian only two months when on the way home to his wife and two young children one evening in November he was caught in the horrendous fire at King's Cross station, an unprecedented Underground disaster that shocked the nation. It killed 31 people. Bates lost the skin from his face, all his hair, and both hands were badly burnt. In his long recovery he suffered psychological trauma that included involuntary playbacks of the minutes when, in the dense smoke blackout after a fireball had swept up an escalator and through the ticket hall, he bumped into travellers who he later realised had not escaped. He had managed to get back down the escalator and survive, in great pain, beneath the fire until he was rescued.[5]

The day after the fire, the scheduled meeting of Preston's heads of department, his HoDs, went ahead as usual. For the first time they were shown dummy pages from what would be the most radical and complete redesign in the Guardian's history to date. What better way to announce to the world that the Guardian had new presses than through a completely new look to the paper? The new design had been a remarkably well-kept secret, and was to remain so until its first public appearance three months later. The design editor Michael McNay had first gone to see Preston in July to propose that the conjunction of new presses with direct input by journalists called for a root and branch redesign of the Guardian - by professionals. Preston agreed immediately. McNay nervously raised the question of cost. 'PP notoriously spent the Guardian's money as though it was coming out of his own pocket so, holding my breath, I said that it would cost more than tuppence ha'penny. He didn't blink, so I guess he had redesign on his mind.'

The idea of engaging professional designers was a heresy and happily both Preston and McNay were heretics. 'You were surrounded by people [sub-editors and some section editors] who thought it a mark of their manhood that they were design people too.' The prevailing culture was one of the reasons, apart from the obvious need for commercial secrecy, why knowledge of the redesign project was confined to the smallest possible number of people. Secrecy concealing urgent activity suited Preston's talent and temperament perfectly. A biblical phrase to describe his general animation in this period came to McNay's mind: 'Behold, he cometh leaping upon the mountains, skipping on the hills.'[6]

After an initial failed attempt with one outside designer, Preston, on McNay's recommendation, hired David Hillman of the graphic design partnership of Pentagram. Hillman had previously worked as a designer on the Sunday Times magazine, and redesigned parts of the paper for Harold Evans. That was where McNay first became aware of him, while doing moonlight shifts on the sports pages in the 1970s. Since then, Hillman had been art director, then deputy editor, of the magazine Nova, and worked on the design of several European newspapers.

McNay went to see Hillman at the Pentagram studios in Notting Hill. 'He was obviously excited by the prospect of redesigning the Guardian from scratch, and asked whether he could redesign the masthead as well. That hadn't occurred to me but clearly it's the first design statement a newspaper makes.' Preston, happily, agreed.

It made one paragraph in the design briefing that McNay dispatched to Hillman shortly after their meeting. It was a momentous project for McNay too. He was coming up to a quarter of a century on the Guardian, which he had joined in 1963 as a news sub-editor. In 1970, McNay became the Guardian's first arts editor, and eight years later rose to assistant editor in charge of design. McNay had successfully argued the case for a modular design to be applied to the news pages and this had met with the approval of Phil Osborne, who had succeeded Preston as production editor. No one had looked forward more to release from the Gray's Inn Road presses than McNay (except maybe Preston), and now an eager impatience was apparent in McNay's brief to Hillman.

It opens with an interesting remark: 'We expect, initially at any rate, to remain a broadsheet paper.' With the Independent gaining ground, with the unknown reader reaction to conversion to tabloid, with uncertain commercial implications and other considerations, Preston had decided that now was not the time to indulge his long-term wish to see the Guardian as the first quality tabloid in Britain.

What followed, McNay explained, was for guidance, not to restrict Hillman's thinking. 'I think "feel free" is pretty well the order of the day. There is, as you know, some trade mythology about not shocking and shaking off readers of a well-loved journal by sudden traumatic change, but as far as we know it is only mythology.'

McNay provided a physical description of the Guardian, explaining why the various sections followed the order that they did. Pages from which advertisements were restricted were also identified. The brief was loose: 'We regard ourselves as basically a text paper but with decided ambitions to use pictures better than before ... We decidedly don't want a déjà-vu appearance like the Independent's, however elegant. We want to look modern.'

Hillman took the brief away with him on his August holiday. He was to come back with two separate proposals, one for a 'tidy-up' with the minimum basic change and the other for a total redesign, as already favoured by Preston. A preliminary fee of £15,000 was agreed – the final payment to Pentagram for the entire design project was in the region of £40,000.

In September, Hillman asked McNay to call round again. 'He showed me some page dummies that would constitute a total revolution for a British quality newspaper if we were to accept them. I was bowled over.' On a subsequent visit, Preston and McNay sat on one side of a desk while Hillman put his pages in front of Preston. The biggest surprise for the editor came towards the end of the presentation when Hillman slipped a tabloid across the table. Hillman recollected, 'I wanted to know how far he would go - and I always said that when the blood started to drain from his face I would know we were probably pushing it.' In fact, it was not a full-blown tabloid proposal. It was for a tabloid sheet wrapped round a folded broadsheet paper. Preston turned it down there and then on the grounds that what was being proposed, without that, was revolution enough. But on the overall design he was captivated, and, in McNay's words, 'went into overdrive sorting out the running order of pages, making sure that the distinction between news and comment, and news and features, would be absolutely clear'. McNay and a thoughtful Preston returned to Farringdon Road - typically for Preston, on the bus. McNay recalled, 'I was shocked but exhilarated, and I guess Peter Preston was too. The difference was that as editor he would carry the can if we were wrong.'⁷ Once back in the office McNay rang Hillman and told him of the silent bus ride. 'Is that good or bad?' Hillman asked. 'I don't know,' said McNay. The next morning Preston walked over to McNay's desk and said, 'Tell him to go ahead.'

About this time Ed Vulliamy found himself standing next to Preston in the lavatories - there were no 'executive toilets' - and took the opportunity to ask what the new design looked like. 'Preston said, "Well, we've got a choice between radical and very radical." I said, "Well, which are we going to do, Peter?" And he said, "Very radical," zipped up his flies and walked out.'

Many of the elements of the finished designs were present when the HoDs were allowed their first glimpse of some dummy pages on 19 November. Hillman had found an ingenious way of distinguishing between news and features. News would have headlines throughout in the sans serif typeface Helvetica, features would have headlines in elegant Garamond italic. The text of all news stories would be justified, that is in vertical alignment left and right. All features articles were to be set left, ragged right, that is unaligned and irregular on the right. The masthead would combine the two in a way that would become emblematic of the Guardian. The 'The' would be in Garamond italic and the 'Guardian' would be in Helvetica bold. Above the masthead, in place of the contents teasers that had run down one side of the front page, there were to be headshots of people featuring prominently in stories on inside pages, or – another radical departure – in the second, features section of the paper. A minimum number of words would accompany these 'Horsemen of the Apocalypse', as Hillman called them.

Hillman's proposals in the context of British newspaper design up to then were revolutionary throughout. The structure was built on an eight-column page, with a 17-line eye line across the top of each one, creating the space within which the headlines were to be placed (Hillman had been an admirer of the use of white space in the Guardian of the 1960s); headlines were to be restricted to just four sizes, with the possibility on news pages of varying headline type between Helvetica bold and light fonts; the layout of pages was to conform to a grid, dividing the page horizontally into quarters and sixths; there were to be no dog legs, that is stories in columns of unequal length; there was to be no bastard setting, that is columns departing from the standard column width; each story was to start with a drop capital in the same typeface and the same size as its headline. There were rules to fit all eventualities, helping to guarantee that adjacent pages laid out by different hands did not look unrelated. The aim was to bring order, clarity and coherence, with a modern, elegant, European appearance and a recognisable Guardian identity.

Not everyone was impressed. And at an even later stage when training and preparation for the Hillman design was well advanced and the heroic David Watts – Harold Jackson's brilliant deputy systems editor – had been working day and night writing new programs for it, an alternative design was proposed. A key member of Preston's bunker – the fingers all pointed towards Ian Wright, the managing editor – had asked Dennis Hackett, a former art director and editor of Nova, to produce some dummy pages. 'Had I known he was in the background at that stage, I would have walked out,' Hillman said. McNay was eventually called in for a chat with Preston and Ian Wright. McNay was furious since the proposals undermined elements in the Hillman design that were precisely what made it distinctive. 'I pointed out that creative tension did not work once a design was up and running: it would produce all the muddiness and clutter that we had designed out of the paper.' Preston accepted this, although Wright remained unhappy - particularly about the inside pages, which he thought lacked vitality.[8] Wright was not the only one with misgivings. There were rumblings from the news desk and the sub-editors' benches. One senior sub-editor mistook the recently arrived Ian Mayes (myself) for Hillman. He pinned me to the wall and asked me whether I was trying to ruin the Guardian.

Friday 12 February 1988 was the date now set for the debut of the redesigned Guardian. The newly clothed paper was sufficiently controversial within the office for the approaching day to be viewed with a degree of apprehension. Naturally, it was heralded to the outside world with every show of confidence. The word relaunch was used cautiously, since, although what was about to appear would have a radically different appearance, and be printed with an unaccustomed clarity on the new presses, the content would be essentially the same. The advertisements that started running in the national press in January seemed to promise that. In the text, the Guardian allowed itself an opening swipe at the Independent. 'No one else has managed to produce a paper that's better than the Guardian, so we decided to do it ourselves,' ran the headline. One of the ads specifically promised, 'Different look; same outlook.'

The most tantalising - or let us say optimistic - ad was the one that guaranteed that 'From February 12th, one hallmark of The Guardian will be just a fond memoyr' [sic]. This ad brought a quick response from one devoted reader:

> Sir, - I have come to regard the many literals and 'typographical inscrutabilities' - as your leader of January 25 has it - as a lovable idiosyncrasy, a sacred tradition and a constant source of merriment. Who but the Grauniad could inform its readers that specially trained 'gods' were employed to sniff out truffles? I shall mourn the disappearance of such gems. - Hilda Morris, Great Henny, Suffolk.

Time must have provided considerable reassurance.

A great deal depended on the first edition of the new paper. A Marplan poll had been commissioned on the state of the parties to provide a story if all else failed. According to the recently appointed news editor, Paul

Johnson, 'Preston said, "*Newsnight* are coming in to film the birth of the new Guardian - let's make sure we've got a good story, we don't want to rely on the poll." It got to the day and I rang round the specialists and there was nothing at all. It was unbelievable because we'd had a very, very good record of exclusives. So when *Newsnight* turned their cameras on I had to walk into Peter's office and say, "Great news, Peter, we've got a terrific poll to lead on," and he literally punched the air, and said, "Fantastic!" I knew he thought I'd done a lousy job but you wouldn't know it.'

Newsnight viewers had the first glimpse of the new Guardian. What would the readers think? Would the migrants be persuaded to return, or would it stimulate a further exodus? The first issue brought a huge response, both positive and negative. Carolyn McCall, who had not long arrived in the ad-planning department, was one of half a dozen people who had volunteered to take the telephone calls, starting at 7am. 'The phones rang off the hook and they did not stop ringing until midnight ... You know, the readers took it so personally.' It was a formative experience for McCall, here on the first rung of the ladder that took her to the office of chief executive. 'I was talking to readers for the first time, and what I realised was that they own the paper ... It taught me a lot.'[9]

It was a foretaste of what was to follow, an influx of criticism, with which the Guardian, in characteristic manner, chose to flagellate itself over the next several days. The letters made lively reading. The restaurant designer Enzo Apicella offered the benefit of his experience: 'When an established restaurant starts losing customers you don't call in the interior decorator, you change the menu.' The following *cri de coeur* came from 'Horrified of Bayswater,' also known as the multi-talented comedian Spike Milligan: 'My God! What have you done with the Guardian? What was *wrong* with the old one? Don't you know when you reach perfection the only way is *down*!' Joyce Pitt of Bromley in Kent made a heart-rending plea, 'Confused by all this change, I made a soft cuddly blanket from copies of the old (real) Guardian and now, cocooned, won't come out until you stop messing about.'

There *was* praise for the new Guardian. From Paul Cookson, of Reddish, Stockport: 'Congratulations are in order ... The style is clear, readable and retains the Guardian qualities.' Michael and Mariella Chance of Birmingham: 'Such a surprise, so enjoyable, clean, easy to read - layout with computer logic - but what an overload of goodies for one day!' Vera and Roger Batt of Tunbridge Wells: 'Our Guardian was always THE paper but setting the definite article in italics is a subtle stroke of typographic genius. It is now *the* newspaper.'

It was probably a signal experience for the new wave of journalists who had been swept into the Guardian to find that its readers held them personally and individually responsible for its welfare. Now there was no turning back: for the rest of 1988, and longer, the competition would be even more intense.

Chapter 6
The Changing Agenda

'To everything there is a season.'

Richard Gott quoting Ecclesiastes

There were two significant casualties in the transition from the pre-Hillman Guardian to the paper that followed the radical redesign, or three if you count an important change in the conduct of the letters page. The two were Richard Gott's Agenda page, and Victoria Brittain's Third World Review, both of which limped on briefly in the new paper before finally expiring.

Both pages were characteristic of Preston's Guardian in the 1980s, often controversial, influential, sometimes touched with perversity. Both ventured into places where other papers rarely trod. They were not, in terms of revenue, of very much value, although the Third World Review was born of an extraordinary sponsorship deal that underwrote its first three years, more on which below. But in terms of editorial content, they both spoke strongly of the character of Preston's paper during the Thatcher years.

Amid the great many changes of the time, their departure, particularly to those working on these pages, seemed peculiarly like waving goodbye to the decade and to the flavour of the 'old Guardian' with it. The feeling was accentuated by a more or less simultaneous change in the editorship of the letters page, over which Christopher Maclean had presided since shortly after Mrs Thatcher's accession. For most of the 1980s Maclean provided a redoubt and rallying point for the anti-Thatcher forces that came to dominate the page. All three, Gott, Brittain and Maclean, stood well to the left of the Guardian's generally perceived editorial position.

Agenda had been Preston's idea, although Richard Gott quickly made it his own, describing its policy as akin to Mao's 'Let a hundred flowers bloom.' Agenda was a page of political debate of the broadest possible spectrum, derived largely from outside contributors rather than staff journalists. It might be seen as a precursor of the Comment and Analysis pages that followed through the 1990s – although their primary forerunner was another Preston innovation, the 'facing page' or 'op ed' page, which is where staff journalists were more likely to appear at that time. It could perhaps be seen, not too fancifully, as an early pointer towards the Comment is Free section of the website, since it was a forum for debate between contributors and readers presided over by the Guardian.

The Agenda page was introduced in July 1979, hard on the heels of Margaret Thatcher's election victory in May, and edited by Gott until the new Guardian design was launched in February 1988. In fact, under the editorship of Martin Kettle it did continue for a time in the new two-section broadsheet but, perhaps inevitably, it did not last for long. It was one of those pages that Gott handed over with a symbolic washing of hands, in the form of some 1,200 words by Gott on the page itself, under the heading 'Agenda: Goodbye to all this'.[1] Gott opened his valedictory address by quoting Ecclesiastes, 'To everything there is a season.'

This peculiar Guardian farewell is worth quoting since it is difficult to imagine such a public handover taking place on any other paper. Here it seemed that what Kettle was handed was little more than an urn with rapidly cooling ashes in it. 'We live in revolutionary times, yet it is not a revolution in which the left or the centre take part ... "Which way for Labour?" used to be a meat and drink question for this page, but until the baleful Kinnock/Hattersley clique are got rid of it hardly seems worth asking. "Whither the Alliance?" might have got a few readers a year or so ago, but now only a handful of MPs and their parents would fail to turn immediately to another page. Even the views of the Tory "wets" (those of them that could ever be persuaded to raise themselves from their 18th-century sofas to write) are not in great demand.'

Students of intra-Guardian communiqués in this period and of Gott's individual brand of scorn would see the reference to the Kinnock/Hattersley clique as a mild dig at Preston, who sometimes referred to Kinnock affectionately as 'his gingerness'. He had also provided Hattersley with a platform for his Endpiece column since 1982, and Hattersley continued to write for the Guardian throughout his tenure as deputy leader of the Labour Party. Gott's suggestion of a geriatric boredom descending on supporters of the Alliance was a jibe at the considerable Guardian faction who had gone that way. And the remark about Tory 'wets' was an oblique criticism of editors who commissioned John Biffen and others from the civilised wing of the Tory party for the facing page.

The Agenda page was set against all this debilitating moderation. The list of contributors to whom Gott paid his parting respects is indicative, starting with 'Tony Benn and Enoch Powell, long my political favourites, men who ... look forward to something different: a Britain free from entangling military alliances, a Britain free from nuclear weapons and the myths of nuclear deterrence, and a Britain capable of renewing ancient links with Russia while gently detaching itself from the coils of American global power.' Still more controversially, he went on, 'Writers with a soft spot for Pol Pot have also not been turned away.' On occasions such as these Preston was likely to shake his head and say, 'Ah, Ricky.'

Gott acknowledged with pride that for practically a decade he had orchestrated 'a sometimes wayward political and cultural debate through the Thatcher years'. He had not done it alone. 'It is a task in which I have been aided and abetted by Chris Maclean, the benign and mischievous editor of the Guardian's letters page. Now is a time for both of us to do something different.'

To more than one senior Guardian executive, Christopher Maclean, who was letters editor from 1980 to 1987, was more than mischievous – one described him as 'a truculent Trot', an affiliation that he vehemently denied as an affront to his lifelong unclubbability.[2] He was allowed, recklessly in the minds of some, a great degree of autonomy in his choice of correspondence to print.

Paul Johnson, writing in the *Spectator* in 1982,[3] remarked on the over-representation of the radical left in the 'lively and often savage' letters columns – possibly, he mused, because they were better at organising letter-writing campaigns. 'Certainly there seem to be an awful lot of university lecturers who have nothing to do except to write to the Guardian.'

There were informal guidelines, a 'formula' that both Preston and Maclean believed they had clearly understood and agreed upon, for, as Maclean put it, 'the weighing of opinion' in the conduct of the page. 'It was called "the proportion of the postbag",' Maclean recalled. So, for example, if 30 letters were received in support of the leader line in favour of maintaining the nuclear deterrent and ten against, the letters editor would aim to print three of the former and one of the latter. In fact this was one of a number of issues where the postbag ran quite contrary to the editorial opinion of the paper. The Social Democratic Party, according to Maclean, made greater inroads into the editorial staff of the Guardian than into the readership, at least as it was reflected in the letters intended for publication.

Many found this difficult to believe. Complaints from Shirley Williams among others led to surreptitious checks being carried out on the letters when Maclean was away from his desk. David McKie, Preston's deputy editor until 1984, made several such inspections and found they endorsed the balance of opinion reflected on the page. 'I thought well that's OK, but I realised after a time that all newspapers are a marketplace to some extent. We had created a market in which people writing to the paper thought the letters page is for leftwing letters and not for others. So I think we deceived ourselves on that basis.'

Only on very rare occasions did Maclean try Preston's patience beyond its normal generous limits. One of these occurred in 1987 at a time when management and journalists were embroiled in a dispute over the introduction of the new computer technology. Maclean managed to include among his selection of letters one from Peter Hildrew,[4] the father of the chapel, the Guardian office branch of the National Union of Journalists, who wanted to draw attention to 'a penal clause in an otherwise acceptable disputes procedure'. Preston did see the letter before the edition went away, but too late for him to do anything about it. He settled for, by his standards, a stiff memo to Maclean.

Nowhere was the letters page more roundly criticised than in Geoffrey Taylor's volume of the Guardian history in which the author, reviewing the state of the paper as the Independent began to make alarming inroads, notes, 'Not only was the Guardian missing editions through labour disputes but its once important letters column had become a playpen for paranoiacs, nihilists and hard-left freaks, who were a caricature of the paper's following and with whom more serious readers clearly did not wish to be identified.'[5] He then points to the dive of 50,000 in the Guardian's circulation over the 18 months after the appearance of the Independent, which during the same period had soared to 376,750 from a standing start.

The implication that the letters page was a major stimulus for the exodus is too simple. But there was a feeling within the office that the letters page was contributing to a perception that the Guardian had too narrow a focus, while readers of the Independent were enjoying a broader view. To some extent this was manufactured. Rusbridger had noted that Matt Hoffman, the letters editor at the Independent, was commissioning some of its letters. 'They thought, "we want to be the noticeboard of the establishment", so they did ring up bishops and generals. It was a very clever thing because it made it look as though all these people were reading the Independent.'[6] It was briefly tried at the Guardian, but Maclean and others objected to it as a distortion of the authentic voice of the readership.

A reshuffle was in the offing. Maclean gave way to Jeannette Page, and eventually left the paper at the end of 1989. Richard Gott continued as features editor until June that year, when Rusbridger succeeded him.

A little distance has allowed the Agenda page to be seen as an important part of the Gott era. Some of his critics pointed out that the moderate views of the centre were frequently ignored. Gott's justification for that was that these were more than adequately represented elsewhere in the paper, and increasingly so since it was towards the centre that the paper was being led.

The demise of the Third World Review was also considered by some Guardian journalists, and readers, to indicate a slide in the wrong direction. It started as an experimental co-production with Third World Media, a new company whose editor-in-chief was Altaf Gauhar, to whom the page owed its title. Gauhar was a former senior civil servant in Pakistan who during the 1965 war with India over Kashmir had been President Ayub Khan's press secretary, effectively his appointed censor, working in conjunction with the foreign minister, Zulfikar Ali Bhutto. It was in this role that Peter Preston first encountered him, having been sent to Rawalpindi to cover the war for the Guardian, his first big foreign assignment after joining Hetherington's paper a couple of years earlier. 'We did not love him when our stories mysteriously went astray,' Preston recalled. 'I complained about this to the foreign minister, Mr Bhutto ... He smiled and told me not to fuss. "All your copy comes to me, and then ..."'[7] Gauhar later became editor of the country's main English-language newspaper, Dawn, in Karachi, a role that in the early 1970s led him into conflict with Bhutto, then in charge of martial law, who twice imprisoned him. A question to arise later was whether Gauhar used the Guardian to strike back at Bhutto while the latter was under sentence of death in Pakistan during the military dictatorship of President Zia.

Gauhar was not the most controversial thing about Third World Media. The company was backed by BCCI, the Bank of Credit and Commerce International, founded in 1972 by a charismatic Pakistani financier, Agha Hasan Abedi, described as 'a Muslim, a mystic and a poet'.[8] BCCI had made an astonishing start in life, benefiting from Abedi's close relationship with the ruler of Abu Dhabi and president of the United Arab Emirates, Zayed bin Sultan al-Nahyan, and receiving an immediate boost with the oil embargo that followed the Yom Kippur war of 1973.

By the time the Third World Review started in 1978, BCCI had almost 146 branches in 32 countries. It had grown so rapidly in Britain in 1977 that the Bank of England had ordered it to stop branching, and the following year declined to give it 'recognised bank' status. Two writers who examined it declared it to be at that time 'by any measure the fastest growing financial institution in the world'.[9] Very few at the close of the 1970s, and no one in Farringdon Road, heard alarm bells or suspected that the bank in less than a decade would be on the very edge of ignominious collapse. By then, the end of the 1980s, the deputy director and later director of the CIA, William Gates, said BCCI was known in the financial world as 'the Bank of Crooks and Criminals'.[10]

All that was in an unforeseen future. Gauhar was introduced to the Guardian by a journalist and media consultant, Judith Vidal-Hall. She recalled, 'Some time in 1977 I was asked by Altaf Gauhar, to whom I had been introduced by a mutual friend formerly of the World Bank, if I would be what is known technically as a "bare nominee" in the purchase of the Observer, which David Astor was then thinking of selling in the face of continuing huge losses. The financier was Abedi of the BCCI. This did not work out.'[11] (It is interesting to speculate what might have been the fate of the Observer if that sale had gone through.)

'I was then asked to advise on setting up a magazine in London to deal with third world affairs. I advised strongly against this and suggested setting up a partnership - a piggyback - with an established paper. I thought people needed to learn how the media in this country worked before plunging naked into what was a pretty rough game.'

After a failed negotiation with the Financial Times, Vidal-Hall introduced Gauhar to the Guardian, prompted by the sponsored supplements devoted to individual countries the paper had lately begun to run under the title of 'special report'. Michael Simmons had been recruited from the FT in 1977 to edit these, bringing with him an established expertise on eastern Europe and the Soviet Union. He also served as an adjunct to the foreign desk, first under Ian Wright and then – after the Third World Review started – with Campbell Page and Martin Woollacott as successive foreign editors.

The 'special reports' had been running in the Guardian for some time, very much as an advertising initiative, but with the support of authoritative and informative articles, which it was assumed nobody read. Oddly, only a few months before Simmons arrived, there had been one special report that was conspicuously successful, both commercially and in editorial terms. This was the seven-page special report on San Serriffe, a small group of islands, the main ones of which were Upper Caisse and Lower Caisse, which together, as the map showed, formed the shape of a semi-colon. The president of this tiny republic was General Pica. So closely did it tease the reader with its claim on credibility that an occasional reminder of reality was sought. It was found in a glance at the dateline: 1 April 1977.[12] San Serriffe set a new standard for newspaper hoaxes on April Fool's Day. The advertisers had wholly entered into the spirit of the thing – the Access bank claimed credit for the development of its currency; Costain announced that they were building the new harbour. However, attracting advertisers to the special reports that Simmons was now to edit proved more difficult.

Before signing up to a deal, the Guardian turned back to Judith Vidal-Hall to give a clean bill of health to Gauhar and his money, and this, insofar as she was able to do, she did. There was no secret about the link between the new venture and BCCI. A senior executive from the bank came for lunch with Preston and Wright at Farringdon Road to discuss the arrangement.[13] Third World Media, backed by BCCI, was able to guarantee about a quarter of a million pounds over the first three years, with £96,000 in advance for 1978/79, and a further £120,000 in 1979/80.[14] At the end of such a hungry decade this was manna from heaven: it was money being offered to the paper to do at someone else's expense, and with a profit, what it wanted to do anyway, which was to develop its interest in developing nations.

The Third World Review began on 6 March 1978 as a monthly four-page supplement within a normal Monday Guardian (it later became two pages fortnightly, then one page weekly). In a prospectus it set out an ambitious programme: 'This is the first in a series of reviews ... devoted to the social, economic and political developments in Third World countries ... The aim of the reviews is to bring into sharper focus happenings in the Third World, where, too often, the standards of news reporting by the newspapers of the developed world have been inadequate, bland or superficial.'

For the first crucial two years BCCI regularly placed quarter-page advertisements in the Review. Its support continued indirectly through Third World Media, which regularly advertised its various publications, particularly the highly regarded Third World Quarterly, which Gauhar launched just before the arrangement with the Guardian began, and which has continued in publication for over three decades.[15]

Simmons recalled, 'Third World Review was launched with me as editor, Ian Wright at my shoulder and Peter Preston always interested and enthusiastic.' Gauhar, who appeared on the published pages as 'co-editor', was an ambitious and energetic partner, suggesting both writers and subjects and contributing articles and interviews himself.

In editorial terms, the Third World Review was an immediate success, recognised and applauded for its innovatory journalism. In its first year Altaf Gauhar and Ian Wright, who described himself as 'a kind of god-father'[16] of the project, won the prestigious David Holden prize for it in the British Press Awards. It immediately announced that the £250 prize money would go towards a one-off third world travel grant for students. A couple of years later, the Review was again picked out, this time in a commendation of the Guardian at the United Nations Association's first peace prize ceremony in London. It was doing what it set out to do, lending an ear to voices otherwise unheard, attending to the political and economic development of vast swaths of the post-colonial and developing world, and publishing interviews with heads of state and other leading figures.

Already, however, serious questions were being raised about the Third World Review's source of funding. In October 1981, the *New Statesman* in three consecutive weeks ran anonymous articles attacking BCCI and questioning the motivation for its connection with the Guardian. The articles suggested that the paper's journalistic integrity had been compromised. It also published an extraordinary attack on

Gauhar that purported to be part of a death-cell testament by Bhutto, written as a riposte to a Guardian article about him by Gauhar, published on 21 February 1979, which Bhutto had read in prison. The *New Statesman* said that, although Bhutto was not stainless, Gauhar in this piece made him out to be 'a drunken megalomaniac, militarist and anti-democratic'. Publication of Gauhar's article, it contended, could be seen as 'a remarkable penetration of western news-media by a highly partisan Third World propagandist'. Furthermore, the article seemed to assist General Zia's efforts to sanctify an act of 'judicial assassination'. Bhutto was hanged on April 4, just six weeks after Gauhar's Guardian article appeared.

A couple of months later, Gauhar announced that he was to sue the *New Statesman* for libel. The action centred on the allegations that the Third World Review was 'not editorially independent and was sycophantic towards dictators' and that during Gauhar's time in Pakistan 'he had been involved in subversive activities'. Gauhar strongly contested all this and, in an out-of-court settlement in November 1983, he received more than £10,000 in damages, plus costs.

Part of Gauhar's case had been that the Bhutto prison document was a forgery, which was something the New Statesman never quite conceded. The Guardian, which insisted that the Third World Review *was* editorially independent, did not join in the action, although its lawyers had an interest in the wording of the apology. That apart, Preston had settled for a letter to the New Statesman shortly after the articles appeared, commenting on inaccuracies and dismissing the three pieces as 'a pretty tatty bag of investigative journalism'.[17]

The Guardian in a report of the settlement, two years after the anonymous New Statesman articles had appeared, for the first time identified the author of them as the radical writer and activist Tariq Ali. The following day, the Guardian publicly retracted this at the request of Ali, who feared for the safety of members of his family who were still in Pakistan. As for the Bhutto prison document, Ali had believed it to be genuine at the time and he maintained that Benazir Bhutto had subsequently told him that she had no doubt that it had been written by her father.[18] Time has certainly vindicated Tariq Ali in his criticism of the bank and its affairs. The authors of one study of BCCI called his New Statesman series 'the first major exposé' of the bank,[19] coming as it did a full decade before its final forced closure.

The last advertisement for BCCI in the Third World Review appeared at the end of March in 1980, more than 18 months before the New Statesman articles were published. But the page continued as a cooperative venture with Gauhar's BCCI-funded Third World Media for another two years. Publication of the New Statesman articles in October 1981 undoubtedly caused a crisis in relations. Gauhar wrote to Preston in the month after they appeared, 'I was dismayed that a four-year-old association, developed with such care and mutual respect, should have been summarily terminated.'[20] In fact, the editorial arrangement with Gauhar and his company continued for another six months or more after that, finally petering out in the summer of 1982. Gauhar was said to have been disappointed that he had not received more support from the Guardian over his libel action. Preston's letter to the New Statesman had not been quite the wholehearted endorsement he might have desired.

The relationship between Third World Media and the Guardian was never a particularly easy one. The Guardian was zealous in exercising editorial control over the page, and Third World Media was equally keen to protect its own copyright interest in material that appeared on it. The week after Preston's letter appeared in the New Statesman, the magazine published one from Rory Flanagan, the former business and syndication manager of Third World Media, who complained about the Guardian's penny-pinching financial dealings with his company. 'The professional ladies working Park Lane who can spot a petro-dollar at 1,000 paces could learn a lesson or two from the Guardian.'

However embarrassing all this was, there was no lasting acrimony directed towards Gauhar. Victoria Brittain, who had become sole editor of the page in the mid-1980s, co-edited with Simmons an impressive compilation of pieces from the review.[21] Thanks are extended in the acknowledgements to Altaf Gauhar 'who cooperated so closely when the original idea was being nursed to life'. Later still, when Gauhar died of cancer in December 2000, Simmons wrote his obituary for the Guardian.[22] Gauhar was described as 'a man of extraordinary versatility, charm and intelligence' who had endeavoured 'to do what he could to improve the lot of the world's poorest'. The president of Pakistan, Muhammad Rafiq Tarar, attended his funeral.

BCCI was finally forced to close in 1991 at the summit of its notoriety. The authors of one study of the collapsed bank claimed that it had never had more than a facade of respectability, greatly assisted by its associations, including that with the Guardian: 'BCCI was a criminal enterprise that catered to some of the most notorious villains of the late twentieth century', including Saddam Hussein and several international drug cartels and warlords. 'BCCI not only assisted others in committing crimes, the institution was itself a fraud.'[23]

On this last point, those who have studied BCCI appear to agree. When the bank was shut down, the Guardian ran a story declaring its own connection.[24] The article, headed 'Using charity and prizes to fuel rapid growth', implied that the Guardian, with others, had allowed itself to be used to enhance the bank's credibility. According to a front-page story in the Guardian, the forced closure of BCCI in the summer of 1991 left more than 40,000 creditors and former employees in Britain owed at least £3 billion.[25]

That the Guardian Third World Review survived, indeed succeeded, for more than a decade - the last page under its banner appeared in June 1989 - was due largely to the indefatigable efforts of its combative editor for most of that time, Victoria Brittain. Third World Review occupied an uneasy position within the office, even though practically all the Guardian's leading staff foreign specialists and correspondents wrote for it occasionally. Brittain recalled, 'It was completely groundbreaking for British newspapers - and it was incredibly unpopular [within the office]. The concept was that we would have articles from places in the third world by people from there, journalists, intellectuals, even heads of state, so it was extremely eclectic, somewhat in the Gott tradition. The office found it bewildering and it wasn't subbed in the foreign department.'

The last page to be flagged Third World Review appeared in June 1989, the month that Alan Rusbridger succeeded Richard Gott as features editor. Preston, in the end, so he told Brittain, thought it had come to seem a bit old-fashioned. Brittain said, 'Almost 20 years afterwards, I still found that people would come up to me, like someone at a recent conference who said, "I've never been able to thank you for my PhD - I wrote it entirely using your articles from Third World Review".' More often, she would be attacked for ending it, as though the decision had been hers. Everything was changing. To everything there is a season, to quote Gott quoting Ecclesiastes.

Chapter 7
The New Look Guardian and the Birth of Weekend

'That British oxymoron, a tabloid with brains.'
Flyer for the new Weekend Guardian, December 1988

It was pretty obvious fairly soon that the redesign was not achieving all that had been hoped for in the form of increased circulation. Only briefly did the Guardian's lead over the Independent exceed 100,000 again, and occasionally the independent audit, the monthly ABC figures, depressingly, would show the Times ahead of the Guardian. In this context, the Hillman design was the cause of a good deal of tension at Farringdon Road. It was difficult to tell whether some of the resistance to the new design rules was wilful, whether there was some deep-rooted conditioning at work - old habits dying hard - or whether it was simply that some were taking longer to learn than others. Hillman was around for some time, both to protect his creation from abuse, but also to help it to adapt in a compatible way to the demands of daily use. Thereafter the onerous task of walking the floor fell principally to the design editor Michael McNay and Bernard Jolly, who had risen from the sub-editors' benches. They became quickly known as 'the thought police', with McNay cast - in his own words - 'as a died-in-the-wool Mujahideen brooking no departure from holy writ'.[1] There were frequent complaints that pages were now 'design led' rather than content led.

It was true that tighter discipline came in with the new design. Commonly now, a length to write to would be stipulated in advance. For the first time reporters were required to hit grid lines, meaning cuts were obligatory when stories ran over. Sometimes, to mild astonishment, a reporter would be asked to write more. The complaints were by and large exaggerated. As CP Scott used to remark to Crozier: 'There is very little written for a newspaper that would not be improved by being made shorter.'

There was also the matter of the four heads, Hillman's four 'horsemen of the Apocalypse' strung across the top of the page above the masthead. These became a major preoccupation. Great efforts were made to avoid ending up with four white males: there was a constant search for women, for the young, the old, for those of ethnic origin other than Anglo-Saxon. Subtler distinctions according to sexual orientation were sometimes considered. The prominence of the heads meant, so the argument went, that they would be taken together as emblematic of Guardian values. The search ranged wide. The writer rather than the written-of soon began to appear, and quite often a 'thing' appeared in place of a human head. By June 1990, after almost 18 months, the heads had been abandoned completely and replaced by written teasers, still occasionally illustrated.

On the inside pages, the bylines of the paper's main columnists and commentators were illustrated by portrait line drawings. The artist was Su Huntley, who worked from photographs. It would be invidious to name the few writers who protested at an absence of 'likeness'. One or two who had protested over byline photographs continued to do so when the drawings were introduced. Harry Jackson's riposte to one complainant was sometimes quoted: 'We can only work with the material to hand.' Despite these touches of vanity, Huntley's portraits lasted much longer than the front-page heads and did not finally disappear until the late spring of 1995. They had supporters, significantly among them Michael McNay, who thought these light and airy drawings added variety and texture to the page.

Preston was coming quickly to the conclusion that something must be done about photographs. Improvement in the print quality brought about by the new presses - with the exception of colour, which was already causing worries - had exposed both the strengths and weaknesses of Guardian photography. Many editions were liberally peppered with single-column mugshots. They had been banned on the old presses because they were often over-inked. Now they were about to be banned for the bitty appearance they gave to Hillman's pages.

In many ways the best photos were products of the paper's revered northern pictorial school, archetypically represented by images of fell and viaduct, often producing pictures of startling beauty, particularly in the black and white work of Denis Thorpe and Don McPhee. They constituted one of the elements that did not appear to have changed with the new design; indeed, many would have considered that suggestion a heresy.

In the meantime, the Independent had enjoyed a head start in terms of picture quality, before the Guardian's new presses came on stream. Preston found this another source of irritation. Retirement on the picture desk was soon to bring changes. While acknowledging all the effort and achievement of the paper's picture editors in the past, Preston was determined to take the opportunity to bring in fresh blood. Brian Whitaker on his arrival from the wreck of the News on Sunday had been asked by Preston to do two things: take care of the early development of computer graphics on the newly acquired Mac, and look at the operation of the picture desk that Preston described as 'a sweet shop'. 'I discovered that what he meant was that the day's pictures were spread out on a table and people came and took what they thought they might have for the page they were editing. He wanted a much more proactive picture desk.'[2]

Word that Preston might be looking for a picture editor quickly spread through the now dispersed Fleet Street, and one of the people it reached was Eamonn McCabe. McCabe had worked as a freelance at the Guardian in the mid-1970s, and since 1976 he had been a sports photographer for the Observer. He was a member of an extraordinary group of photographers associated primarily with the Sunday paper that included Neil Libbert, Jane Bown, Nobby Clark and another award-winning sports photographer, Adrian Murrell. There were many distinguished predecessors at the Observer, including McCabe's personal hero, Don McCullin, famous above all for his war photography. Print quality for these photographers had been much better than any achieved at the Guardian.

After being briefly lured away to work for Robert Maxwell's glossy but short-lived Sportsweek, launched in September 1986, McCabe returned to the Observer early the following year. By now he had acquired a great reputation. He had been sports photographer of the year four times. The second book of his work had just been published and he had been included in an exhibition at the Walker art gallery in Liverpool. Within his book was a photograph that might be seen as the psychological end of that phase of his career. It was taken at the Heysel stadium when 39 Juventus fans were crushed to death before their team's European cup final match against Liverpool in May 1985. McCabe wrote movingly in the Observer of how he had gone to photograph the Juventus star Platini and ended up photographing something like war. The experience left a lasting impression. For various reasons, he was ready for a new challenge.

He rang Preston's office and said he'd like to pitch for the job. The interview was not without Prestonian touches. McCabe recalled, 'He said, "Well, we'd like to offer you the job," then suddenly asked me, "How would you get pictures out of Red Star if the office was closed?"' Red Star was British Rail's registered package service that the Manchester photographers would use to send their pictures down to London. 'All I could think to say was, "Well, I'd just have to get a jemmy and break in."' It was 10.30am and Preston ushered him out through the discreet back door of his office. A minute later McCabe realised he had left his briefcase in Preston's office. He went back in through the same door and walked straight into Preston's morning conference with 20 or so of the paper's leading journalists. 'By the time I got back to the Observer in Battersea everyone knew I was coming to the Guardian.'[3]

He was 40. Up to that point his only experience as a picture editor was his five months on Robert Maxwell's failed enterprise. McCabe was picture editor of the Guardian for the next 13 years and won picture editor of the year six times in the annual press awards. He had a wonderfully disruptive effect on the picture desk, where staff photographers found themselves competing with agency, freelance and 'star' photographers whom McCabe began introducing to the pages. He also started to encourage bigger and bolder use of pictures, bringing complaints from journalists who saw their chances of getting their story prominently displayed reduced. Now the complaint was that the paper was being not just design-led but picture-led as well. McCabe was unapologetic: 'It seemed to me that they had redesigned the paper but they hadn't thought about the photographs ... Really I was just putting back into the paper the visual confidence that had been lost by custom and practice that said just anything would do.'

The biggest impact was on the front page, sending out the strongest signal that a major if somewhat belated change was in progress. As the Hillman design had bedded down in the body of the paper, the front was the one page that was clearly still not working. McNay recalled, 'It hadn't moved out of the groove of having between six and eight stories on the page even though pagination had risen and it would have been perfectly possible to use the front much more as a display page.'

Late in the summer of 1988 Preston suggested that when McCabe arrived at the beginning of October McNay should temporarily move on to the front page as the layout person, before handing the job over to Michael Pilgrim. McNay recalled, 'Peter in his winning way put it to me that it would be handy for Eamonn to have a friend on the front page when he started. I worried that nothing major in splashy terms might happen in a three-month period but Peter just said to play it as it came – play what's in front of you, as sports coaches say.'

McNay's worries about the lack of weighty events were quickly swept aside. In the second week in November, George HW Bush succeeded Ronald Reagan to become president of the United States. In mid-December there was a triple train crash during the morning rush hour at Clapham Junction in London in which more than 30 people died. And just before Christmas, a terrorist attack brought down Pan Am Flight 103 over the Scottish town of Lockerbie, killing 270. Each of these stories commanded the whole of the front page. The Bush election victory brought the first front page to use an eight-column photograph right across the page. The front-page report of the Clapham crash was accompanied by a deep five-column picture of the scene. And on the first of two Lockerbie front pages the four heads above the Guardian title were also dropped, setting a pattern for the presentation of such cataclysmic events in the future. Pages such as these were demonstrating what many critics had doubted, that there was flexibility in the Hillman design.

Paul Johnson bore the brunt of much of the subsequent protests from reporters. 'It caused awful trouble at the time. People were complaining that hundreds and hundreds of words of their stories were being lost because we were putting pictures in on this unprecedented scale. In the end someone produced a front page one night with just a single column mugshot as the central picture. We showed all the reporters this and said, "Look, there are more words on that than you'll find on the front page of any other paper. Now do you think you'd buy that paper or the Times or the Independent?" And I think they started to get the point.'

These early McNay-McCabe front pages were all produced on the Atex system, still without the benefit of whole-page on-screen make-up, agreement for which had not yet been reached with the NUJ chapel.

Their strongest supporters in the field were the night editor, Phil Osborne, and the new deputy editor, now happy to participate in competition with his old newspaper, Jonathan Fenby. He was, McNay testified, 'an absolute livewire. He was on his toes constantly and I can say that the best months of my newspaper life were working with him on the front. Eamonn, of course, was great ... He got a kick out of producing the best, and I did too.' Suddenly the paper and the Hillman design were looking bold, confident and competitive.

While this was happening on the news front, Preston was planning his most innovative move yet in the features department. This was to be a new tabloid second section on Saturdays to replace the broadsheet Choices section, which had failed to establish any real identity. The blurb for the first edition of Choices back in February 1988 perhaps explains why: 'Saturday's second section is the new Choices Guardian, a leisure and activity blend for the weekend ... with Travel, Food and Drink, Motoring, Gardening, Impulse Fashion [whatever that was], Chess, Bridge, Property, top job advertisements, Event listings - plus Money Choices, the authoritative guide to personal finance. The cartoons and Quick Crossword are inside the back, together with Obituaries and Sunday's TV and Radio.' It sounds like a ragbag, or a scatter of groundbait in the hope that advertisers would bite. And that is largely what it looked like despite the valiant efforts of Bill Smithies, the very experienced journalist who was given the job of editing it. In fact, in the Guardian manner of the time, he was not the editor of the entire section, but only of the front several pages, after which the arts pages fell under the remit of the arts editor, and the finance pages under the city editor and so on. The greatest sympathy went to the obituaries editor, who was obliged to park his bodies in a kind of noisy corridor - three vertical columns alongside Sunday's television and radio schedules.

Not surprisingly, the set-up did not inspire the sub-editing staff assigned to help Smithies bring it out. When the arts editor of the time, Roger Alton, asked Desmond Christy what he was doing one day, Christy replied, 'Subbing'. When Alton asked, 'Where?' Christy replied gloomily, 'Lack of Choices'. No one was more aware of the problems than Smithies. Less than two months after Choices was launched, Smithies wrote to the features editor, Richard Gott: 'Choices is OK so far, but let no one pretend it is terrific. It could be and should be, and I know how to do it, but it can't be done unless there are some important changes ...' Three weeks later Smithies wrote again to Gott, this time copying in Preston, asking to be moved off to something else. 'Enough is enough. I am being prevented from doing the job that needs to be done with Choices. I will not continue after today.'[4]

The section nevertheless limped on with Smithies still nominally in charge, despite his evident frustration. Preston and Smithies lunched on Tuesday 13 September to discuss the issue. The date is significant. The previous Saturday the Independent had launched an impressive magazine under the editorship of Alexander Chancellor. Set beside this, the deficiencies of Choices seemed startlingly apparent. Preston's post-prandial memo summed up their discussion. 'Bill: Thanks for lunch. I felt pretty cheery afterwards. Really, I think, it comes down to this. Richard and I would like to move you back to the centre as Assistant Features Editor (although the titular side of things is easily fettlable) responsible for special projects and colour' - editorial colour, Preston said, was something 'dear to my heart'. Smithies must have breathed a sigh of relief. 'Running Choices,' he later confessed, 'was a nightmare.'

Preston had in fact already found someone to take over. In his survey of available resources, he scanned the ranks of the 'King's Own Fine Writers'. This was a semi-scornful and possibly envious epithet applied to the journalists, and quickly adopted by them, who were conspicuous for the quality of their writing. Characteristically, Fleet Street had a cliché at hand to describe anyone considered to be in this category: he or she was said to 'write like an angel'. Among those in this small elite corps at the Guardian were Terry Coleman, Matthew Engel and Alan Rusbridger. They had been liberated from the normal departmental structure and made the responsibility of the deputy editor, Peter Cole. Part of the thinking had been to protect these angels from the temptation of higher salaries elsewhere, by allowing them to range freely and to write at length. Coleman had become one of the best interviewers working anywhere in Fleet Street; Engel was in the process of broadening his range beyond the cricket pitch on which he had had a long and scintillating innings; and Rusbridger, recently returned to the Guardian after his period away on the Observer and London Daily News, had already reminded his peers and Guardian readers what a loss he had been: to lose him twice would be unfortunate.

It was Rusbridger to whom Preston turned. The announcement that he was to become the editor of the new Weekend Guardian prompted a mixed reaction. Some thought it not a good idea because he had no experience as an editor; others questioned the appointment because they thought it was 'a waste of a really good writer', as one put it. Preston had no qualms on either score. 'I thought Alan would be the obvious person to try for this. Remember if you are running a diary - as I had done and as Alan had done - intrinsically you are editing. You have to say, is this good? Does that bowl with that? Can we have a change of pace here? He had been totally ace at all that. So I was always sure that he could edit as well as write.'

Preston wanted a weekend magazine that would compete in a Saturday market that was slowly beginning to show interesting signs of life, especially in the case of the Independent. But as always there were financial constraints. 'We were never swilling in cash,' Preston said. 'It was an endless hassle. You couldn't just waltz in [to the group board] and say, "Can you give me X for a 72-page full-colour glossy magazine with a staff of X and a budget of whatever." Life was just not like that.' Guardian Weekend was an ingenious compromise; it was to be a 48-page news-print tabloid - published with a 48-page careers and jobs supplement, which was expected to contribute an extra £10,000 towards the cost of the Saturday paper.[5] The advertising department with characteristic efficiency had this ready a couple of weeks ahead of the editorial venture, so it was published by itself for two consecutive weeks.

In fact Preston had been involved in what he revelled in - secret planning sessions for the new supplement. He had appointed Rusbridger about two months before his transitional lunch with Bill Smithies, and in mid-August - a month before the Independent's Saturday magazine first appeared - a design dummy for Guardian Weekend was produced. This was the work of Dennis Hackett, then nearing 60, the vastly experienced journalist whose alternative to the Hillman design for the main paper had so inflamed McNay. The Guardian Weekend dummy was a partner-ship project with the almost equally experienced graphic designer Celia Stothard. But the resulting dummy, dated 13 August 1988, although it had a faint echo of the Hillman Pentagram design, had none of its fresh order and flair. The employment once again of Hackett strongly suggested that somewhere deep in the bunker the lack of confidence in Hillman's design persisted.

The dummy pages were laid out for inspection on the boardroom table at 119 Farringdon Road. Rusbridger, who was still marshalling his ideas for Weekend - even the title was only tentative - was acutely aware that he had never edited anything, except his school magazine, the Cranleighan, and, in his words, 'didn't know the first thing about design'. Nevertheless, he instinctively rejected the pages spread out before him, thinking them densely uninviting. He had his own form of non-verbal communication. He indicated a negative view by momentarily lapsing into a state of inertia, as though temporarily deprived of all sensation.

I myself (Ian Mayes) also felt little enthusiasm for them. I had recently been recruited as Rusbridger's deputy, after dividing my time as a sub-editor between the arts pages and Richard Gott's features desk. The recruitment procedure had been deceptively casual. Rusbridger had tossed a weighty manila folder into my lap and with no further explanation asked me if I'd take a look at the contents overnight. It contained Rusbridger's plans, pretty much fully formed, for what became Weekend Guardian. The following morning I told him I thought it looked 'interesting' and Rusbridger said, 'Well, how would you like to come and help me do it?'

I jumped at the opportunity. Just before Christmas 1987, Preston put me on the staff. When we began working together in the few months before Guardian Weekend first appeared, I was 52 and Rusbridger 34. Rusbridger showed every consideration to his older colleague. When I logged on to the Atex system in the morning a message from Rusbridger would come up on my screen telling me, 'Today is Tuesday. You are at the Guardian. The weather outside is quite nice. The next meal is lunch.' Possibly due to a certain suspicion and hostility directed towards the new venture from elsewhere in the building, an excessively informal style of communication developed between us. We addressed each other as 'Darling' and 'Sweetheart'. When a temporary male secretary, G, who was standing in for the admirable Pauline Willis, heard one of these exchanges one morning, he said, 'Oh, I think I'm going to enjoy working here.'

The third new member of the staff was Brian Whitaker, who had no time - quite literally - for any of this nonsense. He had a wide brief, part managing editor, part production editor, part graphics editor, organising the flow of copy through the week. He was known to have been a cross-country skier, driving himself across frozen wastes, the way ahead illuminated by the light from a lamp on his head. He pursued his vital tasks on Weekend with much the same sort of single-minded determination. The other members of the team had all worked with Bill Smithies on Choices: Chris Maclean, Murray Armstrong, Stuart Legge and Denis Piggott, making (with Pauline Willis) eight in all - a much smaller number than would have been required to produce a full-blown colour magazine.

Rusbridger had developed a very clear idea of what he wanted it to be, and that was something that Preston too had long desired: 'That British oxymoron,' as Rusbridger put it, 'a tabloid with brains.' The language comes from the four-page glossy flyer produced by the Guardian for the trade press just before first publication. 'Printing a quality weekend section in tabloid size is not a marketing trick - it has a double logic of its own,' Rusbridger said. 'First it sets the tone midway between newspaper and magazine. Second, it enables you to print an extraordinary range of material in a comfortable and orderly way ... The Weekend Guardian', he promised, 'will be something of a new journalistic form in Britain.' Illustrating this statement was a mugshot of Weekend's youthful-looking editor, alongside photographs of myself, McCabe and the Weekend's new food and drinks editor, Matthew Fort, who was to spend more than 20 years writing for the Guardian. 'I would not say Matthew Fort was greedy,' Rusbridger wrote. 'I would not even say he is a glutton. That he takes an inordinate pleasure in food is apparent from the gusto with which he has written about it.' That was what Rusbridger wanted: gusto.

Taken as a whole, the four-page flyer gave a remarkably accurate outline of what was to come. One of the new features - Gallery - embarked on the fairly hazardous venture of a weekly full-colour page aimed at putting artists in direct touch with buyers. 'We shall charge no commission, we shall simply stand back and wait for the stampede.' And stampede there was, with the result that there was soon a cupboard stacked with transparencies. A similar free service was Booksearch, enabling readers to track down long-sought-after volumes. This too proved to be hugely popular. Then there was a 'Sod the public' section, where 'fed-up consumers can ventilate their lungs', and a Forum page, also given over to readers, who were invited to start or enter a debate on any topic close to their hearts. It was here that Rusbridger in a small way started to define the new kind of interactive relationship between the Guardian and the reader that became a basic principle, even the underlying philosophy, of his editorship in the digital age.

An innovation was a New Age page covering 'everything from herbal therapy and healing to allergies, telepathy and acupuncture'. There was a page devoted, more or less, to domestic matters called Home Front. A regular feature of this was the Bad Housekeeping column written by the novelist Sue Limb under the pseudonym Dulcie Domum. She and it were to enter history for introducing into the English language the term 'bonkbuster'. Weekend also introduced into the Guardian the Doris cartoon by Ros Asquith. Doris, distinguished by her head-scarf with its polka-dot pattern, was a cleaner – a subtle, or perhaps not-so-subtle, way of acknowledging that many Guardian readers employed such domestic staff. Doris ran in the Weekend Guardian for 10 years – many years later her progenitor still missed her. 'To me, she represented a figure in all of our lives: that of the barely visible worker, mother, grandmother, aunt, undervalued by the society whose wheels she is oiling. Doris endured many insults, but perhaps her highest praise came from a reformed convict who told me: "I love Doris. My mother was a cleaner. I used to sit in the corner while she tidied little Tarquin and Amanda's nursery. I couldn't wait to grow up and rob the lot of them."'[6]

Among other features, McCabe ran a series called Image Makers in which he expounded on the work of contemporary photographers. I edited a series on Design that ran alongside, featuring contributors such as Jeremy Dixon, Paul Smith, Anthony Caro and Molly Parkin. This column, like the Diary, made an unashamed bid for celebrities who had an area of expertise or an informed opinion about something and who could write well. Rusbridger said, 'They were places where outsiders could write. That was the whole idea, because it struck you that one of the faults about the Guardian was that it seemed closed, while the Independent seemed open to the world.' Rusbridger and I rapidly extended our contacts books by frequenting publishers' launches, often working a crowded room from opposite ends to sign up contributors.

It had been quickly resolved to bring back Hillman to provide a design that was both compatible with the broadsheet and had a bit of independent zip about it. Hillman recalls this as being very much a last-minute job: as he put it, the dummy and the first issue were one and the same. He provided exactly what was required, a versatile and stylish design for varied and lively content.

Eamonn McCabe, who was already having a beneficial impact on the front page of the main paper, demonstrated his brilliance as a picture editor in the photographers he deployed on Weekend. He made the pages a showcase for some of the best newspaper and magazine photography available. A particular asset in establishing the look of Weekend was the photographer Nobby Clark, known especially perhaps for his portraits of actors. He took the cover portrait of a naked Richard Boston, a Tandy covering any indiscretion, that announced Boston's report of a visit to a naturist town in the south of France. Boston, like another fine writer, Peter Lennon, was never on the staff of the Guardian but had a long career as a highly regarded freelance, so closely associated with the paper for so many years that for a large numbers of readers his witty and often lightly erudite contributions were of the essence.

Rusbridger demonstrated that the format could equally well carry more obviously serious subjects. Six weeks after the launch he swept away the regular sequence of features to run as the cover story an essay by the American academic Paul Fussell, under the heading 'Thank God for the atom bomb'. It followed the death of the wartime leader of Japan, Emperor Hirohito. Fussell argued - over five inside pages - that those who condemned the bomb ignored the experience of the frontline soldiers who believed that the bombs on Hiroshima and Nagasaki shortened the war, saving thousands of American - and Japanese - lives.

The article was predictably controversial and hundreds of letters quickly piled up on Rusbridger's desk. Many of them were published over the next couple of issues. It was a subject of passionate interest to Guardian readers. In a readership survey the previous year, Guardian readers had placed nuclear weapons second in a list of the most important issues facing the country, after unemployment. Fussell's essay was the first major piece that Rusbridger ran as an editor that was deliberately calculated to challenge the sensibilities of many, or in this case probably most, Guardian readers. He came to consider it a matter of editorial health to do that fairly often.

The following week Weekend entered an even more difficult area with a cover story written by Swee Chai Ang, a doctor who gave up her NHS career to help Palestinian refugees in Lebanon. Her article, written in the heat of the Intifada, recounted her experiences in Al-Ahli hospital in Israeli-occupied Gaza, giving graphic details of the injuries she had treated, many of them sustained by children. Again, a great deal of correspondence was generated. This article demonstrated not only that the tabloid format was perfectly capable of carrying self-evidently serious content but also that some special value and force were added when the writer gave his or her testimony directly without the mediation of a reporter.

Rusbridger saw no incompatibility between this kind of witness reportage and the lighter material that appeared elsewhere in Weekend. What had taken the Guardian so long to see the reader as, whatever else, an intelligent consumer? 'It was extraordinary that you should still be having these debates about whether Guardian readers could also be consumers. We had got ourselves into such a Maoist frame of mind about our readers.'

It was presumed that Peter Preston agreed. On the day before the first issue was published he had arrived at Rusbridger's desk to look at an early copy. Leafing silently through the pages, he suddenly banged an arm down on top of a metal filing cabinet with alarming force, and then walked away. No one knew exactly what that meant.

The new publication had an immediate effect on Saturday sales, putting them up by 40,000, an increase that was sustained and later improved upon, although not sufficiently to stop the Independent further closing the gap. But more than six months after the launch the Guardian's former editor Alastair Hetherington, now the chairman of the Scott Trust, expressed his delight at Weekend's 'extraordinary success'. In passing it might be mentioned that this was the closest the Guardian had yet come to a 'through-edited' section or supplement with an editor whose influence extended from the front page to the back.

Readers by and large loved the tabloid format. One wrote, 'The tabloid format, combined with an intelligent content, is remarkably attractive. Why not turn the Guardian into the first true quality tabloid? I'm sure there'd be a market for it.'[7]

Once again, there was that idea.

Chapter 8
A Beeline to Beijing

*'John Gittings came through from Beijing on a Sunday morning.
I was on the roof inspecting my beehive and I talked to John
with the phone under my bee suit.'*

Ian Wright on the near strike of 1989

The introduction of new technology at the Guardian in these years immediately after Wapping kept the management of the paper and the journalists' union, the NUJ, in a state of almost constant negotiation and dispute, marked occasionally by a work-to-rule or a protracted mandatory chapel (office branch) meeting. Routine gatherings were sometimes held in the [Karl] Marx Memorial Library, nearby on Clerkenwell Green, an appropriate place for a show of unity perhaps, but much too small for most purposes. Nearly all the big meetings in this period were held in a venue that embodied an idea even closer to the hearts of modern Guardian readers, perhaps, than the philosophy of Marx: Finsbury Library, a pioneer of open public access information.

Preston's style was to represent the editorial management side personally. 'But I hated in the end those endless NUJ negotiations because it was very draining.' He dealt with a very effective succession of people in the role of FoC, the father of the chapel, or journalists' shop steward: Mick Downing, referred to affectionately by Preston as 'Father' Downing; Aidan White, whose voice had been one of the few raised against Preston at the staff meeting during the Sarah Tisdall affair; Peter Hildrew, the Northern Labour correspondent; and Seumas Milne, Downing's deputy for some of the negotiations in the late 1980s, before becoming FoC himself. They were difficult years all round.

Across the dispersed Fleet Street there were moves to de-recognise the NUJ, ending its right to negotiate pay on behalf of its members in favour of universal personal contracts. There was no concerted move for de-recognition by the Guardian management, but the union's blanket resistance to personal contracts was strongly felt to be cramping Preston's style when it came to signing up star journalists. Reason eventually prevailed and a limited number of such contracts were allowed.

The disputes procedure that Harry Roche had been so keen to see introduced in 1985, when finally in place, may have had the desired effect of cutting stoppages, the spectre of which hung around long after the printers had gone. Whether it actually did or not was itself a matter of dispute, since the NUJ had rarely been responsible for stoppages in the past. Seumas Milne thought the union had been misguided to accept it; in his view the disputes procedure - which moved in timed stages until it culminated in mediation under the auspices of the government-sponsored body, Acas - complicated rather than simplified things. 'The Guardian was a relatively small workplace with about 250 journalists. We didn't need somebody [from outside] to tell us what the settlement of our dispute should be, when it was something that should be settled between the chapel and the management ... It meant that in a lot of the disputes over the next few years there was an undercurrent or subtext: we were trying to use the disputes procedure for industrial advantage, but also to show that it was a) unnecessary and b) disruptive. So there was a dispute under this procedure every year for the following four years, certainly up to 1991.'

No dispute took the Guardian closer to a strike than the one that began in the late autumn of 1988. Even in the early stages, Harry Roche, who was now the group chairman, had forecast that it would be protracted. There were 'difficulties' with the NUJ over new technology, he reported to the Scott Trust in November. And he allowed himself to lament, 'The Guardian is now the only national [newspaper] with a closed shop.' Alastair Hetherington, nearing the end of 19 years on the Scott Trust, the past five as chairman, independently made the same point. To most in the Guardian's editorial management it was not a hot issue. Peter Preston, who, as well as being editor of the Guardian, had succeeded Harry Roche as chairman of the Guardian board, Ian Wright the managing editor, and all the senior editorial executives - the denizens of the bunker - were members of the NUJ, nominally at least. Wright explained, 'We regarded the NUJ as our colleagues, we understood the sentiment that made most people, including Peter and I, subscribe to NUJ funds quite willingly - as members - and we [also] understood that there were many people who felt it was a small thing - a bit like going to church and putting money in the collection box for overseas missions ... The closed shop had never been formally abolished, but it was understood that it was not something that anybody was going to go to the wall for.'[1]

Wright was critical of what he saw as Harry Roche's generally 'macho approach', although he understood the necessity for the Guardian to have its house in order to maximise its energy to compete. There was no disagreement on the principle; only the manner was in question. Roche, whom Wright thought was still flushed with success from his battle with the NUJ in Manchester, wanted 'what you might have called an unconditional surrender document from the NUJ'.

In the long series of disputes accompanying the introduction of new technology, Wright had tried to foster an alternative conciliation service. He often had informal conversations at such times with the deputy father of the chapel, John Gittings, for many years the Guardian's principal China expert. Some of these were telephone conversations when Gittings was in Beijing in the immediate run-up to the student protests at Tiananmen Square.

On one occasion, Wright had been at home, attending to the beehive he kept on the roof of his house in one of Islington's elegant squares, when a long-awaited call from Gittings in Beijing came through. Wright recalled, 'It was quite difficult in those days to get through from Beijing but he came through on a Sunday morning. I was on the roof inspecting my beehive and I talked to John with the phone under my bee suit ... So we had this private call, a call that didn't exist: he's not going to tell the NUJ and I'm not going to tell the Guardian management. But what are we going to do to bring together these people who have dug themselves into such holes?' Gittings agreed, 'We were a sort of unofficial back channel quite frequently throughout the whole business.'[2]

The dispute that ran on through the first six months of 1989 was about a range of issues involving pay, new technology and working practices: and a feature of almost all the disputes of these years were concerns about RSI, repetitive strain injury, which had already reached epidemic proportions throughout the industry following the introduction of VDUs (visual display units). Sub-editors working long hours against deadlines were particularly susceptible to the condition. A number felt inhibited in talking about their experience by confidentiality clauses written into the terms of their severance agreements.

Anne McHardy, the night news editor and a former Northern Ireland correspondent, was among the most badly affected. It troubled her for the rest of her career. She wrote about her experience in April 1990 and again in 1994.[3] Celia Locks, who had just started chief-subbing on the home news desk, was another whose life was practically blighted by the condition and was still affected by it when she left the Guardian in 2012.

Some 30 people at the Guardian were seriously affected by this miserable and initially mysterious accompaniment to the new technology: they used to hold meetings occasionally to compare notes, and to shore up morale. McHardy's articles were part of the forward march in knowledge that informed not only her colleagues but also the doctors, physiotherapists and others who were treating them. The NUJ incurred huge costs in trying to bring legal cases throughout the industry. 'Hundreds of journalists [were left] in constant pain, many for life; for some their careers were ruined.'[4]

Serious though this and other issues were, from the management point of view the crucial issue in the 1989 dispute was the need to reach agreement at long last on electronic page make-up. It was the final element of new technology that would complete the replacement of the old hot metal process that had ended almost two years earlier. The management had offered £500 to the limited number of people who would operate the page make-up terminals. The union was asking for more than twice that figure, £1,200, and furthermore it wanted it to be paid as a flat rate to all NUJ members, not just those working on electronic page make-up.

Towards the end of January, the union and the company went into formal dispute. In the spring there was a conciliation meeting at Acas that was, in the word used to report the outcome to a board meeting, 'unfruitful'. Later in April the two sides were back at Acas for a meeting with the mediator, Lord McCarthy. In May, McCarthy made his recommendations. He said salaries should be raised by 6% (inflation meanwhile had moved above 8%); and he recommended that a flat rate annual payment of £750 a year should be made to those operating full-page make-up.

The last week of May found the two sides still unable to agree. Milne felt unable to commend McCarthy's proposals to his colleagues. 'Lord McCarthy did a perfectly good job but, as mediators and arbitrators generally do, he split the difference. And that didn't really reflect either the strength of feeling in the chapel, or [the fact that] some people would have been worse off than they had been under the previous offer. So we just reserved our position. We took on board the McCarthy report and then said, "And now we'll proceed to ballot for industrial action." And I think the management was upset about that.' At the ballot, 'We had an enormous "yes" vote. We then held a mandatory chapel meeting, and at that we had a huge vote for a strike.'

Harry Roche was watching the situation closely, but the main protagonists now were Jim Markwick, who had succeeded him as managing director of the Guardian, Peter Preston and Seumas Milne.

Both Preston and later Rusbridger had an equivocal attitude towards Milne. Preston, who had hired him in 1984, never quite got over the feeling that he had somehow been slipped to him. It was a thought that troubled him quite frequently once Milne, only a year after his arrival, had plunged into union activities, and even more so when he was elected to the national executive of the NUJ, on which he was to serve for a decade. Preston, while conceding the demands that the union made on Milne's time, felt, as he put it, somewhat deprived of his company. In a way he blamed Richard Gott, who, in an outburst at a heads of department meeting, had complained that they were all growing grey together and needed more very bright young people. Almost coincidentally Andrew Knight, at that time editor of the Economist, followed up a lunch with Preston by sending him a handwritten note to say he had a very bright young man on his staff who might be more stretched on a newspaper such as the Guardian. 'The message from Richard and the HoDs had been clear, and here was God handing me Seumas with a personal recommendation from Andrew.'

Milne allows himself the flicker of a smile at this account. 'I think Andrew Knight had the feeling that maybe I wasn't an entirely appropriate person to have working for his organ, that politically I was too leftwing, a cuckoo in the nest. He never expressed it quite like that but I think they were quite keen for me to go.'

Milne for his part was aware that his devotion to union matters had not done his career a lot of good. 'I think subsequently there was a feeling by Peter Preston in particular that he had been distracted from the full level of attention he should have given to the challenge of the Independent by endless negotiations with the NUJ.' Certainly Preston was desperate to avoid a strike, which he was convinced would damage the paper's competitiveness.

Milne recalled the dramatic moment: 'We had the authorisation to go ahead with the strike and we were having a committee meeting to draw up the strike rotas.' Suddenly Preston appeared. 'He flung open the door and said, "Do you want to negotiate then?"' An almost interminable round of negotiations restarted but again little progress was made.

It may have been at this time that Markwick said to Milne, 'Criticise the play by all means but stop short of burning down the playhouse.' Milne said of Markwick, 'He was the one person I dealt with in the Guardian management who just didn't take it personally. For him, not that it was a game, but he saw negotiations with unions as a completely ordinary part of management business. You know, you played hardball, you reached agreement and made your settlement and that was that. I remember in one dispute Preston saying about me and Markwick, "You two just love this, don't you?"'

On Tuesday 30 May, the union passed a resolution: to take strike action for 24 hours from 2.30am on Thursday 1 June (which would prevent publication of the paper on Friday 2 June); to work to rule; and to inform freelances not to file copy intended for use on Friday 2 June. In addition, the mandatory chapel meeting was set to resume at 4pm the following Monday, 5 June, itself eating disruptively into peak production time for Tuesday's paper, with the threat of further strike action to follow.

Jim Markwick, who had been in Edinburgh for part of this escalating phase of the affair, caught the 7am plane back to London. He told an emergency board meeting that evening that there were two courses available to the management: either resume negotiations or seek an injunction to prevent strike action. There was little appetite for the latter course of action. It would be back to the negotiating table.

Negotiations went on through the following day and into the evening, in the boardroom in Farringdon Road. Jim Markwick at a very late hour had taken a break to go to the lavatory and on the stairs had bumped into the arts editor Roger Alton. 'I told him, "It's not looking too good." I always remember what Roger said: "Oh fuck it, it's become a big dick contest."' It caused some welcome laughter when he reported this exchange back in the boardroom. Seumas Milne had an encounter that evening too with one of the senior sub-editors. 'He came up to me at about nine o'clock that evening and said, "Don't do it, Seumas, don't do it." He knew that in the past the troops had all been marched up the hill only to be marched down again and he was in a terrible state that this time they would now go over the top.'

But this time the ticking clock had successfully concentrated minds. A deal was finally agreed at 1.50am on 1 June, and the strike that had been due to start just 40 minutes later was called off. The talks, agreeing a new deal, went on into daylight. The basic increase on salaries was 5%, but taken altogether the deal would add an average of almost 9% to journalists' salaries. It was too late to get more than a brief note on the front page of the final edition of that day's paper: 'Guardian strike called off'. A fuller story appeared in the Guardian for 2 June, the paper that would probably not have appeared had the strike gone ahead. From the management's point of view it cleared the way for the introduction of full-page make-up. From the union's point of view it made the long drag across the previous six months seem more than worthwhile. Milne, looking back at that night more than 20 years later, said, 'It was a very good agreement, probably the best we've ever had.'

Two weeks later Ian Wright told the Guardian board that trials of full-page make-up were to be held immediately and that the tabloid Weekend Guardian would be entirely prepared on full screen by early August. It would then be rolled out across other departments, with the whole paper being brought onto the News Layout system within 12 months. Another step forward had been taken, and this time a sizeable one.

Chapter 9
The Shock of the New

'There's enough success to go round.'

Attributed to Jocelyn Targett

The end of the NUJ action that brought the Guardian to the brink of a strike in June 1989 also marked further changes in the features department, with the role of features editor passing from Richard Gott to Alan Rusbridger. The move, coming at the end of several years of technological upheaval, signified a degree of fatigue on the part of Gott, who had done the job with distinction for a little over a decade. But the change also recognised the part Rusbridger's Weekend had played in just seven months in bringing new life to the Saturday paper and beginning to beat back the Independent's challenge.

Journalism at the end of the eighties, after Wapping and the destruction of the old printing unions, was a career that offered unprecedented scope for ambition. It was a period of extraordinary fertility. Among those entering the profession at this time who were to play a significant part in the changes taking place at the Guardian were Jocelyn Targett, James Wood and David Rowan.

Jay Rayner, who was to find fame as the Observer's food critic, was also part of that talented generation, and his fortunes in the early years to some extent were linked to Targett's. Rayner, the son of the agony aunt and NHS campaigner Claire Rayner, recalled, 'Jocelyn had a theory which I think was right - that for all our liberal-left credentials we were Thatcher's kids to the bone. We had soaked up enough of the prevailing political culture to believe that there was absolutely no reason why we couldn't just get stuck in, if we had the balls.'[1] David Rowan attributed a similar view to Targett. 'Jocelyn said something that I still quote which is, "There's enough success to go round." His view was if you make an effort rather than sit around and envy those who are already in good positions then you too can make something of yourself.'[2] Contemplating his career 20 years later Targett wondered whether his 'gene of ambition' might not have been overdeveloped.[3] From the Guardian's point of view they brought in necessary fresh air and energy.

In 1987, Targett, Wood and Rayner all figured in the National Union of Students/Guardian Student Journalism awards. Targett won a special award with his precocious creation Parade, swiftly renamed Plural for the magazine's second and only other edition to avoid confusion with the soft porn magazine of the same name. James Wood, his close contemporary and friend at Cambridge, was voted student journalist of the year.

Rayner, a student at Leeds, was also shortlisted that year in the best college magazine category. Those three were to win for the Guardian the Young Journalist of the Year award in successive years, Targett in 1989, Wood in 1990 and Rayner in 1991. Rayner, unlike the others, was never actually on the staff of the Guardian, a sore point with him as the paper claimed him as its own in a trade advertisement bragging of its success in the press awards, misspelling his name in the process.

Wood and Targett had arrived at Cambridge via different routes. Wood had been educated at Eton; his father was a professor at Durham University. Targett had gone to a north London comprehensive of which his father Peter Targett (later dubbed 'Red Pete' by the Daily Mail) was the progressive headmaster. Meeting the challenge of survival as the head's son equipped him with a useful resilience, he believed.

Before long, Wood and Targett were working together at Cambridge, not only editing the student newspaper but becoming members of the same student pop band. As soon as he had won the student journalist of the year award, Wood wrote to the literary editor of the Guardian offering his services as a reviewer. Waldemar Januszczak had by then embarked upon a brief and iconoclastic stint in charge of the books pages. He had recently decided not to carry any review of Rushdie's The Satanic Verses on the grounds that it was of insufficient merit to warrant such a distinction.[4] He did however inaugurate James Wood's career as a literary critic when he commissioned him in mid-November 1988, making Wood the first of this group of graduates to be published in the Guardian.

Of the Guardian intake at this time, none had a trajectory quite as conspicuously and controversially brilliant as Targett's. It did not have a totally smooth launch. Targett had pitched several ideas to Rusbridger after meeting him at the 1988 student journalism awards. Rusbridger eventually asked him to do 2,000 words about a council housing estate that was being yuppified, and to 'Bring it in'. After fortifying himself with a fried-egg sandwich at Boggi's, a nearby café much frequented by Guardian journalists, Targett handed the piece over to Rusbridger, who read it there and then with no appearance of great enthusiasm. (It did get into Weekend eventually - four months later.)[5] So it was quite unexpected when Rusbridger suddenly asked him, 'How would you like to edit a special edition of Weekend Guardian?' Weekend had not yet been launched, so Rusbridger showed Targett one of the dummy issues. 'He said, "I'll give you five hundred quid to do an edition about 1939." [Later this was raised to £800.] Naturally I said yes, but then I asked him, "Does it matter that I don't know anything about 1939?" His reply to that was "Learn."'

This was to become the first of many newspaper supplements that year to mark the 50th anniversary of the outbreak of the Second World War. Targett was 22 when he was given the job, and just 23 when that issue came out on 11 February 1989. It was an unusual achievement, the first of several single-issue editions of Weekend in its early months, a model of bold and imaginative commissioning, with an arresting use of pictures and layout. The contributors included Stephen Spender, Spike Milligan (who seemed to have got over his complaint about the 1988 redesign), the poet Roy Fuller, and Tom Hopkinson and Bert Hardy, respectively editor and chief photographer of Picture Post in the 1940s. It set the pattern for future single-subject editions of Weekend in that all its regular features were recruited to the theme, including the arts pages (Dilys Powell on the wartime cinema; Cyril Cusack describing theatre performances that carried on with the sound of shrapnel hitting the roof). Even the bridge and chess columns looked back to great games of the time.

The real Targett touch, it can be seen in retrospect, was to commission pieces from two of the Mitford sisters, Diana - Lady Mosley, the wife of the British Fascist leader, Sir Oswald Mosley - and Jessica Mitford, whose communist affiliations had led to what was to be a lifelong split with her sister. Neither, according to Targett, knew in advance of the other's contribution. Jessica Mitford was in London when the 1939 issue came out, and a couple of days before publication Targett took her out to lunch, carrying with him proofs of the pages. When she saw that she shared the issue with Diana she was, Targett declared, 'incandescent with rage'. Lunch, he recalled, was an uncomfortable affair.

For Rusbridger, the 1939 issue confirmed his view of Targett. 'I thought he was one of the most extraordinary young journalists I'd ever worked with. I thought he was a completely, fantastically precocious, brilliant, likeable, bumptious, ambitious person; I mean Tigger-like in his enthusiasms.' Preston was impressed too. On 1 May 1989, on Rusbridger's recommendation, Targett was awarded a contract in the features department, starting at £18,000. Targett had murmured something about being offered more by the Independent and Preston had replied, 'I don't want to pay you too much now because I want to be able to pay you more later.' Targett was still pondering that when he received Preston's equally enigmatic welcome note, in which he was told not to say 'much of a word to Mother' about his salary.

In September, Jocelyn Targett was put on the staff as an arts sub-editor, working to Roger Alton, the arts editor. Three months later, Alton became editor of Weekend to replace Ed Vulliamy, who held the editorship only briefly after Rusbridger, and Targett joined him as deputy editor. Unusually, Alton and Targett had been invited to pitch for the jobs together, and they had a joint audience with Preston at which, Targett believes, the seeds of future discord were sown. Targett remembers Preston saying something along the lines of, 'Right, this is going to be perfect. I regard you two as the dream team. You, Jocelyn, with all your dash and innovation and style, and Roger - you'll make sure it gets done on time.'

Targett quickly rose to the challenge by producing another impressive 48-page special issue of Weekend on the theme of the eighties, to mark the end of the decade. The contributors this time included Alan Bennett, Jeffrey Bernard, JK Galbraith, Robert Kee and Edward Said. Julie Burchill was also among the contributors, complaining that the eighties were marked and marred by 'the pathologisation of pleasure', the rise of a cult of miserabilism among the young that saw a problem behind every pleasure. This was not Burchill's first bylined piece in the Guardian. That had been her scathing review three years earlier of *A Concise History of the Sex Manual* by Alan Rusbridger, illustrated by Posy Simmonds.[6] (Rusbridger clearly did not bear a grudge: from 1998 to 2000, Burchill wrote a regular column for the Guardian of which Rusbridger was by then editor.) Long before that, with Toby Young and Cosmo Landesman, she founded the Modern Review, and that small magazine, as we shall see, became a significant player in the revolution that was sweeping through the features department.

This eighties issue of Weekend also provided David Rowan with an entry into the Guardian. He and Targett had also been at Cambridge together. Individually or jointly, Targett, Wood and Rowan had all had turns at editing the student newspaper, Stop Press.[7] Rowan: 'We had an all-night paste-up session once a week, making pages up with wax and rollers. It forged a bond.' He and Jay Rayner knew each other too. They had been together, although a year apart, at Haberdashers' school in Hertfordshire.

On Rowan's 21st birthday, still a student, he had his first piece on the main features page of the Telegraph, about entrepreneurial activities among his fellow students. He embarked on an enterprise of his own immediately after taking his finals, making crêpes for Oxbridge balls. He mentioned this hesitatingly in an interview with Charles Wilson, the editor of the Times. Wilson told him that was just the kind of entrepreneurial spirit they needed and took him on to the graduate training scheme, at the end of which the Times offered him a job as an environment reporter, which he declined. He was doing some shifts on one of the dummy editions of the Independent on Sunday when he had the call from Jocelyn Targett to help him put together the eighties issue of Weekend.

From that moment, Rowan's career went on apace. He had a talent for innovation. Once on the Guardian, he pitched and provided a language column called Lingua Franca to Roger Alton's arts pages, and then he was asked to do an arts diary. His first contribution to that was an exceptionally well-informed item about the number of free tickets being distributed at the Royal Opera House, Covent Garden, allegedly keeping up the price of tickets available to the general public. It caused a rumpus at the Opera House and a hunt for the mole.

Preston had noticed Rowan's activities, and about the middle of March he called him down to his office in the bunker. The conversation, according to Rowan, went something like this: 'We have a tradition of April Fools at the Guardian and I'd like to do a Sunday Guardian. We're not actually going to launch a Sunday edition but we're going to pretend that we are and we're going to give it away with the Saturday paper. I'd like you to work on it.' Brian Whitaker, the managing editor of the features department, had been given the job of editing it. It was thought his previous connection with the News on Sunday, which he had edited for a very brief spell, along with Rowan's earlier shifts on the dummy of the Independent, would lend the exercise a worrying credibility. Putting the wind up Stephen Glover and his team was what it was all about.

The 36-page newsprint tabloid was published on Saturday 31 March with the giveaway dateline Sunday 1 April 1990. It was two months after the launch of the Independent on Sunday. On the front page of the Guardian for Sunday there was an exclusive story revealing that Mrs Thatcher was putting her family home in Dulwich on the market since she had decided to reside permanently in Downing Street, not quite an unimaginable event in 1990. Another feature was Salman Rushdie on 'A room of my own'. Rushdie, who had been in hiding since the fatwa the previous year, described a room in a clapperboard [sic] building in the Falklands Islands. The photograph showed an orange 'Neighbourhood Watch' sticker in the window. The books section reflected the not uncommon view that such pages were customarily in the hands of a small elite. Martin Amis reviewed Margaret Drabble; Drabble reviewed Blake Morrison; Morrison reviewed Julian Barnes; Barnes reviewed Martin Amis ... and so on.

The impending publication of the Guardian for Sunday had been reported po-faced as a real event in the trade press, and champagne now had to be dispatched to all the trade reporters who had been taken in. 'I don't think I've had so much fun since then,' said Rowan.

Shortly after this, Rowan was called down to Preston's office again. Just nine months after crossing the Guardian's threshold he became the launch editor of eG,[8] a weekly education section set up in the wake of the Education Reform Act of 1988, which brought in the national curriculum in state schools in England and Wales. It was another product of Preston's fertile mind. 'I invented it sitting in the back of a car in Chelsea, scribbling on a piece of paper.'[9]

Meanwhile, Targett's upward trajectory was also continuing. The Independent on Sunday courted him in the period before the paper was launched at the end of January 1990, to no avail. It came as no surprise when he won the Young Journalist of the Year award, commended for 'vivid writing, complemented by all-round ability in editing, design and organisation'. It was assumed that the last of these qualities was to be attributed to his way with editorial content rather than people.

As well as attracting interest from other newspapers, Targett was also doing his best to attract the attention of the Guardian's newish fashion editor Judy Rumbold, who had been recruited in 1987 from Company magazine. In the view of many, Rumbold had lightened the Guardian's drabness. Preston, encountering her in a corridor of the Farringdon Road office, as she was setting off, bespangled and besequinned, for an evening engagement, had said, 'It's great to have a fashion editor who looks like a fashion editor for once.' Recounting the story, she said, 'It's not to say the others were dowdy, but I love dressing up. Call me shallow but it's part of the fun, and for me, fashion is fun.'[10] The convention of the time for male journalists, even on the second floor where suits were already rare, was to keep at least a tie in a desk drawer in case you had to interview the prime minister. Targett was among the first seriously to challenge the convention, not by 'dressing down' - a tendency that seemed to come naturally in features - but by dressing up in the latest designer fashions. To what extent Judy Rumbold was treating him as her personal clotheshorse became a matter for speculation. The attraction had become mutual and they were now an item; their enthusiastic terms of endearment, escaping across the Atex system, earned Targett his first of many appearances in Private Eye: 'Some of the more staid and ancient hacks at the Grauniad ... have been complaining that obscene sexual suggestions keep appearing on their computer screens. An in-house investigation reveals that the messages are computerised *billets doux* between two of the paper's youngest hacks - Jocelyn Targett, the peroxide-blond 23-year-old toy boy who is now deputy editor of the Weekend Guardian, and Judy "Rumpy-Pumpy" Rumbold, the paper's teenage microskirted fashion editor with whom he is besotted.'[11]

This was not quite what it seemed to be. Targett was already being seen as the instrument of undesirable changes that Rusbridger was introducing, particularly after the latter became features editor in June 1989. He became a focus for many of the otherwise generalised fears caused by the great changes taking place across the features department, among them that the paper's leftwing politics were giving way to a soft centrist liberalism, and that at the same time it was drifting downmarket. A tendency to take Targett less than seriously was inadvertently helped by Nicholas de Jongh, the paper's arts correspondent. In editing the *Bedside Guardian* for 1990, de Jongh had included a piece by Targett. Unfortunately, in the 'Notes on contributors' at the end of the book, de Jongh had described him throughout as 'she', which was quickly seized upon by Private Eye, who referred to him thereafter as 'Miss' Targett.

Early in 1992, a couple of things happened that intensified Private Eye's interest in Targett. The first was a probably libellous profile he wrote of one of the founders and former editor of Private Eye, Richard Ingrams, published on 17 February to coincide with the launch of his new magazine the Oldie. The heading set the tone: 'The Monday Profile: Old, cold and past it - This doyen of dinosaur hacks, this gerontosaurus rex, cares only about his class, sex and generation. Sod the rest. Jocelyn Targett, 26, profiles Richard Ingrams, 54, editor of a new magazine, the Oldie'. It was a vigorous, even vicious attack. 'The ex-editor of Private Eye - once a man of cheek and gall - is now a shambles of decrepit jokes and potty, unshakeable prejudices,' Targett wrote. He ran a list of Ingrams' 'hates', including 'pooves' and Jews. Ingrams responded with a complaint to the Guardian's ombudsman, Professor Hugh Stephenson, objecting to the implication that he was anti-Semitic. Stephenson upheld it, finding 'no justification' for the assertion in the article that 'he hates Jews'.

The second development, little more than a week later, was Targett's sudden elevation to replace the extremely well-liked Helen Oldfield, the arts editor. They were swapped over, with Oldfield becoming deputy editor of Weekend, working once more with Alton, whom she had succeeded as arts editor. Targett's tenure of the arts desk was brief and almost continuously controversial. His displacement of the popular Oldfield, and the picaresque nature of his own conduct of the job, guaranteed a constant feed of titbits to Private Eye, and his profile of Ingrams guaranteed that there would always be an appetite for them there.

He had pitched for the job in a 2,500-word manifesto, submitted to Rusbridger at the beginning of February. It was punchy stuff. 'What is the best arts section in British newspapers actually like? It is sharp-witted and creative in its commissioning, adept at coming up with fresh and challenging angles on the arts issues of the day. It is first with the big stories ... It stimulates debate and isn't shy of courting controversy. From time to time, it becomes something of an event itself - newsworthy and widely discussed.'

He then proceeded to criticise what had been on the arts pages over the preceding three weeks. The pages did not span the broad range of the arts. They did not make good use of their 'star' critics, Michael Billington,

Nancy Banks-Smith, Derek Malcolm, or the newly appointed arts correspondent, Joanna Coles. The exceptions apart, the arts pages were now
'a faculty of nonentities, tenured wasters'.

As for the main weekly showpiece for the arts, Review Guardian,
which appeared on Thursdays, he declared, 'The pages require a vision
and an ambition they have never had. Appointing a new deputy arts editor
will not give it this. It will merely consolidate a reign of dire mediocrity.'

It would not be going too far to say that in his year as arts editor Targett
polarised not only the arts desk, but also the entire features department,
and to some extent the paper as a whole. This was partly due to what
some saw as a pathological ambition. When his age - 26 - was mentioned,
he was said to have pointed out that CP Scott was only 26 [sic][12] when
he became editor of the Manchester Guardian. As his profile of Ingrams
had shown, he was inclined towards generational warfare. Discussing his
new role with a friend on the phone, he was heard to say there was a lot
of dead wood that would have to be cut out. Some of the dead wood was
apparently within earshot. Several well-respected critics, including Judith
Williamson and Gilbert Adair, soon disappeared from Targett's arts pages.

Targett caused an early sensation with a piece by Jay Rayner, whom
he had rung up in search of ideas. Rayner had noticed that there were a
couple of sculpture exhibitions focusing on the male form. 'I suggested
to Jos that I do a piece about the uncircumcised penis in art. After all,
Michelangelo's David was a nice Jewish boy, but he was still intact. Jos
said yes, and so I wrote 1,000 words of whimsy about foreskins. I thought
little more about it, until Jos called me the next morning both horrified
and mischievously thrilled by what had happened. He had illustrated
the piece with Robert Mapplethorpe's photograph *Man in Polyester Suit*.
When you opened the second section you were confronted by a close-up
of a man's open fly and, hanging from it, 10 life-size inches of uncircumcised cock. It ran under the headline "Boyz 'n' the hood".' Rusbridger
was alerted by the editor: 'I got a call from Peter Preston saying, "Do you
realise there's a picture of a black man's penis in the arts pages?" And I
had to rush in and take it out, as it were.'

The corps of critics suffered in a variety of ways. One or two were
left to languish, without loss of contract. One of these was the radio critic
Val Arnold-Forster, who had been writing regularly for the Guardian for
the past 18 years. For the last couple of months of Targett's tenure her

column wasn't used, nor was she ever told why. It was also suggested, erroneously as it happened, that the theatre critic Michael Billington had had one of his reviews spiked. A piece in Private Eye commented, 'Billington was furious, natch.' (Since 'natch' was a favourite word of Alton's, all eyes employed in the search for the mole turned towards him at this point.) Strenuous denials from both Billington and Rusbridger were carried in the next issue of Private Eye.

Others were put under pressure through the introduction of a rival critic whose work they would find running alongside or above their own efforts. Targett's main accomplice in this was Toby Young, the son of Lord Young of Dartington, who had written the Labour manifesto for the 1945 landslide election. Rusbridger thought he detected a certain eccentricity in the elder Young's pitches for Guardian features, which led to his referring to him affectionately as 'Barmy Lord Young'. As previously mentioned, Toby Young was the co-founder of the Modern Review, published beneath the banner 'Low Culture for Highbrows'. 'The point,' Young declared, 'was to champion the kind of mainstream schlock that the chattering classes regarded as beneath contempt.'[13] Young quickly established a presence on Targett's arts pages, but not without meeting some resistance: witness this fax, from Young to Targett, which also found its way to Private Eye: 'Here is the piece on multimillion dollar art movies ... This is the best piece I've done for you - please sub it yourself so nothing gets fucked up. The only way we can beat them is by doing good work.'

The Guardian's long-serving film critic, Derek Malcolm, a champion of European and world cinema, in particular found himself frequently squeezed on the page by Toby Young's reviews of the latest American blockbuster. There had been a direct conflict with Malcolm's views when Young challenged the critical reception given to Terence Davies's *The Long Day Closes*, released in May that year. Every serious British film critic, he complained, had chosen to make this the lead review while relegating *Wayne's World* to the bottom of the page. Malcolm had written enthusiastically about Davies's work and had chaired a special Guardian/NFT preview at which he described Davies as a 'treasurably original filmmaker'. Young, by contrast, thought the film 'wilfully inaccessible' and a 'depressingly predictable' portrait of working-class life, 'reminiscent of nothing so much as a Hovis commercial'. (Derek

Malcolm was to survive Young's assault: he remained the Guardian's film critic until 1997, when he 'retired' at the age of 65, though he continued to write; a book of his 100 best films appeared in 2001. Publication was marked by the following correction in the Guardian: 'The details of Derek Malcolm's new book, page 5, G2, January 18, were correct except for the title, publisher and price ...')

Running alongside this was a certain amount of turmoil on the arts desk itself. There was head-on conflict between Targett and the sardonic and rather volatile Deborah Orr, who was armed with an unrivalled fund of experience in magazine design and publishing. Cries of anguish pierced the features department from time to time. Orr, three years older than Targett, had joined the arts desk under Helen Oldfield and had shared the general shock at Oldfield's sudden departure. Her background was very different from Targett's. She came from a gritty Scottish working-class environment in Motherwell, where her father worked in the steel industry and as a postman. It was a bleak landscape dominated by the Ravenscraig steelworks, a childhood environment about which Orr wrote vividly. 'Sometimes, turning a corner or reaching the top of a hill, the huge industrial complex would spread out before us, stretching to the horizon. That filthy, black steam-soaked, smoke-belching sprawl should have been ugly. Instead it was overwhelming beautiful.'[14] Orr went to St Andrews University, afterwards arriving in Edinburgh amid rising unemployment, where she benefited from the Thatcher government's enterprise allowance scheme, working briefly as an assistant magazine designer before moving to London. By then the recession was in full swing. Unemployment was moving rapidly towards its peak in 1986 of well over 3 million. Back in Scotland, Orr's whole family was now out of work. For a time she lived in a squat, eventually finding magazine work, before a stint at the terminal City Limits led her to the Guardian.

In her year subbing in the features department she had not been oblivious to the tensions that were accompanying the huge changes taking place. Rusbridger had not been universally welcomed as a replacement for Gott as features editor, and his continuing rise was both predicted and resisted by what Rusbridger had termed 'the old guard'. Their main complaint was that he had 'no politics'. Similarly, Alton, the new Weekend editor, had 'no politics' and in addition was considered 'a dreadful lightweight'. As for Targett, who was now in charge of the desk on which Orr was working, not only did he have 'no politics', he was despised by the old guard as Rusbridger's pet young find: flashy, ambitious, pushy and inexperienced. 'It was quite hard to work out what, in the seething mass of resentment, was genuine criticism and what was bitter tribal alliance,' Orr commented.[15]

'Jocelyn and I couldn't get on,' was her rather understated assessment of the situation. The situation was not helped when in mid-July, while Targett was away on paternity leave, Orr accidentally sent him a message saying that she wanted to kill him - 'figure of speech', she explained. That found its way to Private Eye even faster than its fairly rapid progress round the office.

Whatever their differences, Orr, whose designation was 'assistant arts editor', continued to commission pieces and also to contribute interviews and articles, mainly on film, and at the same time she became a regular reviewer on the books pages - now edited by Richard Gott - where guerrilla fighters could always find a refuge.

Targett was also by no means paralysed by this conflict. In the autumn he made a snap signing of David Mellor, the heritage secretary. Mellor had resigned in disgrace from John Major's government in September, not because of his earlier affair with an actress, Antonia de Sancha, but after courtroom revelations that in 1990 he had taken a month-long villa holiday for himself and his family in Marbella, paid for by Mona Bauwens, whose father was said to be a financier of the Palestine Liberation Organisation.[16] Mellor wrote a very good insider's column that ran on the arts pages of the Guardian for three years.

Another stroke of Targett's was to sign up William Cook as the paper's inaugural comedy critic. The paper had been covering comedy, or cabaret as it was usually called, pretty much since the current wave of stand-up comedy had started with the opening of the Comedy Store - Britain's first alternative comedy club - in an attic above a Soho strip club in 1979.

Now Cook, concentrating almost exclusively on comedy, became an acknowledged guide to a burgeoning genre.

At the end of 1992, Targett had a call from Andrew Neil, the editor of the Sunday Times, who offered him a job starting the paper's Culture section (what emerged clearly owed a debt to the Modern Review) and relaunching its Style section. Targett believed that, ironically, it was through Private Eye that Neil first noticed him: he couldn't imagine that Neil spent much time perusing the Guardian's arts pages. Targett had been arts editor of the Guardian for slightly less than a year when he sent Preston a note, sounding a bit like a parody of one of the editor's own: 'Dear Peter, I'm off to the Sunday Times on March 1st 1993, with a knapsack full of memories and second thoughts. All the best, Jocelyn.'

At the end of February, before he left the office on the eve of his departure, he sent an emotional message via the Atex system to Rusbridger. He said how much he had valued him as a model and a mentor, and went on, 'Right from the start you've been magnificently constructive ... Quite how you put up with the petulance, arrogance and childishness I don't know! And your successes and creativity make me proud to be a journalist. I've felt hugely flattered to have been "chosen". Much love, Jos.' It is possible that drink had been taken. He was not allowed to go quietly. When he arrived in Farringdon Road on his last day he found the huge advertisement hoarding on the opposite side of the road entirely taken up with the words, 'Thanks, Jocelyn' and an invitation for Guardian readers to follow him to the Sunday Times, rather suggesting that it might have had something to do with his new employer.

Toby Young swiftly disappeared from the arts pages of Targett's successor - me - given that my knowledge of and interest in whole swaths of popular culture were minimal. However, the paper's infatuation with the Modern Review did not end. In 1995, there was thought of buying it, though it eventually came to nothing. Young wrote, 'The Guardian made it clear that the magazine's original formula - smart writers on dumb things - would have to be updated if they were to remain interested. Too many broadsheet journalists were now pulling the same stunt. It no longer gave us a distinctive editorial identity.' Later that year he took the unilateral decision to pull the plug, and the original Modern Review was scuttled.

The effect of the Modern Review on the Guardian, especially in Targett's time, was seminal. Almost all those involved in it were to write or otherwise contribute to the Guardian at one time or another. The founders, Toby Young and, later, Julie Burchill wrote extensively for the paper. The third co-founder Cosmo Landesman appeared occasionally. Among others, Tom Shone, Nicholas Lezard, Will Self, Charlotte Raven, Suzanne Moore and the cartoonist, Martin Rowson, all became regular contributors.

The Modern Review's basic idea, that popular culture could be treated seriously, had more or less won the day. Nicholas Lezard, reflecting five years after its demise, wrote, 'The magazine let you liberate yourself from the tyranny of reflexive disdain ... what it really taught was that there is no "high" or "low" culture ... there is culture and individual responses to it. It's what's upstairs that counts.'[17] Not everyone agreed. Auberon Waugh, in an editorial in his Literary Review, protested that the popular mass culture that Toby Young championed was 'the enemy of all truth, beauty and wisdom in the modern world'. Even Young's enemies at the Guardian probably thought that was going a bit too far.

Helen Oldfield looked back on her former domain with something close to equanimity. She felt the inevitable pangs of regret that some of her favourites had disappeared so swiftly. What she particularly regretted was the relative neglect of the corps of regional critics, the largest group of whom worked under the direction of the Manchester office and the northern arts editor Robin Thornber. She was the last arts editor under whom they did really well. 'Jocelyn wanted that Modern Review aesthetic and he wasn't much interested in reviewing what went on at the Bolton Octagon. You know, I can see the point. In retrospect what we were there to do was interest the most possible readers and not to be too anxious about the relatively small number who would go to an art exhibition in Salford.'[18]

There had been another development in June 1989, the month in which the advent of Rusbridger as features editor had stimulated the growth of something like a youth culture on the second floor at Farringdon Road. That was the long-awaited announcement of a launch date for the Sunday Correspondent, less than three months away on 17 September. As the Correspondent struggled for life, rather like a fish driven into the shallows, derisory funds from Farringdon Road were one of the causes for its floundering. Did the Guardian really want it to thrive, or was it simply seeking to keep it alive to prolong its agony?

Chapter 10

Ethical Issues as the Correspondent Dies

'The months of the paper's existence seemed like
a continuous emergency board meeting.'

Peter Cole, editor, Sunday Correspondent

The Guardian's sudden decision to renege, as Peter Cole saw it, on the promise of £2 million in pre-launch funding for the Sunday Correspondent, did not kill off the embryonic paper as he had told Preston it would in their manic taxi ride across London. An alternative backer in the form of the Chicago Tribune was quickly found, the required total of £18 million was achieved and Cole went ahead with his plans for the birth. It was to be an extremely uncomfortable pregnancy and, alas, a very short life. Andreas Whittam Smith's assurances that the Independent would not publish a Sunday title in 1989 proved to be true, but only just. Its ambitions towards the Sunday market had by no means been abandoned. Even in December 1988 the Independent had eyes on the Observer - which it had codenamed 'Andrew' - and was prepared to bid £55 million for it, five years before it made a more determined effort.[1]

The Guardian, with its protracted NUJ dispute a preoccupation, dithered. It might, subject to certain stringent conditions, still make a contribution to the Sunday Correspondent, Harry Roche told the Scott Trust in February 1989. Ominously, from the Correspondent's point of view, the Independent was producing dummies for a proposed Sunday newspaper, driven by Stephen Glover, throughout June. There were still arguments at the Independent over whether it should pursue its bid for the Observer more vigorously or go ahead with a Sunday paper of its own, and there were many who did not think diverting resources into a Sunday newspaper was a good idea at all. Nevertheless, at the end of the month, when the Sunday Correspondent announced its launch date of

17 September, Glover for a moment entertained the 'mad idea' that 'we might pre-empt its launch'. 'Mad' because the in-house row still raged: nothing had been decided. Mad, too, because to try to bring out a competitive paper in less than three months would have been to invite disaster. Instead he took a more practical view and went on with plans to produce an Independent on Sunday dummy. This when it was circulated among media correspondents in mid-August scored a notable success over the dummy for the Sunday Correspondent, which had been shown only to its own readership panel and selected advertising agencies. Among the latter, according to Georgina Henry, the Guardian's media correspondent, its reception had been lukewarm.[2] Henry observed, 'The irritation and frustration felt by the Correspondent's team at the Independent's tactics is understandable, even if they pretend they are ignoring it. Peter Cole, the Correspondent's editor, testily tells inquiring journalists that he is not going to participate in a comparison of the two papers when he and the rest of the team are concentrating on getting their own paper right.'

Before the end of the month there was a mildly bizarre development. With only three weeks to go before the launch of the Sunday Correspondent, Richard Branson intervened to try to divert the two newspapers from their potentially disastrous collision course. The agent in this was Mick Brown, whom Cole had hired on the Correspondent, and whose biography of the Virgin boss had come out earlier in the year.[3] Cole explained, 'Mick Brown was close to Richard. And it was Mick who came to me and said, "Richard is appalled by what he hears and wants to try and bring you all together, can we do this?"' Shortly afterwards, Branson had telephoned Whittam Smith from his boat 'somewhere off the West Indies', according to Glover, to suggest the meeting. The approach caused huge glee at the Independent, and 'put Andreas into a kind of ecstasy'. 'Our guess,' wrote Glover, 'was that they had seen our dummy and panicked.'[4]

By the evening of 29 August, when the two sides gathered at a table beside the swimming pool at Branson's home in Holland Park, Cole had already had a couple of preliminary meetings with their host. He thought Branson's attempt to broker a deal 'entirely well-intentioned'. On the Correspondent side were Cole, the chief executive Nick Shott, David Lipsey and David Blake. The Independent team included Andreas Whittam Smith, Stephen Glover and Matthew Symonds. Cole thought the atmosphere 'incredibly frosty', despite Branson's best efforts. 'It became clear that all Andreas wanted was for us to announce that we'd been taken over by the Independent, which we couldn't actually do – I mean nothing to do with emotion – because we were launching two weeks later. We'd hired the printing presses, we'd produced the dummies and we had £18 million of other people's money, which we were contractually obliged to spend on launching the Sunday Correspondent, so it was a nonsense.'

The event left Whittam Smith and his colleagues with an encouraging view of a weak opposition. 'Their very presence at such a meeting so close to their launch showed how unsure they were of themselves,' wrote Glover. The next morning the board of Newspaper Publishing, owner of the Independent, met and, in a conclusive rejection of the Branson peace talks, decided that the Independent on Sunday would make its debut on 28 January, four months after the first appearance of the Sunday Correspondent.

There were now two Sunday newspapers recruiting staff, greatly increasing competition in the quality market. The nightmare vision of a mass exodus of the Guardian's best people never materialised, but in the mind of Guardian management it emphasised the paper's vulnerability to predatory rivals, especially as it was hampered by the NUJ's resistance to personal contracts. This was only resolved months later with limited concessions to Preston's requirements.

The Sunday Correspondent had proved particularly attractive to staff at Wapping, whence came its largest number of recruits, including another of Cole's former five-a-side teammates, Simon Freeman, who became chief reporter. It also picked up two exceptionally bright graduate trainees, Jonathan Freedland and Ian Katz, contemporaries at Oxford. It had been David Lipsey's idea to employ trainees, as an expression of 'belief in the future', Cole explained wryly.

The Sunday Correspondent had launched as planned on 17 September, striking a jaunty note in its advertising, promising – in a poke at both Murdoch and Rowland – that it would be 'Great, but not Wapping. Concise, but not Tiny.' The inaugural print run of 610,000 sold out,[5] but it was a figure that no one expected to be sustained. The target over the first year was 362,000. However, after that first edition it lost sales faster than expected. Its own figures charted the rapid decline over the first weeks: 610,000; 517,000; 420,000; 390,000 and falling.

There was some faint cheer to be had in the Correspondent camp when it transpired that the Independent on Sunday's penultimate dummy, published in early January, had contained a libel for which it had to pay out £5,000 in damages, plus 'several times that' in costs, a possibly unique occasion when a newspaper libelled someone from a dummy before its first issue had appeared.[6]

But whatever cheer there may have been was quickly dissipated. The Independent on Sunday had recruited 86 star-studded editorial staff, 24 of them from the Independent and the other 62 from the rest of 'Fleet Street'. Its launch issue on 28 January sold 760,000 copies of the 1.2 million that had been printed. It had a disastrous impact on the Correspondent, which was harder hit than any other Sunday. Its last issue before the launch of the Independent on Sunday sold 309,000. On the day of Glover's launch, sales of Cole's beleaguered paper plummeted to 230,000. The sales on the Independent on Sunday were soon plunging too, also somewhat faster than expected. Their figures for the first six weeks were: 760,000; 540,000; 480,000; 425,000; 395,000; 383,000. By April sales were down to 333,000. Glover commented, 'Our only compensation is that the Sunday Correspondent is going down faster still, a crazy shooting star in front of our more sedate meteorite.'[7]

The impending launch of the Independent on Sunday had concentrated minds at the Guardian. Three weeks ahead of its appearance the Scott Trust devoted virtually the whole of its January meeting to the deferred question of investment in the Sunday Correspondent. The sum being proposed was now £4 million - twice the amount Peter Cole thought he had been promised a year earlier. There was still a degree of uncertainty, although Hugo Young, the new chairman of the trust, believed the general feeling was that the Guardian needed to do something because a successful seven-day operation by the Independent would be, as he put it, bad news. Would it not be better, one trustee wondered, to increase investment directly in the Guardian? Jim Markwick explained that this had already been done. An extra £5 million had been spent on a number of editorial projects over the past year, Harry Roche confirmed, including the Weekend Guardian. The Correspondent money, Roche told the trust, should be seen as a tactical investment that might damage the Independent and therefore be good for the Guardian. An acute reader of the minutes might imagine eyebrows being raised at this point. If the investment went ahead, said Hugo Young, then it should be made clear to the Correspondent that the Guardian would expect to play a positive journalistic role. These were the mildly expressed beginnings of what was seen by its proponents as an ethical argument destined to become heated over the coming months.

Within little more than a week of the Sunday Correspondent's launch, there was a flurry of meetings culminating in the Guardian's decision to invest, in the end, £3 million in the already flagging newspaper. It gave the Guardian a 16.6% shareholding, slightly less than that held by the Chicago Tribune with 17.7%, and it placed Jim Markwick on the Correspondent board. The sudden urgency was due to several factors. The Guardian had picked up rumours that the Independent board had designs on the Sunday Correspondent. The Independent on Sunday was proving to be a continuing drain on resources at a time when a downturn in the advertising market meant that the daily Independent was also running at a loss. Newspaper Publishing was keen to remove this element of competition as soon as possible. It was itself now facing the need for further financing. Markwick told his fellow directors that it would be extremely dangerous for the Guardian if the Correspondent folded or was taken over by the Independent. One of the main reasons for the Guardian's investment was to keep the Correspondent publishing throughout 1990, maintaining pressure on the Independent. Keeping the Correspondent going for a whole year even then seemed a tall order.

It was becoming apparent that the paper could not continue for much longer without a further injection of funds. Jim Markwick had reported that a Correspondent board meeting had gone on for 22 hours, with several of the shareholders wanting to call a halt to the whole thing and to try to recover some of their money. Others, including the Guardian, wanted to continue, having come to the view that leadership was part of the problem, an intimation of the vulnerability of Peter Cole. Sir John Nott, the former chairman of Lazard Brothers, had been appointed adviser to the Correspondent and was drawing up a cost-cutting plan, with the possibility of printing on the Guardian presses. He was also acting as a broker, exploring the option of merging the Correspondent with the Independent on Sunday or the Observer. None of these things came to pass.

It was Liz Forgan, then in her first period of service on the Scott Trust, who this time raised the recurring question, seeking assurances that the

Guardian's interest was not solely in trying to make life difficult for the opposition. Preston provided the stock answer. It was commercially important that the Guardian had a relationship with a Sunday paper.

Meanwhile, Andreas Whittam Smith believed he had persuaded the Chicago Tribune to dump the Sunday Correspondent – which he had now codenamed 'Granny' – and throw its resources into the Independent. He was sufficiently confident that in July he called a meeting of his senior staff to announce it. Under this plan Whittam Smith would get approximately £15 million from the American publisher in exchange for a large shareholding in Newspaper Publishing, the Independent holding company, £6 million of which would be used to cover the cost of closing the Correspondent and taking 25 of its staff. He believed most of the readers would move over to the Independent on Sunday. There was one snag. It depended on the Guardian, the other big media investor in the Sunday Correspondent, guaranteeing that it would not launch its own Sunday newspaper within 12 months of the closure. The Guardian team was unlikely to agree to this. They had deliberately allowed rumours of plans to launch a Sunday Guardian to go uncorrected. The April Fool's 'Guardian for Sunday' that year helped to feed the paranoia.

While Whittam Smith was trying to close the Chicago Tribune deal, Sir John Nott and the chief executive of the Correspondent, Nick Shott, had been desperately trying to put together an alternative £9 million refinancing package to relaunch the Correspondent as a tabloid under a new editor. On 31 July, they told the Guardian team that a replacement for Peter Cole to edit the planned tabloid Correspondent had already been approached.

It was a fairly complicated package. Lonrho would put in £3 million, provided both the Chicago Tribune and the Guardian put in more money. Two Middle East investors offered £1.5 million each, but only if Lonrho was kept out of the picture. The Chicago Tribune was willing to put in another £1 million but only if the Guardian put in £2 million and any contribution from Robert Maxwell was limited to 10%. That meant that Maxwell, who had offered £3 million, could only be asked for £1 million. And then half a million would be sought from existing institutional shareholders.

The Correspondent board was meeting the next day, 1 August, and it required a letter of intent from each of the investors, declaring what they would put into the Correspondent if the offer from Andreas Whittam Smith was to be rejected. All but one of the Guardian group directors rejected the proposal to send such a letter. Ahead of their own GMEN[8] board on 2 August, Jim Markwick, in a long, written memo, ran them through the whole saga, concluding with a strong plea to join in the refinancing because that would be 'best for the Guardian'. 'Without GMEN the refinancing will probably fail and the Independent will gain. It can be made perfectly clear that this subscription is our last.' Markwick, the keen cricketer, finished with a cricketing analogy: 'The development of the Guardian as a paper continues with two launches planned for September [Guardian Europe and eG]. We seek to keep our eye on team and pitch alike.'

But were the tactics in keeping with 'Guardian values'? Was it cricket? The question was to come up again, this time generating unprecedented heat, when the board gathered. Appropriately enough, the directors met in the middle of a record-breaking heatwave with the temperature in central London exceeding 35C. By then the new editor of the Correspondent, John Bryant, whom Preston described as 'an excellent journalist', had agreed to join, taking the job after it had been turned down by Preston's own deputy, Jonathan Fenby. Peter Cole would leave just before the tabloid relaunch in September.

Preston believed the Guardian should continue to back the Correspondent at least until it was clear whether or not the tabloid version had achieved the desired breakthrough. Hugo Young, the chairman of the Scott Trust, had indicated that he was in favour of further investment, as was board member Ray Tindle, who pointed out that the group, with cash resources in excess of £60 million, could well afford to invest the £2 million being sought.

Among those against were Harold Lever (Lord Lever of Manchester), the former Labour Cabinet minister; the long-serving group finance director, Stanley Porter; and, significantly, Harry Roche. The Correspondent circulation was now down to 160,000 and falling. Relaunching it at this point, it was argued, would be much more difficult than the original launch. It was now seen by readers and advertisers as a doomed paper.

Of the seven directors present, four were against the investment and only Markwick, Preston and Tindle were in favour. Markwick and Preston in particular clearly felt passionate about it. Preston accused his fellow directors of first encouraging Markwick to pursue the matter to this stage and then pulling the rug from under him. Markwick felt that there was 'a vote of confidence factor' in the decision. Harry Roche rejected any such suggestion and proposed a compromise where the fact of a majority in opposition would be recorded but the minority allowed to prevail. That idea was swiftly rejected by the other opposing directors. Markwick, making the point that it was not entirely a commercial issue, wondered whether the decision should be left to Roche and Preston, who as well as being directors of the group were both members of the Scott Trust. Harry Roche quickly dismissed this; the constitutional implications of that for the Guardian would have been interesting, to say the least.

There was one point of unanimity. There would be no undertaking that a Sunday Guardian would not be published. But that was little consolation to Markwick. He felt badly let down and indicated that he would have no option but to tender his resignation to the board of the Correspondent. It did not come to that.

Less than a week later there was another meeting of the GMEN board to consider a plea from Sir John Nott, via Jim Markwick, to invest a compromise £250,000, preventing the Guardian's equity shareholding in the Correspondent from falling below 10%. The new editor of the Sunday Correspondent, soon to take up his appointment, had expressed concern that the Guardian had refused backing. This time the board, with a larger number of directors attending, agreed to invest this sum by nine votes to one. The one dissident was Stanley Porter. He remained against the decision because it would have the effect of either deliberately or cynically misleading the new editor about the true position of the Guardian's future commitment. Porter wanted it to be recorded that he was increasingly unhappy over the attempt to damage by indirect financial means a highly regarded newspaper.

But minds were made up. Markwick wrote to the Correspondent confirming that the Guardian would put in £250,000 on two conditions: that the Chicago Tribune invested a further £1 million; and that it was understood that no further investment would be required from the Guardian. The refinancing package was put in place. The relaunch of the tabloid Sunday Correspondent went ahead without Peter Cole on 30 September.

On 13 November Markwick told the Guardian group board that, although the conversion to tabloid had gone well, major long-term financing was for the Guardian no longer a strategic matter. Closure seemed inevitable and might as well be sooner as later. It was sooner: on 25 November 1990 the Sunday Correspondent breathed its last. It had survived for 14 months, less than two of those months as a tabloid. About 100 journalists lost their jobs.

Peter Cole, looking back, said, 'The 14 or 15 months of the paper's existence seemed like a continuous emergency board meeting. We had a lot of refinancing along the way and I'm afraid that in the end we spent about £30 million. But I will always say I would never not have done it. I found it incredibly exciting. They were a wonderful team of people. There is hardly a person who has not prospered since. That was satisfying. But at the same time I was out of work thinking, "Was I foolish?" You get that business where everyone says, "You'll be all right, won't you? I'm sure the phone hasn't stopped ringing." It didn't ring at all.' Preston did not ring, except belatedly and apparently after a prompt from David McKie. 'But Andrew Neil just phoned up out of the blue and offered me a job on the Sunday Times, which was, you know ... Everyone shitbags Andrew Neil but he phoned and others didn't.'[9] Cole edited the News Review section of Neil's Sunday Times for a period before entering academia as a professor of journalism.

Why did the Guardian get so agitated by it all? There were many reasons. The downturn of advertising as the recession took hold was much worse than expected. There is an argument that it was this more than the conflict with the Correspondent that caused problems for the Independent after the costly launch of the Independent on Sunday. But most disturbing from the Guardian's point of view, despite the success of the Weekend supplement, was the fact that the Independent had continued to close the overall circulation gap, reaching its closest point in August when the controversy over investment in the Correspondent was at its height. A further depressing note was added by the Times's circulation. In the autumn of 1989 it had crept marginally above that of the Guardian and begun a game of leapfrog between the two papers that continued over the coming months. Now in August 1990 the Times stood well clear at 417,696. It was a turning point, the last time for three years that it was allowed to lead. It is a measure of the energy that the Guardian was now bringing to the battle, both in management and in editorial strength, that until Murdoch initiated the price war in 1993 the Guardian led both the Times and the Independent, the three forming a contesting trio that seemed doomed to an eternal jostling for second place after the Daily Telegraph.

One of the things that the upheaval in the British newspaper industry at the end of the 1980s and early 1990s demonstrated was the stimulating effect on subsequent careers of the period's failed enterprises. In terms of the long-term benefit to the industry it could be argued that they had not failed at all since they projected so much useful experience into established newspapers in the process of modernisation.

The failure of the Correspondent was no exception. An obvious example was the Correspondent's former chief reporter Chris Elliott, who went on to a career in the upper echelons of the Guardian, first as managing editor and then as the paper's third readers' editor. Catherine Bennett, a talented interviewer and writer of profiles, was another major gain. She had gone to the Correspondent from the Times, where she had spent about a year writing to the features editor, Richard Williams, who also joined the Guardian later.

Ian Katz and Jonathan Freedland were similarly important acquisitions for the Guardian. Both were soon being spoken of as potential editors of the paper. Their lives had to a quite extraordinary degree run along parallel lines since they were pupils together, age 11, at University College School (UCS), in Hampstead, north London. Both are from Jewish families, something of significance, in particular to Freedland. Both studied politics, philosophy and economics at Oxford. Both were conspicuously involved in student journalism: Katz founded a magazine called Twist, which he co-edited with Marianne Macdonald, for which Freedland wrote. Katz recalled, 'I remember Jonny, age 19 or 20, writing the most poised interview with Bron [Auberon] Waugh and being absolutely devastated by it because it was so far ahead of anything that I or anyone I knew could do. In fact I remember saying to him, "How did you write that piece?" And he told me his technique, which was to type the whole transcript and then cut it physically into pieces, cut the quotes into pieces, and then assemble them on the floor. And suddenly I thought, God, I've finally discovered the secret of how you write a feature.'[10]

After graduation, both did shifts on the Evening Standard Londoner's Diary, before being recruited as trainees on the Sunday Correspondent. Katz had written to Peter Cole, saying 'New paper – you need new blood.' It was the kind of impetuosity that became a distinguishing mark of Katz's career. 'It was an unbelievably bumptious letter. I can't believe he let me in the door.' At the Correspondent he and Freedland were given closely adjacent desks. Freedland recalled, 'I think it was a deliberate ploy to introduce creative tension: we were both at the bottom of the ladder, and the idea was to see which one would survive.'[11] Freedland left the Correspondent before the paper folded to join the BBC's graduate trainee scheme. He came on to the Guardian in 1993 through an ingenious scheme of his own devising whereby he proposed to Peter Preston and the BBC, that they share him, dividing the cost and jointly reaping the benefits. Remarkably, they both accepted it. Both Katz and Freedland later won Stern fellowships to work for a period on the Washington Post. In their Guardian careers Katz was to become deputy editor of the paper after setting a new record for long service as features editor (by then editor of G2), and Freedland was to become one of the paper's leading correspondents and columnists.

Katz's entry into the Guardian took place in a flamboyantly daring fashion, after the Correspondent asked him to cover the run-up to the Gulf War. 'It was a measure of how chaotic that place was that a 21-year-old cub reporter with no real reporting experience could end up in Baghdad.' Back home in November 1990, just after the Correspondent had folded, he was asked by the Sunday Express to cover the story of some British hostages who were being released in Iraq. Katz was worried about the validity of his visa, but he was determined to travel to Iraq and get the scoop. As the plane took off, Katz's anxieties came to a crisis, making him think he had better stay on board when it landed in Baghdad. And then something extraordinary happened. 'As we were approaching Iraqi airspace the captain came back and said, "I'm sorry about this but we've been denied permission to land in Baghdad, so we're going to land in Amman instead." It was just as if Christmas had come early. We landed in Amman, where new plans were made to pick up the human shields, not from there but from Frankfurt, where they had been delivered in an Iraqi airlines jumbo.' Katz filed a piece for the Sunday Express as agreed, and then he rang Jonathan Fenby, the deputy editor of the

Guardian, and offered to file for the Guardian. His report appeared on 11 December 1990. A month later he began his first real job on the paper, editing Young Guardian,[12] a weekly page aimed mainly at readers aged 16 or under.

The Correspondent also provided the future Guardian foreign correspondent Luke Harding with his first job in journalism after Oxford, where he had edited Cherwell for four terms after Jonathan Freedland, and written book reviews for the Ian Katz-Marianne Macdonald magazine Twist. They were all in the year above Harding, whose immediate and near contemporaries included the future Guardian journalists Alex Bellos, Vikram Dodd, Sarah Ryle and Will Woodward, all of whom cut their teeth on student publications. The Guardian/NUS student journalism awards acted almost as a shopping list for newspapers seeking bright recruits as the pace of change in the industry increased. But in many cases their careers also emphasise the value of training on regional newspapers. Luke Harding's career had both of those elements, but also contained another element that, having been exceedingly rare, was to become less so as the Guardian expanded and sought to sharpen its competitive edge. Let us call it the Mail factor.

Harding was not the first recruit from the Mail. John Illman, who had been the Mail's medical correspondent for five years, joined the Guardian as health editor in 1989, after a brief interval as a freelance. Illman found one striking difference between the Mail and Guardian cultures. 'The Mail is top-down. The Guardian is bottom-up. Shortly after joining the Mail I met the editor, Sir David English, in the lift. He asked about my plans for the day. I told him. Thirty minutes later, Paul Dacre, then news editor, roared: "What the hell are you doing telling the editor things before telling me?" I have never learned so much before or since from 20 seconds in a lift.' Despite this harsh induction to the culture, Illman had no regrets about working there. 'I was a career journalist. It made me a much better reporter and feature writer ... The divide between the Mail and Guardian was irrelevant. Bugger the politics.'[13]

Illman joined the Guardian only a month or two before Catherine Bennett, who had worked for a period on the Mail on Sunday earlier in the 1980s. She began at a time when personal contracts were an issue with the union, of which she had not been forewarned. So she was somewhat taken aback when one of her new colleagues hissed at her as they filed in for a chapel meeting, 'We know what you are earning.' She particularly resented their resentment since she had taken a substantial salary drop to come to the Guardian. From Rusbridger's point of view she was worth every penny of her reduced salary. Her features were well researched despite often being written at alarmingly short notice; her profiles were written with disinterested inquiry and wit, with no adjustment for any ambient ideology or office politics. At the Mail she had once been warned, when assigned to an interview, that the subject was a friend of the editor and if that was likely to be a problem she had better not do it. She said it was, and so didn't. Now at the Guardian she was assigned to write a profile of Michael Ignatieff, the future Canadian politician, at the time a columnist on the Observer, and - something that no one told her in advance - a friend of Rusbridger's. Her time with him expired before she was able to discover any innate modesty in her subject, and she allowed him to lament, 'Someone like me does not exist in America, and that seems to me to be terrible.' Rusbridger never mentioned it to her. The freedom in her new environment impressed her.

Some nine months after Bennett arrived from the Mail, Stephen Bates followed the same path when he joined in the senior role of education editor. And in September that year, 1990, he was joined by another former Mail man, James Meikle, as education correspondent. Bates's appointment, and to a lesser extent Meikle's, were regarded at the time as ill omens by the internal dissidents displaced and/or dismayed by the changes taking place at the Guardian.

What did the Mail factor bring to the Guardian? Ideologically, the liberal Guardian and the rightwing Mail were poles apart, each anathema to the other, something about which Polly Toynbee frequently reminded her readers. Emily Wilson, at the time an assistant features editor, remembered the awkward shuffling caused at one of the editor's morning conferences when Toynbee said that people who had worked at the Mail 'shouldn't be allowed to work here'. 'There was a short silence as we ex-Mailers counted up how many of us were in the room.'[14]

Nevertheless, among others, a sneaking regard for the professionalism of the Mail, detached from its content, was sometimes cautiously murmured. Stephen Bates summed up what was generally appreciated about time on the Mail: 'I spent three years there and now don't regret them because they certainly toughened me up professionally and sharpened my journalism skills. It was hell at the time, for a sensitive soul, of course.'

The catalyst for the late movements from the Mail to the Guardian may have been Kevin Toolis, a frequent contributor to the paper. In November 1996 he had contributed a long piece to the Guardian Weekend, recording a disastrous clandestine visit to Afghanistan for the Mail on Sunday. 'To be truthful, I hated every minute I worked at the Mail. Personally, I was, and am, a liberal leftie and republican to boot.'[15] This was confession, to be followed presumably by absolution.

In the summer of 1997 a young Irish News journalist, Rory Carroll, the son of a famous Irish Times man, Joe Carroll, moved from Belfast to London as a freelance. He became a researcher on a Channel 4 documentary produced by Toolis but ended up working primarily for the Daily Mail. 'It was a formidable, aggressive newsroom culture. Lots of bullying, fear and ambition. I hated it. But an amazing learning experience. The Mail was a machine and knew what it was doing. I was seconded to the showbiz desk, for which I lurked at film premieres (trying to get a quote from a stony Salman Rushdie, among others) and followed (stalked, I guess) celebs.'[16]

In September, thanks to Toolis, he got a second interview at the Guardian with Alan Rusbridger and Georgina Henry. 'I'd been advised, shrewdly I think [by Toolis], to play up my Mail experience even though I'd been there only a few weeks. "Act like you open doors with your forehead." I didn't quite go that far. The other card I had was recently winning Northern Ireland young journalist of the year. A few days later Alan called me while I was in the middle of some barney at the Mail's showbiz desk, people yelling. He offered me a staff job on the Guardian. Deliverance.' Carroll became in sequence Africa correspondent in Johannesburg; correspondent in Baghdad, where in January 2005 he was kidnapped and held for a day before being released unharmed; and then in 2006 Latin America correspondent based in Caracas.

The award-winning investigative reporter Ian Cobain - who had worked as the Mail's New York correspondent before joining the Guardian in 2005 - also placed a positive value on his Mail experience. 'There are some similarities between the two newspapers, as they were, although I accept that quite a few readers of either would be horrified by that suggestion. Essentially, there's a self-confidence, which stems from a reasonably clear idea of who your readers are, which allows each organisation to plough its own furrow ...[17] One of the major differences, politics and place in the market aside, is that the Mail, like most London-based newspapers, is still a centrally organised and controlled news organisation in which reporters are, to too great an extent in my view, expected to make stories "stand up" in a particular manner.'

Jeevan Vasagar, who had joined the Guardian from the Mail as a reporter, concurs. 'The Mail's news desk had a *dirigiste* approach to news. At its best this meant they clearly defined the objective and guided a rookie reporter on how a piece should be written to fit the paper's template. At its worst, of course, this approach can mean that a reporter merely chases facts to fit an agenda.'[18]

The relationship between the Guardian and the Mail was mutually obsessive, even more so with Dacre in charge than when English was editor. According to a recent 'unauthorised' biography of the Mail,[19] some of its journalists explained the obsession on its side by the absence of any real mid-market rival since the decline of the Daily Express. But that seems to overlook the ideological and psychological elements. More plausibly an anonymous Mail executive, describing the paper in the mid-1990s, is quoted: 'They were utterly obsessed with the bloody Guardian, it defines exactly what they do *not* want their Daily Mail to be. Dacre would grumble away to himself under his breath about "Polly fucking Toynbee" as he marched to the lift.'[20]

Chapter 11

Europe and Journalism Without Borders

'Peter Preston, editor of the Guardian, to lunch at Brooks's. I found him remarkably agreeable: not difficult to talk to as I half-expected, very European, well-informed, and sensible on practically everything.'

Roy Jenkins, diary note, 8 May 1978[1]

One way in which the Guardian, raising its head from the preoccupations of Farringdon Road, acknowledged the new order of things in the world at large was in the creation of a section initially called European Review. It was designed to exploit and reflect the new mood in Europe with the fall of the Berlin Wall and the end of the Cold War. *Alle Menschen werden Brüder,* and so on. Or, in the words of a headline in the handsome but ill-fated dummy issue, dated 7 April 1990 (after the election in which the East Germans voted freely for the first time since Hitler came to power): *Wir sind ein Volk.* The new weekly section was to have little directly to do with the fluctuating argument about Britain's role in the European Community, nor was it meant to replace the Guardian's routine coverage of European news. Instead it aimed to stand alongside it, and to bring to it a fairly revolutionary new dimension in which Europeans spoke for themselves.

Although, in the manner of many newspaper enterprises, it never emerged in the form originally planned, it did for several years in its eventual form as Guardian Europe, under the sympathetic editorship of Martin Kettle, give readers the feeling that they might be part of a genuinely European conversation. It did this at a time when Euroscepticism was rampant: it was launched just a couple of months before the Sun sent its famous front-page message to the president of the European Commission: 'Up yours, Delors!'[2]

The leader of the Guardian's European tendency was undoubtedly its editor, the outward-reaching Peter Preston. Throughout his editorship he was a dedicated European, to a degree that others sometimes found surprising. Roy Jenkins, while president of the European Commission, in Preston's early years as editor, had found him 'very European, well informed and sensible on practically everything'.

The message of Preston's Guardian was that Europe, In the aftermath of conflict, should be reaching for its shared values, and going beyond that in search of closer political ties. Under Preston, as Geoffrey Taylor noted in a previous volume of Guardian history, 'the political integration of Europe indeed became one of the Guardian's liveliest concerns', with no serious hesitation about Britain belonging to Europe.[3]

That in itself was an achievement. It is doubtful whether there has ever been total agreement between members of the editorial staff of the Guardian on this (nor perhaps on any other issue). But arguments over Europe have generally been about detail and degree rather than the big question of to belong or not to belong. One notable exception came in the autumn of 1962 when, under Hetherington, the Guardian for a time turned against entry into the European Economic Community, the EEC, but even then it was only (in the familiar phrase) 'because the terms were wrong'. That apart, the Guardian's view has looked from a short distance like consensus compared with the view of post-war governments of whatever persuasion, at least up to Blair. The history of official attitudes, as Hugo Young has pointed out in his remarkable survey of the subject,[4] is one of vacillation, prevarication and ambivalence. A thesaurus rifled to describe a position that could be summed up in a word as 'wobbly'. (Young did not live to see the UK referendum on Europe in 2016.)

When Britain finally entered the Common Market on 1 January 1973, the paper was in favour, although careful not to overdo its enthusiasm. 'We're in - but without the fireworks', said the front-page headline. From the time Preston became editor in 1975, the Guardian progressively became the most consistently pro-European among British papers. Preston's own Europeanism developed over time. As late as 26 February that year, he was calling himself 'a moderately inert agnostic' on Europe. It would be another 20 years or so before his views and those of Hugo Young, another 'agnostic' of the time, converged in passionate advocacy (Young's support extended to arguing for Britain's full integration into Europe, including adoption of the euro). The referendum on whether Britain should stay in or come out of the EEC, promised in the Labour manifesto the previous year, was, a leader on 27 February 1975 declared, 'a mistake' but 'inevitable'. The Labour Party itself was deeply split on the issue: at a special one-day conference at the end of April the vote was almost two to one in favour of leaving the EEC.

The heading on a leader three days before polling day – 'Britain and Europe – partner or voteless hanger-on?' suggested that there was only one possible answer to the 5 June referendum. It acknowledged that it was urging a Yes vote for an imperfect and inchoate institution (most of Fleet Street urged a Yes vote), but at the same time it had no doubt that 'Britain ought to remain in what is potentially the most important democratic grouping in the world', which it saw not least as a prop to world peace, a buffer zone between the Soviet Union and the United States. Across the United Kingdom the answer was a resounding Yes, by roughly two votes to one.

It was Hetherington rather than Preston who wrote the key leaders. They were the last editorials that Hetherington was to write for the paper he had edited for almost 20 years. His leader on 7 June welcomed the 'unambiguous' result. 'It is a tonic for Britain and a tonic for Europe.' Preston took over from Hetherington officially a little over a week later, on 16 June.

Guardian Europe coming almost 20 years later was to be concerned not so much, then, with the continuing arm-wrestling over the developing EC, but with a broader cultural dimension. It reflected an instinctive desire shared by many members of the liberal press across Europe to reach out through the often-depressing clamour of their front pages towards a new and deeper understanding of each other. The project was to suffer a few false starts before it reached its final form.

Preston from the beginning of his editorship had encouraged and quickly established ties with a number of newspapers in Europe. Among them was the Spanish newspaper El País, born in 1976 during the period of transition to democracy after the dictatorship of Franco. A pre-launch detachment had come from Madrid to the Guardian's new home in Farringdon Road for consultations and Preston had become friendly with its founding editor Juan Luis Cebrián. Friendship between the two editors may have cooled a little by the time Guardian Europe was being planned. Jim Markwick thought that Cebrián had been dazzled by the light of the Independent rising above the horizon, and was shifting his attention towards it. Otherwise the friendship might have been tested when Preston persuaded the Guardian group board to put £250,000 into what was to become El País's main rival, the tabloid El Mundo. The paper, which like El País was based in Madrid, was launched in October 1989, with Preston as an adviser and the Guardian represented on its board by Richard Gott, whose Chilean Spanish apparently caused some amusement among his fellow board members. A year later El País and the Italian paper La Repubblica each invested about £10 million into the Guardian's main rival, the Independent.

Preston, although he was annoyed by this temporarily rejuvenating injection for the Independent, generally regarded these events as no more than the restless jostling of an industry in its usual ferment. It was his element. During the early 1980s he had acquired a home in Spain, and his visits there quickened his interest in the possibilities of intelligent tabloid newspapers like those he found in the Spanish press.

In the mid-1980s he joined the International Press Institute, of which he was later to become president. The IPI had been established in 1950, with the aim of promoting international understanding in the post-war world through a free and independent press. Preston was the first editor of the Guardian to make any systematic attempt to forge links between the paper and others sharing its liberal values in Europe and the wider world.

Preston's experience of the press in the United States had been formative. 'I had come to the conclusion that America - huge continent, many states and very few national newspapers - could nevertheless have a debate with itself through syndicated columns, that is you could have opinion in newspapers that operated from Anchorage to Florida and influenced a nationwide debate. The difficulty in Europe was that Europe had no means of talking to itself at all.'[5]

It was increasingly apparent this needed to change. During the political upheaval that followed the fall of the Berlin Wall in November 1989, Preston had become frustrated with what he termed the 'snapshot journalism' through which European countries reported each other's activities. He had responded positively to an idea promoted by Helmut Schmidt, the former German chancellor, who in 1985 had become the joint publisher of the intellectual weekly Die Zeit, and who a couple of years later attempted to set up an international publishing venture, with the provisional title Voice. It was to be an uncompromisingly upmarket tabloid, similar in format to Le Monde and in tone to the Economist. Preston had been unable to attend the first formal two-day meeting in Hamburg, and the representatives of the Italian papers La Repubblica and Corriere della Sera, and the Rotterdam daily NRC-Handelsblad, which had also shown interest, had not made it either. Nevertheless, six papers in addition to the host Die Zeit were at the table. They were the Swiss paper, Neue Zürcher Zeitung; El País, Madrid; Il Messaggero, Rome; Frankfurter Allgemeine Zeitung; Dagens Nyheter, Stockholm; and Le Monde, Paris. The range of papers indicated the ambition of the project.

Apart from Schmidt, the key person was a distinguished American journalist, Philip Foisie, formerly of the International Herald Tribune, whom Schmidt had commissioned to carry out a feasibility study. Foisie delivered his 75-page 'preliminary study' to Helmut Schmidt in mid-August. It was not wholly encouraging. All options appeared costly. Nevertheless the Guardian contributed £30,000 towards the cost of further market research. There were other concerns. Jim Markwick was worried about the welfare of the Guardian Weekly, in which he had a special interest, having spent three years in New York in the mid-1960s controlling this highly regarded digest of the Guardian. The Weekly, which had been established in 1919, had quickly gained readers in the United States. By the end of the 1980s worldwide sales had climbed to almost 72,000. Schmidt's weekly would to some extent become a competitor.

However, the project failed to survive in its original form and the idea of providing a European voice in the American political debate gave way to what would be primarily an intra-European 'conversation'. A dummy was produced – now renamed the Continental – but again the research results were not encouraging when they became available later in 1988. It became apparent it would be much more expensive to produce than had been supposed, and there was little prospect of pan-European advertising. So towards the end of the year Schmidt's idea finally expired and the Continental followed the Voice into oblivion.

Preston had returned to Farringdon Road from these meetings convinced that with a different approach the idea remained a good one. There were several factors that made the moment seem right, even urgent. There was the prevailing atmosphere of optimism, certainly from 1989, that a new Europe was in the making. The Guardian for once (although, as it turned out, not for long) was actually making some money. 'There was a mood to compete, to add things and do new things,' Preston recalled. The Independent was strong on Europe. In addition, the word had long been on the street that Robert Maxwell was planning a pan-Europe paper, and it was assumed that that was still on, even though Maxwell's first projected January 1989 launch date had come and gone. There was a suspicion, later hardened into certainty, that in planning his weekly, the European, Maxwell had the benefit of comprehensively leaked details of the Schmidt project. In fact, according to one of his former editors, Roy Greenslade, 'Maxwell had taken part in an outrageous act of industrial theft to steal the whole idea.'[6]

By January 1990, however, Schmidt's plan had failed, there would be no Voice, or Continental, and Maxwell was only now putting serious effort into the European, although the revised launch date was still five months away. Inside the Guardian, Richard Gott was looking for a new role on handing over the features department to Alan Rusbridger. It would be understating things to say that Rusbridger and Gott did not regard each other as natural allies. Gott, however, was one of Preston's most valued and trusted lieutenants, or rather generals, and they went back a long way together, to university in fact. The esteem and affection in which he was held by Preston was indicated by the nicknames conferred on him - so in the morning conferences Gott was often Ricky, or occasionally the more lavish Riccardo. Among older colleagues he was sometimes referred to as El Gotto.

Gott had been discussing his future with Preston on and off for at least a year. As early as the summer of 1987 Preston had somewhat controversially considered making him the foreign editor.[7] It did not happen. Gott had probably returned more urgently to the question of a move towards the end of 1988 when Preston's first tabloid baby, Weekend, was being planned. Its founding editor, Rusbridger, reported directly to Preston and there was no communication between Rusbridger and Gott. This led to a certain tension. Staff for Weekend were appropriated from elsewhere in Gott's features department with little or no consultation. Furthermore, as the new Weekend began to appear, Gott made no attempt to conceal a disdain bordering on contempt, directed not only at the product but, it seemed, at the producers. Even worse, in terms of the features succession it became clear that Rusbridger was the chosen one. The 'sandpit', as Gott referred to Weekend, was to be extended to cover the entire features department, and from 1992 the main receptacle for Guardian features, the tabloid G2, became the 'comic'.

In the event Preston came up with a brand-new project for Gott, developed out of the failed Voice and Continental ideas – a Guardian-led and as-yet-untitled venture devoted entirely to Europe. He offered Gott a twin job, as editor of the projected new section and as the Guardian's director on El Mundo, which Gott quickly accepted. Almost as his first act, he signed up the new Spanish paper as a partner in a venture that at last had fired his imagination.

Delighted with the new appointment, Gott embarked on an extended tour of Europe. By the end he had assembled a remarkable consortium of partners. In a number of them he already had friends of his own. This was true of the Frankfurter Allgemeine Zeitung, which was one of his early trips, and of Dagens Nyheter in Stockholm, where he knew the writer, philosopher and economist Sven Lindqvist, who had a long association with the Swedish paper. He went with his Guardian colleague John Rettie to Helsinki, where the daily Helsingin Sanomat was signed up, and then beyond the boundaries of the earlier projects to Moscow, where both Komsomolskaya Pravda and Literaturnaya Gazeta joined. He also talked to Adam Michnik, the founding editor of Gazeta Wyborcza in Warsaw, which first appeared in May 1989 as the voice of Lech Wałęsa's Solidarity movement in the run-up to its landslide victory in June. In Copenhagen he met the legendary Herbert Pundik, the executive editor of the influential daily Politiken, who was later revealed to have worked for Israeli intelligence throughout the 1960s. There was indecision over whether to approach Le Monde or Libération in Paris. In the end both agreed to take part. The other papers signed up were De Volkskrant in Amsterdam, Lidové Noviny in Prague, and the prestigious Swiss daily Neue Zürcher Zeitung. Including the Guardian there were 15 of Europe's leading newspapers, eager to reflect the zeitgeist across the whole of the continent.

The plan Gott discussed with them was to make available to each of the partners a free selection of articles and editorials from the others, with the Guardian acting as a sort of clearing house, and individual newspapers being responsible for their own translation and presentation.

His plans were ambitious. On the completion of his tour he set about selecting content for a couple of dummy issues, enlisting the help of the chief features sub-editor, Douglas Morrison. He also brought David Hillman back to the Guardian. Hillman loved working for both Preston and Gott because they gave him a brief and then left him to get on with it 'without interfering'. Two black and white dummies of the European Review, as it was now being called, were produced before the end of 1989. The second, produced in December, combined characteristic Hillman virtues of clarity, refinement and bravura, with dramatically big head-lines. A small but very experienced team had now been gathered, noted in egalitarian alphabetical order inside: 'Copy for this issue selected and edited in London by Desmond Christy, Richard Gott, Martin Kettle, Seumas Milne, Doug Morrison and Paul Olive.' A list of partner papers shows that Gott was still recruiting, with Gazeta Wyborcza in Warsaw and Lidové Noviny in Prague yet to be signed up at this time.

Gott's position on Europe was complicated and somewhat radical. Underlying his feelings for the continent there was a thread of anti-Americanism, at least towards its political and cultural imperialism, particularly its militarism. In the early 1960s he was a research assis-tant at Chatham House, the Royal Institute of International Affairs, and was there when his first book *The Appeasers*, a study of British attitudes towards Nazi Germany, was published.[8] He was 24. The book, which quickly became a bestseller, was completed as the Cuban missile crisis dominated world news. Those sweaty-palmed days confirmed Gott and his circle in their view of the Cold War. 'We just thought the whole thing was a complete nonsense. It seems odd now because people imagine the Cold War as this terrible thing, but I think most of us just thought that the struggle between Russia and the United States was totally ridiculous and that countries in Europe should have a position in between.'[9] It was at this time, as he later revealed, that Gott was first approached by people from the Russian embassy, who he said he found a lot more interesting to talk to about foreign affairs than the people at Chatham House (for more on Gott's interesting new contacts, see Chapter 23).

Now the Cold War had ended, the new supplement was to provide a forum for some of the continent's progressive voices. Hillman's brief was to create that forum in the shape of a 32-page tabloid weekly magazine, to be produced on high-grade newsprint, and unlike the first two dummies it was to make generous use of colour. The content was drawn from the partner papers over the previous couple of months. The finished product admirably illustrated the potential of the magazine in editorial if not in commercial terms. As an object it was a thing of beauty in which both Hillman and Gott had excelled themselves. The cover - a red rectangle with the hammer and sickle of the Soviet Union replaced by a hammer and dollar sign - reflected the theme of the magazine's first double-page spread, an interview by Serge July, the editor of Libération, with Leszek Balcerowicz, 'the market revolutionary in Warsaw who is leading Poland towards western-style capitalism', as the standfirst described him. The dummy issue also included a piece by Norberto Bobbio about the transformation of Italy's Communist Party (from La Stampa); an interview with Claude Silberzahn, the head of the French equivalent to MI6 (from Le Monde); a column by the Soviet writer Maya Ganina (from Literaturnaya Gazeta); an article about Hobbes' *Leviathan* by Sven Lindqvist (from Dagens Nyheter); and a review of Simone de Beauvoir's collected letters to Jean Paul Sartre (from Le Monde). It also contained, a shade optimistically as it turned out, large dummy ads for Bosch, Fiat and Volvo.

Fate was about to take a hand. Finished copies were to be ready for display to the European partners at a weekend meeting at the Waldorf Astoria in London in early April. Hillman recalled, 'I think one of the reasons for printing it was that everybody felt it was so different from everything else that we'd been doing that it would be a good idea to see it on the kind of paper that we were talking about.'[10] The Waldorf meeting was an overnighter, with no expense spared: a get-together dinner, and then a meeting the following morning. About 500 copies of the dummy had been printed and they were kept in advance of the meeting in Jim Markwick's office in Farringdon Road. According to Gott, Markwick had a standing arrangement with the night cleaner that in the occasional chaos of his room, anything on his desk must be left alone, and anything on the floor could be swept away. Somehow the dummies had ended up on the floor. Years later, for Gott, the recollection still prompted dual feelings of pain and shame. 'As with John Stuart Mill and Carlyle's manuscript,[11] the copies went the way of all flesh, and we had a solitary single copy to pass round at the meeting.'

Douglas Morrison recalls the Waldorf meeting as an example of perfidious Albion. 'After a day of discussion it seemed to be understood that the partner papers would allow us to choose pretty much whatever we liked from them in politics, culture and economics features, and the Guardian would reciprocate. There was a break in the proceedings for this to be considered and when they came back Richard Gott and Ian Wright boldly announced that everything was agreed, but instead of the partners having access to pretty much all Guardian material, which they seemed to be expecting, we would send them a weekly list of articles selected by us. There was a sharp intake of breath.'[12] There were complications over copyright – the Guardian at that time quite often carried contributions where the copyright was retained by the author. There were also concerns about encroaching on the territory of the Guardian's syndication department, which meant that the same material could not be made available to competing papers. Despite these potential complications, agreement was reached, and the general view of the Guardian dummy among the partners was favourable.

Momentarily the cautionary tales of the Voice and the Continental seemed to have been forgotten. But the disaster of the trashed dummies had filled Gott with foreboding, and his fears were soon borne out. 'I thought it was such a beautiful artefact. And everybody was rather keen on it. We were all ready to roll. But when it came to taking the magazine to the marketing department and whoever it was who was basically going to have to fund this operation, they said this is a no-no; this is not an add-on to the Guardian, this is a financial add-off.' How much of an 'add-off' was already known to the Guardian management. A couple of weeks before the Waldorf meeting Ian Ashcroft, the finance director, had been asked to provide a broad annual costing for the Review as a separate magazine to be inserted in the main paper. His memo was addressed to the marketing director, David Brook, and copied to Caroline Marland, Jim Markwick, Peter Preston and Ian Wright. Richard Gott was not on the circulation list. The total annual cost came to a startling and prohibitive £4.1 million. It was an abrupt reality check.

So the European Review became the third attempt at a pan-European cooperative publishing venture to be abandoned. Preston kissed goodbye to Hillman's elegant tabloid with some regret. He had by now invested considerable time and money in the exercise. Perhaps there was a way to salvage the project? He asked Gott to stay with it and edit it as the leading pages of the second section on Fridays, displacing Environment to a place further back and accommodating both at the relatively modest cost of an increase in pagination.

Gott turned it down. 'I felt that I had invested too much in the beautiful Hillman supplement, and in roping in all the partner papers who would feel let down by the rather meagre end result, so I said I didn't want to go on.' He asked to take a year off to write a book instead.

There was a feeling among some of those involved that Gott had called the disaster down upon himself, that there was an element of 'Hier stehe Ich'. Indeed there was. Gott recalled his response when the compromise proposal was put to him: 'I just said, "Fine, but you can't count on me. I've done my bit and if you don't like it ..."' He consoled himself with the thought, perhaps partly true, that the European Review had been dumped not on cost grounds alone but because it was thought to be too intellectual. This was a view guaranteed to attract sympathy from his large circle of admirers, especially those who thought they detected anti-intellectual tendencies in the Rusbridger features department.

Oddly, Martin Kettle at one time might have been among these. In the upheaval that accompanied the rise of Rusbridger he had even considered leaving. In the end Kettle took a pragmatic view. For him journalism, as well as politics, was the art of the possible. He believed that the form now proposed for the survival of the project could be a good and worthwhile outcome in the circumstances. Furthermore, he felt his own European credentials were as good as Gott's.

Gott found no consolation whatsoever in handing over to Kettle, whom he thought worthy and admirable in many ways but whose work was not associated, in his mind, with the éclat that surrounded his own efforts. Perhaps Preston felt a touch of this too, for when he handed the project, now called simply Europe or Guardian Europe, to Kettle, it came with a few words of Prestonian advice: 'You've got to make sure that every now and again there's a flash of thigh.' There was a note of urgency if not desperation in Preston's voice. He had already been associated with three failed attempts to launch a pan-European project. And in the interim, Robert Maxwell, bouncing back after the failure of the London Daily News, had used the vacated premises to launch the weekly European, his commitment to which he had publicly repeated in June 1988.

Jim Markwick, like others, was now sure that Maxwell had also by now received intelligence about the Guardian's failed European

Review. Maxwell's paper was a broadsheet, strong on editorial colour, with a tabloid arts section called Élan. Markwick might have taken some comfort from the fact that Maxwell's losses on his version were substantial, reported to be £1 million a month.[13] Sales never achieved the desired levels. But at least Maxwell's paper had made it out on to the strassen, strade and boulevards. According to Maxwell himself the initial print order had been for 1 million, but, by the time the first audited figures were available early in 1991, the figure had already slipped below a quarter of a million. By then it was being referred to by Private Eye as Le Piss-Pauvre. In October 1991, in a desperate measure, Maxwell announced a US edition – shades of Helmut Schmidt's original idea, perhaps. Maxwell's US venture failed too. That was among the least of his troubles. On 5 November, Maxwell disappeared from his yacht in the Mediterranean and drowned.[14]

By then Kettle's Europe was making a very respectable showing. It had been launched on Friday 7 September 1990 with a public blessing by Peter Preston. In a signed editorial on page one of the new section, he wrote, 'These are pages for Guardian readers, edited in London and using all the Guardian's own correspondents across the continent. But they have the vast resources of 14 quality European newspapers to draw on. Each day our partners make available to us the cream of their comment, a series of unique perspectives.' And Prestonologists will have registered his concluding words as a coded message, quite possibly intended for Richard Gott: 'This isn't some visionary venture. It is, we believe, a practical exercise in cooperation which aims to lower some barriers to understanding as the economic barriers come down: a window swinging open on a new world.' He might have added, 'At last.'

Martin Kettle, now charged with making the most of Guardian Europe, had come to the paper in 1984 after a spell on the Sunday Times. He had interesting credentials. He was born in Leeds in 1949, the son of Communist Party intellectuals and activists. His father Arnold Kettle taught English literature at Leeds University, writing the books that made his reputation as Martin was growing up – the two volumes of *An Introduction to the English Novel* and a 1963 biography of Karl Marx. Martin Kettle was a history boy, and his route to the Guardian was via Leeds Modern School and a scholarship to Balliol. From there he trod a broad left-liberal path, first to the National Council for Civil Liberties, then to New Society in 1977. It was Kettle's writing in New Society that caught the eye of Hugo Young, then deputy editor of the Sunday Times. While working for the Sunday Times in 1982, Kettle first met Tony Blair and began a friendship that was to endure, surviving the Iraq war, to which Kettle was opposed. Kettle was to be more influential in the Guardian than many with a higher public profile. Not long after his arrival in 1984, he began his long career as a leader writer, although not without excursions. One of these occurred shortly before Rusbridger became features editor, when Kettle had a period on the features desk as an assistant to Richard Gott. They did not exactly hit it off. His friendship with Blair was not something likely to endear him to Gott, whose relationship with desk colleagues who fell short of his total approval was not always, let us say, relaxed: strong men were occasionally seen to weep.

Kettle inherited the team that had worked on the project with Gott. It included, apart from Douglas Morrison, Desmond Christy and Madeleine Bunting, who, like Kettle, owed her introduction to the Guardian to Hugo Young - she had worked as a researcher on a television series that Young made. Christy was, relatively speaking, an anachronism in a generation of graduate journalists. He had left school without going to university, and was essentially self-educated. He had come up through the provincial press, first in Northampton - where he became deputy to another non-graduate, the features editor, Ian Mayes (myself) - and then in Birmingham. Christy learned German by spending time in Hamburg and immersing himself in German culture, where he came to swim freely. Alex Duval Smith, an accomplished linguist, was also part of the original Europe gang, as Preston called it. She had been working sub-editing shifts and now saw the opportunity to apply for a staff job. 'I could read several of the partner papers without a dictionary, all those in French, Norwegian, Swedish, Danish, German.'[15] She got the job.

The team was completed by David Hearst, who had just returned from Northern Ireland. He was a lightly seasoned reporter. Among his imperishable memories was one of having his head pressed to the ground by the avuncular hand (his term) of Martin McGuinness when a Loyalist gunman opened fire on mourners at an IRA funeral in 1988.

Kettle's editing experience was mainly confined to the uncomfortable period on Gott's features desk, but he had a good team, with Morrison now his deputy. And this time the figures, at a fraction of the total estimated for the European Review, seemed to allow the possibility of survival if not of profit. Much more use was to be made of the Guardian's own corps of correspondents, and the section's own talented staff could translate some of the chosen pieces themselves to keep costs down. This time it would be printed in the normal way on the Guardian's new presses, and obviously there would be no need of extra outlay for insertion (paying the newsagent to insert a supplement into the main paper). The total annual cost was budgeted at around £350,000.

The first issue was indeed a lively one, complete with Preston's 'flash of thigh' - taken almost literally, in the form of a piece from La Stampa about the burgeoning sex industry in Hungary. Beneath it was a report from the Süddeutsche Zeitung on bicycle thefts in the Netherlands - neither perhaps likely to have been first choice for the European Review. As the front of a second broadsheet section, Guardian Europe now conformed to the Hillman Garamond and Helvetica combination of 1988. One element retained from Hillman's design of the European Review was the use of capitals for all headlines. For the lead (actually page 25, following the 24-page main news and comment section of the paper), Hugo Young had flown to Frankfurt to interview the president of the Bundesbank, Karl Otto Pöhl, on the movement towards a European Central Bank, still eight years away. It was illustrated by Pancho, the cartoonist of Le Monde and Le Canard enchaîné, appearing in the Guardian for the first time. There were several compilation features culled from the partner papers in short snippets. A page of European business and another devoted to culture completed the package.

From the beginning, Guardian Europe benefited from a high standard of translation, although a rare lapse would occasionally provide a moment of hilarity, as, for instance, when the supposed byline on a piece from Helsingin Sanomat turned out to be not the name of the author but the Finnish for 'continued on the next page'. But, not surprisingly, Guardian Europe provided a portal through which a number of journalists with a good command of languages gained entry to the Guardian, among them Dan Glaister (Catalan and Spanish), Clare Margetson (French and Italian) and Isobel Montgomery (Russian), all of whom went on to distinguished careers.

Kettle, in fact, quickly proved to be a very good editor, whose colleagues generally liked and respected him. According to Hearst, 'He was very committed to the idea of Europe, a shrewd editor and not at all heavy-handed.' And he admired Kettle's erudition: 'He was very, very well read.'[16]

In March 1992, Europe had acquired another gifted linguist in Dominique Jackson. She had studied languages at Oxford – she was fluent in seven apart from English – and then worked for Reuters and as a foreign correspondent. However, six months after she joined, sweeping editorial changes were introduced with the birth of the tabloid G2 edited by Rusbridger. Europe lost its place as a practically free-standing front feature in the broadsheet and became a cluster of pages well back in G2. Kettle decided not to go on with it. He went back to writing, then became editor of the comment pages.

The Europe section was not the biggest casualty of the reshuffle caused by the advent of G2 – that was probably the obituaries page, which never looked comfortable in the G2 format. But Guardian Europe, although the quality of the content was more or less maintained, had lost its profile. It was not a happy ship. It carried on in this fashion for about 18 months before it was effectively killed off, with the staff either leaving or finding jobs elsewhere in the Guardian. The enterprise was not given the coup de grâce until quite late in 1995 when John Hooper, the energetic correspondent in Rome, reported mutterings among the European partner papers who no longer knew to whom to turn when they wanted to use or offer something. The newly anointed editor, Alan Rusbridger, sent a memo to Ian Wright and foreign editor Simon Tisdall, 'Perhaps we should put our heads together to determine what future we see for Guardian Europe.'[17]

The answer was none, at least in that form. Paradoxically, as enthusiasm for Guardian Europe as a separate section had withered and died, interest in Europe had increased, perhaps stimulated by the opening of the Channel Tunnel in May 1994. At the same time the paper had strengthened its corps of correspondents around Europe. Apart from Hooper, there was Jonathan Steele in Moscow, Ian Traynor in Vienna, David Gow in Bonn and John Palmer in Brussels. If anything, the paper's international outlook, in Europe and beyond, was stronger than ever. The 'local' voice was also by now a well-established part of foreign coverage. Something that had been deliberately promoted by such ventures as the Guardian Third World Review, and Guardian Europe, was to become an integral part of the Guardian in the internet age.

In October 1998 the Guardian's international edition, a pared-down version of the paper circulated in Britain, was revamped and renamed Guardian Europe. It did in any case always draw most of its circulation from Europe, with only a thin spread throughout the rest of the world. Now it was able to focus on the demands of its main market. Simultaneously, the Guardian Weekly was improved and vigorously promoted as the Guardian's main international organ. By now the Guardian presence online was developing, with the official launch of Guardian Unlimited in January 1999 a turning point. It is perhaps remarkable that the international paper edition went on for more than another decade, until the autumn of 2011. When it finally closed, editions were being printed in Frankfurt, Madrid, Malta, Cyprus - even in New York. But although the combined total number of copies was 12,000 to 15,000, only 3,500 to 5,000 were actually being sold (copies distributed abroad counted in the circulation figures of UK papers whether they were sold or not). By way of consolation, perhaps, the number of people accessing the Guardian online was now exceeding 3 million a day and growing fast.

Chapter 12
A Post-prandial Nap and a Rude Awakening

'It would be nice to imagine, as 1989 looms ... that we would begin to settle down and move towards sunny uplands. Alas, the prognosis is not good.'

Richard Gott to his staff, December 1988

In June 1989, when Alan Rusbridger took over the features department, Richard Gott had been in the job for just over a decade, the longest period that anyone had served since the post was introduced in 1959. Rusbridger was the proverbial new broom. He quickly introduced sweeping changes that reached every corner of his inherited empire, changes that were often made against a resistance, initially sometimes a degree of resentment, as fresh ideas were brought to bear on the department. The department had already undergone a period of exhausting change. Gott had indicated a couple of years earlier that he was getting bored and restless and wanted to do something else. But with the introduction of the new technology then getting under way and the arrival of the Hillman redesign imminent, he was persuaded to stay in place to lead the largest department in the paper through the upheaval.[1] They had been a wearying few years.

At the end of 1988, Gott had circulated a lengthy sitrep to the features staff, partly in response to the house agreement recently negotiated with the NUJ, which had called for a system of regular meetings to discuss 'problems, performance and prospects'. It is a Gottian document. 'We have surmounted many hurdles in the months since we embarked on the Atex system, took over the work of the Manchester features department, moved into a new part of the building, suffered the exigencies of the redesign, and absorbed a significant number of new people ... We have also had a disproportionate number of casualties, which has at intervals left us denuded of necessary talent. A particular burden has been taken up by sub-editors who have effectively been deskilled and then reskilled in an exceptionally short space of time. All in all, it's been an heroic year, and if we gave medals for Stakhanovite endeavour almost everyone would qualify.' Gott then went into a detailed analysis of the future challenges. 'It would be nice to imagine, as 1989 looms (the 200th anniversary of the French Revolution), that we would begin to settle down and move towards sunny uplands. Alas, the prognosis is not good. On at least three fronts there is likely to be further change and upheaval.' These three fronts were the move to full-screen make-up, almost there; the extension of the nine-day fortnight or 35-hour week to a greater number of journalists, many of whom were working a coveted four-day week; and changes in practice for page editors, involving them more in copy-editing and page layout, and not solely in the commissioning of material.

Had there really been a time when Gott and his small team on the main features desk - his three assistant editors, latterly Chris Dodd, Tim Radford and Bill Smithies, the Surrogotts as they called themselves - could concentrate on core content, and when the other semi-autonomous islands in the sprawling features archipelago, including Roger Alton's arts desk, could be left to run themselves? It had all seemed to evaporate incredibly quickly. When the first refugees from the disasters elsewhere in Fleet Street had begun to arrive, the features department had appeared to them like a haven of tranquillity, as they imagined a gentlemen's club in St James's might be,[2] quiet enough for the freelance writer (and enthusiastic campaigner for real ale) Richard Boston to enjoy an uninterrupted post-prandial nap, or occasionally an overnight stay in any of the glass cubicle offices that happened to be conveniently vacant. Alcohol had flowed freely, particularly among the sub-editors. Desmond Christy's life, seriously affected by his health problems, had been further imperilled when, forbidden alcohol himself, he mistakenly swigged hard liquor from an open Coke can left in the fridge door by an alcoholic motoring correspondent. The tide of alcohol would soon begin to ebb, perhaps out of the necessity of focusing on the Atex monitors. Organisational demands intensified. Excursions such as Gott's long visit to Bolivia in the autumn of 1987 served to accentuate the tedium of his deskbound admin duties back in the office. When the moment of handover to Rusbridger came, Gott saw it not as the putsch that some in his department suspected, but as a welcome 'escape', wrench though it still was.

Rusbridger's Weekend had been coming out for slightly less than six months when Preston told him that he wanted him to take on the entire features department. Rusbridger immediately instigated a major shake-up, as was the custom: Preston had done it when he succeeded Christopher Driver in 1968, and Gott too in 1978 when he took over from Harry Jackson. It seemed to happen about once a decade. Rusbridger now faced a features department larger than at any time in its history, and one that would continue to grow. It was also a department agitated by all the recent changes, and somewhat divided in its opinion of Rusbridger's agenda.

Rusbridger decided from the outset that as many people as possible would individually accumulate a variety of experience within the paper, changing jobs every two or three years, a policy that he generally applied from then on. It was called career development, and for many it worked admirably. He moved on to the features desk with Whitaker, who became managing editor of the department, and me, who continued as his deputy. Physically, the distance from the cluster of desks that made up Weekend to the warm seat vacated by Richard Gott was no more than six or seven paces. In all other respects it was a huge leap.

Ed Vulliamy - whose experience of editing at that point was nil - had been appointed as the new editor of Weekend in the Rusbridger manner. 'Alan came wandering up to my desk and said, "I want you to have a go at Weekend." I said, "What do you mean?" "Edit the Weekend Guardian." And that was it.'[3] It was not exactly random selection. Vulliamy was a wonderfully articulate writer with a knowledgeable passion for the arts. He had followed what was then an unusual route to the Guardian, combining employment in both the printed press and television. After graduating from Oxford, he had worked for local papers in Devon, then for Granada Television, eventually becoming an award-winning reporter with *World in Action*. He joined the Guardian at the beginning of 1986. When Rusbridger approached him he had very recently been invited to apply for the job of head of arts at Channel 4, something he discussed with the Guardian's literary editor and art critic, Waldemar Januszczak - somewhat awkwardly, it turned out, as Januszczak had applied for it too. The offer had come from Liz Forgan, the former women's editor of the Guardian who had become director of programmes at Channel 4. Januszczak got the job, leaving Vulliamy free to become the editor of

Weekend. Private Eye was quick to pick up on the commendably frank biographical note he was said to have offered the Guardian's press department: 'I was born and grew up in Notting Hill, west London, and drew my cultural education from Portobello Road, family holidays in Italy, the Isle of Wight rock festivals, the Roundhouse and the Proms. I lost my virginity on the floor of a church crypt in Chicago in 1971; I support Queens Park Rangers and my favourite subject at school was history, at which I was quite good.'

Rusbridger in nominating him as his successor on Weekend was retrospectively seen to be formulating a technique that he continued to practise throughout his career, of making appointments that surprised the recipients with a perception of talents they did not know they had. Only rarely did it turn out that they did not have them after all. Occasionally it induced a post-acceptance panic in the journalist suddenly elevated in this manner, for which Rusbridger was not always sympathetic. One time I was dispatched with a message for someone who, having accepted a key job, after a complex chessboard of deployments changed his mind: 'Tell him if he doesn't do it, he's dead in the water.' He went on to do it quite successfully.

Vulliamy, on the other hand, admitted to struggling from the outset. 'Genius though he is, not even Alan always makes the right appointment. I am the living proof of that.' Weekend, already, was regarded as a great success, editorially and commercially. It was to be imitated by both the Times and the Independent. Great expectations accompanied Vulliamy's appointment. Yet the dynamic of the desk was not ideal. Vulliamy was not allowed to choose his own deputy. The person appointed to the role was the incumbent chief sub-editor, the former letters editor, Chris Maclean, with the close support of Murray Armstrong. Vulliamy admitted: 'Murray saw me I think as a political comrade, but a useless editor, and that's a pretty fair assessment.' One or two changes that Vulliamy wanted to make to regular features were vetoed by Rusbridger, who had, after all, so recently set them up.

Vulliamy happily delegated much of the more mundane parts of his role to others, starting with Maclean, whom he found slightly intimidating ('He knew what he was doing and I didn't'). He also delegated staffing matters to others, which was a mistake, responsibility for the welfare of the people on the desk being a section editor's cardinal duty. Before long a tremendous row broke out over the recruitment of a sub-editor, the appointment of whom was thought to have been motivated more by political than professional considerations. Vulliamy was called down to Preston's office, where he found an incandescent Rusbridger, who wanted to know why he had not been consulted. Vulliamy recalled, 'It's the only time I've seen Alan really angry. He saw it as an attempt to undermine or humiliate him.' The appointment did not go ahead.

Vulliamy concentrated entirely on content, with the clear aim of taking Weekend much further upmarket. Extracts from Umberto Eco's new book *Foucault's Pendulum* were carried, although a cover story by Eco was pulled at the last moment when it was discovered that neither Vulliamy nor anyone else could quite understand it. It may have lost something in translation.

Some time before he took over as editor, Vulliamy had told Rusbridger that he would like to write 'a big piece' on Wagner. The words 'big piece' uttered by Vulliamy did not yet set alarm bells loudly ringing. He began working on the article immediately. 'Now several months later I found myself in charge of the magazine that had commissioned it.' He handed to Chris Maclean for editing a first draft of about 8,000 words, three or even four times longer than the average cover story. The finished article was still almost 6,000 words spreading over several pages, displacing some of the regular features. As the author conceded, it seemed to 'go on and on'.[4]

The final act came on 9 November 1989 with the fall of the Berlin Wall. It was more than Vulliamy could endure to sit at a desk at a time like this. 'The world was going crazy.' He asked Maclean to take over, rang his brother, and said, 'Come on, let's go to Berlin.' In army terminology he went AWOL. He and his brother caught the first available flight and spent the next three days 'drinking and celebrating and hacking into the wall'. He did file a vivid mitigating piece for Monday's front page, recording 'the biggest weekend party of the 20th century'.

What happened to him next is an interesting illustration of the difficult-to-define 'Guardian culture'. In doing what he did, Vulliamy had declared his true vocation, and, blistering annoyance though there was, it was recognised that he had in a sense simply answered the call of the wild. 'Typically, and kindly, rather than sack me, Peter, Jonathan [Fenby] and Alan suggested that Weekend was not quite the job for me, and changed my life by introducing me to the foreign editor Paul Webster,[5] and sending me to Rome.' He left Weekend with feelings of guilt and gratitude. 'It was Alan's baby. I felt I had let him down by not looking after it, and in fact nearly throttling it – and he was very, very decent about that.' In February 1990, Vulliamy moved to Rome and into a bare attic with views across the rooftops and began what he looked back on as four of the happiest years of his life, notwithstanding that he soon had cause to recall Preston's prescient briefing: 'Your job is to cover Italy but we want you to keep an eye on Yugoslavia ... You might have to go there twice a year.' The following year the country erupted into civil war.

Weekend was to become for Vulliamy's successor, Roger Alton, what it was for Rusbridger: a launch pad into the upper atmosphere of the organisation. He had only one way of editing, and that was vigorously, even physically. His favourite recreational activities were running, cycling, climbing and skiing. He pursued them wholeheartedly and fearlessly, and attacked journalism in the same full-blooded way. Although he would have been embarrassed to be caught theorising about journalism, he had very strong ideas about his craft, not dissimilar to those of Peter Preston, with whom his relationship went beyond respect to mutual devotion. To Preston, Alton was always 'Rog'. They had trodden similar career paths. At Oxford both had edited the student newspaper Cherwell, Alton in 1968, when he succeeded in getting it banned by the university after he had carried a story about the expulsion of a number of students for drugs offences. Both he and Preston trained on the Liverpool Post and went from there to the Guardian, where Preston arrived in 1963, Alton in 1974. Alton certainly wrote less frequently than Preston; he seemed to underestimate his own talent as a writer. A difference between him and Preston was in their family background. Preston was a product of Midlands trading and building interests. Alton was a son of academia. Alton, progressing through the Guardian from sports to arts to features, never corrected the impression sometimes formed that he was cut from different cloth.

He was dismissive of anything that seemed in the slightest way pretentious, and some mistook this for impatience with anything 'serious'. In fact he had an eclectic range of interests. He inspired unusual devotion in close colleagues, a possible exception to the general rule being Jocelyn Targett, who as we saw earlier had been put in as his deputy. Alton later expressed his own view of Targett in a remark that was both compliment and criticism: 'Jocelyn is a hugely talented man but he is not one of life's deputies.'[6] Nevertheless, Weekend under Alton became a hub of dynamic activity.

Meanwhile, Rusbridger was busy signing new talent. He was trying to reinvigorate the features department by lowering the average age of its journalists. His hiring of comparative juveniles led to the false conclusion that he was prejudiced against more mature talents. It became his habit when these accusations were cautiously put to him to point at me, barely visible at that time in a cloud of cigarette smoke. But he might have pointed to his hiring, or rather rehiring, of Peter Lennon, aged, it turned out, 59. Lennon had been the paper's Paris correspondent in the 1960s, when a friend and regular drinking partner was another Irish exile, Samuel Beckett, and he had enjoyed success with a remarkable autobiographical documentary film, *Rocky Road to Dublin* (1967). Lennon's reappearance in the office caused a passing commotion in the bunker, all the members of which, unlike Rusbridger, recalled the circumstances surrounding his departure in 1969. He had sued the paper over the meagre severance payment with which after a decade his contract had been suddenly terminated, a measure taken under the stress of dire economic straits. He finally succeeded in extracting more money after his lawyer threatened to impound copies of the Guardian intended for distribution in France. Upon his resurrection 20 years later, all was quickly forgiven, if forgiveness was needed. The intelligent, articulate and sometimes mercilessly observed pieces that began to grace the pages again argued his case for him. He continued to write for the paper to within months of his death in 2011 at the age of 81 (as it was discovered with some surprise).[7]

If there were mildly shocking arrivals, there were departures that were more shocking, notably that of the incumbent women's editor Brenda Polan. She had the distinction of being the first person that Rusbridger ever 'fired', the word she used. Polan had joined the Guardian in 1977, covering fashion, initially somewhat against her better instincts. But she took the job and became an adjunct to Liz Forgan's women's desk, 'the boiling heart of the feminist revolution', as Forgan described it. Polan eventually became women's editor in 1985 after two others had had a go at it. Preston, having passed over her twice in fairly quick succession, had interviewed her in a wine bar off Farringdon Road. This time she was armed with an offer to edit Good Housekeeping. Preston had reacted to this news by dropping his pipe and, according to Polan, practically setting fire to his trousers. 'With an offer like that why would you want to edit the women's pages of the Guardian?' he wondered. 'Because I've wanted it since I was 13 years old,' she told him.

Now, three years later, Preston had the uncomfortable task of sanctioning her removal from the job. Rusbridger had indicated his decision over lunch with her in a restaurant in Clerkenwell Road. 'The first thing he said was, "Am I right in thinking that you are producing the very best women's page you know how?" It is burned on my memory. And I said, 'Well of course.' And he said, "Ah, in that case I am going to move you because I want a very different women's page."'[8] The women's page, especially as the heat of feminism cooled slightly, was subject to practically continuous reappraisal by an almost entirely male senior editorial staff sensitive to what it could term 'dull' or 'worthy'. This view was not aided by the reflections of Dennis Potter's psoriasis-racked Singing Detective upon his appearance (played by Michael Gambon) in 1986. He believed that thinking of 'something very very boring' such as 'the Guardian women's page' might help him control lustful thoughts while a glamorous nurse was greasing the lower parts of his body, although in the end it didn't help, a failure that might almost be taken as an oblique compliment to the page.[9] But clearly Rusbridger did not think the existing page was, in the purely journalistic sense, 'sexy'.

The incoming women's editor was a New Zealander, Louise Chunn, who had been in England since 1982. She had been a successful editor of Just Seventeen before moving to the newly launched UK edition of Elle. She met Rusbridger when he joined others to judge an Elle writing competition. He called her up afterwards and asked her if she would like to be women's editor of the Guardian, not mentioning at that point that there was an incumbent.

When she arrived to start work she brought with her Andrea Chapman, who had been the chief sub-editor at Elle. The dull air of the second floor parted as they entered, making them aware that they struck an exotic note in the male-dominated domain. Chapman and Chunn were both dressed in black chic as though they had stepped from the glossy pages of Elle. They were closely followed by two very large bouquets of white lilies from well-wishers. 'No one could even tell us where to find vases,' Chunn complained.[10] Annie Taylor, the incumbent assistant/secretary who had started a few months earlier – who, with her multicoloured hair extensions and heavy boots, was to be a vivid punk presence on the desk for the next decade – noticed the immediate change. 'When I started, Brenda had the page organised down to the last word. From Louise onwards everything changed and became more immediate and we became much busier.'[11]

It became a very lively desk, introducing to the Guardian, for example, Suzanne Moore, Suzie Mackenzie and Jan Moir, who all began writing for the Guardian during Chunn's tenure. The then unpublished novelist Claire Messud worked on the desk as Chunn's deputy from 1990 to 1993. (She and James Wood, who was producing the Guardian's books pages with Richard Gott, married while working at the Guardian.) Esprit de corps was fostered by occasional parties in an upper room of the Eagle in Farringdon Road.

An innovation by Chunn was a competition among students to pitch for the job of women's editor – to pitch for her job in fact – with the winners brought in for a fortnight to plan, commission and write the material that then appeared through the second week. One of the winners was Katharine Viner. She had just graduated from Oxford, and jumped on the train to London with no clear idea of a career. Her student journalism was confined to one piece, written while still at grammar school in Ripon, about being part of the last year to take O levels. She sent it to the Guardian because that was her family's paper (both her parents were teachers), and it was published on the Young Guardian page, still under its inaugural editor Tim Madge. The excitement had passed, but came back during this fortnight and never went away again. Towards the end of the exercise Louise Chunn took her aside and said, 'Kathy, you know I really think you could be a journalist.' 'I felt that Louise unlocked something for me just by saying that. Even though we'd done these pages, everyone had loved them, and I was really proud of them, I still didn't assume that journalism was for me.'[12] Katharine Viner eventually joined the Guardian in 1997 and became editor-in-chief in 2015.

Among the pages put together by Viner and her co-winners was one concerning the implications of HIV and Aids for the safe sex lives of university students. It was a discussion of the subject in terms that perhaps few if any other national newspapers would have carried at the time. If talk of sexual matters had long been frank on the women's pages of the Guardian, it became franker under Chunn. On one article by Katie Campbell, Chunn recalled, 'I had to go down to Peter and say, "I've got this great piece about the use of the word cunt, and my question is can I use it at all, or once, or all the way through?"' Preston's decision was that it could be used once, presumably to remove any possible doubt about what was signified by the asterisks that were to be used thereafter.

Chunn believes that the pages during her term – four years in the end – did help to make the Guardian 'more a part of modern British life'. There was thought to be a sort of compatibility between Elle and the Guardian; they jointly produced a 24-page tabloid supplement, *Men and Women*, which contributed to the Guardian winning the prestigious Medium of the Year award for 1992; *Campaign* magazine called the cross-promotion 'a publishing first in the UK'. The Guardian was rapidly overcoming its historical aversion to fashion and glamour.

But while these changes were taking place, Chunn had been changing too. And probably what had brought that about was increasing contact with readers. A survey of readers that asked them questions about the practical realities of their lives produced a huge response. 'Interestingly, the thing that got the biggest postbag was an anonymous first-person account by a woman of 40-something who had been married for 20 years. She said I love my husband, I love my children, life is great in so many ways but I absolutely don't want ever to have sex with my husband again ... It drew a huge postbag, and we took an extra page to carry some of the letters. A lot of what it was about was the menopause. But if I'd said, I'm going to do a big thing about the menopause ... I think the response might have been, "Haven't you got anything a bit jollier?"'

Andrea Chapman ended up serving as the page's sub-editor for the extraordinary period of 22 years (before moving to Weekend in 2011). She was well aware of the recurring question as the page passed under the care of a succession of women's editors. 'I think there was a definite feeling that grew over the years that the women's page was something of an anachronism, that stories of interest and relevance to women should have a place in the main paper, if you like, rather than being ghettoised. But I think every editor who came in realised that there was something unique about the page, something that readers really related to and about which they felt both passionate and possessive.'[13]

The features department under Rusbridger continued to evolve and expand, often at a dizzying pace. The workload and pressures referred to by Gott in his sitrep at the end of 1988 had grown since then. Occasionally simply bringing enough people to bear on the day-to-day task of producing the paper was only achieved by extraordinary means. One sub-editor, while his dialysis was in progress at Bart's hospital in Smithfield, and blood was coursing through various tubes, was delighted to see a visitor from the Guardian, only to be asked whether he would be free to do a shift in features the following day.[14]

Chapter 13

Comment, Cartoons and a Touch of Poetry

'I remember Ronan [Bennett] saying, "How's it going?" to Roger [Alton] at some Guardian do, and Roger would go, "Nightmare, nightmare, nightmare, mate" – and Ronan saying, "I hear you're the nightmare."'

Georgina Henry on Roger Alton

While Rusbridger's mini-revolution was taking place across the features department, there was one section that came in for particular scrutiny since most of it was controlled and commissioned directly by him and his assistants, the successors to the Surrogotts. This was the comment section, comprising at this time just two pages, the leader/letters page and the facing page or op ed page, now bearing the rubric Comment & Analysis, but in fact very much as Preston had invented it some 20 years earlier.

The leader page, with the benefit of the Hillman redesign, had acquired an extra degree or two of texty elegance, the leaders stripped across the top of the page or run vertically down the two left-side columns. But even that was a format that had been left basically unaltered rather than created by Hillman. The letters, as before, occupied the remainder of the page, making way only for another daily institution, the Country Diary and, once a week, a column that ran across the foot of the page, usually an essay loosely related to the news. This acquired some distinguished exponents, including Geoffrey Taylor, whose column Terms of Reference, a combination of lightly borne erudition and wit, enjoyed a final run on Mondays through the greater part of 1991. It was then followed by Roy Hattersley's long-running column, Endpiece, relocated from the facing page. One or sometimes two single- or double-column cartoons, usually, in the early part of Rusbridger's tenure as features editor, by Hector Breeze or Merrily Harpur, illustrated the letters.

Theoretically, the key people on this page were the editor of the paper, with whom the leader writers conferred every day, and the letters editor, a proxy for the editor and also supposed to confer daily with him, who nevertheless, as we saw earlier, enjoyed a high degree of autonomy. The letters editor also edited the columns that appeared on the page and was responsible for choosing the illustrations. Rusbridger's influence over the page, at least while he remained features editor, was quite limited.

The facing page was another matter. Rusbridger was entirely responsible, as Gott had been, for the content, tone and appearance of that, and it was this page that naturally seemed to invite a direct comparison with that commissioned by Richard Gott and his Surrogotts. Rusbridger ran it from 1989 to a few months after the advent of the tabloid daily features section G2, not finally surrendering it until early in 1993. As it happened, shortly after that he became a member of Preston's bunker as deputy editor when once again he assumed a direct interest in the Comment pages. As features editor, his conduct of the two pages, together constituting a kind of forum, began conservatively and became more adventurous, both in presentation and content.

The content of the facing page had always combined domestic and international affairs: Richard Gott had seen to that. If anything, commentary on foreign affairs became more dominant under Rusbridger, and so did the proportion of expert or 'participant' outside contributors - those directly involved in the news - who appeared on the page. A shift of emphasis was not surprising considering the enormous changes that were taking place throughout the world in those years. It was a time marked by the fall of the Berlin Wall, the release of Nelson Mandela, the first Gulf War, the Middle East hostage crisis, the coup attempt against Gorbachev, the war in former Yugoslavia, the end of the Soviet Union, the end of the Cold War and the supposed beginning of a New World Order. At home, it brought the end of the Thatcher era, with the lady herself, the noise of the poll tax riots fading, finally giving way to the sleaze-plagued government of John Major.

There was a notable change in the appearance of the comment pages in this period. The paper's principal columnists, Hugo Young, Ed Pearce and others, began appearing at the top of the leader page. The facing page at the same time became a showcase for the development of graphic art. Peter Kennard's photomontages made a number of powerful appearances on it. What probably became his best-known image from this time – the shaking of hands through the breached Berlin Wall – was published the year before the reunification of Germany. Peter Clarke's surrealistically distorted portraits, memorably of a long upper-lipped John Major, also appeared regularly on the pages.

The facing page was the platform from which the Polish cartoonist Andrzej Krauze first addressed Guardian readers. He made his debut in the paper in December 1989, illustrating an article in which Francis Fukuyama defended himself against the critics who had taken issue with his influential essay, 'The End of History'. Rusbridger had called Krauze out of the blue to ask him to illustrate it. He came up with a bleak landscape of fallen and broken classical columns, in what quickly became his instantly recognisable strong linear graphic style.

Krauze had moved to England from Poland in 1982 at the age of 35, the year after a small but impressive book of his cartoons was published in London. *Andrzej Krauze's Poland* featured a preface by the Hungarian-born George Mikes, a former contributor to the Observer and the author of *How to be an Alien* (1946) (among his observations: 'Continental people have sex lives; the English have hot water bottles'). He saw Krauze's use of metaphor as a way of protecting himself against the communist censor in his native land. Between artist and reader and censor there was a tacit agreement to pretend that no one really knew the wolf was Brezhnev or that the crow was Wojciech Jaruzelski. Jaruzelski effectively cut off Krauze's return to Poland when he declared martial law in December 1981, and closed the weekly publication Kultura, which had been Krauze's primary outlet in his home country.

By the time Krauze and the Guardian found each other his work had been appearing in the New Statesman and New Society and elsewhere, although it still provided him with little more than bread and butter. Before long he could be seen in the Guardian at least twice a week. 'The Guardian was a big change in my life,' he said.[1] He was the artist most associated with the running commentary the paper was providing on all the changes that were taking place in what was soon the former Soviet Union. A lesser artist might have been trapped or typecast by finding himself constantly called upon to comment on events to which he was so close; Krauze was saved from any narrow confinement by the metaphorical language he had developed. A Krauze illustration, while fitting its original purpose, often achieved a universality that would continue to give it relevance and resonance.

The most enduring mark, however, was to be that made by the sudden promotion of Steve Bell to the Comment and Analysis pages, taking over from the New Zealander Les Gibbard. He thus became part of a distinguished Guardian chain. In the post Second World War period, it began with another New Zealander, David Low, who became the Manchester Guardian's chief political cartoonist in 1953 and continued working for the paper until a few months before his death in 1963. He was succeeded by the South African William Papas, although, in the judgment of design editor Michael McNay, 'political satire was not Papas's true métier ... His style was closer to Ronald Searle than to Low or the savagery of ... Steve Bell.'[2]

Les Gibbard took over from Papas in 1969, and his work appeared in the paper for the next 25 years. He was the last cartoonist in this high-profile political role at the Guardian whose work was, so to speak, tainted by kindness. This was not a characteristic that could be said to be often visible in the work of Bell, who had been nursing, or perhaps indulging, a searing hatred of Mrs Thatcher and all she stood for. Fans of his 'If ...' strip, which had been running in the Guardian since 1981, were used to finding him in the nether regions of the paper, lately at the foot of the curious hotchpotch of the Personal page. A permanent element of this was the Obituary, itself full of surprises in the hands of WL Webb and Christopher Driver. The obituary might be sharing the page with a Law Report, or the Face to Faith religious column, and, below all this, the quick crossword and the strips: as well as Bell's 'If ...', for a time a resurrected Krazy Kat by George Herriman (1880–1940), and Gary Trudeau's Doonesbury.

Bell arrived at the Guardian (from City Limits) in time to run a ferociously bizarre commentary on the Falklands War. Mrs Thatcher was his muse, as Preston rightly remarked, and never failed to stir his inkpot. Preston came to regard him as a genius, and Rusbridger shared that opinion. It was Rusbridger who called Bell as the political conference season approached in 1990 and told him he would like him to take on the additional task of producing a big single-frame political cartoon for the Comment pages.

Bell started with the Labour Party conference in Blackpool at the beginning of October, producing not what Rusbridger had in mind but an extended two-deck strip in the style of 'If ...' The first had an autobiographical theme, with the artist himself as a grizzled refugee from the Left Bank, lamenting that all he could see of Neil Kinnock from his place below the conference podium was 'Ze turp of 'is 'ead!!' Rusbridger made a mild protest over the result of Bell's first effort: 'But it's a strip.' Bell reflected, 'All the ones I delivered from the conferences turned out this way. I've always been very slow to adapt.'[3] But the message was taken to heart and in November the first of the big single-frame political cartoons made their appearance.

From Bell's point of view events had provided the perfect occasion. On 15 November 1990, he responded to deputy prime minister Geoffrey Howe's devastatingly critical resignation speech by depicting Thatcher caught round the neck by the liana she had hoped to swing free on, with Howe, the sheep, clinging to her feet, and - hanging on to the sheep's tail - Heseltine as Tarzan (both nicknames they had acquired in the 1970s).[4] Bell's cartoon on 23 November - the day following Mrs Thatcher's resignation - stretched across the full eight columns and, like the earlier one, no words were required. It showed Michael Heseltine, with Howe at his heels, leading Douglas Hurd and John Major as crocodiles bearing the defeated Thatcher suspended from a pole carried between them; crocodile tears were shed by all.

This was one of Major's last appearances in a Bell production before his irrevocable transformation into 'Hedgerman' - as he was transiently called - soon to be instantly recognisable by the pair of Y-front underpants drawn on over his trousers in parody of Superman. Once on, the underpants would never be cast off. The underpants were emblematic of what Bell saw as Major's appalling boring suburban normality (qualities that in the turmoil of Brexit, almost three decades later, appeared to enhance his nostalgia value).

Once the Gulf War began, Bell was enlisted to provide two Comment cartoons a week. From that time he never looked back, except for during the party conferences when for some reason the copiously worded multi-frame strip took over again. No one seemed to object, except on the occasion when he depicted Tony Blair in a negative light at his first conference as party leader, in a 14-frame cartoon on the front page.[5]

Rusbridger, by now the deputy editor of the Guardian, speaking to a media audience shortly after this, reasserted his commitment to the cartoonist. 'Steve Bell is a genius,' he declared. 'The problem is that most readers are not geniuses. Or they are geniuses without a sense of humour. Anyway, they don't see the funny side of Steve Bell. Quite a large number of them think he is completely awful and should be banned from ever appearing in the paper.'[6]

The Comment page proved to be a space that offered ample room for development of this form in Bell's long career with the Guardian. Peter Preston paid his own tribute in 1999. 'Steve Bell is a genius. He may not look like one (unless genius is bearded, bulky and has been wearing the same black woolly sweater for the past 20 years). He may not sound like one (conversations are mostly laddish and jovial until they turn to money). But the affability and the timewarp kit, in a sense, make the genius more astonishing.'[7] He is one of the great political cartoonists of his day, an opinion endorsed by the many awards showered on him.

Early in 1993, a few months after the creation of G2, the Comment pages team moved to a new free-standing position on the first floor more or less at Preston's elbow. There they had a new editor, Martin Kettle, who by now had handed over the editorship of Guardian Europe to Dominique Jackson. He was assisted in his new role by John Cunningham. Neither Kettle nor Cunningham had been entirely comfortable with the Rusbridger features regime. Now out of both Gott and Rusbridger's shadow, Kettle would have a taste of independence as an editor of pages that were central to the paper's identity and with a higher profile than Guardian Europe.

The new arrangement probably suited Cunningham too. Already some 25 years into his Guardian career (and with a decade still ahead of him) he enjoyed a flourish on the Kettle comment pages in the form of an occasional and extremely witty column called 'P.S.' Its merits said a number of things about its author: that his style had somehow been cramped in the post-Gott features department, that looking askance at the world around him came perfectly naturally to him, that he had an insatiable relish for London life, and possessed an almost surreal way with words. There were altogether too few of these columns, providing only a tiny fraction of the million or so words that Cunningham contributed to the Guardian.

Change in the features department had achieved considerable momentum by the time Rusbridger became deputy editor of the Guardian in May 1993. In February, after four years in the role as Rusbridger's deputy, I became arts editor on Jocelyn Targett's departure for the Sunday Times. It was another Rusbridger-style appointment. We had been driving in Rusbridger's car to Highbury, where we both lived at the time. We were continuing to mull over possible candidates when Rusbridger suddenly said, 'Why don't you do it?'

Over the next couple of years I made more than a dozen changes or new appointments, notably signing up the ballet critic Judith Mackrell and the classical music critic Andrew Clements, a champion of new music, both of whom began careers on the Guardian that would last more than 20 years. Mackrell ran alongside and in the end took over from the critic and ballet historian, Mary Clarke, whose own greatly valued connection with the Guardian went back to the end of the 1950s.

Another venture was a series of Guardian New Poetry commissioned from Simon Armitage, who selected and edited it. The series opened at the end of September 1993 and ran irregularly until early June 1994. It began with one of Armitage's own poems and included Lavinia Greenlaw, Ian Duhig, Michael Donaghy, Selima Hill, as well as then better-known poets such as Ted Hughes, Carol Ann Duffy, Hugo Williams and Tony Harrison. The regular publication of original poetry was not sustained in the Guardian until it found a place in the sheltered accommodation of the (Saturday) Review in the new millennium.

I also revived the critics' meetings, which had been held occasionally in the past but had been set aside by Targett. Preston, invited to attend the first, seemed to be more alarmed than impressed by the massed weight of critics that were assembled, between 20 and 30, the cost of whom he appeared to be silently totting up. The great majority were free-lances. Amid all the changes very few of the critics, perhaps none, had met all the others – a pity therefore that in my introductions I suddenly blanked the name of the paper's primary rock reviewer Adam Sweeting. Sweeting, a former features editor of Melody Maker, had by that time contributed more than 1,000 reviews and interviews to the Guardian over the past seven or eight years and might have hoped that at least his name would trip off the tongue. Sweeting and Caroline Sullivan, also formerly of Melody Maker, together with the jazz critics John Fordham and Ronald Atkins, formed a uniquely strong front line. It was made even stronger by the journalism of Robin Denselow, an informed advocate of folk and world music. Denselow combined his work for the Guardian with a career as a leading current affairs reporter - he was one of the original team that launched the BBC's *Newsnight* programme in 1980.

I also held a critics' meeting in Manchester, where Robin Thornber's band of regional critics were experiencing frustration increasing in proportion to the rate at which the space made available for their reviews was diminishing.

One of the points of the critics' meetings in London was to give everyone on the arts desk the chance to meet, mingle with and get to know the critics. The desk during Targett's time had been a place fraught with tension and sometimes audibly rent by it. It was symptomatic that Clare Margetson, whose talent and contribution to Guardian Europe had been noticed, had now been recruited to the arts desk not directly by the arts editor but by the triumvirate running the main features department: Rusbridger, Brian Whitaker and myself. Margetson joined a desk that, with Targett as arts editor, included Deborah Orr, Stuart Jeffries and Stephen Moss. 'From day one you noticed the tension between Jocelyn and Deborah ... Jocelyn was keen to shock and ruffle the feathers of the arts community,' Margetson remembered,[8] with Toby Young his main ruffling agent.

My successor Claire Armitstead had joined the Guardian from the Financial Times in February 1992 as a theatre critic, supplemented by a couple of days a week subbing on the books pages. Armitstead recalled, 'My own career as a theatre critic was pretty stymied because, for all the revolution at the centre, no one had tackled the outdated system of regional theatre reviewing. Basically, Michael Billington reviewed all the major London shows, while Robin Thornber, in Manchester, ran a fleet of local critics who filled the early regional editions, or (more often) filed to the spike [at one time literally and dangerously a vertical metal spike on which unwanted copy was impaled]. I remember turning up at the Lyric Hammersmith one day to review an adaptation of *The Ragged-Trousered Philanthropists*, to find at least two, or maybe even three, Guardian reviews pinned up in the foyer from the show's travels around the country before it arrived into London.' Sorting all that out was one of the tasks left for me to tackle.

Stuart Jeffries was nominally my deputy, and somehow managed to combine the role with his studies for a degree in philosophy from Birkbeck. He and Armitstead had been contemporaries at the Ham & High (the Hampstead and Highgate Express) in north London. What was then a highly cultured, wide-horizoned weekly paper was one of several staging posts on Jeffries' route from home in the Black Country, via Oxford, to the Guardian, where he arrived in 1990. His journalism, especially his interviews with writers, academics and actors, would be an asset to the paper for the next two decades and more, by which time he had had a period as a television critic and Paris correspondent. Combining the esoteric and the prosaic was one of Jeffries' specialities. When his autobiographical account of growing up with television - *Mrs Slocombe's Pussy* - came out in 2000, some critics discerned a touch of Proust in his writing. The Daily Mail called the book 'hilariously Proustian', and Kathryn Flett, in a review in the Observer (that was so scathing that it had to be toned down before publication, according to Roger Alton), wrote of 'a long Proustian reverie about eating custard tarts with his brother while watching *Bill and Ben*'.[9]

Georgina Henry replaced me as deputy features editor. Hers was probably the most important appointment Rusbridger made at that time, and can be seen in retrospect as marking the beginning of a new phase in the ascent of women to which Preston willingly subscribed. At the time that Rusbridger approached her, Preston had been talking to her about the possibility of being a home news reporter. The job in features, on the face of it, was much more attractive, but Rusbridger drove a hard bargain. He did not want her to give up the job of editing the media pages, a big revenue earner for the features department. She was already used to a heavy workload. 'I worked a six-day week for years. I'd work a full week as the media specialist on the news desk and then I'd be frantically running around on Friday trying to do the media pages, and then I would be in every Sunday to see those media pages sent to press. I was bonkers.'[10]

She was only with Rusbridger for a few months before he became deputy editor of the paper and Roger Alton became features editor - Deborah Orr succeeded Alton to become a brilliant and by comparison gritty editor of Weekend (its fourth editor, and the first woman in the role). The pace of activity on the features desk increased under Alton, something that Henry was in the best position to notice. 'Roger inherited me and would have been quite within his rights to get rid of me, but he didn't and we got on quite well.' Henry described Alton as 'very different, loud and charismatic. He swore a lot and he was funny; he used to wander past and make jokes.' Once he became features editor Alton was determined to mould G2 into a coherent entity and sought to achieve his aim in bursts of dynamic activity. 'Roger was famed for disappearing in the afternoon. I remember being enraged by that – the number of times I had to make decisions because the production schedules required decisions to be made in the afternoon and Roger would not be there and then he would come back and unpick those decisions. I remember once literally pushing him into his office and just beating him up.' Henry was married to the author Ronan Bennett and he was familiar with her circle at the Guardian. 'I remember Ronan saying, "How's it going?" to Roger at some Guardian do, and Roger would go, "Nightmare, nightmare, nightmare, mate" – and Ronan saying, "I hear you're the nightmare." Roger was absolutely infuriating but at the same time it was enormous fun.'

Alton's forte was to pounce on breaking stories and turn them round extremely quickly. These were not always front features for G2 but would require space elsewhere in its pages with very little or no notice. 'There was a strong sense of demarcation, which Alan found infuriating and was constantly trying to break down, between arts and women for example, and, you know, all these places which said, "No, hands off." Alan was gradually breaking that down when he went off to be deputy editor. Roger really carried it through. He would say, "Mayesie, Mayesie, you've only got two pages today because I need a little page to do this."'

Once or twice the 30 or 40 people present in the features department would be entertained to a stand-up shouting match in the middle of the floor, which naturally Alton always won. For better or worse – opinion was divided – he became in that sense the first editor to really push the concept of 'through-editing'. It was, he might have argued, in a phrase that was just beginning to creep into the Guardian, a 'no-brainer'.

Chapter 14

A Tale of Two Exiles in a Time of Turmoil

'This is what he thought: I'm a dead man. He wondered how many days he had to live and thought the answer was probably a single-digit number.'

Salman Rushdie, *Joseph Anton,* **2012**

From time to time the Guardian became part of the events it was reporting, or something of them blew in with the dust and exhaust fumes of Farringdon Road. In the autumn of 1988 the solid shape of 34-year-old Kharkov-born writer and journalist Vitali Vitaliev appeared at the Guardian to start a month-long 'educational' visit. Vitaliev was an award-winning journalist in the Soviet Union, contributing investigative articles to several leading journals, such as Ogonyok, but especially the satirical weekly Krokodil. Alan Rusbridger had invited him to England at the suggestion of Martin Walker, the Guardian's man in Moscow. 'Martin Walker and the Guardian changed my life,' Vitaliev declared.[1] The features and reviews he contributed to the Guardian in the four weeks of his visit - the first time he had been anywhere outside the Soviet Union - were to lead to a book offer and a regular slot reporting from Moscow in Clive James's television show, *Saturday Night Clive*.[2]

Walker had first met Vitaliev the previous year, when he went to the offices of Krokodil to interview him. 'We had lunch and became friends. At the time he was passionately pro-Gorbachev and pro-perestroika and one night over vodka even thought aloud about joining the Party ... By early 1988, when the economic disruption and the internal party counter-attack against Gorbachev were emerging, Vitali became very depressed about the future, convinced that the hardliners were coming back, along with more anti-Semitism. Skinheads were becoming a problem, tough young nationalists who would beat up blacks and people from Abkhazia, and Jews as well if they recognised them.' Walker himself was arrested and beaten up while covering a Jewish demonstration.

'We talked endlessly, as I did with other Russian friends, about perestroika and its prospects and the way it was going wrong ... The economic system was fundamentally rotten, the farms unproductive, the infrastructure crumbling and industrial output declining.'

Vitaliev's view was equally gloomy and becoming gloomier. The contrast with the life he found in England on that first visit struck him forcibly. Walker recalled, 'When he came to London, I met him at Liverpool Street station, drove him around the sights, took him to his first supermarket and down to my parents-in-laws' place on Church Square in Rye. It was like watching someone fall in love: the old town, the medieval church, the cobbled streets and teashops, the shops in general, and visiting the Guardian. He was spectacularly happy.'[3]

In the office he was placed in the care of John Cunningham, at the time a staff feature writer, who took him on various excursions, including a day with Thames Valley Police in Oxford that deeply impressed him (he took a policeman's helmet back to Russia). He went to an Arsenal match at Highbury with Roger Alton and Alan Rusbridger; the latter's home was within earshot of the ground. With the literary editor WL (Bill) Webb he visited the Traveller's Club, where the doorman provided the necessary tie.

By the time Vitaliev left at the end of his month he had been given a richly flavoured taste of England. His impressions of the Guardian itself have been a recurring element in his work ever since: 'Here dozens of journalists were sitting next to each other, yet the huge room was immersed in silence, strangely enhanced by softly purring telephones and whispered conversations. No one bothered raising their voice. Twice a day a food trolley was rolled into the newsroom by a white-robed young man from the canteen. The journalists bought their tea and sandwiches and consumed them there and then at their desks. When the trolley was about to leave, the young man shouted: "Trolley going!", at which point the hacks would look up from their computers and chant in chorus: "Bye-bye, trolley!" This little ritual was as sweet and spontaneous as only a children's game could be.'[4]

Russia upon his return provided an even sharper contrast. The economic situation had deteriorated further, crime was on the increase, food shortages were growing. Vitaliev and his colleagues were shaken when Gorbachev launched an attack on press and publishers, including the editors of Ogonyok and Krokodil, accusing them of exaggerating the difficulties that perestroika was encountering. By the spring of 1989 the editor of Ogonyok was asking all his journalists to sign every fact and figure: 'If they make one mistake they can't work for us any more.'[5] There were personal difficulties for Vitaliev. His phone was bugged: he heard KGB voices on the line once while talking to Jonathan Steele, the Guardian correspondent who had taken over from Martin Walker in Moscow. He started to get threatening calls, implicitly directed not just at him but his young son. About a year after his return he made up his mind to defect. On 30 January 1990, he said a final goodbye to his mother. The following day his train crossed the border into Poland at Brest.[6]

This time when he arrived in Britain on the ferry from the Hook of Holland his wife and son were with him, and Alan Rusbridger was at Harwich to meet them, waving an advance copy of Vitaliev's first book in English, *Special Correspondent*. For the first few weeks after his arrival, Vitaliev and his family lived with the Rusbridgers in Highbury. 'He supported me strongly in my decision not to return to the USSR and said that if "they" tried to do anything to my mum in Moscow in revenge, the Guardian people would demonstrate at the Soviet embassy! The Guardian played an enormous role in building up my self-confidence - as a journalist, as a writer and as a free human being.'

Vitaliev wrote for the Guardian for the next five months until, encouraged by Clive James, he took up an offer to go to Australia to become a senior staff writer for the Melbourne's Age and the Sydney Morning Herald. In 1997, back in the UK, he was given a regular column in the Guardian that ran for about year under the title Outside Eye, a name that Vitaliev never liked because by then, he said, he no longer felt like an outsider. Nevertheless, the title fairly described the special perspective he brought to his work in the west.

Another such unusual perspective was provided by the Rugby-educated son of an Indian Muslim family, who was to make headlines of his own in the year that Vitaliev was back in Russia, making up his mind to defect. Salman Rushdie was to become the most celebrated exile of that era - an outcast in his own land.

On the day that the dying Ayatollah Ruhollah Khomeini declared a fatwa on Rushdie, effectively sentencing the writer of *The Satanic Verses* to death for alleged blasphemy against Islam, Rushdie himself was making what was to be his last public appearance for a very long time. It was 14 February, Valentine's Day, 1989. He had gone to the Greek Orthodox Saint Sophia Cathedral in Bayswater to attend the memorial service for the travel writer Bruce Chatwin. There were many friends at this gathering of literary London, among them Paul Theroux, who leaned over to offer Rushdie dubious words of comfort: 'I suppose we'll be here for you next week, Salman.'[7]

Bill Webb had asked John Cunningham, Vitali Vitaliev's minder, to go to the service in his place. In a short piece about the memorial service Cunningham, with some understatement, observed that Rushdie 'looked tense'. Rushdie, with Marianne Wiggins, his wife of little more than a year, had driven away from the cathedral to begin the shadow life of an internal exile, nine years that he describes vividly - writing in the third person - in his memoir *Joseph Anton*. It was an exile that began in a basement flat in Lonsdale Square, Islington, an area densely populated with media people including several from the Guardian, none of whom apparently observed the clandestine comings and goings.

Angela Carter had reviewed *The Satanic Verses* enthusiastically for the Guardian, calling it a 'populous, loquacious, sometimes hilarious, extraordinary contemporary novel'.[8] It was highly praised elsewhere too, and won the Whitbread for the best novel. This accolade was very shortly followed by the public burning of the book in Bradford and the withdrawal of copies from WH Smith branches. The action by Smith's was noted in a column of nibs (news in brief) on the front page, which also included an item reporting that Gorbachev had told Thatcher he would like to visit Britain. Bill Webb was called upon to comment on these parallel threads in a facing-page article: 'As Stalinism recedes and the culture of one kind of world faith begins to recover its nerve, another militant ideology revives heresy hunts, telling its faithful to stop up their ears.'[9] Not only the Guardian itself, but many of its commentators in this pre-fatwa phase supported Rushdie in an unconditional defence of the principle of free speech. Ian Aitken referred to the book as a 'controversial and brilliant novel'.

Then came the fatwa. The Guardian leader, under the heading 'The poison of defeat and of hatred', placed it in the aftermath of the disastrous Iran-Iraq war, and in the context of rising and increasingly violent

Islamic fundamentalism. '[Rushdie] is denounced everywhere by the same extremist passions which (on a wider canvas) are wrecking the chance of a new beginning in Afghanistan [after Gorbachev had opened the way for the Russian withdrawal]. Yesterday's pronouncement by Khomeini is of an extreme, ungilded nature which defies justification by those who are (and should be) seeking to understand the Iranian revolution. The issue goes far beyond that of book banning or even of book burning.'

A month later in another leader the Guardian was urging the British government to consider breaking off diplomatic relations with Iran.[10] This was a view the paper arrived at despite the existence of several British hostages in the area: Roger Cooper, who was being held in prison in Tehran on unsubstantiated charges of spying, and the hostages in Beirut, among them the journalist John McCarthy, the Irish teacher Brian Keenan, and the Archbishop of Canterbury's envoy Terry Waite, who was taken hostage while on a mission to secure the release of the others. Guardian journalists, and the NUJ, were particularly active in support of the Friends of John McCarthy and for a long time a banner calling for his release hung on the wall of the Farringdon Road newsroom.

A couple of weeks later the plight of the hostages was weighing heavier in the collective mind. The Iranian Majlis or parliament had issued a three-point ultimatum, including a demand that the British government denounce the 'anti-Islamic' novel. The Guardian leader suggested a diplomatic solution: 'It may be argued that Sir Geoffrey [Howe] cannot properly say anything about the book. But how about something like, "We profoundly regret the distress that publication has occasioned to sincere followers of Islam?"' The Guardian was suggesting precisely the same form of words that Rushdie had used two weeks earlier, which had proved singularly ineffectual. Two days later at least 12 people were killed in India when police fired into a crowd of Muslim protesters against Rushdie. The death of Ayatollah Khomeini in early June brought about no immediate improvement in the situation.

All points of view were expressed in the Guardian's pages, many challenging the leader's position. Hugo Young, initially at least, took a hard line. He quoted Muslim leaders in Britain who were saying Rushdie must hang. In response, Young said, 'a kind of mesmerised terror had descended on the guardians of liberty'. The toleration extended to those who made such remarks had, he suggested, been excessive. He went so far as to suggest that those unable to accept the requirements of the law in Britain might find it more congenial elsewhere and – naming one of the locations where anti-Rushdie demonstrations had occurred – asked: 'If not Gravesend, why not Tehran?'[11]

In March, the Guardian, along with newspapers in 15 other countries, published a whole-page advertisement carrying a statement by a thousand internationally known authors defending Rushdie's right to publish his novel 'free from censorship, intimidation and violence'.[12] The signatories included Samuel Beckett, Graham Greene and Harold Pinter. The statement was the first act of the recently formed Rushdie campaign committee, which had the support of the Society of Authors, the Publishers' Association and the NUJ.

Michael Foot, who was one of the signatories, wrote a spirited defence of Rushdie for the Guardian's Friday Review.[13] 'The killings [in India] are not attributable to Rushdie's book: not a single sentence within it incites people to kill or offers excuse for the killers. On the contrary, the reason for the killing is to be found in the religion of those who have incited them to kill.' Khomeini, not Rushdie, was to blame, he said.

Among the Guardian's own, none was more forthright in Rushdie's defence than Melanie Phillips. 'Those who have faith should be free to practise it so long as that practice does not stifle the freedom of others – so no censorship, no book-burning, no murder. That is why those who support the ban on the book, whatever their weasel words about abhorring violence, connive at the establishment of a medieval and theocratic lynch-mob.'[14]

The Guardian found its clearest voice in the leader that marked the first anniversary of the fatwa, stating at the outset that 'Salman Rushdie is not a victim of Islamic law but of Iranian politics.' It strongly criticised the attitude of the British government, whose response had lacked authority and decisiveness. Then it came to the great pending decision of whether there should be a paperback edition of *The Satanic Verses*. Here it took issue with some of its own contributors, including its principal political commentator Hugo Young – who had moved somewhat away from his initial stance, having recently suggested Rushdie should renounce his book – and gave an unequivocal statement of the paper's editorial position. 'There can be only one answer: that the paperback must be published. To stop it now would be to give in to terrorism.'[15]

The same issue carried three opinions representative of the continuing debate about the paperback publication. Nadine Gordimer was in favour of its publication; Louis Baum, the editor of the Bookseller, wanted it to be published by syndicate; and John le Carré was against publication. Le Carré argued, 'Absolute free speech is not a god-given right in any country ... Nobody has a right to insult a great religion and be published with impunity.'[16]

What should be made clear in considering all these expressions of opinion is that they were made a little over a week after the relatives of four of the British hostages had issued a public appeal to Penguin to 'forgo' paperback publication. The statement, issued via the Archbishop of Canterbury on 5 February, declared that publication would be irresponsible and would cause further damage to community relations. 'We believe the time has come to balance the principle of free speech against that of self-restraint.'

Salman Rushdie's 7,000-word apologia, 'In Good Faith', appeared in the Independent on Sunday the day before the hostages' relatives made this plea, and it contains no direct reference to their position. Lamenting the wobbly nature of some of those who had first expressed support, Rushdie wrote: 'It has been that sort of year. Twelve months ago, the Guardian's esteemed columnist, Hugo Young, teetered on the edge of racism when he told all British Muslims that if they didn't like the way things were in Britain, they could always leave ... now this same Mr Young prefers to lay the blame for the controversy at my door ... No doubt Mr Young would now be relieved if I went back where I came from.' John Berger and John le Carré are also chastised.

In December 1991 Rushdie marked more than 1,000 days living under the threat of the fatwa with a surprise appearance at Columbia University in New York to speak on the 200th anniversary of the First Amendment guaranteeing freedom of speech to citizens of the United States. By then the British hostages held in Lebanon had all been released. Rushdie had been flown to the United States on a military aircraft, his first trip out of Britain since he was forced into hiding. He was greeted by a prolonged standing ovation.

Rushdie was reported as saying, '*The Satanic Verses* must be freely available and easily affordable, if only because if it is not read and studied, then these years will have no meaning.' The text of Rushdie's speech had been published in the New York Times and a substantial part of it, some

2,500 words, was given on the main Comment page of the Guardian under Rushdie's byline.

Publication of the article led to an unfortunate altercation between Rushdie and the features editor of the Guardian, Alan Rusbridger, a few weeks later. They met in London on 24 January 1992 and Rusbridger was somewhat taken back to find himself accused of stealing the piece. Clearly stung, he wrote a lengthy note of explanation on the following Monday:

> It was good to meet you the other night, a meeting marred only by our inability to agree on whether the Guardian had acted honourably in carrying the text of your extremely thought-ful talk to Columbia University. You described the publication of your speech as "theft". This was based on your belief that a) the Guardian is not a subscriber to the New York Times News Service; and that b) your agreement with the NYT was, in any case, for one use only.

Rusbridger pointed out that the Guardian had been a subscriber for well over a year, and he also dug out the original wire copy, which carried the clear rubric: 'For use by NY Times News Service Clients'. He continued:

> If you truly had a one-use only agreement with the New York Times, then you have been badly let down. But your grievance is against the New York Times, not the Guardian.

Le Carré and Rushdie were the principal protagonists in a more serious argument that ran over several days on the letters page of the Guardian five years later, in 1997. Raw nerves were touched after Le Carré had given a speech in which, having been accused of anti-Semitism, he had spoken of the pain of being misunderstood.[17] Rushdie wrote to say, in effect, that this was a bit rich coming from Le Carré in view of the latter's misunderstanding of Rushdie's motivation for writing the book – he had accused Rushdie of profiting 'from the notoriety he must have known would result'. Christopher Hitchens became a participant, with a particu-larly abusive attack on Le Carré.[18] William Shawcross, the chairman of Article 19, which was coordinating the campaign to defend Rushdie, then wrote rebuking Rushdie, Hitchens and others for their misdirected abuse of Le Carré.[19] Alan Rusbridger, by now the editor of the Guardian, rang Rushdie to offer him the space to respond. Rushdie rather sourly declined.[20] (Harmonious relations between Rushdie and Le Carré were not finally restored until 2012.)[21]

In April 1998 the Guardian announced that a paperback edition of *The Satanic Verses* was at last about to be issued by a publisher in Britain, not by Penguin, but by Random House. Rushdie later described the Guardian story as 'provocative', presumably because it predicted that paperback publication, even now, was 'likely to inflame hardliners in Britain's Muslim community and elsewhere'. Happily the prediction was not borne out. In August a writer in the Guardian was able to say that publication had passed off 'with hardly a murmur'.

There were changes on a wider scale. Within a few months of the paperback publication Salman Rushdie was free, or relatively free. The front page of the Guardian on 25 September 1998 was a memorable one: 'Rushdie's nightmare is over: Iran disavows fatwa and bounty'. The leader the following day explained: 'For Britain, the end of the fatwa is a breakthrough - one for which the Foreign Secretary [the new Labour government's Robin Cook] deserves real credit ... Credit should also go to the Iranian people. Last year they elected a relative moderate as their president [Mohammad Khatami] - a clear signal to their leaders that they no longer wanted to be a pariah nation.'

For the Guardian, the Rushdie affair tested its liberal principles. On the safety of Salman Rushdie it was absolutely clear: it condemned the fatwa and declared that the state should protect him. On his right to publish *The Satanic Verses*, it was equally clear: he had a right to free thought and expression, subject to the law. But to what extent that right should be qualified or modified was a recurring question. Among the matters to be considered were: the principle of the right to offend; the necessity of trying to understand the nature of the offence to those who sincerely felt it; the murder of one translator and attempted murder of another; the deaths of a number of protesters in related riots; the fate of the western hostages in Iran and Lebanon; and the effect on minority populations and social cohesion at home in the United Kingdom. At stake was the very principle of free speech, which, as ever, the Guardian sought to protect and promote.[22]

The unlovely Guardian building in Farringdon Road in the mid-1980s. It stayed unchanged as Peter Preston presided over the paper through the whole 20 years of an innovatory editorship.

Melanie Phillips in 1985. Marked by Preston for stardom, she was a controversial choice as news editor before becoming an incisive columnist, sometimes shocking colleagues with her 'un-Guardian' views.

Hugo Young, political columnist and chair of the Scott Trust, with Paul Johnson (RIGHT) at the Press Awards in 1986, shortly before Johnson became news editor.

Andreas Whittam Smith (FRONT) and staff on the launch day of the Independent, October 1986. The Daily Telegraph was the expected target but it was Preston who found their tanks on his lawn.

The siege of Wapping, 1986: police and pickets clash after Murdoch migrated his papers there. Some of the 'refuseniks' found a new home for their energies at a welcoming Guardian.

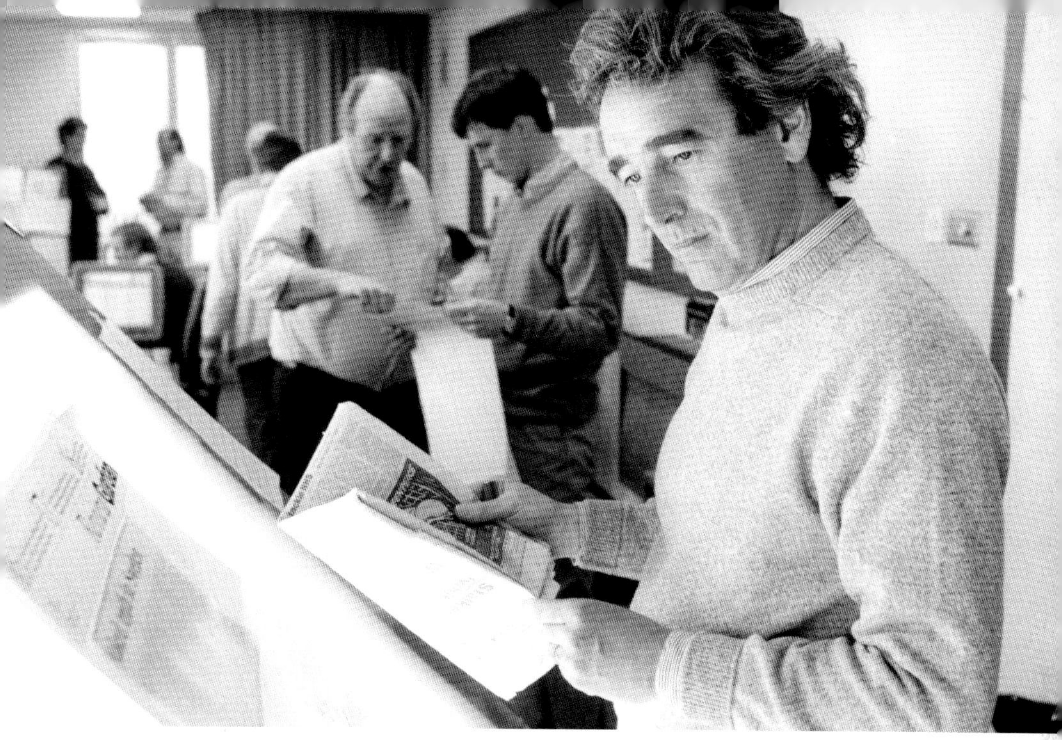

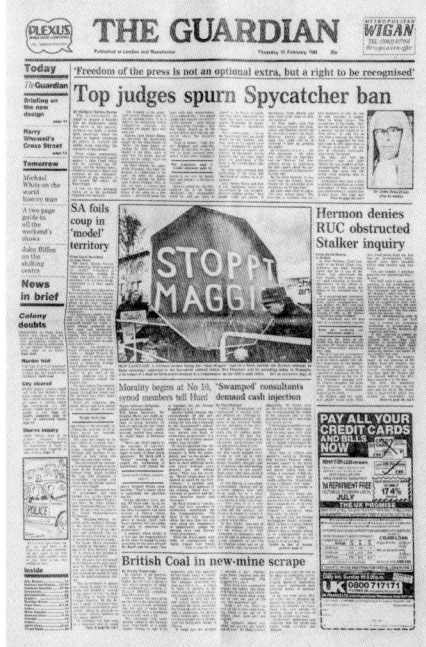

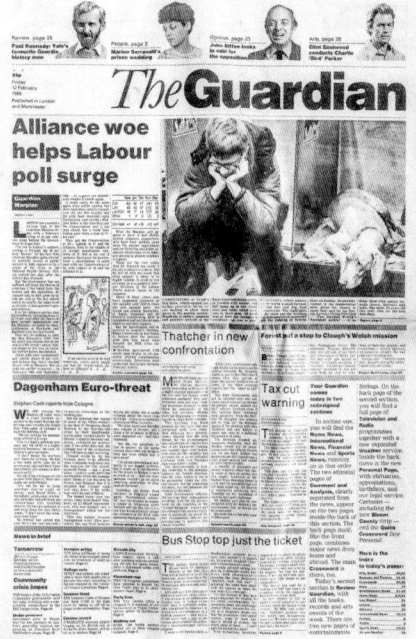

David Hillman at work on the redesign of 1988, the biggest in the paper's history up to then. In true Guardian fashion, not everyone approved.

THE GUARDIAN

Published in London and Manchester

Today

'Freedom of the press is not an optional extra, but a right to be recognised'

Top judges spurn Spycatcher ban

SA foils coup in 'model' territory

Hermon denies RUC obstructed Stalker inquiry

News in brief

Morality begins at No 10, synod members tell Hurd

'Swamped' consultants demand cash injection

British Coal in new-mine scrape

PAY ALL YOUR CREDIT CARDS AND BILLS NOW

The Guardian

Alliance woe helps Labour poll surge

Thatcher in new confrontation

Dagenham Euro-threat

Tax cut warning

Bus Stop top just the ticket

News in brief

Before and after the radical redesign. The first front page was unhelped by the hangdog picture, but Hillman's typographic innovations were soon widely copied.

ABOVE Louise Chunn arrived in 1989 as a modernising women's editor challenged with providing dynamic pages relevant to readers' lives in a rapidly changing world.

LEFT Deborah Orr, the first female editor of Weekend. Amid the glamour she provided a gritty commitment to the serious side of life, rooted perhaps in her Ravenscraig background.

The first front page of the revolutionary G2, 12 October 1992. In retrospect Alan Rusbridger thought it screamed, 'Don't read me!' But readers loved the idea of a serious tabloid.

Monday
12 October 1992

Media jobs start on page 18

Arts 8/9
Julie Burchill: why I write books

Architecture 4
On a wing and a stair: the buildings that think they can fly

Profile 10/11
Monsieur Habitat: after decades of marketing French design to the Brits, Sir Terence Conran is now flogging English coziness to the French.

Women 12/13
When your husband starts wearing your clothes

Obituaries 14
Victoria Lidiard: Suffragette

Media 15/17
Why the running dogs snapped: the Tory press falls out of bed with John Major

Television 32; Weather 30
Radio 31; Quick crossword 31

2
The Guardian

PHOTOGRAPH: SEAN SMITH

THE CEMETERIES are full. Now families dig up football pitches to bury their dead. Veronica Horwell experiences daily life under siege in Sarajevo

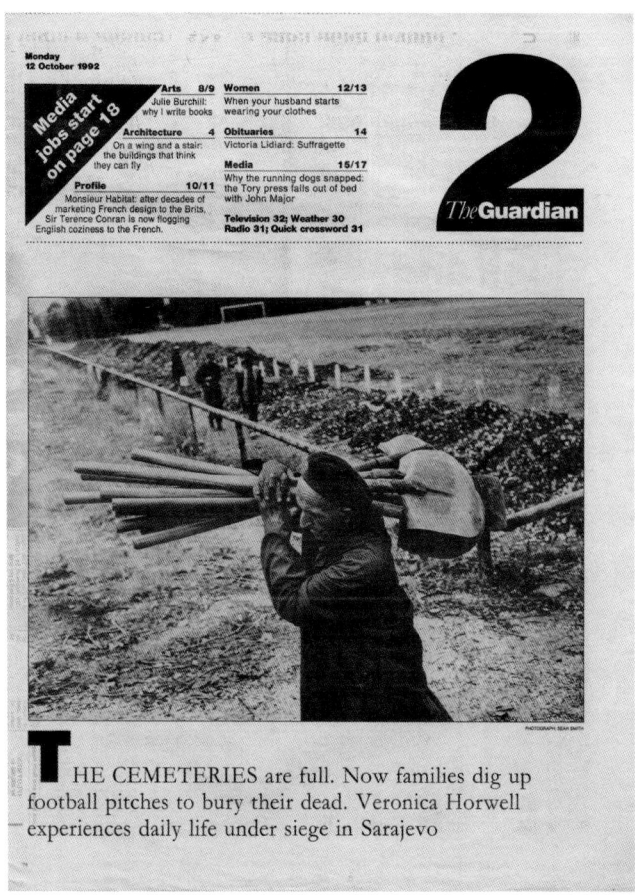

The tableau in the press room for the birth of G2:
(l to r) Camilla Nicholls; Jocelyn Targett; Brian Whitaker; Peter Preston; Jim Markwick; Alan Rusbridger; Ian Mayes.

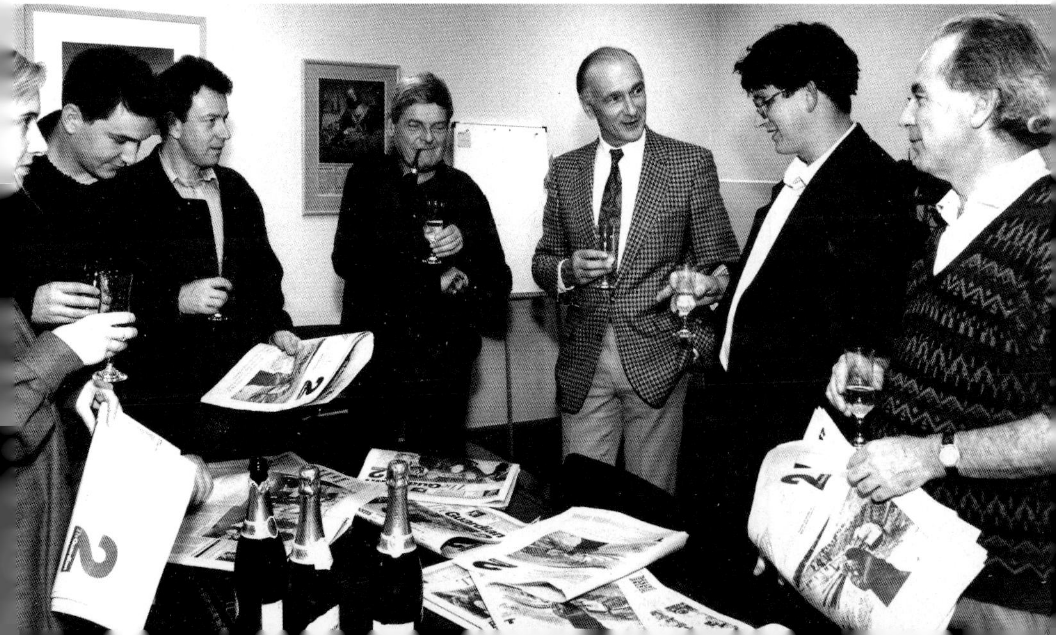

Matthew Engel in Kuwait, 1991, where he brought his distinctive descriptive powers to bear in the war that ousted Saddam Hussein's invading Iraqi army.

Maggie O'Kane in Bosnia, 1993. Her war reports so impressed Peter Preston that he said, 'Tell her there's a job on the Guardian waiting for her when she comes home.'

Donald Trelford and the staff of the Observer in the late 1980s, determined to fly the flag despite the intrusive ownership of Tiny Rowland.

Jonathan Fenby in 1993, the first editor of the Guardian-owned Observer. It was supposed to be 'a marriage made in heaven' but, despite Fenby's brave efforts, he resigned 'by mutual agreement' after 18 months.

ABOVE Peter Preston,
the editors' editor at his
desk in Farringdon Road
in 1994 - a stubbornly
courageous man, always
with the human touch
that endured through
thick and thin.

LEFT Alan Rusbridger,
c. 1994, Preston's choice
as his successor - and
the journalists' too. His
boyish look belied his
experience, energy and
flair for innovation.

Chapter 15

War over Kuwait: A Lion Among the Gazelles

'Was this the global community, the new world order,
enforcing its resolutions? Was this the era of peace and order,
in the wake of decades of Cold War, finally dawning?'

Guardian leader, 17 January 1991, as Desert Storm hits Iraq

The Guardian had not allowed the upheaval that had been taking place in Farringdon Road and in Fleet Street at large to limit its horizon. The strength of the Independent's foreign coverage had been an additional spur to its own, not that the Guardian's seasoned and vigilant foreign desk feared competition. Nevertheless, it was now about to intensify.

The Guardian in the late eighties had not failed to recognise the evils of the regime that Saddam Hussein presided over in Iraq. It had been quick to condemn as war criminals, for instance, those responsible in the closing months of the Iran-Iraq war for the poison gas attack on the Iraqi Kurdish town of Halabja. Several thousand people, overwhelmingly civilians, died agonised deaths in the attack on 18 March 1988. The paper's vastly experienced man in the Middle East, David Hirst, had been among the few western journalists helicoptered to the scene by the occupying Iranian forces. His detailed report on the front page of the Guardian was, as the leading article that followed it said, 'unusually horrifying, even in an age of worldwide public violence'.[1] The editorial described the attack as an act of genocide against the Kurdish people.

Two years after Halabja, when the Iranian-born freelance journalist Farzad Bazoft, working for the Observer, was hanged in Abu Ghraib prison in Baghdad - a prison yet to plunge to the full depth of its notoriety - accused of spying for Israel, attention was again focused, to quote the Guardian's leader, 'on one of the world's most savage regimes'. 'Mr Saddam and his crew are thugs', it concluded.[2]

Sanctions, in essential partnership with diplomacy, remained the Guardian's strongly preferred response to the brutal excesses of the regime. That remained the case as the war that Saddam, and not only Saddam, seemed bent on instigating over Kuwait loomed larger from the summer of 1990. When Saddam began his massive movement of troops to Iraq's border with the emirate, an area sweltering in a heatwave with unusually high temperatures soaring over 50C, the Guardian, practically alone among British newspapers, continued to urge the case for cool diplomacy. Its position was spelled out and reiterated in a long sequence of leaders, very often written by John Gittings but in many cases by the editor, Peter Preston.

The paper stood firmly against the use of force, even after Saddam Hussein had chosen invasion as his way to resolve disputes with Kuwait over national debt and oil and territory. The historian of the Times was right when he described the Guardian as 'the most reluctant convert' to the use of force to drive Saddam Hussein away from his prey.[3] But Saddam, with his appetite and regional ambitions, was a lion among the gazelles, as David Hirst would describe him, a lion made more dangerous by the physical, psychological and economic wounds suffered in eight years of bloody war with Iran.

On the eve of the invasion, Gittings had collated what the Guardian regarded as the impossible financial demands that Saddam was then making. As the leader noted, 'The total shakedown could be of the order of 25 billion dollars (plus tracts of territory and oil wells), which is a lot to have extracted from your wallet on a quiet day.' Talks in Jeddah had failed. It seemed the lion had already decided to leap.

The front page of the Guardian the following day, Friday 3 August, told the story that even then not everyone had been expecting: 'Superpowers unite on Iraq: Overwhelmed Kuwaiti forces continue to fight invaders'. No one seriously expected Kuwait by itself to offer significant resistance. Iraq, even after the depletions of the war with Iran, still had an army of around a million to call upon. The number serving in the armed forces of Kuwait at the time of the invasion was about 20,000: as gazelles go, the emirate was little more than a juicy morsel.

Among those caught by surprise by the invasion of 2 August, it would transpire, was the United States. Towards the end of the month, the investigative journalists Bob Woodward (of Watergate fame) and Rick Atkinson would be able to piece together the American reaction to the invasion in a carefully researched piece for the Washington Post, also carried in the Guardian. The article related, in the words of its subheading, 'how Bush's advisers were caught on the hop',[4] despite the Pentagon's monitoring of the build-up of Iraqi forces on the Kuwaiti border. Once the invasion had taken place, President Bush's deliberations still went on for 115 hours, Woodward and Atkinson reported with some precision.

The Guardian, in the first leader after the invasion, headed 'Paying the price for past error',[5] called for all legitimate means short of military action to be used against Saddam's regime. 'The isolation of Saddam Hussein should in theory be a relatively easy matter for instant and collective resolve.'

Elsewhere in this edition, David Hirst predicted: 'A military response seems improbable. Six US warships have gone on alert in the Gulf. But the Iraqi leadership have threatened to "make a graveyard" of Kuwait should anyone try to prise it from them ... Sanctions would appear to be the only option. The most effective would of course be a boycott of Iraqi and Kuwait oil production.'

That was Saturday. On Monday 6 August, the improbable military response suddenly looked possible. The front-page lead read: 'Bush hints at military action against Iraq'. At the United Nations, the Security Council was locked in talks over 'an almost unprecedented package of measures against Iraq', as the Guardian's Washington correspondent, Simon Tisdall, reported. The sanctions, including a worldwide arms and oil embargo, were imposed later that day. Fears were already growing that Saddam, pumped up by the ease with which he had gobbled up Kuwait, might be entertaining wilder thoughts about Saudi Arabia and the oil wells that lay not so far over its border.

John Gittings was again entrusted with the leader and once more he advocated a peaceful solution. 'Frustration in the Gulf leads temptingly to the invocation of task forces and tactical bombing, but the military option is no option at all. The emergence yesterday of a potential hostage problem of vast dimensions only emphasised that this is far too complex a crisis for gunboat diplomacy. Loose talk of "carpet-bombing" Baghdad should be put back in the bottle of theoretical but unacceptable scenarios.'

During the next few days things began to move with 'frightening speed', as Martin Woollacott wrote on 8 August. The headline that day read: 'US troops heading for Saudi'. The following day's front page reported that the UK was following suit. A huge coalition force was being assembled, ostensibly for defensive purposes to deter an 'imminent' Iraqi attack on Saudi Arabia.

The media on both sides of the Atlantic were now moving on to a familiar war footing, with some of the coverage in Britain strongly reminding the leader writer on 11 August – David McKie – of the rhetoric of a previous conflict. The Sun set the standard, running a front page (9 August) with the Union Jack and the Stars and Stripes together and the massive headline: 'Our boys go in'. McKie wrote: 'Suddenly we are back with "Rejoice" and "Here we go" and "Gotcha". It's the Falklands war all over again.'

By the middle of August the Guardian was confidently of the opinion that the United States, however much it emphasised a defensive role for the coalition that it was now vigorously canvassing, was marching to a different drummer. A leader declared: 'Washington has left no room for doubt that it wants Saddam removed from (a) Kuwait, (b) the presidency of Iraq, and (c) this mortal coil. Its motive is to protect its oil supply, however much it may also be concerned to support its loyal and terrified Saudi ally.' The leader is attributed in the cuttings file to David McKie and Dan van der Vat, a Guardian journalist since the early 1980s and at that time beginning a parallel career as a military historian.

At the end of the month Mrs Thatcher recalled parliament for a two-day emergency debate on the Gulf crisis. Thatcher was, metaphorically speaking, once again in tank turret mode (an image that Les Gibbard used in his cartoon to accompany the report of the debate). Only a handful of Labour leftwingers, led by Tony Benn, opposed the military option. A vote gave the government a majority of 402.

On 24 September King Hussein of Jordan wrote a front-page article for the Guardian beneath the somewhat histrionic headline, 'King Hussein says world is stumbling into replay of 1914 war'. It misconstrued the point he was making, which was that it was the process, with the ineffectiveness of the diplomatic efforts, that the world seemed to be in danger of replaying rather than anything comparable to the First World War itself. 'Are we embarked on a noble mission to establish a new world order of peace and justice and the abolition of aggression? Or are we witnessing a replay of the quixotic events of August 1914, when the world stumbled into a war it did not want but could not stop? Let us hope that a new world order can be established, but its foundation must be based on conciliation, not conflagration, and on distributive, not selective, justice and morality.'

By now it was estimated that more than 1,000 British citizens were being held hostage in Iraq. Edward Heath flew to Baghdad via Amman in mid-October and his progress was chronicled by Patrick Wintour, who would spend the rest of the month in Baghdad. David Austin, whose pocket cartoons on the front page ran in fine form throughout the crisis, depicted a biblical Heath in Arab dress making the reasonable request, 'Let a few of my people go.' A couple of days later, Heath was able to fly out with 38 British hostages. The modesty of his achievement was underlined by the almost simultaneous release of more than 200 French hostages.

Both Hugo Young and Ed Pearce made a similar point on the comment pages. Young, in a column headed, 'Averting our gaze from the blood of war', wrote: 'No modern war has been so deliberately prepared for as the one that now seems about to happen ... The closer war looms the less we want to look it clinically in the eye.' Ed Pearce, writing the following day, in a column headed 'Monstrous anger of the guns' (echoing the First World War poetry of Wilfred Owen), began, 'I make no apology for the fact that like Hugo Young yesterday I mean to go on about the unacknowledged horrors of a war our rulers plan to fight with the gay hearts of children preparing for a party. In a climate of shallow abandon, two of us dissenting is not too many.'

Before the month was out, Margaret Thatcher had stood down and John Major had taken over. On 29 November, the Security Council authorised the American-led coalition to use force to drive the Iraqis out of Kuwait unless they withdrew by 15 January. A glimmer of hope that war might still be averted was raised at the beginning of December when Bush offered to receive the Iraqi foreign minister Tariq Aziz in Washington and to send US secretary of state James Baker to talk to Saddam Hussein in Baghdad. Gittings welcomed what on the face of it seemed to be an eleventh-hour change of tactics by the Americans, at the same time arguing that the time frame was unnecessarily tight. 'This is real war we are talking about, not games in the sandpit. The world has at least six weeks. The Guardian would have preferred to wait at least six months.' Iraq accepted the offer of talks. It also made the surprise announcement that it would release all the many hundreds of foreign hostages it had detained.

'The pieces begin to fall for peace' was the headline on Preston's leader on 7 December. 'Now, with luck and judgment, there need not be a war.' Preston declared that new evidence made it absolutely clear that sanctions were working, a point that Gittings underlined in his leader ten days later: 'Why don't the allies trumpet this success? Why don't they repeatedly hail the economic noose that unprecedentedly effective, concerted world action has slipped around the transgressor's neck? ... Sanctions have idiotically become a code word for "appeasement" in the current context.'

John Ezard went to Baghdad to cover the release of the hostages, and his reports appeared on the front page on 10 and 11 December. It was on 11 December that Ian Katz made his debut in the Guardian. As we saw in an earlier chapter, he had been on the British Airways Boeing 767 that had gone to pick up some of the hostages. None of it had gone smoothly, from from his own anxieties about his visa onwards. The Iraqis refused permission for the plane to land in Baghdad. It sat first on the tarmac at Amman. Then it flew to Frankfurt, where it finally collected its passengers and presented them with the challenge of drinking 400 quarter-bottles of champagne on the 90-minute flight to London.

On 9 January 1991, six hours of peace talks in Geneva, covered by Hella Pick, produced nothing. Baker told a news conference, 'We are now at the point of war.' The sentence - a ready-made headline - ran across the width of the front page the following day. Saddam Hussein in Baghdad warned that if US troops launched an attack to liberate Kuwait he would 'make them swim in their own blood'. There was more than a touch of pathos in Martin Woollacott's front-page Eyewitness dispatch from Baghdad. It was, he reported, a day like any other, or at least the pretence of one. '"Nothing important has happened here today," a government driver said. "People are shopping, working, walking in the streets, doing their jobs. That's all."' The Guardian declined to abandon all hope. 'If there is the chance of a peaceful settlement, it will come not at the eleventh hour, but at the twelfth or even the thirteenth.'

At the end of the first week in January the media editor, Georgina Henry, looked at the way in which the world's journalists had been drawing their own battle lines. 'If it comes to war with Iraq, two things will distinguish the media coverage from previous wars. One is the technology: the Gulf area is already bristling with satellites which have been transmitting news of the crisis for five months and there is the potential, as never before, for continuous television coverage of events. The second is the number of journalists from different countries on the ground: this will not be a war like the Falklands, witnessed only by British journalists controlled by the Ministry of Defence under the longstanding conventions of government secrecy. Other countries which make up the allied force have more liberal attitudes to a journalist's right to ask questions, although it is already clear that Washington, after its experience in Vietnam, is trying to take a more British approach to media control ... Journalists who want to go to the front, in the case of British journalists, in "media response teams" (MRTs), have already been told they will work under ground rules laid down by the military authorities and have their pictures and reports "vetted" by military personnel ... Already there are signs of tension over organisation and rules.'[6]

The drama of the countdown to expiry of the deadline for Iraq to withdraw from Kuwait was perfectly captured in the pages of the Guardian, not least in the leaders. Readers who turned to the leader page on 15 January found the Guardian's view expressed in a long editorial, unsigned of course, but in fact by Preston. 'Let us explain, one more time, why the first allied policy - sanctions and a defensive ring - seemed the right one to this paper,' he wrote. 'Take the CIA's own figures. Ninety-seven per cent of Iraqi exports have stopped. Saddam's life support system is cut. It is only a matter of time before sanctions bring him down. Ah, the immediate counter cry, but how long could you give that first, more peaceful policy? Three months? A year? Three years? It is a facile debating point, easily turned upon the proponents of war. How many casualties are they prepared to endure? Three thousand? Thirty thousand? How long are they prepared to fight for? Three days, or months, or years? How much of Kuwait City are they prepared to flatten in the exercise, the liberators of Dresden?'

A great deal about the Guardian of the time, and indeed about its editor, is to be found in that leader. The views expressed in it were at odds with, among others, those of Hugo Young voiced on the adjacent page under the headline: 'Brutal price that has to be paid'. 'Sanctions,' Young declared, 'are the all-round moralist's alternative. Caring, agonised citizens, deeply anxious not to appease Saddam, hang on to them as a golden promise, the perfect instrument of his painless destruction. But unfortunately this skirts too easily past aspects of the real world.'

The war started on the night of 16 January. All other news was swept from the front page of the Guardian for the following day, Thursday 17 January, an edition produced in the early hours of the morning. A stark headline ran across the top: 'Desert Storm hits Iraq'. The report was put together from agencies in Baghdad - most of the western media having been expelled - and by David Fairhall in Riyadh, and Larry Elliott and Martin Walker in Washington.

There were few foreign journalists in Baghdad. Among those allowed to remain were the staff of US 24-hour station Cable News Network (CNN), whose correspondents, John Holliman and Peter Arnett, were able to broadcast live from their ninth-floor hotel room in the al-Rashid hotel in the centre of the city. The Guardian carried graphic snatches from their commentary as an Eyewitness column at the foot of the front page. Explosions ringed the city - some close enough to rock the hotel - as they described the anti-aircraft and tracer fire rising into the night sky.

The CNN team became very possessive about their equipment, causing Alfonso Rojo of El Mundo, whose reports were being shared on a reciprocal arrangement with the Guardian, to complain a week into the war that Arnett had refused to let him file via the channel's satellite telephone line. Rojo, the last western newspaper reporter left in Baghdad, claimed, 'He has not even allowed me to tell the paper where I am and how I am, with the excuse that we are in competition.'[7]

The leader writer who had been kept up late to respond to the onset of the war was again Preston himself. His leader was headed: 'Suddenly the sky turns orange'. The report began: 'So, with scant pause, with no let or hindrance, it begins. Desert Shield turns to Desert Storm in the middle of America's evening news bulletins. There could, in terms of United States opinion, be no more dramatic moment ... There is an instant feeling of a war like no other in history, a war of demonstration and of orchestration ... Was this the global community, the new world order, enforcing its resolutions? Was this the era of peace and order, in the wake of decades of Cold War, finally dawning? We who have watched over the months in some anguish, and know in the end where we stand on the arguments, must also feel a chill as we confront those questions.

The world, at prime time for television, in sadness and apprehension, has embarked on a new chapter.'

Coverage of the war throughout the paper on the following day, 18 January, added up to around 30,000 words, mainly spread over 12 pages. Preston's leader outlined the military strategy so far. 'First, using every resource of high technology, pound Iraq from the air. Pound airfields and missile sites. Pound communications centres. And then, as necessary, pound the hundreds of thousands of Iraqi troops dug deep into trenches along the Kuwait border: blasting them to smithereens. This is the "softening up". Only when the enemy has been suitably softened - it may be days, it may be weeks - are we likely to see the inevitable infantry and marine attack that will seek to reclaim Kuwait.'

Not all was going the coalition's way. There were losses, among them at least four of the RAF's Tornado fighter-bombers. The two-man crew of one of them had been captured and paraded on Iraqi television with five other coalition aircrew. On 19 January the reporter David Sharrock, whose dispatches from the Gulf throughout the conflict were a model of their kind, contributed an extraordinary Eyewitness to the front page. It was headlined: 'Tornado pilots tell of lost friends and fear of dying'. Three RAF crew members who had lost members of their squadron confessed to something that British servicemen were not supposed to be susceptible to: one broke down in tears while talking to Sharrock. Pictures of the RAF prisoners were run across the front page on 22 January beneath the headline 'Bush rage at human shield', a response to the news broadcast by Baghdad radio that prisoners of war were being placed as shields against attack on strategic targets. An ominous paragraph in the accompanying report by Martin Walker in Washington, with Hella Pick and John Mullin, read: 'Mr Bush's fury and an incensed US public opinion may now rule out any prospect of an interim diplomatic solution or a ceasefire. It is likely to widen the US war aim from the liberation of Kuwait to the elimination of President Saddam, and war crimes trials for Iraq's leaders.'

Finding and destroying Iraq's mobile Scud launchers became a very high priority as further missiles landed on Tel Aviv. Washington urged restraint. At least for the time being, Israel seemed prepared to accept that a retaliatory strike might well damage the coalition more than it damaged Iraq. The search for the Scuds took a desperate turn when it was suggested that some of the Scud launchers, hardly more conspicuous in the desert than an individual grain of sand, might actually be decoys constructed of plywood and cardboard. On 24 January, David Austin's front-page cartoon showed an RAF pilot returning from a mission over Iraq triumphantly telling his commanding officer, 'We've taken out the cardboard factory, Skipper.'

Bizarrely, given the Guardian's dogged anti-war stance, the photo-montage artist Peter Clarke was indirectly responsible for the paper's unlikely participation in the Gulf War in the form of a Jaguar ground-at-tack bomber with its nose labelled in four-inch letters *The*Guardian*Reader*. The pilot, Squadron Leader Mike Rondot, was a friend of Clarke's and the cartoonist had sent him a Guardian T-shirt and a copy of the paper, asking him to have his photograph taken with them in the cockpit of his aeroplane. Apparently Clarke had wanted to annoy anti-war colleagues. One thing had led to another. During Desert Storm Rondot flew 29 combat missions in *The*Guardian*Reader*. This was not something that the Guardian bragged very loudly about: there were a couple of mentions in Andrew Moncur's Diary.

The allied pilots were certainly kept busy. The 50,000 crack Iraqi troops - members of the Republican Guard - dug in around Kuwait were subjected to a relentless pounding from B-52 bombers. An Iraqi incur-sion into Saudi Arabia at the end of January only added to the urgency. The Iraqis set fire to Kuwaiti refineries, and, as John Vidal reported early in February, two huge converging oil slicks were threatening the fragile ecology of the Gulf. A ground war was now inevitable.

Paul Webster, the foreign editor, did his best to penetrate to the reality of the war - a reality masked by the carefully controlled presentation of it as an affair of hi-tech and practically bloodless precision - by setting some of the Guardian's best journalists on the task. Among them were David Beresford, in 'normal' times the paper's South Africa correspondent, and Matthew Engel, a writer of distinctive descriptive power. Beresford, inci-dentally, was not a 'pool' reporter required to share his dispatches with other publications in exchange for a certain amount of privileged but supervised access to the fighting. As a non-pooled Guardian correspond-ent he was theoretically free to roam outside certain forbidden areas. In fact he encountered no objection to his entering those as well. Various experiences that he recounted in a book almost a decade later led him to believe that the free-range journalists were subject to just as much official effort to manipulate their reports as the rest. 'The pool positions, although much fought-over, would have been distrusted by editors, in that they were completely controlled by the military. So let loose 1,000 more "irregulars", make them feel that they were independent and feed them with lies.'[8]

Webster also had the services, already noted, of El Mundo's Alfonso Rojo. On 11 February, Eyewitness reports by Beresford and Rojo ran side by side, but from opposite sides of the conflict. Beresford was in Saudi Arabia, and his piece – headlined 'Arab blood brothers in war' – opened with the unusual scene of an Egyptian colonel and Iraqi lieutenant and colonel amiably sitting together and discussing military positions. Beresford went on, '[The] sense of identification between Arab forces facing each other across the front lines is almost palpable. The Egyptian troops rarely, if ever, refer to the Iraqis as the "enemy", reserving their antipathy for President Saddam. A young captain in the mechanised infantry told me how another group of Iraqis had surrendered to them last week after a shouting match across the desert. "Are you American, or Egyptian?" the Iraqis had yelled. "Why?" shouted back the Egyptians. "Because the Americans shoot, the Egyptians will not." "Egyptians!" "OK, we're coming."'

Alfonso Rojo, meanwhile, was making the hazardous journey south. 'The 400-mile ride south from Baghdad to Basra is an adventure in itself. Every time you see the smoking carcases of vehicles blasted from the air the previous night – the travelling bomb in which you are riding, its boot filled with four jerrycans of precious black-market petrol, hardly bears thinking about.' At Basra he checked into an empty, candlelit Sheraton hotel. '"Don't get worried when the Americans turn on their discotheque [the nightly bombardment] at 8.30, 12.30 and 4.30," says the maid, pointing to the roof.'

The war in the beginning and the end was one-sided. As David Sharrock put it, 'Public opinion on what is taking place, as seen so far through the eyes of pilots and the censored images of airborne video recorders, may have greater difficulty tolerating an exercise which every day more resembles shooting fish in a barrel.'[9]

On a typical day, Sharrock reported, allied aircraft carried out 650 raids on the area. Inevitably, a civilian disaster soon occurred. On 13

February a pair of 2,000lb laser-guided 'smart' bombs dropped by two US F-117 stealth bombers penetrated a shelter in a suburb of Baghdad and incinerated some 400 civilians, many of them women and children. The US claimed it had been an Iraqi military command control bunker. The evidence was otherwise. Alfonso Rojo, now back in Baghdad, was among those who went to the scene. His Eyewitness account appeared on the front page. 'From time to time, firemen, their faces blackened by the smoke, would emerge dragging a blanket full of human remains and throw it into the back of a lorry. The corpses, which looked as if they were made of pumice, were very small and seemed to have been shrunk by the heat of the fire. When the lorry was full, it started off for the Yarmuk hospital where a group of women, with their heads covered, laid out the corpses in the yard – 47 black bundles laid out in a line.' The leader ran: 'This is a moment of truth ... You cannot, in the words of one US pilot yesterday, "see miles of blackened earth and bomb craters" below without killing people. You cannot pound Baghdad or Basra from on high, daily, without dire consequences.'

On the comment pages that day the distinguished American professor of psychiatry Robert Jay Lifton wrote: 'The communications revolution has taken us amazingly close to the war zone but, psychologically speaking, further than ever from the war ... This form of dissociation can be called psychic numbing, the diminished capacity or inclination to feel.'[10]

Several days later it was revealed that the Al Amiriya shelter had not been the only civilian area disastrously hit that day, 13 February, by coalition bombing. A bomb dropped by a British Tornado had veered off target and hit the crowded marketplace in Fallujah, killing up to 130.

During the following week, last-ditch talks in Moscow failed to bring about a pause in preparations for the ground war. Bush swept them aside with a blunt order to Iraq to get out of Kuwait by noon (5pm GMT) on 23 February. The Guardian leader that day continued to insist that peace should be given a chance: 'Diplomacy must not be allowed to turn to dust ... Mr Bush had an air yesterday of stepping forward as the commander of a war which no longer needed referral to wider international judgment.'[11]

In the printed press, it fell to the Sunday papers to report the massive allied assault – the biggest since the Second World War – that began at 1am

GMT, two hours before dawn in the Gulf and eight hours after the expiry of the deadline, as late editions of the Observer reported. The Guardian headline on Monday was: 'Iraqis reel under invasion'. The coalition forces made rapid advance amid many thousands of surrendering Iraqis. Matthew Engel crossed from Saudi Arabia with Kuwaiti soldiers, having camped in the desert with them. They were a 'raggle-taggle force of escapers and exiles' who were returning to reclaim their country. As they came to the border, Engel asked the Kuwaiti commander whether he had any fear. 'He looked bewildered. "I have no fear," he said, "I am going home."'

The front pages conveyed the swift progress of the action. Tuesday 26 February: Baghdad 'issues order for troops to leave Kuwait'. Wednesday 27 February: 'Allies go in for the kill'. Thursday 28 February: 'Bush halts Gulf action and states his terms'. A down-page story on Thursday's front contained clues to the wider horror of the past day or two. The headline summarised something that General Norman Schwarzkopf, leader of the coalition forces, had said, 'The gates are closed ... there are no ways out.'

A sentence in the story hinted at the monstrous reality. 'In the narrowing neck of land leading out of Kuwait to the north, a river of Iraqi vehicles fled for home, pounded continuously by allied warplanes in what one pilot called "a turkey shoot".' This was the so-called Highway of Death. The most graphic account of it published in the Guardian appeared on page six on 4 March, taken from the New York Times, written by Joseph Albright and Marcia Kunstel. The opening paragraph: 'Kuwaiti looters and a few US soldiers strolled down the blasted and burned highway of death on Saturday, like picky shoppers in a macabre 10-mile-long mall. They held their noses as they passed charred bodies rotting inside the twisted tanks, trucks, fire engines, ambulances and luxury cars commandeered by Iraqi soldiers desperate to make a quick getaway. The fleeing Iraqis ran into fierce air and ground allied attacks. When the lead vehicles in the cavalcade were stopped by the shooting, traffic backed up for 10 miles, only to be blasted by more air attacks from the rear.'

The Observer the day before this appeared in the Guardian had conveyed in a single image what it called in the headline that ran above it, 'The real face of war'. The caption is sufficient to evoke it for anyone who saw it: 'The charred head of an Iraqi soldier leans through the windscreen of his burnt-out vehicle, attacked during the retreat from Kuwait'. The photograph, by Kenneth Jarecke, failed to find a publisher in the

American media.[12] Only the Observer published it in Britain.

The burned Iraqi pecked at the conscience. On 18 March the Guardian devoted half of its comment page to the first publication of a poem by Tony Harrison that had been inspired by the image, titled 'A Cold Coming', which opened with the lines: 'I saw the charred Iraqi lean towards me from bomb-blasted screen'. It was in fact the second of Harrison's Gulf War poems to be published in the Guardian. The first, 'Initial Illumination', had appeared a couple of weeks earlier.

Alan Rusbridger, in a contribution a few years later to a Festschrift for Harrison on his 60th birthday, wrote, 'We carried the poems on the main editorial page since it seemed to us important that they be seen as a commentary on current events and not as a piece of contemporary Eng Lit, which would undoubtedly have been the case had they been consigned to the arts or features pages.' Carrying the poems in this way, Rusbridger wrote, 'was such a success that we asked Tony Harrison to accept a regular retainer in return for a few poems a year on contemporary themes; in effect to be the Guardian's Poet Laureate'.[13]

On 3 April 1991, the UN Security Council passed its wide-ranging Resolution 687 setting the terms with which Iraq now had to comply, including the destruction of all chemical and biological weapons, a ban on the development of nuclear weapons, and granting access to UN inspectors to confirm that the steps demanded had been taken. Martin Walker commented, 'The implications of the small print of UN Resolution 687 – passed last week and by far the longest such resolution ever to emerge from the Security Council – are only now being fully understood. It extends international law, widens the rights of intrusion into the internal affairs of UN member states, lays down precedents for the role of the UN, and is described by senior US officials as "the first legal basis" for President Bush's new world order.'[14]

On 28 February 1991, the day the Guardian announced in its headline, 'Bush halts Gulf action and states his terms', Austin's pocket cartoon summed up the new reality. It showed two diplomats conferring, one saying to the other: 'It's the New World Order. The New World gives the orders.'

Chapter 16
Order, Disorder and the Message from Mesopotamia

'Out of these troubled times ... a new world order can emerge:
a new era - freer from the threat of terror, stronger in the
pursuit of justice, and more secure in the quest for peace.'

George HW Bush, 11 September 1990

The Guardian's 'New World Order?' series ran over three weeks in March and April 1991. It was an enterprise of Rusbridger's features desk, still responsible at that time for the daily Comment and Analysis pages. There had been causes for optimism. Waves of euphoria had followed such events as the fall of the Berlin Wall in November 1989 and the release of Nelson Mandela in February 1990. George HW Bush and Mikhail Gorbachev at the Helsinki summit in September 1990 had jointly opened the prospect of a new world order based on international cooperation. They did so as the clock ticked on the UN deadline for Saddam Hussein to withdraw his forces from Kuwait. In October the reunification of Germany was formally concluded. As we have seen, the brief and, so far as it went, brutally effective Gulf War of January and February 1991 expelled the Iraqi dictator from Kuwait but left him free to turn vindictively on the elements in his country that the west had encouraged to rebel, in particular the Kurds of northern Iraq. Six months later the rump of Moscow's old guard would mount a coup in an attempt to unseat Gorbachev and by the end of the year the Soviet Union had ceased to exist. It was in the midst of these changes that the 'New World Order?' series was commissioned, with seven leading contributors offering their assessments.

The series opened with an essay by Denis Healey, who through most of the Thatcher years had been the shadow foreign secretary. He provided a lucid and hardly optimistic view of Bush's conduct during the Gulf War. He concluded: 'The United Nations must be the foundation of any New World Order, if only because some of the major problems of the next century will defy handling on a purely regional basis.'[1]

Bleak though this was, Noam Chomsky presented a much bleaker picture, summing up the central message from the White House as 'We are the masters, and you shine our shoes.'[2] He mocked the intellectual community's response to the war: 'When Bush announced that there would be no negotiations, a hundred editorials lauded him for his extraordinary efforts at diplomacy. When he proclaimed that "aggressors cannot be rewarded", instead of collapsing in ridicule responsible commentators stood in awe of his high principles ... In such ways, the ground was prepared for the merciless slaughter.'

JK Galbraith, at the time emeritus professor of economics at Harvard, argued that poverty had to be addressed as a prime source of world disorder. He also declared that 'the UN must be a great deal more than it is now. It cannot, as in the Gulf war, be the justifying instrument of American policy. It must have a higher authority of its own.'[3]

The fourth article in the series was arguably the most important since it was the only one that came from an Arab writer. Abdelrahman Munif, 'one of the foremost novelists of the Arab world',[4] had become a writer in his early 40s. Such is the lack of curiosity for the culture of the Arab world in the educated English-speaking world that little of Munif's large output has been made available to the English reader, although it has been translated into more than 10 languages. Munif was the son of a Saudi Arabian father and an Iraqi mother. He was brought up in Jordan and studied law in Iraq, but was later expelled for political activity. He was also stripped of his Saudi nationality for similar reasons. It became something of a pattern that he would share with his books, which were also banned from several Arab countries. His contribution to the Guardian series (translated by Atif Saweries) pretty well justified the whole exercise.[5] It began by saying that the war in the Gulf was the worst possible start for any 'new' world order. 'The new world order that ordinary people seek is one free from the fear of weapons and wars, an order based on cooperation, mutual exchange, and equality. Its fundamental basis would be democracy, the safeguarding of human rights, and protection from pollution, epidemics, and everything that threatens humanity now or in the future.'

It was also something of a coup to persuade Eduard Shevardnadze to contribute to the series, achieved with the help of the Guardian's Moscow staff. Shevardnadze had resigned as Gorbachev's foreign minister in December 1990. He was known for his almost unique accessibility to journalists for a Soviet politician at his level, but if he readily gave interviews he very rarely wrote directly for the press himself.[6] He was an admirer of the Guardian and asked to be paid with a year's subscription to the English edition of the paper, and that was arranged.

He was frank about the current problems in the Soviet Union. 'The very fabric of our civil society has been torn apart by philosophical divisions and irreconcilable attitudes. [But] I strongly disagree with those people in my country who suppose that force and punishment are the best means of restoring law and order. To the same degree, I cannot support the point of view that force can safeguard international peace and stability.' He was another who advocated a strengthened and extended role for the United Nations to deal with the threat posed by weapons of mass destruction and to regulate the arms race.

The series concluded with articles by Francis Fukuyama and Theo Sommer.[7] Fukuyama suggested that one strong lesson from the Gulf War for any potentially aggressive rising regime was that there were no military short cuts to becoming a modern country, 'no escape from the dull work of economic development'. The world would continue to be subject to bloody struggles and revolutions but they would have little impact, he predicted, on the growing part of the world that was democratic and capitalist.

Theo Sommer, the author of the final article in the series, was editor-in-chief of the influential German newspaper Die Zeit and also held several academic and government posts concerned with defence and international relations. He swiftly rejected any notion that the Gulf War had ushered in George Bush's promised New World Order. That, he said, 'lost its moral underpinning when the Kurds were callously left to Saddam Hussein's slaughter squads'.

The Gulf War, he said, was 'a sideshow of secondary importance. The most significant event of the past few years was the end of communism and the dismantling of what used to be the Iron Curtain. Now that it has finally happened, it must be the primary task of all Europeans to help the two long-divided halves of Europe grow together again.'

The question for the Guardian was how to cover these challenges to global stability in such fast-changing times. For three of their leading foreign correspondents - Martin Woollacott, Jonathan Steele and a younger colleague, James Meek - this quest led them to the very heart of the historic events that dominated the headlines in the immediate aftermath of the Iraq war.

In April 1991, the terrible consequences of the war were still unfolding. Martin Woollacott had been in the Middle East for several weeks, for some time in a hotel in Amman where David Hirst was also staying, somewhat to the consternation of the cost-conscious managing editor Ian Wright, fretting in Farringdon Road. Wright, like Woollacott, went back a long way. Both had reported from the Vietnam War and both had been foreign editors. Now, as managing editor, Wright was responsible for budgetary control, and the cost of keeping two journalists on the periphery of the action was beginning to worry him. The investment, however, was about to prove worthwhile.

Paul Webster, the foreign editor, set the scene: 'It was the chaotic end of the Gulf War. Saddam Hussein had unleashed his troops against the Kurdish uprising and we were beginning to get reports of great bloodshed. Somewhere in the middle of this awful mess was Martin. He had more or less disappeared. It was a very worrying and dramatic time because for days we simply didn't hear from him. I became more and more alarmed and was in contact with Mori, Martin's wife, and in constant discussions with Ian Wright and Peter Preston about how we should respond. Finally, they were sighted. We got a call from ABC News [whose correspondent Charles Glass was with Woollacott]. The caller said they'd been spotted somewhere in Kurdistan and that they were safe and they were trying to get back across the border into Turkey. They'd crossed the whole of northern Iraq.'[8]

For Woollacott, in fact, the story had begun in Damascus rather than Amman.[9] 'Giving up on trying to get into Iraq from Jordan, I went to Syria where a small group of us, including Jon Randal of the Washington Post, Charlie Glass, Julie Flint of the Observer, and Geraldine Brooks of the Wall Street Journal, managed to secure the help of Jalal Talabani, the Kurdish leader in exile there. With *laissez passer* from him we drove to the northeast of Syria and crossed the Tigris into Iraq on makeshift boats.

'We had (primitive) computers but communications in Iraqi Kurdistan were almost non-existent, so they were useless. Satellite phone calls involved a huge, cumbrous, and unreliable piece of equipment, which only ITV had – you needed a Land Rover or a jeep to transport it. I only got one piece out by satellite and that was thanks to a Kurdish satellite that they let us use on one day only. The other copy went out by Kurdish couriers to the Iranian border and thence to Tehran and on to cable there. We scoured Dohuk and Mosul for typing paper and typewriters, or hand-wrote in block capitals. We puzzled over how to keep copies of the stories, whose arrival in Britain or France or the United States was obviously highly uncertain, thinking we might have to send them again. Writing them out twice would be laborious. Then someone remembered an antique item called carbon paper. So there was *some* copy – one lengthy news feature by satellite and two or three pigeoned pieces [ie sent via the couriers] – and so we had not quite "disappeared". Although I suppose we did disappear when Kurdistan's brief moment of apparent victory came to an end with the arrival of Saddam's tanks on the outskirts of Kirkuk – there was no way of filing while we were, essentially, running away.'

The story that Woollacott filed by telephone from Van in eastern Turkey to the Guardian copytakers was foreign reporting at its best, told in direct and urgent language. It began: 'A monstrous crime is being perpetrated in Kurdistan. As the Kurdish people's brief springtime of freedom ends, they are, and will be, subject not only to the effects of a war waged in their own cities and towns without restraint or morality, but to the reimposition of Saddam Hussein's brutal rule and his revenge on those who have challenged him.'[10]

Paul Webster said, 'The copy was brought to me take by take [sheet by sheet] as Martin dictated it. I took the first sheet straight to the duty editor who that day was Jonathan Fenby and he decided immediately that we were going to clear the front page ... It was still at that time unusual for the front-page of the broadsheet Guardian to be devoted to a single story.'

It ran with a six-column picture of refugees waiting to hear if the Turkish authorities had granted them asylum.

On 2 April, the day before the report appeared, Turkey's National Security Council said that more than 200,000 people fleeing Iraq, mostly women and children, were in danger of death near the border between the two countries, pursued by Saddam Hussein's advancing armies. Woollacott described the exodus over the mountain passes: 'Up the rock-strewn hills, through gorges bristling with dwarf oaks, and over rushing grey streams, a miserable procession of people claws and staggers its way out of Iraqi Kurdistan. There is no road, only a horse track that winds endlessly upward, normally used only by smugglers. Babies cry, old people stand panting by the side of the pass ... This is the middle class of stricken towns like Kirkuk and Tuz Kurmatu.'

The middle class? They do not often figure in the forefront of reports of fleeing refugees. Woollacott's eye for detail took the reader closer to their plight. 'They are ill equipped for the trip. High-heeled shoes buckle, badly secured possessions are swept away in the first stream, one woman in a leopard-skin dress walks along with a box containing shampoo, conditioner, and hair tint ...' Under the constant threat of Iraqi bombing, class distinctions dropped away.

Woollacott, giving voice to the questions the Kurds were themselves asking, moved with increasing passion into closer identification with their cause. 'Why didn't the US and the allies [intervene]? God knows, we bent international law and the UN Charter whenever we wanted to in the effort to free Kuwait. We spent millions and killed many thousands to punish President Saddam's aggression and, bluntly, to bring him down. Why then this sudden excess of legalism, this prating about internal affairs, these oh-so-wise thoughts about the undesirability of a divided Iraq?'

Persuaded by Woollacott's account, the Guardian changed its leader line and came out for intervention, preferably with but if necessary without UN sanction. It was written by Peter Preston. 'Nothing Mr Bush (and Mr Major) can do now is right. They can only step into a mire. But they cannot, knowing all they know now, condone massacre upon massacre. It will be hard, going on impossible, to secure UN backing for intervention. But that effort on simple humanitarian grounds is inescapable: and will redefine what we mean by a new world order.'

We know what happened in the Guardian office in Farringdon Road that day because the media editor Georgina Henry recounted the story a fortnight later in a piece for eG, the weekly education supplement. Under the heading 'Hold the front page', she described the whole day, outlining its progress from 10am as the choices presented to editors changed or developed. '11.30am: the leader writers' conference begins. There is a choice of topics for consideration: should the Guardian say something about the hostages in Beirut now that Roger Cooper has been released? What about the teachers' conferences? The question of the Kurds is left until Martin Woollacott's piece arrives, although there is some disagreement on what the paper should say: should it continue to oppose military intervention by the Allied forces?' Woollacott finally came through at 3.10pm. By the time of the full news conference at 6pm Peter Preston had decided that the piece was so powerful that there should be an editorial calling for action. As Georgina Henry noted, this was 'a change of stance for the Guardian'.

Woollacott said, 'I was amazed and very heartened by the paper's decision to project the story as powerfully as it did. There is no denying that the piece crossed the line that should divide reporting and advocacy, as did articles by the other journalists who were there.' Taxed about that in a subsequent interview, Woollacott remarked, 'The combined impact of reporting out of northern Iraq, television particularly but press as well, played a significant part in John Major's decision to intervene by ordering what the British called Operation Safe Haven and the Americans called Operation Provide Comfort. It is the only time I have been certain that reporting (not just mine, of course) changed government policy and the only time I have ever felt completely unreserved admiration for a Tory politician.'

Woollacott became journalist of the year in the British Press Awards when they were announced in February, the judges citing 'the dignity and enormous influence' of his reporting from Kurdistan. The following year he won the James Cameron award, the judges on that occasion praising him for 'work that combines moral vision and professional integrity'. Woollacott, as we shall see, would not be the last Guardian journalist to be tugged over the border into involvement in the story he was reporting.

Just four months after Martin Woollacott's flight across the mountains from Iraq into Turkey a story with even wider implications jumped into prominence in the Soviet Union. On 4 August 1991, President Gorbachev had left Moscow for a holiday with his wife Raisa at his state dacha at Foros, the southernmost point of Crimea, looking out over the Black Sea. A fortnight later, shortly before he had been due to return to Moscow, he was placed under house arrest as communist hardliners, seeking to forestall the break-up of the Soviet Union, staged a coup in the capital and ordered KGB troops to surround the presidential dacha: the head of the KGB and the minister of defence were among the plotters. The Guardian's Moscow correspondent, Jonathan Steele, became the only British or American journalist to reach Gorbachev as the putsch flopped and the president was liberated. It had been, as the Guardian put it a day or two later, 'the most revolutionary week in Russian history since October 1917'. The story completely dominated the front pages of the paper from Tuesday to Saturday, by which time the Guardian had carried a total of more than 40 broadsheet pages devoted to it.

President Gorbachev had been cut off from contact with the outside world from the middle of Sunday afternoon, 18 August. The public were told he was ill. Rebel tanks took to the streets of Moscow later that day, surrounding the parliament building. Boris Yeltsin, the new president of post-Soviet Russia, emerged to challenge the coup leaders, making a defiant speech while symbolically standing on one of the tanks. The opposition of Yeltsin and others, greatly assisted by the incompetence of the plotters, guaranteed doom for the coup.

The Guardian's headlines that week capture the extraordinary drama and speed of events: 'Yeltsin rallies resistance against "eternal night"' (Tuesday 20 August); 'Protesters confront tanks in Moscow street fighting' (Wednesday); 'Yeltsin triumphant as Gorbachev flies back' (Thursday); and 'Defiance at the dacha: how Gorbachev refused deal' (Jonathan Steele's exclusive on Friday).

Wednesday had been an extraordinary day for Steele. It had started in the crowded gallery of the Russian parliament and ended almost 1,000 miles away, interviewing a shaken but determined Gorbachev at his dacha in the Crimea. Steele later reflected, 'As with most scoops, it was 90% luck and 10% intuition ...' Frustratingly, there was no immediate way of getting the story out – all normal communication between Foros and the outside world had been cut. Steele was only able to file after getting back to Moscow early on Thursday.[11]

The opening paragraph of his story, carried in Friday's paper, read: 'It was a tanned and tired-looking President Gorbachev, his body visibly trembling with excitement, his face expressing relief at being free, who received a small group of journalists at his country house in the Crimea less than an hour after he had learned that the way to Moscow was open again ... Mr Gorbachev said no physical intimidation had been used against him, but indicated he had been under pressure to make a deal with the coup leaders. Had he done so, he said, he would have had to kill himself.'

Gorbachev had been in 'complete isolation for almost four days and nights', he said. But the coup was over quickly. Two of the coup leaders had arrived at the dacha earlier on Wednesday, perhaps, as Steele later suggested, looking for a compromise that would somehow legitimise their behaviour.[12] Both were arrested immediately on their return to Moscow. 'Mr Gorbachev told us that the main reason the coup had not succeeded was that Soviet society had changed. It was a triumph for perestroika.'

Steele's account of how he got his interview formed a substantial part of a report of nearly 2,500 words, carried on pages two and three of Friday's paper, under the headline 'Flight to the Crimea'. On the Wednesday, Yeltsin revealed to parliament that he had been contacted by the coup leaders and was proposing to fly down to the Crimea to bring Gorbachev back to Moscow. After a short break in proceedings, he then returned to make a sensational announcement: he had been told that a convoy of ZiL limousines carrying the plotters was heading for Vnukovo airport. It looked as though the coup was on its last legs. He asked the deputies, 'Do I have your authority to arrest them?' The question was greeted with a huge cheer and shouts of 'Yes'.

Steele said, 'I was actually sitting with Mark Frankland from the Observer [at this stage still owned by Tiny Rowland] and I said to him, "Let's get to Vnukovo [about 17 miles from the city centre]. If we see the arrest of the coup leaders it will be an incredible story." My car was some way off because the whole building was surrounded by volunteers and barricades, and then there were all kinds of roadblocks and checkpoints. But eventually we managed to make our way on to the ring road going towards the airport. Flights were taking off normally but there were no buses going to Vnukovo, so people were walking to the airport carrying suitcases and babies to get away on holiday. So we gave - I mean it was pretty mad because we were in a hurry - but we gave a couple and their child a lift. We were going to the VIP terminal, separate and some way from the main airport building, but we took them as far as we could.

'The VIP terminal looked completely dead behind huge grille fences, no sign of anything. There was a man in an Aeroflot uniform standing near one of the buildings. We asked him, "Have you seen any sign of ZiL limousines, any planes taking off?" He said, "No, no, no it's all quiet."' They then asked the same question of a passing policeman and were told the flights had already left. 'We were on the verge of leaving when I said to Mark, "How do we know he's telling the truth? Perhaps they still haven't arrived."'

They had started driving back into town when they saw a small convoy of black Volgas coming out from Moscow towards Vnukovo. 'I said to Mark, "Let's follow these people and see what this is." So I did a U-turn, overtook various cars and managed to look as though I was the final car in the motorcade. They didn't go to the VIP bit of the airport where we'd been before. The convoy drove towards the civilian terminal, through a special gate for VIPs and straight on to the tarmac. I was the fourth or fifth car, also black, and they didn't have time to slam the gates shut after the Volgas because I was so close behind. The cars all came to a screeching halt and I saw [prime minister] Ivan Silayev and [vice-president] Rutskoy getting out of them. And I suddenly realised, "Of course, this is the delegation going to the Crimea." You know we'd completely forgotten about it. We had been so obsessed with getting the scoop of the arrest of the plotters.

'I rushed to the foot of the steps and there was a man I knew from the press centre who recognised me ... Two other journalists followed me on to the plane, one from AFP [Agence France Presse] and the other from [the Spanish newspaper] La Vanguardia. We went right to the back of the plane and tried to be as inconspicuous as possible in case they changed their mind and decided to throw us off ... You can imagine the phone in the Moscow office ringing off the hook later that afternoon with Paul Webster [the foreign editor] saying, "Where the hell is Jonathan?" I think eventually they must have done a ring-around and Mark said, "Well, actually, he's gone down to Foros."'

Mark Frankland summarised the extraordinary outcome of the failed putsch in Sunday's Observer. It began, 'President Mikhail Gorbachev last night resigned as General Secretary of the Soviet Communist Party, and suggested that the Party Central Committee take the "honourable" decision and dissolve itself.' At midnight on 31 December the Soviet Union came to an end.

Jonathan Steele was named the David Holden International Reporter of the Year in the British Press Awards for 1991 for his 'brilliant' coverage of the Gorbachev coup – the same year of Martin Woollacott's triumph. Steele also won the London Press Club's Scoop of the Year award. Almost 25 years later, Gorbachev himself referred with some warmth to 'my old British friend, Jonathan Steele, the correspondent of the Guardian'.[13]

Steele's career with the Guardian would eventually span four decades, having started in the early 1960s while he was still a student. After Eton (as a King's Scholar) and a double first at Cambridge, he then went to Yale on a Harkness Fellowship. He arrived there in September 1963, the month after Martin Luther King gave his 'I have a dream' speech. Two months after his arrival Steele found himself driving with three fellow students the 1,300 miles or so to Vicksburg, Mississippi, to join other students campaigning for 'Negro' voting rights. 'We saw a lot of brutality and violence. That was the first radicalising thing.' The following year, he spent a month in what was called the Mississippi Summer Project. It brought his first exposure to the virulence of Ku Klux Klan racism. The experience produced his first piece for the Guardian, published on 8 July 1964. Shortly afterwards, he was taken on by the Guardian as a trainee.

The Yale students had all absorbed the same message: they were expected to 'bear witness'. 'I think that's stayed with me ever since, so that 45 years later I still feel I'm bearing witness, because I have the chance to go to places which most people don't get to or don't want to get to – and it is important that people know.'

The third of the trio of exceptional foreign correspondents covering the tentative new world order was James Meek. His first piece for the Guardian was a front-page story on 2 December 1991 datelined Odessa, jointly bylined with Jonathan Steele and Marta Dyczok, a Ukrainian stringer, both of whom were in Kiev. It was concerned with the perennial subject, the relationship between Ukraine and – still at that time – the USSR. Ukraine had declared its independence just three days after the abortive August coup against Gorbachev. Now it was being put to a referendum. Gorbachev had warned that if Ukraine went ahead with independence it would be a disaster for itself, 'for Europe and the world'. Nevertheless, almost 93% voted yes.

Not many Guardian careers are launched on the front page. For Meek, however, it was still a relatively inconspicuous way to start. He would quickly make a reputation not so much for contributions to the necessary write-throughs (compilations from the reports of more than one correspondent) but for solo reports of a distinctively engaging character. He was highly effective writing about domestic matters in Ukraine: the tensions between the state and rapidly developing free market, the impact on the lives of Kievans of the unpredictable fluctuations in price or availability of everyday items. Ignatsevna Lubov, aged 70, tells him – this is January 1992 – 'If meat is 150 roubles a kilo now, what can I buy for my 400 roubles pension? Me and my husband saved 2,000 roubles for funerals, but now it's not worth anything. You can't even die properly.'[14]

From the beginning Meek was a wonderfully readable writer with the ability to carry a great deal of information lightly. His fans at the Guardian were many and included in his immediate orbit Martin Woollacott, and, only slightly grudgingly, David Hearst. Hearst took over from Jonathan Steele as the Moscow correspondent, worked with Meek for a time and was then succeeded by him. When Simon Tisdall, the foreign editor, had been about to move Meek from Kiev to Moscow, putting him on the staff, Peter Preston, mischievously, sent Hearst a cryptic message saying, 'Let not the Meek inherit the earth.' Hearst said, 'That's exactly what happened. While James was still in Kiev and getting around in the Caucasus and elsewhere, I said, "He is brilliant: he absolutely must come." He also spoke much better Russian than I did – he was just all-round very, very assured and competent, a very good colour writer who grew in stature before my eyes.'[15]

Meek's route to the Guardian and Moscow was interesting. He was born in London of Scottish parents in 1962; his father eventually became deputy governor of a couple of Borstal institutions for young offenders in Scotland. The family settled in Broughty Ferry, Dundee. 'As the Jewish-by-descent, church of England-christened, Scottish Episcopal Sunday-school-going son of an Anglican mother and a nominally Kirk father who late in life converted to Catholicism, with one sister a Buddhist nun and the other a follower of [the Indian guru] Sri Chinmoy, I suppose I'm typical of the religiously uprooted mass who have forgotten what it is like to belong to a faith community,' he later remarked.[16]

Meek, more than he wanted to be a journalist, wanted to write novels.[17] Looking back on his first job in journalism at the Chronicle and Echo in Northampton, he said, 'Just to walk into ordinary people's houses and ask them searching questions about their lives – it was like being in a story really, in a work of art.' His first novel was accepted for publication while he was there. He was also given scope to write at some length, perhaps 2,000 words, just sufficient to open a door into what was later called 'long-form' journalism, of which Meek would become a maestro.

He went from Northampton to Edinburgh and the Scotsman, edited at the time by Magnus Linklater. It was Linklater who sent him to the Gulf as the selected representative of the three Edinburgh titles - the Scotsman, Scotland on Sunday and the Edinburgh Evening News - who were allowed to nominate one person between them. Meek was 28 and had no experience as a foreign reporter, let alone of war - well, he had accompanied a charity convoy to Bucharest, a couple of months after the execution of the Ceaușescus, bearing from Scotland essentials such as a truckload of frozen kippers. But now it was the real thing. Crossing into Kuwait with Egyptian forces, he found himself moving through a landscape of littered mines, burnt tanks and surrendering Iraqis.

Edinburgh after that had seemed rather tame. He made a reconnaissance trip to Ukraine and decided that Kiev was where he would start life as a freelance. 'I handed in my notice to the Scotsman early in August 1990. I held the letter over the postbox for a second and then I let it go ... that Monday the Gorbachev coup happened.' Three months later, when his period of notice expired, he packed a few belongings into a Volkswagen Polo and drove from Edinburgh to Kiev. It took him five days. 'My idea was to write my fiction and to do journalism to make money.' His Russian came on quickly, partly with the assistance of long convivial journeys on night trains when vodka among strangers flowed liberally. He married his last interpreter in Kiev, Yulia Petrova, and she moved with him to Moscow.

One of the benefits of the Hearst-Meek arrangement in Moscow was that the former, the bureau chief, excelled at the big political stories, and the latter was at his best when released to rove across the vastness of a former Soviet Union that was in the process of adjusting, sometimes violently, to the new order of things. Meek in the summer of 1994 had thus been able to set off on what was intended to be an east-to-west tour of the Caucasus. (Only slightly earlier, Suzanne Goldenberg, after a period as the Guardian correspondent in India, had done a similar thing, navigating the Caucasus and writing a book about her experience.)[18]

About the time Goldenberg's book came out, Meek had found himself in Makhachkala, the capital of Dagestan, on the Caspian Sea, sharing a hotel with the football team Lokomotiv St Petersburg, who were on their way to play in Chechnya. 'I got talking to their manager and he said, "Why don't you come with us?" It would be Saturday, there was no paper on Sunday and I was going to Grozny anyway. It was a beautiful day, and Grozny seemed absolutely peaceful ... I was very much in holiday mode.' He went to the match, which ended in a goalless draw. A chance remark from a stranger about 'a big fight' the previous day in Grozny passed him by. 'I got back [to Makhachkala] four or five hours later and the lead on the BBC World Service reported that a major conflict had broken out in Chechnya ... I had completely missed the story. I felt very bad about it. The next day I got up at six o'clock and was back in Chechnya by noon, trying to recover the situation.' As Meek reported in his account in the Guardian, perhaps 10 people had died in what by Chechnya standards would become more minor than major.

Meek moved on to Starogladovskaya, about 50 miles north-east of Grozny. He wrote, 'I found a village where these old Cossacks were living, and an amazing storm started to gather where the sky gets terribly dark and dust devils start blowing in the streets but it doesn't actually rain, and there's a real sense of something ominous brewing. And as I drove there I passed Russian soldiers washing their armoured personnel carriers in the stream like eighteenth- or nineteenth-century cavalrymen washing their horses, and the geese belonging to the Cossacks had been eating fallen mulberries and the juice had been dribbling down from their orange beaks and staining them black as if it was blood ... the whole atmosphere was just incredibly sinister and pregnant with menace ... I tried to say some of that in the piece I filed ... I don't regret screwing up on the other story because I did get the chance to go there. It was one of those times that allow little observations to break through the skin of the news.'[19]

Before the year was out Russia had begun a full-scale invasion and the first Chechnya war had begun. Meek's experience of it changed many things. For example, he would see 9/11, 'terrible though it was', through the prism of having watched Grozny, 'a modern city, being destroyed and people being slaughtered, and nobody really caring. There was something shameful about looking the Chechens in the eye ... the world did nothing and the shells kept falling.'

David Hearst had been in Chechnya to cover the early days of the war from the invasion on 11 December and then Meek took over at the end of the month. 'There was one very long day when there were Russian aircraft actually firing rockets at the place where I was.' He had gone to Shali, about 20 miles south-west of Grozny, a town that was repeatedly attacked by Russian planes dropping cluster bombs. Over 40 people died that day. 'The hospital itself was being evacuated after it too was bombed. Shrapnel littered the ground. Most windows were shattered. Three corpses lay on stretchers outside the surgical unit. Inside the dead and wounded filled the corridors and rooms. A boy of eight or nine with a white bandage wrapped round his head lay dead on a wire bed-frame.'[20]

Even on this occasion, as he was caught in the raid himself, Meek shied away from the use of the first person in his report. 'I was in the early stages of doing that thing which is enormously questionable - I don't mean it's wrong but you always need to question it - namely the business of putting yourself in the story ... Once you do it, it becomes seductive and you are tempted to do it more often than you should - there's an argument that you should never do it.'

Meek continued to write from Russia, latterly as the bureau chief in Moscow, until 1999. He did not cover the even more brutal second Chechen war, which broke out in August 1999, as he had returned to Britain a few months earlier and had briefly become the Guardian's religious affairs editor. He would later return to war, to Afghanistan in 2001, and to the Iraq war in 2003. In 2005 he published his 'Russian novel', *The People's Act of Love*, which he had begun writing in Moscow ten years earlier. The huge success of the book was one of the things that enabled Meek to leave the Guardian in 2006 to devote himself to his writing.

Chapter 17

The Guide: A Little Thing That Meant a Lot and Led to More

'He was a very live wire. He never seemed to walk anywhere.
He always ran, and he was full of ideas and very receptive to new ones.'
Ian Wright on Tony Ageh

To a journalist, the pages of television programmes and entertainment listings are not usually a source of professional excitement. The events described in the previous chapter and elsewhere are more like it. With such distracting noises off, not all newspapers saw the possibility of an immediate advantage over their rivals following the deregulation of TV listings on 1 March 1991. But it was an event of significance. It ended the duopoly of the Radio Times, the BBC programme magazine, and the TV Times, which presented the schedules of the commercial companies, making it possible for newspapers for the first time to run programmes for an entire week in advance. When the moment came, only a few jumped at the chance immediately and the Guardian was not among them, although it had been building its listings service across a broad entertainments field for several years and had toyed with the idea of acquiring two of the metropolitan listings magazines when they ran into difficulties. But in the end, the way in which the Guardian responded to the opportunity was to start far-reaching changes that played an important part in modernising the Guardian, particularly in the eyes of its younger readers.

Television listings were still potentially rich in promise. Before the advent of commercial television in Britain and the accompanying launch of TV Times in 1955, the BBC's Radio Times had been the biggest-selling magazine in Europe, with a circulation peaking at an astonishing

15 million. By 1991 this was down to about 2 million and falling.[1] Up to this point, newspapers had been restricted to publishing television and radio schedules just a day in advance, with extensions for weekends and national holidays. Newspapers attempted to minimise any frustration to readers by carrying extensive seven-day previews of television programmes (and some radio programmes) on Saturdays or Sundays, with day-by-day previews during the week. In the Guardian this task for two decades was in the capable hands of Sandy Smithies. She carried out the job, before and after deregulation, from 1980 until the end of the 1990s, with an apparently inexhaustible diligence.

With deregulation, a round of intense competition was initiated. Over the next year practically all national and Sunday newspapers greatly extended their listings, often in the form of separate television and entertainment sections. The popular newspapers led the way, with the Daily Mirror and the Sun responding immediately with seven-day television sections. Many others followed suit.

On the face of it the Guardian was well set up to take advantage of the new situation. To explore and exploit the possibilities that deregulation offered, it had recruited two people, both very talented. One was John Mulholland, who later became editor of the Observer. The other – at that time, so it seemed, by far the more ambitious of the two – was Tony Ageh, who went on to become controller of archive development for the BBC and led the team that invented and developed the iPlayer.[2]

Mulholland, after studying media and communications at Dublin City University and California State University, Sacramento, had joined the new Independent in 1986. Within months he was recruited to the arts desk of Robert Maxwell's London Daily News, working on the excellent Metro listings section. After the collapse of Maxwell's short-lived paper he became the deputy editor of a new company, Listings Limited, which rose phoenix-like from the ashes of Metro. It provided a comprehensive listings service for the Guardian, its main client, from the time of the Hillman redesign of 1988. Mulholland was the principal contact with the Guardian and Ian Wright asked him if he would like to work on the paper's response to deregulation. He joined the Guardian, initially on contract, and stayed.

Tony Ageh was recruited not by editorial but by the Guardian management. At 31, Ageh brought an unusual intensity and passion to whatever he did, which, in the turmoil of the time, led to suspicions that he was some kind of fifth columnist set on undermining the old Guardian. In a way he was. He was certainly an enemy of the status quo and had a loathing of anything that seemed to be complacency.

In his MA-1 jacket, he seemed to have arrived ready for combat. Although he was born in Chelsea, he had had the formative experience of growing up in Walthamstow, a mixed-race child in a white family in what was then very largely a white community. Ageh's formal education was bumpy and limited: he came to feel he had collaborated in his own humiliation. Two years after joining the Guardian he wrote with memorable force about his experience growing up in that time and place.[3] He recalled crying because he was not white. 'Why wasn't I born the right colour? The white colour. My brother was. I wanted to be like him.' Ageh mixed a concoction of bleach that he intended to apply to himself, but a boy at school was taken to hospital after inhaling the toxic fumes.

He was asked to leave a couple of schools, although not exactly expelled, before ending up at the McEntee Technical School in Walthamstow, which he left at the age of 16 with two O levels. He got a job with a small government department, based in the bowels of Bush House, with the BBC broadcasting from the upper floors. Then he became an advertising copy-chaser for a publishing company owned by a young Richard Desmond, later the publisher of several soft porn magazines as well as the Daily Express. Ageh worked on the Home Organist – there was no double entendre; it was a magazine for music enthusiasts – before going to work for Richard Branson, who was launching a listings magazine called Event to exploit the opportunity created by a staff strike at Time Out, where the egalitarian collective was coming to a traumatic end. During the four months it was off the streets some of the striking journalists made plans to start a rival magazine, which was to become City Limits, and by October 1981 all three titles were jostling for attention.[4] But where for a decade or so City Limits maintained a presence, Branson's Event lasted only a year.

After this failure, a brief incursion into mortgage magazines led Tony Ageh back to listings, this time as publisher of City Limits, now about five years old. It had been one of the early projects of the rapidly rising graphic designer and typographer Neville Brody, later to redesign the Guardian. The joint editors were John Fordham, who had been writing about jazz for the Guardian since 1978, and a former writer for the satirical magazine Oz, Nigel Fountain: he wrote and edited for the Guardian for more than 20 years from the mid-1980s, spending a long period as a valued member of the obituaries desk. Other City Limits alumni who moved to the Guardian included Ros Asquith, Deborah Orr, Steve Bell and Duncan Campbell, who became the Guardian's crime correspondent.

When Ageh arrived in 1986 it was still a workers' cooperative, but no longer a happy ship. According to Ageh, it was practically insolvent. The staff were often not taking salaries. At one point he negotiated a tax rebate of about £30,000 for the staff, who had been taxed as though they were earning continuously. There was passing consideration that the whole sum should be put on a horse.

While Ageh was contemplating a bleak future he discovered that the unrelated magazine City Life in Manchester, had been bought by the Manchester Evening News. Seeking similar salvation, he arranged a meeting with Jim Marwick at the Guardian. He went with Mick Quirk, the magazine's advertising sales manager. They told Markwick that the money would run out in a matter of months. What they did not know was that almost a decade earlier Branson had asked the Guardian to take over his magazine, Event. Ian Wright had looked into that and wisely advised Markwick not to go ahead with it.

This time deregulation was nearer. Furthermore, as Ageh and Quirk argued, there was potential synergy: City Limits was a radical publication, as was the Guardian, relatively speaking. There was already some overlap of staff. The whole might exceed the sum of the parts. Again Ian Wright was asked to look into it, and meanwhile Markwick took what was on the face of it the extraordinary decision to put a substantial sum of money into the magazine so that it would at least keep going while the Guardian considered whether or not to buy it. Wright went to the City Limits office for what he thought would be a fairly brief Saturday afternoon chat with Ageh and left five hours later. Ageh made a big impression. 'He was a very live wire. He never seemed to walk anywhere. He always ran, and he was full of ideas and very receptive to new ones.'[5] Again, in Wright's view, buying the magazine would not be a good idea. He described it as 'a financial hole in the ground'. But he told Markwick, 'It would be a good idea to get Ageh on board as soon as we can.'

By the early summer of 1990 Ageh had resigned from City Limits and gone to Rome for the World Cup in June and July. When his mother rang to say he had had a call from the Guardian, he delayed his response because he thought the paper might be trying to get its money back. To his relief, Markwick instead offered him a job.

Ageh recalled Markwick saying, 'We'd like you to address the listings problem. See if you can solve that.'[6] Then he added, 'See if there's something that we're not doing that in a few years' time you think we'll wish we had been doing - that would be useful to know.' It was an extraordinary brief, calculated to give Ageh plenty of scope. Ageh joined in the autumn of 1990, on a modest contract of £1,000 a month, and quickly brought in one of his closest friends from City Limits, Gary Phillips, a brilliant young designer.

He and Mulholland had both been set the same initial task and Ageh had the impression that Markwick did not mind whether they tackled it together or separately. The allotted working space was a windowless room on the fifth floor of the Farringdon Road building. Two quite different plans emerged - one was for a 16-page Saturday tabloid; the other, Ageh's more radical proposal, was for a compact pocket guide close to A5 in size. His original dummy is dated October 1990. Both used the title *The*Guide - the two title words following what was already becoming the routine practice of combining Hillman's Garamond and Helvetica. And although Gary Phillips had a hand in both designs, both deferred in essential respects to Hillman's overall grid design.

Both plans were presented to the management team before the end of the year. They were scrutinised initially by Jim Markwick, Ian Wright and the dynamic marketing director, David Brook. Brook favoured Ageh's more inventive proposal. But there were financial anxieties. Readers' expectations of a comprehensive listings service after deregulation had to be measured against production costs and the degree to which these could be offset by advertising. There were cautionary words from Ian Ashcroft, the finance director. It was less than a year since his costing of the projected Gott-Hillman European Review had led to its being scrapped. From a budgetary point of view deregulation was not necessarily a positive development. Seven days' television and radio programmes would require the equivalent of 14 pages of newsprint. Brook, like Ageh, saw things differently. 'If you take a step back and say, well, what does deregulation – the fact that you can publish seven days of TV – what does that give you the opportunity to do if you combine it with seven days' listings of cinema and theatre and things going on outside apart from television? Can that not be an opportunity for a paper to capitalise on?'[7]

In the end the paper took what in retrospect looked like a very tentative step. After several days of front-page trails, the Guide, with Mulholland as editor, appeared on 4 May 1991 as a weekly 16-page tabloid pullout published with Weekend, but it only appeared in that form in the London area and it still only included television and radio schedules for Saturday and Sunday. It used an outside contractor, Mulholland's former employer, Listings Limited, to provide highlights for the week ahead in cinema, theatre, dance, classical music, opera, rock and jazz and the visual arts. The Guardian's own critics provided regionalised previews and recommendations. It was a strong team, as good as any the Guardian had had – Derek Malcolm on films, Michael Billington on theatre, Tom Sutcliffe on opera, Edward Greenfield on classical music, Mary Clarke on dance, Tim Hilton on visual art, John Fordham on jazz and Adam Sweeting on rock music – although by 1991 there were heretical murmurs that some refreshment might not be a bad thing.

A new classified page called *The*Noticeboard introduced what it was hoped would be a series of services for readers that would also produce some revenue. For the first time in the Guardian, there was a column for what were still generally called lonely-hearts ads. And another innovation was a swap shop: 'Want to swap your Pavarotti tickets for a pair at the Pet Shop Boys? ... Want to sell John Lennon's plimsoll or find Wayne Fontana's original Pamela? ... Whatever your problem, *The*Noticeboard is the answer.' Clearly a gusty wind of change was still blowing, and each gust brought fresh anxieties that something essential might be carried away. After Weekend, here was another tabloid that would have to be watched for populist tendencies.

The effect of the new publication on overall circulation was initially not great. The Guardian had already begun to recover from the shock assault of the Independent. The traumatic moment had come only nine months earlier, in August 1990, when the Independent closed the gap between it and the Guardian to a mere 4,000 copies. Its frequent invoking was calculated to spur on. Tony Ageh when he arrived at the Guardian that summer had a conversation with Preston, in which they discussed the consequences if the Independent overtook them. 'He said, "That would be a disaster. You know, it's not the loss of income from the news-stands that's the problem. It's the impact it would have on advertising, on confidence, on our ability to attract journalists."'

Since then, the Guardian had managed to open out a reasonable gap again. Perhaps the new tabloid Guide was among the factors that helped the Guardian to restore and maintain its lead. The Times and the Guardian had also been running more or less neck and neck, but by the time the Guide first appeared the Guardian had broken ahead. The audited figures for May 1991 were: Guardian 419,949; Times 396,268; Independent 383,017. The Telegraph stood aloof from this close competition with sales still comfortably over the one million mark.

What the Guide in its original tabloid form did do was contribute to the change in readership patterns that was beginning to make Saturday the best-selling day of the week not only on the Guardian but across Fleet Street. In 1988 there was not a single week in which the Guardian's Saturday sales came out as the greatest of the week. But at the end of the year Rusbridger's Weekend made its appearance and that began to make a difference, along with the 48-page tabloid Jobs and Careers supplement. During 1990, Saturday began to catch up with the best-selling days of the week, which were Tuesdays when the education section appeared and, increasingly, Mondays, which carried the media pages. The following year – helped by the advent of the tabloid Guide in May – it led the way for 30 weeks. In 1992 it was the best-selling day throughout the year, with sales showing a marked increase after the redesigned all-colour Weekend magazine made its appearance.

It was not until the Guide was relaunched on 4 September 1993 that it made any real impact. This time it carried seven days of television and radio programmes and appeared in a pocket-size format, an elegant variant of A5, slightly taller and slimmer, a format unique to it that Tony Ageh fought hard to promote as an essential stand-out element of its design. The Guide, as Ageh very justifiably put it, had been 'sitting there, a solution waiting for its moment', waiting, in fact, for more than two years. As it was rolled out over the country to achieve nationwide circulation in the autumn of 1996, it helped to augment the overall rise as Saturday sales increased through a period of intense price war elsewhere in the industry, to achieve in mid-1995 figures in excess of 500,000. That was a circulation that had not been regularly reached on any day of the week since the mid-to-late 1980s, when Guardian sales were at their highest.

Ageh in his first 18 months or two years at the Guardian had been extraordinarily prolific, and was hardly less so for the remainder of his time in Farringdon Road. Initially he had been alone. It was with a sense of some irony that he had invented the title of Product Development Unit (PDU) – 'I thought it was quite funny – I was the unit' – a title that came to him after he was given a set of Guardian business cards describing him as Product Development Manager. Like David Brook, Ageh was a 'contextual' thinker, and the context broadly was the perceived need to shake the Guardian free from the sandal-wearing, muesli-eating image that had been of such assistance to its competitors. The challenge was to do that while reinforcing its essential identity as a non-party, liberal-radical paper actively participating in the same modern world in which its readers lived.

An idea particularly relevant to the role of Tony Ageh's PDU, driven by David Brook and with strong support from Brian Whitaker, the managing editor of the features department, was to put into circulation publications that surprised those they reached by their content, by their unexpected association with the Guardian, or, preferably, by both. In his time at the Guardian Ageh and his department, now working from the basement of Farringdon Road, produced some 200 publications. After the arrival of the designer Gary Phillips, Ageh and he had quickly been joined by Peter Silverton, with whom Phillips had latterly been working at the humorous weekly, Punch. That magazine, although in rapid decline, had been the first UK national publication to adopt full-page make-up via Apple technology and software, a factor in Silverton's hiring. The trio designed and produced many of the publications in the early days of the department, which would eventually grow to more than 30 people including the staff of the Guide.

Silverton formed his own succinct job definition: 'Although it was never spelt out in direct, simple language, it quickly became clear what our task was: the reinvention of the Guardian. We weren't meant to do it ourselves. We were big-headed but not that big-headed. The idea was that we would show others possible ways forward by example and implication rather than direction.'[8] Silverton was one of those arrivals who viewed the Guardian with a combination of admiration, puzzlement and disdain. 'The logo and design of the Guardian had been changed ... I thought this was one of the best rebrandings I'd ever seen ... But a logo change was never going to be nearly enough to recapture the lost readership - particularly the generation of students who had started with the Independent and would, unless the Guardian could achieve something dramatic, stay with it till the grave. The Guardian looked dull. It was dull. It was also naïve and old-fashioned ... Politically, it was still of the opinion that Tony Benn had something to tell us. Visually, it didn't even have a colour section. In fact, there was a general view in the building that colour, in itself, was suspect. Fun and joy should be relegated to their rightful place: in the queue and on the ration.'

The first time he went into the Guardian canteen he thought, 'This is Winston Smith [of Orwell's *1984*] world. A pleasant, liberal version of it, but Winston Smith world nonetheless. This dull, clean, uncomfortable, chummy little lunchroom is the last of the wartime British Restaurants. And the senior editing staff were in there - in such bad clothes.'

The PDU's job was to change this - softly and slowly. To achieve it, they had something the rest of the building didn't: new, reasonably powerful Macs and the knowledge to use them.

Silverton described Ageh as a 'point man, a salesman, a diplomat'. He continued: 'Tony would prowl the building and the local pubs, chatting and charming his way up and down the Guardian hierarchy ... He went out and pitched for work around the building. Bring it to us, he'd say, doesn't matter if it's big or small, we'll do it brilliantly (modesty was not a Tony characteristic) and we'll do it faster than you can imagine.'

This they did. 'Tony would do the deals, arrange the printing etc. I'd copy-edit and write all the display copy - bringing a particular kind of jokey smartassness that was standard on the music press but had, at that point, not made it to the national papers. Gary would design - he was easily the quickest and most literate designer I've ever worked with. We'd bring in an outside sub - final proofreading has never been one of my strengths. We'd do a whole magazine in a few days. We did loads and loads and loads of supplements - travel ones, culture ones. They were, generally, ad-gets, there to entice advertisers - in fact, they were the only place for colour ads in the paper. But they were great ad-gets (I can't see the point of being modest myself) ... We also designed Guardian ads [advertising the Guardian itself] ... We helped pioneer and develop international partnerships, producing joint magazines with a variety of European papers and magazines.'

The PDU's first title (The Gulf Crisis) appeared in October 1990. It was a large-format 68-page survey of the first 60 days of the conflict, and one of its intentions was to demonstrate the strength of the Guardian's foreign reporting team. It was edited by Michael McNay and Quentin McDermott, produced on high-grade newsprint and sold as a free-standing Guardian publication at £1.95. According to Ageh it sold about 40,000 copies. It was followed in December, using the same format, by The Sporting Year 1990 (£2.50), and The Thatcher Legacy (£1.95). Probably the best and most ambitious publication of this kind was The Gorbachev Revolution, which came out in September the following year. It was able to make full use of Jonathan Steele's coverage of the attempted coup against Gorbachev only a week or two earlier.

The PDU output was certainly diverse. It included a programme for performances by the anarchic circus, Archaos, a bestselling guide to the general election of 1992, and a version of the French fashion and beauty magazine Madame Figaro in a co-publishing arrangement which came out at intervals from 1993 to 1995.

Silverton left before the Guardian's association with Madame Figaro ended. He departed in some bitterness in the summer of 1993, asked to leave by Ageh, he says, but not knowing quite why, although there had been some falling-out between Silverton and Gary Phillips, with whom he later worked again when they both followed Jocelyn Targett to the Sunday Times. Silverton acknowledged that he was not easy to work with, adding, 'I don't think I'd like to work with me.'

As he departed, he felt he could look around with some satisfaction at the changes that had taken place in the Guardian, some of which he had worked hard to bring about. There was a change in the ambience too. As he put it: 'To me, the simplest way to benchmark that early 1990s shift was the new canteen at the Guardian. It looked good, it was spacious, it served cappuccino. It was the future. The day I saw it, I knew the Labour Party would win the next election. The Guardian had finally come round to embracing the truth of its readers' desires, rather than the rhetoric of a small, vocal regressive minority. They might want social justice but they want a nice cup of coffee, too - and, like most of us, they wake up thinking of coffee, not justice.'

Not everyone saw it that way, of course. Just before Christmas 1991 an anonymous and somewhat vituperative article appeared in the pilot edition of a magazine called Casablanca, tearing into the evolving - or in the author's view degenerating - new-look Guardian. The article alleged, and lamented, a 'marked shift' downwards and towards the right since the late eighties. Its repeated characterisation of the various disappeared sections as highbrow and their replacements as lowbrow and (even worse) apolitical was clear enough.

The article had obviously been written by an insider, and, as Private Eye described, with only a degree of exaggeration, it induced a 'wave of paranoia' at Farringdon Road. The prime suspect was Casablanca's initial editor, Tariq Ali. Nearly 20 years later, he confirmed it in a telephone conversation.[9] 'Yes, I did write it. We on the left had a sort of love-hate relationship with the Guardian. We couldn't do without it, but we were also very critical of it.' It was a view that reflected the muttered discontents of the Gulshan group, although Ali himself was never a member.

Elsewhere, the new direction gained some surprising supporters. Stephen Glover, arch-critic of the Guardian, writing in the Evening Standard a couple of weeks after the Madame Figaro launch, was moved to pay an unusual and, perhaps, coming from him, unique compliment to the Guardian, although it was clearly in part employed as a rod with which to beat the back of his old paper, the now flagging Independent.[10] In recent years, he claimed, there had been 'a destructive cancer slowly eating away at the heart of the Independent', while a resurgent Guardian had been in the process of 'transforming' itself. The Guardian's glossy edition of Madame Figaro was an indication of this transformation, Glover suggested. 'With this full embrace of bourgeois interests the last vestiges of Trotskyism were squeezed out of the Guardian's soul. The days when the newspaper's letters column resembled the noticeboard of the Socialist Workers Party are long forgotten.' After a thousand words or so of this, one senses that sweat suddenly broke out on the critic's brow: 'Lest anyone should think me starry-eyed, I should stress that even now the Guardian is not quite my kind of paper ... But that is not really the point. The point is that the Guardian has become a class act.'

It was not a position that Mr Glover felt able to maintain and business, to the relief of all concerned, was soon being carried on in adversarial fashion as heretofore.

Chapter 18
'Small but Perfectly Informed': The Birth of G2

'At last I've got something to edit.'

Alan Rusbridger on the first issue of G2, 12 October 1992

When Rusbridger took over the features department the idea of a daily tabloid second section was little more than a twinkle in Preston's eye. More concrete thoughts developed in 1991. But almost three years of the new features regime passed before the tabloid project was finally given the go-ahead, and then, in the usual manner, everything was done in a rush. By the spring of 1992 the time suddenly seemed right. Saturday was now firmly established as the best-selling day of the week. But something, it was generally agreed, needed to be done urgently about the five days that preceded it. There was a fear that the convention of leading second sections with the classified high-revenue earners, in particular media, education and the social services, on Monday, Tuesday and Wednesday - the crown jewels - might be off-putting for readers with no special interest in the day's chosen discipline, and contribute to the irregular buying pattern that was developing on weekdays. Bringing general features to the fore in a tabloid second section while continuing to deal with those core Guardian editorial and commercial interests might help to even out the weekday circulation. It would also be the biggest test so far of the tabloid format.

The Saturday paper, meanwhile, had gone from strength to strength. At the end of February 1992 the broadsheet front news section had been augmented by an analytical comment section called Outlook. Jonathan Fenby, newly recruited from the Independent, was the motivating spirit and the key members of his team included Michael Pilgrim, the editor of the new section, a man of brusque efficiency highly rated by Preston (he had succeeded Michael McNay as the design commissar of the front page), Christopher Dodd, who had been Gott's deputy features editor, Patrick Ensor, a former arts editor of the paper, and Alex Duval Smith, who moved her linguistic and editorial talents across from Guardian Europe.

Fenby undoubtedly added to his reputation with Outlook (and so, of course, did Pilgrim). Fenby was a determined agent of liaison between news and features, whose independence of each other sometimes caused them to be bizarrely out of sync. Overkill was a principal symptom of this defensive departmental autonomy, with sometimes half a dozen different sections and columnists running versions of the same story. This seeming free-for-all was especially puzzling to the growing number who had come into the Guardian from papers where editing was more hierarchical - or, to put it another way, decisive.

Preston had let Fenby know from the outset that he was doing something highly unusual in bringing in an 'outsider' to such a senior position. A certain amount of diplomatic footwork had preceded the appointment. After an initial lunch with Preston, there had been dinner for three at an Italian restaurant in Lamb's Conduit Street to make sure that Fenby and Preston's other deputy, Ian Wright, would be able to work together. Then Preston had gone round to Fenby's apartment in Bloomsbury with a bottle of Côtes du Rhône to complete the signing. Fenby took his appointment as a clear signal that Preston wanted change. 'I tried to contribute towards broadening the paper's approach - I remember producing a singular silence when I told an away-day meeting that if Mrs Thatcher came up with a prescription for everlasting life, the Guardian splash the next day would be, "Thatcher forces people to live longer", and the story would start, "Labour last night denounced the government for interfering with the natural lifespan."' Preston would have been well satisfied to hear his deputy tackling that one. 'It was not simply a matter of editorial approach. The culture at the Guardian was the most conservative I had ever encountered. Hard choices were to be avoided. Fudge ruled. As one old hand told me after I had praised a story at the morning conference, "We don't praise because we don't blame."'[1]

Fenby became an energising presence on the first floor. 'I tried to move across the board, knitting together the various departmental operations and breaking down barriers. This meant changes in the daily organisation, which may seem arcane but were vital. The 5pm conference was an occasion at which department heads read out their stories, and then Peter, on the advice of the night editor, picked the front- and back-page stories and that was that. This meant that things got going quite late in the day. I tried to get decisions moving before lunch and setting up pages and packages in time to bring together words, pictures, graphics and layout, and to coordinate with other parts of the paper, notably features.'

Editorially, Outlook was a great success, at least among those who had felt awash and fearful amid all the recent changes: for them it was as though a familiar coastline had suddenly been sighted. The overall tone was serious and texty, despite the use of large photographs and illustrations. It carried the Saturday comment and analysis page, with the first edition carrying a foreign affairs commentary by Martin Woollacott, who had been named Journalist of the Year the previous week. There was a political column by David Marquand and an arts page featuring a column by Joanna Coles, and the section also included the letters and obituaries pages.

There were lighter touches. David McKie under the name Smallweed treated readers to miscellaneous outpourings of his fertile mind in a column that had been introduced in another part of the paper some six or seven months earlier. Smallweed himself - from Dickens's *Bleak House* - was a know-all, and so in a way was the McKie of Smallweed, sharing the genuine pleasure he derived from a compendious and idiosyncratic knowledge with his readers.

The first issue of Outlook also had 'A Letter from the Isle of Dogs' written by the best-known resident of that part of London, at least to Guardian readers, Nancy Banks-Smith. The term 'television critic' always seemed an inadequate term to describe what she brought to her main task, which was her undiluted self: the writer and the written seemed at one in a way that few achieve. This particular contribution to the first Outlook was not exactly a television review. She described a PR trip on the Thames to publicise a television series about the Isle of Dogs. There on the launch, unable to escape, she was carried past her home and claimed that she saw her dog, Eric, gazing wistfully out at the flowing river. 'In my front window I could see Eric striking his "I am faithful unto death" pose. It is an act which always sits uneasily on Eric, a second-hand dog of imprecise provenance. My glasses misted.'

Perhaps the biggest attraction of Outlook for many Guardian readers was the return of the incomparable Posy Simmonds, whose cartoon strips had run on the women's page for a decade from 1977 to 1987.[2] In her families of Webers, Wrights and Heeps, she drew upon existing stereotypes of Guardian readers, reinforcing them and establishing them perhaps ineradicably. As Suzie Mackenzie described it, 'Her cartoon strip ... was a gentle social satire of well-meaning, woolly-minded liberal intellectuals trapped in ethical and economic insecurity and character-ised by muesli crunching, Volvos, school runs and indulgent middle-class chaos.' Why did something so popular suddenly end in 1987? 'I had begun to parody myself,' Simmonds told Mackenzie. Now she was back with the cash-strapped Miles and Vanessa Upmaster and the Crouch family, 'a new cast of contemporary characters for the 1990s'. How deep was the impression she made was reflected in the comments posted at the end of the piece she wrote for the Guardian in 2012 when her omnibus edition of the Weber family strips was published: an outpouring of love, thanks, nostalgia and admiration.

Outlook, like a good many other innovations, was an indication of the paper's growing confidence. Just a few weeks after the creation of the Outlook section, differential pricing was introduced for the first time in the paper's history. From the end of March, the price of the Saturday Guardian was increased to 45p, making it 5p dearer than the paper on weekdays, a distinction that remained thereafter, although the price difference greatly increased as the Saturday paper put on weight. Outlook became a part of the paper for the next four years, edited by Pilgrim until 1993 when he followed Fenby to the newly acquired Observer, after which it was taken over by the versatile and rising David Rowan.

Outlook was not the only significant improvement in the Saturday package. Much more important in underpinning the strength of the Saturday circulation was the redesign, practically a relaunch, of the Weekend magazine in September. Alton had always been a bit bothered by the newsprint, hybrid nature of Weekend, finding it neither fish nor fowl. Now it was no longer the Weekend 'tabloid'. It was the 'full-col-our Weekend magazine'. Important technical changes were introduced: production was no longer restricted by the capabilities of the Atex system, but was moved on to the more versatile QuarkXPress and Macintosh. The quality of the paper on which it was printed was of a heavier grade than the newsprint used until now.

The first real dummy seems to have been printed at the beginning of June 1992, dated 6 and 7 June, just a few days before Alton had a horrendous accident. Returning to work from Islington on a borrowed bicycle, he hit the kerb by the Betsey Trotwood in Farringdon Road. Colleagues in the Guardian building heard a scream as he fell, and he seriously injured his face. It could be called a sporting accident: he had been rushing back to a pub in Clerkenwell to watch England's televised opening match in UEFA Euro 1992. Alton would later wrest some humour from the trauma. Part of the recovery treatment had involved the grafting of skin from his behind on to his face. 'I am, quite literally,' he would relate, 'talking out of my arse.'[3]

Work had probably begun on the new Weekend in May, giving perhaps no more than four months to get it all together. There was not a great deal of difference between the dummy and the design that was finally settled upon. In a sense it was a typical Hillman progression, becoming by the time of publication bolder, cleaner, clearer. The dummy carried the title *Weekend* **Guardian;** the published version had only the definite article in the italic Garamond with *The* Guardian nestled against the dominant title **Weekend.** The select index across the top of the cover picture in the dummy was swept away in favour of a single heading.

Peter Silverton was a key member of Tony Ageh's PDU in the run-up to the launch of both the colour Weekend and G2. 'I was in the discussion meeting with David Hillman when he presented the design for the new Weekend, and was struck by how clearly and subtly he understood the culture and internal structure of the Guardian. In particular, he knew how production was dominated by subs who had no design training or experience and that, therefore, the design had to be sub-proofed, so that they couldn't alter the essentials.' Hillman had learned long ago that design grew out of content and was not something that could ever be simply or successfully imposed on it. 'I mean, not blowing my own trumpet,' Hillman confided, 'I think one of the reasons I have succeeded as an editorial designer is because I enjoy reading. I hate magazines where you get the sense that the designer has not read one word of the copy. For me a successful anything - successful book, magazine, newspaper - the pictures and the words have to work together.'[4]

Silverton recalled that, as launch day for the new colour Weekend approached, 'Roger [Alton] started worrying in earnest and asked for my help with the flatplan – he'd never flat-planned a large colour magazine before while I'd done it for years. He took me to the Coach and Horses, the dingy pub behind the Guardian, where we sat and did it together in about an hour, working out what would go at the front and the back, which order to put them in, then leaving the big space in the centre for the features. It stayed pretty much the way we worked out for a couple of years at least.'

All these improvements provided the vehicle for some impressive editorial content, the main feature of which for the launch issue was the first of three extracts from *An Evil Cradling*, the memoir of the former hostage Brian Keenan telling the story of his four years of captivity in Beirut. The promotional advertising was powerful stuff. Beneath a stark image of a bandaged, blindfolded and gagged head, the text read, 'You have to die to go to heaven. Unfortunately, Brian Keenan found the same wasn't true of hell.'

There was almost an exuberance about the reports presented to the Guardian board in October, which took place just four days after the launch of the tabloid Guardian 2. The circulation manager David Owen told the board that the Guardian's combined lead over the Independent had moved from 54,000 copies a day in August to 76,000 copies a day in September. 'Clearly our Saturday sale, which was buoyant even before the launch of [the redesigned] Weekend [on 12 September], has been a major factor in our September sales success. Two weeks after the advertising campaign finished our Saturday sales were in excess of 450,000, an increase over the previous year of 25,000.' All in all, he told the board, something that must have been music to Preston's ears, the Guardian now had 'the best possible platform for launching a tabloid second section'.

The idea for G2, as it quickly became known, had evolved along with Preston's recurring tabloid dream. 'Did I think about that when I made Alan features editor? Perhaps,' said Preston. 'I certainly knew that the 1988 redesign was a beginning, not an end. But my central reason for appointing him then, as in other positions, was just that he was the brightest, most innovative talent around.' Fenby almost certainly helped to bring about its final precipitation into reality. 'I recall talking to Peter a number of times about the lack of editorial logic in devoting the second section broadsheet front to whatever was the classified subject of the day (media, education, social services). It was the second-best slot in the paper. Why not use it for a big feature?' Though of course this led to the inevitable question of where the classifieds would go. 'Then I recall going for a walk in Oxfordshire and thinking why don't we do both - a separate features section and a classified section with its own front? I got so excited by this notion that, when I got back to London that evening, I went into the office and wrote Peter a one-page A4 note - I think I scrawled across the bottom of it "and make them tabloid?"'

Preston hardly needed nudging in that direction. His mind had kept returning to the ambition he had probably now had for a decade, to take the whole of the Guardian into tabloid format. 'I thought being first to go tabloid would put us in a special position, with a younger audience, where the competition couldn't easily follow.' Creating a new tabloid second section for features would be a step in that direction. A precedent that impressed him was a daily in Lausanne that printed in a broad-sheet-tabloid combination.[5] The key moment had come when it became apparent that the new presses could do an on-the-run tabloid together with an on-the-run broadsheet. Furthermore, new inserting equipment made it possible to stuff pre-printed tabloid classified sections, G3s, into the new tabloid features G2, and the whole package to be wrapped into the main broadsheet front, G1.

Preston regarded this as a eureka moment. 'The new presses and the new inserting equipment could do all that. Well, why weren't they already doing it? The answer was because no one had actually asked the question.' So the major presumed technical obstacle had not been an obstacle at all. Apparently the crucial piece of equipment needed was something of German manufacture called a slitter. Preston in his glee at this relatively simple solution to the problem referred to it around the office as Herr Schlitter. Herr Schlitter was the Führer who would lead the Guardian into the tabloid age.

Fenby recalled, 'Nothing happened for a time as Peter talked to advertising. Then he told me it was agreed. Who would run the new section? Alan, obviously. Peter took the two of us to the pub across the road for morning coffee, and G2 followed.' Rusbridger recalled this short excursion the few yards to the Surprise public house in Bowling Green

Lane, timed to avoid lunchtime, when there were strippers, to be told in conspiratorial tones of plans for the tabloid second section. 'The message was, "You proved you could do it with Weekend, now we'd like you to do it on a daily basis."'

At the August meeting of the Guardian board Preston told his fellow directors that dummy second-section covers had been prepared (David Hillman had been called in again to help with these), and he briefed them on progress on production and advertising matters. The board agreed it should be launched on 5 October, six weeks away. It proved to be over-ambitious by just one week.

After the 1988 Hillman redesign, the creation of the tabloid G2 was to be the most radical step the Guardian had taken. The formatting problems were considerable, particularly, as it turned out, towards the back of the paper, with the television and radio programmes causing headaches. Rusbridger wanted the first two pages to be left clear for the cover story. (My own contribution to the opening spread was the title Second Front, which ran well into the decade despite its rather *Dad's Army* undertone.) But Rusbridger also had something else up his sleeve. What that was became apparent when he was called down urgently to a planning meeting in the bunker where the formatting team had placed the two daily strip cartoons at the foot of page two. Rusbridger appeared, brushed the cartoons away and said he wanted them accommodated at the back of the tabloid, whatever the problems. Then he produced a double-column printout of a feature that was to become one of the most popular and long-running in the history of the paper. 'I want that to go there,' he said, laying it down at the right of the opening spread. It was Pass Notes, a satirical crib on a leading figure, event or institution in the news. It had been lifted from the dead body of the Correspondent, perhaps with the justification that the Guardian's investment in the Sunday paper amounted to a reasonable fee. To carry it off successfully it required an urbane wit to be exercised on well-researched material. Rusbridger himself set the standard.

Pass Notes had been invented by Rusbridger's friend Henry Porter, and it was not the only feature by him that Rusbridger appropriated for the Guardian. On 8 December 1990, just an indecent fortnight after the Correspondent finally died, the Guardian published its first Questionnaire, an updated version of the Proust Questionnaire, one that had been 'dreamed up in 1989 over supper'[6] by Porter and the critic and novelist Gilbert Adair. The column, compiled by the seemingly indefatigable Rosanna Greenstreet, went on to appear in Weekend Guardian for the next 30 years.

The cover story for the first issue of G2 was hard won. Veronica Horwell, an elegant, eloquent and generally undervalued writer, had been dispatched to join the besieged people of Sarajevo,[7] carrying with her the first flak jacket the Guardian features department had bought, a weighty object acquired near the Elephant and Castle. 'I spent the evening before I flew to Zagreb embroidering my name, newspaper and blood group on the blue twill fabric of the flak jacket, inside, just behind the ceramic plate, where it would be legible, even if I wasn't.'

She arrived in Sarajevo after hitching a ride on a convoy from Split, by then with insufficient money - in the favoured currency, Deutschmarks, tucked into her bra - to stay in the Holiday Inn, where the international press were gathered. 'So I pleaded my way into an apartment block on what turned out to be almost the front line, where the family of a local journalist took me in ...[8] There were no phones and no contact with the outside world. I already knew that the Guardian photographer Sean Smith was arriving on a certain day, and that I'd have to get to the Holiday Inn (it was on a shooting alley) to rendezvous, which we did - and we've been friends ever since. As late as possible, close to the G2 deadline, I had to get out and bring his pictures with me as he was staying on. We were trapped, but Sean persuaded a German journalist, later killed under similar circumstances, to drive me to the UN airstrip in a dangerous, because it was unarmoured, car. I then conned a ride on a UN Antonov [cargo plane], and was dumped off on a runway at Budapest, hungry, dehydrated and shaky.' Her two long pieces from Sarajevo were reporting of a high order, painting a vivid picture of people striving to preserve something of normal life under attack by bomb and sniper fire.

Sean Smith was already on course to become one of the leading war photographers of his time. Not surprisingly, the black and white cover story struck a somewhat sombre note. Smith's photograph showed in the foreground a man carrying some long-handled shovels over his shoulder against the background of an improvised graveyard. The legend underneath read, 'The cemeteries are full. Now families dig up football pitches to bury the dead.' Rusbridger, writing on the 20th anniversary of G2, wrote, 'Looking back at the first issue, I can't help smiling: the cover shrieked, "please don't read me!"'[9] In fact, it seemed to put no one off. On the contrary, the sales were brisk and immediately rose by 2-4% across the country.

In any case, the serious start was a deliberate choice. 'Tabloid' was still a word with downmarket connotations in Britain. It was important that Rusbridger and his features desk, still responsible for the flagship comment and analysis pages in the main paper, broke away from such associations. This was, after all, one of the things that the Weekend and now G2 were supposed to do. That the latter did so successfully was borne out over time by G2's many imitators.[10]

An enormous effort by David Brook's marketing department had gone into promoting both the remodelled Weekend and Guardian 2, the latter under the slogan 'Small but perfectly informed'. A quarter of a million pounds was spent on Weekend, aiming to attract advertisers and new readers. And a total of £345,000 was spent supporting Guardian 2. There were presentations to advertisers in London, Manchester and Edinburgh. Running through October was the biggest poster promotion that the Guardian had mounted up to then, with a national 96-sheet poster campaign on more than 500 prominent sites across Britain. There were daily radio ads, written day by day to promote the changing content.

Reader reaction in the form of letters to the editor was mixed, but in nothing like the volume that had greeted Weekend when it first appeared. Several readers urged the paper to go that step farther. A London reader, Ross Shimmon, wrote: 'When will the Guardian have the courage to adopt the tabloid format for all its sections? When it does, I can at last join the Sun and Mirror readers and read it comfortably on the 188.' Judith Pratt from Gosforth, Newcastle upon Tyne, disagreed: 'No, it just won't do, your new tabloid. Headlines lose their impact on a small page. Large pictures are ruined by the join down the middle. The weather and television may have got bigger, but it is more difficult to read the radio programmes and the quick crossword and, worst of all, Steve Bell is a shadow of his former self. Please return to the old format.' Margaret Midgley from Bacup in Yorkshire encountered a practical problem. 'Now that the Guardian second section is tabloid, it isn't big enough to fit under my cats' litter tray. What am I to do?'

The space liberated in the main part of the paper by the creation of G2 had created the necessity for changes there too. In particular there was an opportunity to strengthen the profile of sport. This was given its own Hillman-style 'front' on the back page of the paper on weekdays, with a kind of reverse index across the top, calling attention to increased sports coverage to be found on the preceding pages.

With the new broadsheet Outlook section and the relaunched Weekend, followed in fairly quick order by the radical tabloid G2, the Guardian suddenly looked in much better shape to take on the competition. G2 in a sense was the Guardian's late-played ace. Caroline Marland told the board, 'We do believe that, of all the recent innovations, the tabloid second section has the best long-term potential as a newspaper sales builder.' In December, the Guardian board was told that the indications were that G2 had increased sales by an average of about 7,000 copies a day. The Guardian was the only title in the quality market to record an increase in its sales over the previous year, with the Times and the Independent both down by about 1.5%. ICM research carried out early in the New Year showed that half of those surveyed thought that G2 had improved the paper, and that the new tabloid was particularly popular among women and younger readers.

Rusbridger would not be left to enjoy his new role with G2 for long. He had indicated the direction of his ambition when he held the new tabloid in his hands for the first time, hot from the presses on the Isle of Dogs. Turning to Brian Whitaker, he said, 'At last I've got something to edit.'

Chapter 19
Witnesses to
War in Europe

*'I was a serious pacifist who believed that all war was
wrong; now I believe that war is necessary to end
things that are even worse than war.'*

Ed Vulliamy

As the cover story of the launch issue of G2 had dramatically portrayed,
the war in former Yugoslavia drew some fine and courageous reporting
from Guardian correspondents, high among them Ed Vulliamy and a
newcomer to the paper, Maggie O'Kane. They won many awards for
their work in this, the first conflict on such a scale within Europe since
the Second World War. Both had made documentary films for television
before covering the conflict for the Guardian, and perhaps it was this
visual sensibility that gave their writing such a graphic, close-up quality.
Neither was naturally a pack or hotel journalist: they were inexorably
and often dangerously drawn to where the action was. Their reporting was also highly controversial for stepping over a line that many,
including some of their colleagues at the Guardian, thought should not
have been crossed. This was the border on one side of which stood
the witness, the 'neutral' observer, and on the other side those actively
caught up in the conflict.

One Guardian critic of the latter approach said that it turned the
reporter into 'an outraged participant', in a popular and usually pejora-
tive phrase of the time. Another of their colleagues, himself a respected
foreign correspondent, spoke of the rise of 'a Maggie O'Kane school of
foreign reporting': 'I think she was the epitome of this kind of journalism.
The sort of print version of TV journalism, where you begin the article
with a close-up of some sort of agonised scene and then you pull back
to the wider context. But everything has to begin with a crying baby, a

starving child, the weeping widow sort of foreign coverage, which was very different from the Ian Wright, Martin Woollacott, Jonathan Steele, Richard Gott approach, which was much more cerebral and analytical.'

On one occasion, after Jonathan Fenby, the deputy editor, had displaced a political story to accommodate another startling dispatch from Bosnia, it was denounced by Richard Gott at a lively morning conference as 'political pornography'.

In fact both styles, whatever the surrounding tensions, ran very effectively side by side in the Guardian throughout the period of this book, and this was particularly true of coverage of the wars in former Yugoslavia, where graphic reportage was constantly accompanied by contextual commentary and analysis. Noteworthy in the latter respect were the dispatches from the Guardian's Europe correspondent, Ian Traynor, at that time based in Vienna, and by his mentor Martin Woollacott. The best of the reporting combined all these elements, carrying context within penetrating reportage, for example in Julian Borger's dispatches covering the terrible collapse of the Muslim 'safe' enclave of Srebrenica; and in the case of Kosovo (covered in the second volume of this book) in the reporting of Jonathan Steele. Between them they gave the Guardian's coverage great depth and texture.

Both Vulliamy and O'Kane certainly became involved partisans, even 'outraged participants', in the cause of the Bosnian Muslims in particular. For Maggie O'Kane, 'There really was no parity of guilt in this.' When linked in to a radio discussion during the war she was aghast to hear a participating BBC female journalist, who, having quoted the Bosnian Serb leader Radovan Karadžić on the subject of rape camps, said, 'Of course we know there is rape on all sides.' 'I thought, well there isn't rape on all sides, and there certainly isn't systematic rape on all sides. And you, because you're trying to appear as a kind of unbiased journalist, are hiding behind this idea of objectivity, and the truth isn't objective. I felt that if I was in the same room with her I would have hit her.'[1]

Vulliamy too saw the Muslims, more than any others, as the 'victim people' of the war, and his reporting became a passionate indictment of their oppressors. Having stepped over the line, he went further than O'Kane and controversially became the first journalist to give evidence to the International Criminal Tribunal for the former Yugoslavia (ICTY), trying war crimes in The Hague. In doing so he went with his conscience against a great deal of advice. 'Some of the colleagues I most admire have counselled strongly against testifying,'[2] he revealed. He subsequently testified in six more trials including that of Karadžić. The war had changed his life. 'I was a serious pacifist who believed that all war was wrong; now I believe that war is necessary to end things that are even worse than war.'[3] He came to call it 'my war'.[4]

Appearing as a witness at the Hague tribunal was something O'Kane declined to do. 'I think it makes it more dangerous and more difficult for us to do our job [as journalists]. We would be seen as a threat and an enemy combatant.' Nevertheless, she did all she could to provide contact details of survivors and witnesses when these were sought by investigators as a result of what she had written.

The war introduced Maggie O'Kane to the Guardian. Her first reports came from Croatia, many from the besieged Adriatic city of Dubrovnik. She had been smuggled into the city through the naval blockade by a sympathetic Croatian crew member who hid her in the bunks on board a ship carrying European Community observers. It was the first of many occasions on which her vivid accounts were to be splashed across the Guardian's front page.

Her reports were notable for the way they gave voice to ordinary people swept up by events. This was especially true of the trapped citizens of the Bosnian capital Sarajevo, a city from which she reported at regular intervals throughout its historically long four-year siege. She made her first visit there in the spring of 1992 – just three weeks after the siege began – making one stage of her journey in a Red Cross convoy that came under heavy artillery fire that killed several people. She left Sarajevo on that occasion in a sombre group of vehicles that carried the coffin of Jordi Pujol, a young Spanish photographer killed in the city by a mortar bomb – his body became their passport through the checkpoints.

Being in Sarajevo then, with Serbian militia firing in at will from the surrounding hills, felt, she wrote, like being in a doll's house from which a giant had lifted the roof. Her gift for the graphic phrase impressed people on the desk in London. Two months later she was reporting from another siege, this time from the topographical point of view of the Serbian forces commanding the mortar batteries around Goražde. Her report began, 'Commandant Slavo Gub stands on top of a mountain and unscrews the legs of a green tripod to mount his telescopic sights.

The streets of Goražde jump up the mountain.' This last phrase gave her report an immediate and startling reality for Peter Murtagh, on duty that evening on the foreign desk in Farringdon Road. 'It was just such a vivid image. I went in to Preston and said, "You've got to read this." He pulled it up on his screen, and while he was reading it [without looking up] he said, "This young woman has written herself into a job."' It was an appointment that Paul Webster, the foreign editor, warmly endorsed. Maggie O'Kane was taken on to the staff of the Guardian and remained on it for more than 20 years, spending her first decade on the paper in a succession of war zones, including Afghanistan, Iraq, Chechnya.[5] She became one of the select group of female correspondents who, quite literally, put their lives on the line in areas where there was no immunity.

O'Kane found that her own background as a Catholic in Belfast provided her with insights that helped her to penetrate the complexities of sectarian rivalries in Yugoslavia. One of her childhood memories was of being woken, aged about eight, by a bomb 'just up the road at the Co-Op', a blast that shattered her bedroom windows, showering her bed with glass. In the prevailing atmosphere of 1970s Northern Ireland, several members of her extended family had been drawn to the periphery of the IRA, and this perhaps accounted for her father's decision to move the family to Skerries, a seaside village north of Dublin, when O'Kane was 12. She started her career in journalism as a crime correspondent for the Sunday Tribune and Magill current affairs magazine. The editor of Magill was the journalist and later novelist Colm Tóibín, who recognised her acute eye for detail and suggested she develop it by reading Truman Capote's true-crime classic, *In Cold Blood*.

She combined a degree in politics and history at University College Dublin with a job at the Irish television channel RTE, and then went on to enrol in a journalism course in Paris, while still theoretically affiliated to RTE. One of her assignments was to file a report from Berlin. She arrived there at the end of the first week of November 1989. Two days later the Wall came down. RTE had no one there. She filed pieces-to-camera filmed for her in front of the Wall by a cooperative Japanese crew. Somewhere in the crowd was the truant editor of Guardian Weekend, Ed Vulliamy.

Their paths were soon to cross. 'While I was in Dubrovnik, the glorious Ed Vulliamy arrived and bought me champagne. He was and is an incredibly generous colleague. He was fantastic and remained fantastic throughout the whole Bosnian war.' Vulliamy had come directly from reporting the battle for Vukovar, the besieged Croatian town, then entering its final and most brutal phase. The four-month siege was to end about three weeks later, to be followed immediately by the massacre of more than 200 people, shot by Serbian militia and buried in a mass grave.

Vulliamy and O'Kane shared an almost ferocious commitment to speaking truth to power. Maggie O'Kane, as soon as she arrived in the comparative safety of Split after that first visit to Sarajevo, wrote an open letter to the prime minister, commanding a whole Comment page beneath the headline: 'Save Sarajevo, Mr Major'.[6] It was a relentless recital of the agony being inflicted on the multi-ethnic citizenry of the Bosnian capital by militia under the ultimate control of Radovan Karadžić, president of what was soon to be called Republika Srpska. 'I've interviewed Mr Karadžić a few times,' she wrote, 'and it seems to me he gets a bit crazier every time.'

Vulliamy, it will be recalled, had been told to keep an eye on Yugoslavia from his base in Rome. While he was in Dubrovnik a flotilla of 30 small ships led by a car ferry carrying medicine and food negotiated its way through the blockade. It also carried the Croatian president of Yugoslavia, Stjepan 'Stipe' Mesić, who had assembled the convoy.[7] Vulliamy had now been in Yugoslavia for more than a month and was due for a break. He also had a ticket for a key Napoli–Milan football match, a passport to sanity, burning a hole in his pocket. 'I figured that what comes in must get out, so I hitched a ride with Stipe Mesić on the car ferry, planning to get to Ancona in time to make it to Naples in time for this game.' Maggie O'Kane stayed on in Dubrovnik for another two weeks.

On 29 July 1992, the Guardian published what was possibly the most startling dispatch from Maggie O'Kane so far. The report, nearly 2,000 words, was splashed across the front page, under the headline: 'Muslims' nightmare under the long hot Yugoslav sun'. It was the first dispatch in which a Guardian journalist had referred to Serbian 'concentration' camps. Maggie O'Kane's language was unequivocal. Referring to the area of Prijedor, 50 kilometres or so north-west of Banja Luka, she wrote: 'In the four concentration camps in this area in the top corner of Bosnia that the Serbs are claiming for their new Serbian Republic of Bosnia there are at least 14,000 Muslims being held.'

O'Kane had reached Banja Luka by bus from Belgrade. The city was in the process of being closed off. The bus, in which O'Kane sat, indistinguishable from her Serbian fellow passengers, had passed check-points where cars carrying journalists were being turned back. When she checked into a hotel she found she was its only resident. At about four in the morning she had a caller. 'It was a Red Cross worker, a young Serb guy, who said, "You have to understand what is going on." He was the one who alerted me.' He took her to a house where boys under 16 and men over 60 who had been released from the camps were staying. Her own efforts to reach the camps were blocked. But among those she interviewed was a family who had been held for a time in what she called 'Trnopolje concentration camp'. One of the other camps she mentioned was Omarska. O'Kane quoted a witness: 'They've been sitting there for two months, there's no cover, no water to wash and no room to lie down.'

The main horror conveyed by this particular dispatch was the plight of women and children packed into a train of cattle wagons. Again she interviewed a witness. 'They had come from Trnopolje camp ... I only saw a few women's faces and they were sticking their arms out of two barred windows high up in the wagon, but I knew the wagons had to be full because of the noise. The women were crying and the children were screaming. They were screaming, "Water!" Just a glass of water. It was a hot day and the wagons were in the open. They didn't have a toilet.' They were being removed to Zenica in an exercise of 'ethnic cleansing'. By the time the train reached the Bosnian city, some 180 kilometres from Trnopolje, five days later, 11 had died.

There was an immediate response to the article from the Bosnian Serb leader, Radovan Karadžić, who had been in London for talks on the day that it was published. In a letter to the editor,[8] he said: 'Your article on the front page of today's newspaper is sensational and cannot be ignored. It is completely false to suggest that the Bosnian Serbs have organised concentration camps or that we hold civilian prisoners ... I have made an offer to British journalists to make a list of places where they believe such camps exist. I will ensure that they can visit them.'

The day that Karadžić made his promise, Paul Webster, the foreign editor, was having a drink with Maggie O'Kane and Ed Vulliamy at the Coach and Horses pub in Farringdon Road. It was a handover meeting before Vulliamy flew out to return to Yugoslavia in place of O'Kane. Vulliamy recalled, 'Paul had given us an unforgettable, terrifying brief – the best any editor has ever given me: "Get into the thick of it, but I don't want to hear a word from you unless you have the splash [the headline story]".' Webster made a call to Karadžić that night, reaching him on his car phone as he made his way to Heathrow. Webster said the Guardian wanted to accept his invitation and was sending someone out immediately. There had been a similar response from ITN, who dispatched their reporters Penny Marshall and Ian Williams.

One of the most controversial episodes of the war was about to unfold. After delays that dragged out for five days as they were passed down a chain of command starting from Karadžić himself, the journalists were escorted on a restricted visit to Omarska and then to Trnopolje. Neither the International Red Cross, nor the United Nations, nor any press had previously been able to visit Omarska. The main argument on the spot concerned the refusal of those in charge to allow the visitors to see inside a large aluminium shed, contrary to the earlier assurance given by Karadžić that they would be able to see whatever they wished to see. One of those held in the camp and interviewed that day said something that Vulliamy years later was to repeat to the war crimes tribunal at the Hague: 'I do not want to tell any lies, but I cannot tell the truth.' Vulliamy wrote, 'So the aluminium shed conceals some secret. It is a secret the international agencies must uncover if the miasma of lies, propaganda, exaggeration, denial, comparisons with the Nazi Holocaust, claims and counter-claims about concentration camps, is to be more than partially penetrated.'

The party then visited Trnopolje. 'At first, I had been reluctant to call Omarska and Trnopolje "concentration camps", because of the many unique facets of the Holocaust and its scale,' Vulliamy wrote. '... On reflection though, I see that "concentration camps" is exactly what they were.'[9] It was in Trnopolje that the skeletal Fikret Alić was photographed and filmed gazing through strands of barbed wire, providing what quickly became perhaps the single image most readily associated with the war. At Omarska, even among the chosen prisoners who were literally run past the journalists, urged at a rapid jog from the aluminium shed in which they were held to a heavily guarded mess hall, there were men whose physical appearance posed challenging questions. One of these, taken from the ITN footage, stared from a photograph across the width of the Guardian front page beneath a headline: 'The shame of Omarska'.[10] The unstated question was: Whose shame? The implied answer was that it lay not only with those operating the camps but also with the international community for not intervening.

Procrastination on the part of the United Nations, failure to agree a course of action among the members of Nato, allowed the terrible toll to continue. 'Safe havens' protected by UN forces were finally established in the spring of 1993, initially around Srebrenica. They proved to be anything but safe. There was no more telling description of what life was like inside Srebrenica than that published in the Observer in mid-April. It was written by Haris Nezirovic, a 26-year-old Bosnian journalist for the newspaper Slobodna Bosna. He described how 35,000 people were living in basements, wrecked cars, destroyed houses and the ruined streets, as refugees flooded in from fighting in the surrounding villages.[11] A week later Nezirovic was telling a story of incompetence, betrayal and corruption within the Bosnian army, again illustrating the complexity of the situation.[12]

The UN resolution ratifying the establishment of Srebrenica as a safe haven on 6 May had come only after Serb forces had already entered the city, which, by then, had been under siege for a year. The Guardian reported the inevitable Serb penetration on its front page on 17 April. A strapline across the top of the page summarising a message from an amateur radio operator conveyed the desperation: 'We beg you to do something, whatever you can. In the name of God, do something.' Srebrenica was given what the Guardian called 'a thin shield' of 220 Canadian soldiers, serving under the UN. Beyond that, there was louder but still irresolute talk of military intervention, falling fatally short of unanimity. The scene was set for the coming tragedy.

A Guardian editorial on 14 August was unequivocal. 'It should be said quite clearly where this paper stands. We would put many thousands more troops, wearing UN berets, into Bosnia; and we would allow them not merely to defend themselves, but to make the havens truly safe and Sarajevo a protected city. Because we *know* what is happening, we see no possibility of walking away.' The headline on an article by Hella Pick, on the same page as that editorial, acutely summarised the mess of indecision: 'Bumbling while Bosnia burns'. Members of Nato had at last agreed that airstrikes could go ahead, but with the proviso that they be limited to supporting humanitarian relief. Pick, one of the Guardian's most experienced foreign and diplomatic correspondents,

243

summed up the polarity in American and British positions. 'London and Washington have been at opposite ends of the spectrum throughout the interminable debate, with the Americans more gung-ho, and deeply resentful of Britain's angst at being sucked into a vicious civil war. The Europeans are not meeting their responsibilities, with Britain the most cowardly of all.'

It was in that month, August 1993, that John Major had initiated what became known as Operation Irma, sending an RAF Hercules to Sarajevo on a rescue mission to bring out five-year-old Irma Hadzimuratovic, who became an international celebrity in the process. Critics saw it as a public relations exercise to divert attention from the lack of productive activity on the diplomatic or military fronts.[13] Irma's mother had been killed in a mortar attack that left her daughter paralysed from the neck down. Maggie O'Kane took to the Comment pages again, accusing Major of cynicism and hypocrisy. 'Every day in Bosnia is an Irma day,' she wrote. 'Irma may survive. But another Irma is dying in Srebrenica, and Goražde, and the crowded hospitals of Zenica. In Sarajevo ... around 1,000 children have been killed by snipers and Serb gunners firing from the hills in the last year.'

Later that month, Maggie O'Kane was able to join the privileged few, the serving soldiers and politicians, allowed to use the Sarajevo tunnel, built by the Bosnian army and completed a couple of months earlier.[14] The tunnel, carrying essential services such as oil, electricity and telephone, began in the basement of a suburban house. It ran for several hundred yards beneath the Serb positions and under the runway of the UN-controlled Sarajevo airport to Bosnian government-held villages beyond. O'Kane made the narrow and muddy passage with a group of disconsolate politicians from central Bosnia who had spent the weekend in conference discussing the peace plan that lay on the table in Geneva. One of the politicians, a man in his 70s, raised a grim laugh. 'This corridor is the way Bosnia will look when they are finished in Geneva. A little hole like this and with us all crowded in.' Days later, the peace talks collapsed.

The siege continued. On 5 February 1994, a 120mm mortar hit the busy Markale open market in the centre of Sarajevo, killing 68 people. It was - the Guardian's front-page report declared - 'the worst single act of butchery in the 22-month siege of the city'. The headline seemed at last to indicate a strong response from the international community:

'UN chief asks Nato to back Bosnian air raids'. But a subheading told the familiar story: 'Allies split on action following massacre'.

Two days later Nato declared an exclusion zone around Sarajevo, reinforced by President Clinton's blunt statement that 'Nato is now set to act'. Martin Woollacott, in a front-page commentary, noted, 'For the first time in the dark history of the Bosnian conflict the West has credibly threatened to use force, and the effects already appear to have been magical - a Sarajevo ceasefire agreed within hours.'[15]

The peace did not last long. The response of Bosnian Serb forces to the declaration of an exclusion zone around Sarajevo was to fight their way into the 'safe area' of Goražde. This finally provoked Nato's first attack in the two-year war: on 10 April 1994, two US F-16s dropped 500lb-bombs on Serbian positions, following up with another raid the next day. In retaliation, the Serbs intensified the shelling of Goražde, seized 150 UN personnel as hostages, killed two SAS men and shot down a British Sea Harrier. The random bombardment of Sarajevo also resumed, and the plight of the other so-called safe areas worsened.

In May 1995, Julian Borger reported from Sarajevo during a week that was experiencing the heaviest bombardment for 18 months. 'The UN has given up all pretence of protecting the six Bosnian "safe areas" it designated in 1993,' he wrote. Borger spoke to a shopkeeper washing blood from the pavement. '"Fuck the UN", was all he said.'[16]

On the same page, Ian Black, the Guardian's diplomatic editor,[17] surveyed the situation in the other five areas supposedly protected by what he called the 'paper shield' provided by the UN. Srebrenica was one of them. He quoted a Bosnian official describing it as 'a hellish place' with large numbers of people in hospital, a shortage of medical supplies, and a population swollen from 5,000 to 26,000 due to the ethnic cleansing taking place elsewhere.

The Serbs continued to take UN hostages, some of whom were used as human shields to deter bombing raids - raids that, in any case, as Ian Traynor reported, had been 'a signal failure'.[18] An editorial in the Guardian attempted an assessment: 'What is to be done in Bosnia? The UN and Nato and all the governments concerned agree on one thing: they don't have the slightest idea.'

Nothing, it seemed, was able to avert the fate of Srebrenica. In July 1995 as Srebrenica was overrun, the 350 Dutch UN peacekeepers who had the impossible task of protecting the area were, it was said, forced to capitulate, after promised airstrikes were abandoned.[19] Srebrenica finally fell on 13 July. Evidence that a massacre had taken place built swiftly, through accounts given by refugees and by the Dutch personnel who had been forced to abandon the UN post. A story in the Observer by John Sweeney and Charlotte Eagar[20] quoted a Dutch army captain: 'The Muslim men were separated from their families and moved to a white building. I heard shots coming from the building.'

The full horror of Srebrenica emerged over the following weeks and months. Early in August the New York correspondent Mark Tran reported that the United States had presented the Security Council with 'compelling evidence', including aerial photographs of mass graves, that up to 2,400 Bosnian men were massacred after the fall of Srebrenica. The UN report, immediately leaked to the Guardian, along with the testimony of Red Cross officials, made clear the probability that the number would be very much greater. A conservative estimate at the time of writing put the number of victims of what the ICTY had termed 'genocide' at about 8,000. The Dayton peace agreement followed only four months after the massacre but it was not until 25 April 2013 that the president of Serbia, Tomislav Nikolić, publicly apologised for Srebrenica. Conspicuously absent from his apology was the word 'genocide'.

At the fall of Srebrenica, thousands fled into the surrounding country seeking to make their way to the safer ground of Tuzla, 100km (62 miles) away to the north-west, where a refugee camp had been set up. The front page of the Guardian on 15 July carried an image that, as powerfully as that of Fikret Alić, became emblematic of the horrors of this European war. Julian Borger provided the words that went with it. 'In a crowd of over 10,000 refugees sprawled across Tuzla's cornfields, a young woman hanged herself yesterday. No one knew her name. No one wept for her when her body was cut down from a tree, and only a single policeman kept vigil over her corpse as it lay abandoned by the gate of the heaving, sweating camp.' She had been, Borger wrote, 'one of the scatterlings of Europe, torn away more than once from friends, relatives and familiar places.'

The photograph by Darko Bandic, a Croatian photographer, breaking all the rules that in normal times would restrain its publication, was here allowed to provide at once an elegy and an indictment. It was some time before her name, Ferida Osmanovic, became known.

Towards the end of July, the Croatian military began an offensive against the Serb enclave of Krajina in Croatia, causing an initial exodus of some 20,000 refugees, a number eventually to grow tenfold. In the Guardian of 5 August, Julian Borger's report from the Croatian capital, Zagreb, was splashed across the front page under the headline, 'Croats launch all-out war'. Ian Traynor, in a profile of the leader of Croatia, Franjo Tudjman, called him 'a president who has passed from communist fanatic to nationalist zealot'.[21] The full nature of the disaster that had overcome the Serbs of Krajina was reflected in the Guardian's front-page photograph of 9 August, showing the logjam of cars, trucks, men, women and children that had reached the border with Serbia, forming a queue that stretched back for 40 miles.

Towards the end of the month, on Monday 28 August, a 120mm mortar shell landed at the entrance to the covered main market of Sarajevo, killing 43 people. Ed Vulliamy wrote the page one story from Zagreb, pointing out the bombing's potential, and possibly its purpose, to stall the US-driven peace talks. The Guardian carried a gruesome eyewitness account from Sarajevo by the Associated Press reporter Srećko Latal: 'Journalists joined taxi drivers and market vendors in heaping bodies into the back of vehicles to rush them to hospital. Some fell apart as they were lifted by the survivors. Blood-soaked material frayed and split and severed limbs dropped to the ground ... policemen collected legs and arms into plastic bags.'[22] The excruciating detail was unusual; it represented an ultimate point of exasperation and despair.

Nato began bombing targets around Sarajevo at 2am local time on Wednesday. Late editions that night were able to carry the story on Wednesday's front page: 'Nato planes bomb Serbs; mortar outrage prompts attack'. The following day's front page carried the headline: 'The defining moment'. Alongside the combined report from Ed Vulliamy, Ian Black and John Palmer was a dramatic photograph of a massive plume of smoke rising from an ammunition dump at Pale, the town near Sarajevo that the Bosnian Serbs had made their headquarters. The report gave details of '18 hours of concerted air and artillery bombardment against Serbian military positions across Bosnia'. An editorial called the bombing 'a major gamble', the test of which was whether it brought a durable political settlement any closer.

Letters to the editor next day, Friday 1 September, carried a range of opinion about the bombing, and about the Guardian's reaction to it. First was a letter from the MPs Tony Benn, Tam Dalyell and others, utterly condemning the marketplace massacre, but also condemning Nato's intervention. 'The international community loses all moral authority when it adds to the many atrocities which have already taken place.' Among other letters was one from Roderick Bridge, of Hailey, Oxfordshire, attacking the 'chattering negativity' of the Guardian leader. 'What an amazing newspaper you are! After weeks of articles implying the need for positive action in Bosnia, and the day after the UN finally and positively acts to counter the appalling situation there, your leader vacillates with negativism and doubt. Suddenly all your letters to the editor indicate opposition to the UN action.'

On 5 September, amid dissatisfaction with the lack of progress in the withdrawal of heavy weapons from the vicinity of Sarajevo, Nato launched a new onslaught on Serb positions in the biggest single operation in its history. Meanwhile America's chief negotiator Richard Holbrooke arrived in Belgrade for talks with the Serbian president, Slobodan Milošević. Jonathan Steele in a comment piece described the American policy as 'bomb and talk, or Vietnam revisited'. The 'Americanisation' of the war was not automatically bad, he wrote, but 'there is always something inherently cowardly and heavy-handed in the choice of bombs'.

On 11 September, the front-page headline reported a new development in the bombing campaign: 'Serbs hit with cruise missiles'. Ian Traynor in Zagreb and David Fairhall, the Guardian's defence correspondent, reported that for the first time in 11 days of combat operations Tomahawk missiles had been launched from the USS *Normandy* in the Adriatic. The main targets were Serb air defence systems around Banja Luka in response to continued Serb refusal to comply with the exclusion zone around Sarajevo. Several days later the front page was able to strike a more optimistic note: 'Bosnia breakthrough as Serbs agree to lift siege'. Once again Nato was to suspend airstrikes for 72 hours on the promise that the rebel Bosnian Serb forces would at last lift the siege of Sarajevo.

One of the last towns to be reclaimed by Bosnian Muslim forces was Donji Vakuf, about halfway between Sarajevo and Banja Luka. Its fall, Ian Traynor reported, represented a huge morale-booster for the largely refugee army that fought for it. Tony Harrison, whose memorable poem 'A Cold Coming' had been published during the Gulf War, now contributed another, 'The Cycles of Donji Vakuf', carried in full on the front page.[23] It was inspired in part by the sight of one of the victors, a Kalashnikov over one shoulder, a looted mandolin over the other, knees bumping his chin as he made away on a child's bicycle.

The war was now in its final phase. In November, representatives of the main protagonists met near Dayton, Ohio, for what a Guardian headline called 'Bosnia's search for Pax Americana'. Their talks were in progress when Karadžić and General Ratko Mladić appeared at the war crimes tribunal at The Hague where they were indicted with specific reference to the massacre at Srebrenica. Milošević – later also to be wanted by the tribunal – represented Bosnian Serb interests at Dayton in the absence of Karadžić. On 21 November, Milošević, Tuđjman and the Bosnian president Alija Izetbegović initialled the agreement, in what the front-page report called the biggest foreign policy triumph – and the greatest political gamble – of Clinton's presidency. As Traynor reported, the conflict had left an estimated 200,000 dead and more than a million dispossessed.

The Dayton accord, in the division of territory that came out of it, seemed a tacit endorsement of the ethnic cleansing of the four bloody years leading up to it, something presented as an essential compromise in the cause of peace. The ideal of multi-ethnicity was abandoned and former Yugoslavia faced a future newly divided along ethnic lines – or, more accurately, religious lines – between the Orthodox Republika Srpska, the largely Muslim Bosnia-Herzegovina and Catholic Croatia. It reaffirmed that Kosovo with its Albanian Muslim majority was part of Serbia. It was towards Kosovo that eyes now turned as the next likely flashpoint.

That conflict, however, still lay several years ahead. Meanwhile the Guardian had to turn to matters at home that perhaps provided an incongruous contrast to the desperate events in former Yugoslavia. Some of these matters had been there in the background over the past two or three years. All newspapers have to deal with this simultaneity of disparate events, what a previous Guardian historian called the 'commotion of affairs'. The domestic matters that pressed the Guardian had grown, and were still growing, in importance. Now they demanded urgent action.

Chapter 20
The Price of Journalism

*'The Guardian is one of the best-edited papers, for its market.
You have to admire the way it hits the target every day.'*

Rupert Murdoch, 1993[1]

The Guardian, with successful deployments at home and abroad, entered 1993 in fine fettle. It was just as well. Before the year was out it would have bought the Observer, entered the libel labyrinth and weathered the first onslaught of Rupert Murdoch's price war.

Early in the year Peter Preston had submitted the first in a new series of three-monthly reports to the Scott trustees ahead of their meeting on 17 February. It was a succinct and upbeat dispatch from the battlefield, brisk in tone and almost devoid of linguistic Prestonisms. The paper, he told the trustees, had 'so far' had an extremely successful recession. 'We have increased our advertising share and circulation share by very substantial amounts, and' – something he had so long desired – 'are now much more clearly thought of as a mainstream and successful paper, the last vestiges of the old, struggling days dispersed from London advertising minds.' Here in a sentence is an explanation of the depth of anxiety he was to feel as the price war acted as a brake on ambition. There was a great deal to lose.

Precious advantages had been gained, he said, and they must not be frittered away. Among the 'bullish pointers' were 'the evident success of the Saturday colour magazine, which has seen our place in the colour market improve, almost at a stroke, from sixth to third'. And a point of relief, the 'slightly fraught' move of the second features section from broadsheet to tabloid had had no adverse effect on classified advertising. In recruitment advertising the Guardian remained the market leader: in the third quarter of 1992, the paper had held 41% of the market, with the next best the Daily Telegraph at 17%. Circulation also seemed to have repaid the effort and innovation that had taken place throughout the year, especially in the autumn with improvements to the magazine and the creation of G2. 'Early research on reader attitudes to the tabloid second section shows enthusiasm levels around 60%, which is remarkable for any change to something as conservative as a newspaper.' The result was to give the Guardian an aggregated lead over its two main rivals of more than 120,000, putting the Guardian at c. 423,000 – 53,000 more than the Times, and 69,000 ahead of the Independent.[2]

It was with clear satisfaction that Preston attached to his report for the trustees a copy of a page from Campaign, the advertising and media industry 'bible', conferring its Medium of the Year award on the Guardian for 1992 – the first time it had won it since 1982. 'The Guardian, with its well-rounded performance, in the end trounced all opposition,' it declared. 'Throughout the year it looked fresh where other media looked tired.'

With the launch of G2, said Campaign, 'the Guardian radically modernised its brand and became the first true broadsheet-cum-tabloid'. It paid an oblique tribute to David Brook's marketing department, and Ageh's PDU, without mentioning them by name, by complimenting the paper on the way it had used its £1.5 million marketing budget strategically – to back product development, and to produce a series of value-added magazines – rather than tactically, in one-off promotions.

Preston made sure that the trustees knew about further innovations that were already in the pipeline. They included extending printing in Europe and the introduction of 'a television and listings magazine of a rather novel kind'. This was to be Tony Ageh's Guide, launched in an edition of 132,000 within the M25 area in September, its appearance coinciding with the start of Rupert Murdoch's broadsheet price war.

Whether the Guardian was to maintain its price or do what eventually all the other mainstream broadsheet papers were to do and enter the circulation war was to become a matter of strong contention. It was a calculation that would have to be made against the background of serious difficulties that were emerging in the Guardian's ownership of the Observer, which it had bought in the early summer, something that is dealt with in later chapters. The Observer cover price had remained unchanged at 90p. For the moment the price war was more a question of calm debate than urgent counsel. Preston's September report to the Scott Trust was written in the pre-panic week before the Times slashed its weekday price from 45p to 30p, making it suddenly 15p cheaper than the Guardian. At the same time, and potentially even more damagingly, Murdoch cut the price of the Saturday edition of the Times from 50p to 40p. This left the rest of the increasingly lucrative broadsheet Saturday editions at 50p for the Guardian and Independent, and 60p for the Telegraph on Saturday.

Preston, in the calm before the storm, did little more than note in passing that the Sun had enjoyed 'relative success' as the testing ground for price cutting a couple of months earlier, when it had come down from 25p to 20p. But as Andrew Culf and Lisa Buckingham reported in the Guardian two days before the real battle was now declared, 'The Sun claims the move has added 300,000 in daily sales.' The Guardian, they reported, made 'no comment'. Hugo Young, writing on the same day, even sounded just very slightly complacent. Murdoch's price war, he said, was 'a tactic the Guardian is better placed than some competitors to resist'.[3] There was some justification in that. Preston's report had been circulated ahead of the Trust meeting as usual, and Young would have noted that, while an overall loss on the year of £3.4 million was still forecast, the Guardian had actually been running in profit for six months, making some £450,000 in the first four months of the financial year. Advertising had run through the summer of 1993 somewhat ahead of expectations.

Emily Bell, interviewing Murdoch in the Observer, estimated that the cut in the price of the Sun was already costing him £800,000 a week, and that the drop in price of the Times would now push that to more than £1 million. Murdoch, unless he spoke with forked tongue, did not think the Guardian, or for that matter the Observer, would be greatly harmed. 'The Guardian is one of the best-edited papers, for its market,' he said. 'You have to admire the way it hits the target every day. The Observer ... is going to start hitting the target - instead of being all over the joint. And I think that's terrific. It's not good for me, but it will put the Independent on Sunday out of business. They will close and the Observer will get their readers.' This was heartening stuff to read in Farringdon Road.

In October, Newspaper Publishing, the company owning the vulnerable Independent and even more vulnerable Independent on Sunday, defiantly put the price of both titles not down but up. The Independent went up from 45p to 50p, and the Independent on Sunday went up by 10p to £1. The increase, ostensibly justified by a revamp of both papers, seemed surprising to say the least.

Murdoch's campaign - successfully tested on the Sun, and on the Times itself in a limited exercise in Kent - immediately changed the nature of the game between the quality papers. It is not difficult to imagine Preston's feelings when he saw, at a stroke, the Times wipe out the Guardian's hard-won lead over it and by Christmas be ahead by some 50,000. It was the first time it had established such a convincing lead since the end of the 1980s and in 1990, when it had been greatly assisted by the alarming exodus of Guardian readers to the Independent. It had been one of Preston's achievements to claw his way back. Now there may have been some consolation in seeing that it was the Independent that was hardest hit. For the time being it looked as though Guardian readers were resisting the temptation of Murdoch's bargain-basement Times – but would they be able to do so at any price?

Eight months later, in June 1994, amid intimations that the price war was about to get quite dramatically worse, Preston made what sounded like a declaration of faith. 'The choice of a newspaper remains a defining one. It tells, in a word, what kind of person you are. It then relates you to the world in a way where that relationship has meaning and consistency. It is, for millions every morning, part of a way of life. That won't be demolished in a trice.'[4]

The Daily Telegraph, Murdoch's main target, had been striving desperately to keep its sales above the million mark, spending huge sums in the process. In May its average daily circulation slipped to 993,395, the lowest for 40 years. In June its owner, Conrad Black, urged on by his editor Max Hastings, took the inevitable step and cut the weekday price from 48p to 30p. Circulation rose once again above the magic million (and was to stay there well into the millennium). But it was a move more costly even than the high figure that had been anticipated. The Telegraph had already warned that joining the price war would cost it £40 million a year. It had held off for almost 12 months. Now the market had its say, slashing 40% off the value of the group's shares. The Guardian reported: 'According to the Times's calculations, the Independent's circulation has fallen by 56,000 copies a day since the Times dropped its price to 30p last year, making it by far the biggest casualty of the war. Sales of the Telegraph fell by just 14,000, and the Guardian's by only 2,000.'[5]

The Telegraph had just one day, Thursday 23 June 1994, priced at 30p, the same as the Times. On that day too, for one day only, the Independent cut its price from 50p to 20p – a kind of tourniquet to try to staunch the flow to the Times, or an even deeper and self-inflicted wound? It was, in any case, as Richard Brooks noted in the Observer, 'a rather pointless move'.

On Friday morning, the day after the Independent's act of heroic folly, its readers were confronted by a front-page editorial signed by Andreas Whittam Smith. 'Two rightwing ideologues, Mr Black and Mr Murdoch, have set about destroying the quality paper market. Men like Mr Black and Mr Murdoch want control. They care nothing for plurality of opinion, nothing for liberal values.'

Murdoch's response - to Black rather than to Whittam Smith - was to fire another shot. That same Friday the Times lopped another 10p off its cover price, bringing it down to 20p - the same price as the Sun. The Sun by now was selling over 4 million copies a day. The Times, even before the latest cut, had climbed to 517,575 (the average daily figure for May 1994). The Sunday Telegraph produced some interesting figures, calculating that to make a profit at 20p the Times would need to sell an additional 2 million copies - or half a million more copies than the combined circulations of all Britain's national quality dailies.

The first real signs of the jitters appeared in the upper reaches of the Guardian during this week, although its managing director, Jim Markwick, gave the appearance of being completely unfazed. He had set out in his Jaguar on Thursday morning to drive to the cricket ground on the Earl of Carnarvon's estate at Highclere Castle, near Newbury (familiar to television audiences 20 years later as the setting for Downton Abbey). There, in the presence of the Queen, a charity match was to be played between an XI captained by David Gower and the first official South African cricket team to visit England since the anti-apartheid embargo banished them nearly 30 years earlier. Once there, Markwick presumably joined what Frank Keating in his report for the Guardian called the 'select throng of 2,000 corporate guzzlers'.

Markwick settled down to enjoy the game unruffled by the call he had taken in his car from a distraught Hugo Young, telling him that the Times was dropping its price to 20 pence. 'There was an explosion down the phone with Hugo saying, "This is the worst example of rabid capitalism. Murdoch, etc, etc ..." And I remember saying to Hugo, "Hang on, hang on, it is his paper. He can charge what he likes. We may not like it but he is an Australian and he will think we're whinging. So let's just see how it goes." ... But Hugo was worried, very worried. I thought about it overnight. I couldn't see it changed anything. I knew loads of people who read the Guardian and wouldn't go and buy the Times [simply] because it was 20 pence. What we had to do in my opinion was to stick it out.'[6]

But in August cracks began to appear in the Guardian's resolve. What had severely shaken it was the decision of the Independent to reduce its price from 50p to 30p from the first of the month. The Independent was in deep trouble. At the end of July its founding editor Andreas Whittam Smith had stepped down after eight years. He was replaced by Ian Hargreaves, the former deputy editor of the Financial Times, whose brief was to turn the paper round. It was a tall order. In the first half of 1994 it was said to have spent £12 million on restructuring. It had also been shedding staff. Since Murdoch first dropped the price of the Times in early September 1993 the Independent had lost about 20% of its circulation. In June 1994 its average daily sale was being held at around 277,000. That changed when towards the end of the month the Times made the further drop to 20p. The Independent was hard hit. Its circulation figure for July was an alarming 257,812, the lowest since January 1987. It had become a matter of survival. The decision to cut the price was finally taken at the end of an all-day board meeting. The Independent came down to 30p, making it 15p cheaper than the Guardian on weekdays.

Peter Preston professed that he was sorry to see the Independent driven into the price war. He told a reporter, 'For ourselves, we continue to watch the situation, which so far has had very little impact upon us.' That was true. In the first full month after war was declared in September 1993 the Guardian circulation stood at 403,124. In June 1994, nine months later – the month of the Independent's one-day price cut – it stood slightly higher, at 404,225. The Guardian, however, had a particularly bad July and August. The figures for August were the worst for more than a decade, with an average sale of 378,987. The Independent over the same period, apparently assisted by its price cut, seemed to be climbing out of the pit, and put on over 32,000 copies to reach an average for the month of 289,403.

Preston, watching the figures as the month progressed, felt he could hold off no longer. On 23 August he tapped out a memo to Jim Markwick, copied to Alan Rusbridger. He was proposing, as necessary advance support for the paper's normal autumn circulation offensive, an immediate drop in the price of the Guardian from 45p to 40p, with the possibility of a later cut to 35p. The time, he argued, would never be more right. In addition he was advocating a simultaneous cut to 20p for students, something he was particularly keen on. He gave his deputy, Rusbridger, the task of collating a blurb for Saturday's paper, which he duly did. The first few paragraphs of the draft were plugging some of the editorial goodies lined up for the paper's autumn sales drive, starting that day in the Weekend magazine with Nick Davies's 'Dark Heart', 'a vivid series of tales from the underside of Britain.' The highlight of September was to be a 'world exclusive', an extract from Marlon Brando's autobiography, *Songs My Mother Taught Me*, the purchase price of which had come as a special dispensation from group funds. Also announced was an innovation that was not to live up to its promise, a new G2 for Fridays, to be called '... Friday' and quickly known as 'dot dot dot Friday', a section that failed to find a convincing identity.[7]

Notice of the price cuts followed. They were to come into effect for the Guardian from Monday 29 August 1994 and the previous day for the Observer, which was to come down from 90p to 70p. But at the time the blurb was being prepared nothing had been agreed, and a row over the issue was still racketing around Farringdon Road. The draft notice included a personal explanation from Peter Preston: 'Through the cut-price wars, the Guardian's reputation for quality and innovation has seen us hold our own and develop. We're very grateful for the loyalty of Guardian readers. What we're missing, however, is the chance to reach out to new readers and to a new generation of young people buying a paper for the first time. That's what we aim to do this autumn.'

Preston was already aware of differences over the issue with Markwick. Markwick saw a cut of 5p as 'the worst kind of tokenism' that would have the negative effect of demonstrating weakness to the other contending parties. 'We're so weak we can only do 5. You can do 25. I mean it is not clever ... Perhaps *you* can go to 20p and live, *we* couldn't go to 20p and live, not possibly. So where does that lead you? It leads you to stick it out.' Usually when the cover price of the Guardian went up or down there was consensus. 'I knew what Peter was thinking. He knew what I was thinking. We would look at each other and see whether we were thinking the same. So this was different because it was disagreement.'

Caroline Marland called their management meetings the 'Peter and Jim show'. She was vehemently opposed to any cut. Her point was that it would not only reveal weakness to competitors, but it would also devalue the paper in the eyes of advertisers. At this point, as deputy managing director to Markwick, her main role was advertisement director. Preston was the chairman of the Guardian board. 'I said absolutely no. Peter and I had a very difficult meeting, totally disagreeing with each other. I felt really, really strongly about it. If we cut the cover price, what were we saying about ourselves? I thought if they cut the cover price I am going to go, I am going to leave ...'[8] That may or may not have happened, but it would have been a dangerous calculation for others to make. She was known as someone who brought great emotional commitment to her work. Markwick when he had appointed her had joked, 'You're not coming to me as my director of over-reaction?' She had left that day not knowing whether the price was to be cut or not. 'We were going on holiday ... My husband was waiting outside. I went off in a great anger and wept for about four days.'

Markwick had been in the position of arbitrator, but unable to achieve consensus. 'In the circumstances, of Murdoch doing what he did, this was such a big item in the day-to-day running of the Guardian – [it was] the concern of everybody ... [A decision to cut the price] really would have had to be consensual. And, to add to Caroline and to me, David Brook and David Owen [the circulation director] were both of our mind.'

A couple of days after her arrival in her Corsican holiday villa, Caroline Marland took a call from Markwick. He had been involved in a flurry of meetings, telephone calls and what he called 'couch management' – informal chats in his office. He told her he had taken a vote and there would be no cut in cover price. The plug for the editorial content was published as planned on 27 August. The Brando serialisation was a huge success. Sales on 3 September when the first episode was published were the largest, at 514,910, since the Independent launched in 1986. Nick Davies won an award for 'Dark Heart'. The announcement of the proposed price cuts was pulled at the last moment.

Marland's reaction need hardly be stated. A champagne cork probably popped in Corsica. Markwick, in retrospect, commented, 'It turned out right. We didn't go down and we held our own and we looked like big boys.' Preston in a sense was right too. He hated the idea of conceding ground to the Independent. 'It was probably one aspect of my continuing feeling, since the Indy was launched, that we'd been too complacent and sportsmanlike about its threat – and that we had to be a more unpredictable and potentially hostile competitor. There was – from the word go – an assumption that we were in our own untouchable cocoon, and this gave the Indy a head start. Here they were, years later, shipping water ... could we help get them drenched?'

'Murdoch wanted to kill it off,' wrote Stephen Glover.[9] So apparently did Preston.

Preston did carry through one price cut. That was his promotion for students, which was finally presented in October 1994. A blurb on the front page on 4 October promised 20p off the price of the Guardian and 40p off the Observer, with a book of discount vouchers that could also provide those essentials of student life: a mug, an alarm clock and a toaster.

Everyone seemed to have drawn something valuable from the thrashing out of views that took place over the cover price issue, not least Rusbridger. The price war would go well into his editorship, the effect exacerbated by huge rises in the price of newsprint. Preston, now in the new role of editor-in-chief of the Guardian and the Observer, continued to complain about the negative aspect of the Guardian's stand. In his briefing for the Scott Trust in June 1995, he said one effect of the price war was to hamper the paper's ability to recruit young readers. That had a malign effect that could only 'grow and rattle' through the years.

It seemed clear that Murdoch's strategy, although he had failed to catch the Telegraph or even to drag it permanently below the 1 million mark, had succeeded in establishing the Times as the first of the rest. In terms of print circulation it was clear that the Guardian would never again lead the trio of quality dailies that trailed the Telegraph (performance on the web would be a very different matter). Nevertheless, the Guardian had done something quite remarkable in very difficult circumstances. It had not simply ridden out the price war. It had produced some of the most riveting and courageous journalism in its history. There was more of that to come. Perhaps most remarkably, it had 'saved' the Observer, although in an act of rescue that sometimes looked as though the consequences would still be fatal. As we shall now see, the two papers, after the Observer's acquisition, led intertwined, even tangled lives, often marked by mutual antagonism and suspicion, confounding the high hopes with which it all started.

Chapter 21

The Observer: A Marriage, but No Honeymoon

'A marriage made in heaven.'

Anthony Sampson

Jim Markwick, arriving late to speak at a lunch for Guardian advertising and commercial staff in 1993, combined his apology with a flourish: 'I'm sorry I'm late, I've been buying a Sunday newspaper.' 'Of course,' Caroline Marland recalled, 'everyone cheered.' In the periodic ructions that followed the Guardian's purchase of the Observer, reverberating through a rapid succession of editors, it was sometimes forgotten what a great coup the acquisition was for the Guardian management team. Harry Roche, the group chairman, had thrown himself 'body and soul' into the task, according to Markwick; and Markwick, the managing director of the Guardian, had led the detailed negotiations. It was a coup too for Peter Preston. He had realised a longstanding ambition to have a Sunday partner for the daily paper. Now he had acquired not just the world's oldest Sunday newspaper but the one long and universally recognised as closest in liberal values and spirit to the Guardian.

'It seemed a marriage made in heaven,'[1] was the initial response of Anthony Sampson, who had played an important part on the Observer in the heyday of David Astor, the editor who, over three decades, made it 'the most radical liberal newspaper in modern British journalism'.[2] Sampson, like Hugo Young and many others, was a 'Golden Age-ist' so far as the Astor era was concerned: he left in dismay after the paper's acquisition by Roland 'Tiny' Rowland, chief executive of Lonrho, in 1981. 'A peach for Lonrho,' Rowland had called it.[3] There would be times when it looked more like a millstone for the Guardian.

There was another factor. In acquiring the Observer, the Guardian had struck one more blow to Andreas Whittam Smith's once almost insufferably successful Independent, which was now beginning to lose some of its shine. Only a month before negotiations over the Observer reached fever pitch in April, the Independent had scrapped most of its much-admired original design for a new look that according to many, including one of its founders, had seemed 'almost a deliberate act of self-destruction'.[4] Now, the Guardian - as though to rub in its victory - installed Jonathan Fenby, an early Independent defector, as the successor to the outgoing Observer editor Donald Trelford.

The Independent itself had indirectly endorsed Preston's high opinion of Fenby by twice trying to secure his return, first as deputy editor of the Sunday paper and later to take over the editorship of the Independent itself from Andreas Whittam Smith. Both offers were declined without too much difficulty. The Scott Trust had unanimously backed Preston's nomination of Fenby as the new Observer editor at their meeting in February. Fenby, on the face of it, was well prepared. He had been involved in planning for a takeover a year or two earlier, when the Guardian had danced around the Observer looking for a more serious sabbath partner after the drawn-out death of the Sunday Correspondent. 'Jonathan had done all the original thinking about how you'd operate for the first hundred days,' Preston revealed.

This time the competition had been fierce. The Observer had been snatched from the talons of Whittam Smith's Independent eagle at the very last moment. When it had looked as though the Independent had the deal in the bag - as reported in the Evening Standard - three of their senior executives had taken a Saturday excursion to Docklands to see the Observer, 'their paper', coming off the presses. Their visit had reportedly travelled the grapevine and was seen as an arrogant and premature act, carried out as though the deal was a fait accompli. This was not the opinion of Tiny Rowland, who, when he heard about it, according to Markwick, was 'mad as a hatter - absolutely incandescent'.[5]

That same evening, 23 April, Robert Lowe, an associate editor of the Observer, had been busy drafting a direct appeal to his proprietor, begging him not to sell to the Independent. In part it read, 'We appeal to you not to allow this great newspaper to be sold to Newspaper Publishing Ltd and merged with the Independent on Sunday. This would effectively mean the death of the Observer.' No one really believed the rumour that the Independent on Sunday would be the one subsumed and the Observer would be the dominant name in the masthead.[6] No one believed that the Independent's pursuit of the Observer was a rescue mission, rather that the idea was to take it over and close it in the hope of helping the Independent out of its own financial and circulatory difficulties.

All the available senior Observer journalists signed Lowe's letter, and that night, after the first edition had gone away, it was delivered by hand to Rowland's London home in Chester Square, Belgravia. Numerous voices in parliament and the press had been a chorus to the negotiations, warning that perpetual ignominy would attend the souls of those responsible for such an act. Tiny Rowland did not want to be one of them. On the Tuesday morning after the sale to the Guardian had been confirmed he called an astonished Robert Lowe from his car phone to say, disingenuously or not, 'I wanted you to know it was your letter that persuaded me to sell to the Guardian and not to the Independent.'[7]

The sale had been an extraordinary cliffhanger. On the day the Evening Standard published its erroneous 'scoop' announcing that Rowland had sold to the Independent, Roche and Markwick were still in negotiation and, possibly buoyed by the news that their milch cow, the Auto Trader, had made a record before-tax profit of almost £9 million, they had increased their offer to £25 million. (As Harry Roche remarked, 'The cash flow from this division is the lifeblood of the Group.'[8]) The deal appeared to be practically sealed by the time Tiny Rowland - who had acquired the Observer in the first place to promote Lonrho's African interests - flew off to South Africa for the funeral of Oliver Tambo, the former ANC leader.

These were busy days before Rowland's departure on Thursday. On Monday, for the first time since the negotiations started, Markwick and Roche met Rowland and his co-director (shortly to become his nemesis) the German tycoon, Dieter Bock, face to face at the Lonrho headquarters in Cheapside, in the City of London. According to a detailed account of the acquisition that Simon Caulkin wrote at the time for the Observer, Rowland told the Guardian pair that for Lonrho it was now simply a question of Yes or No. 'So if you want the answer to be yes, make the highest offer you possibly can.'[9] The following morning there was a breakfast meeting with Nicholas Morrell, who had been leading the negotiations for Lonrho. The Guardian was now offering £27 million, payable in two instalments, the first on completion, the second a year later; Lonrho was to refund £5 million to pay for redundancies and put up an additional substantial sum to cover the severance payment for Donald Trelford. There was a final shaking of hands in the Lonrho offices on Wednesday evening.

On Thursday it was announced that the Guardian had bought the Observer. There was one last hitch. A meeting between Nick Morrell and Jim Markwick had reached an impasse over the sum of £133,000, which Markwick was refusing to pay. Principals were consulted. Roche was easily reached, and backed up Markwick. Morrell announced he would phone Rowland, now mid-air en route to South Africa. Markwick, suddenly becoming the economy-class Manchester Guardian man, said, 'I didn't know you could phone anyone on a plane.' Morrell said, 'You can on this one, it's Tiny's plane.' Rowland's response, delivered from a great height, was, 'OK, bag it.'[10] The deal stayed on course.

It was pretty well bound to. At 10.30 that morning, coinciding with the press release, Donald Trelford briefed his troops. Preston addressed his at noon. Andrew Culf, the Guardian media correspondent, reporting in the next day's paper – 'Guardian wins battle for Observer' – led off with what seemed to be a reassuring remark from Preston. 'Our overriding aim is clear: to help publish an editorially independent and vibrant Observer.' But readers who turned to the continuation of Culf's report on the back page would have found the first public utterance of what was to become a doleful mantra, also from Preston: 'We have to get some mountainous losses down to break even pretty quickly. I know it can be done and the Observer can be a strong and flourishing paper again.'

For the moment there was relief and rejoicing, certainly at the Observer's extraordinary two-tone postmodern Marco Polo House south of the Thames in Battersea, luxurious accommodation that Preston, having in mind perhaps the contrast with his carpet warehouse in Farringdon Road, called 'the stately pleasure dome', after Coleridge. Bottles of the Observer's own-labelled Blanc de Blancs champagne, bought in to mark the paper's bicentenary two years earlier, were dug out and swigged for the benefit of the visiting television crews, albeit from plastic cups. Even at the time of the bicentenary in 1991 there had been a bitter aftertaste. According to one member of staff, the anniversary had been an occasion not for celebration but for 'widespread recognition that the paper was drifting, and probably doomed'.[11]

Observer readers were ecstatic, none more so the 80-year-old Lord [Jock] Campbell of Eskan: 'As an Observer reader for 65 years may I be among the many to rejoice at the prospect of partnership between the two most civilised and cultured newspapers in the English language. May they both flourish.' The Guardian was probably the preferred option of most Observer readers, 30% of whom had been reading it during the week, a higher proportion than turned to any other daily. This preference worked both ways: 34% of Guardian readers chose the Observer on Sundays in 1990, though this had fallen from 44% three years earlier.[12] Ownership, it was hoped, could be used to stimulate and restore that crossover.

In City Road, the home of the Independent, there were mixed feelings. Ian Jack, who had succeeded Stephen Glover as the editor of the Independent on Sunday, commented with apparent magnanimity, 'We wish the Guardian and the Observer well and look forward to the challenge ahead.' The 'southern Europeans', as the Independent called its backers from La Repubblica in Italy and El País in Spain, were relieved that the deal had fallen through. So was its chairman, Sir Ralf Dahrendorf, who thought the Independent would have severely harmed itself had it been seen to shut down the Observer. But for Andreas Whittam Smith this defeat at the hands of the Guardian was, according to Stephen Glover, 'an incalculable blow'.[13] The Independent on Sunday at the beginning of 1993 was selling about 400,000 copies, the Observer around 520,000. Whittam Smith had dreamed of a circulation for the merged papers of up to 800,000 copies.[14] He took defeat badly, strongly suspecting that his bid had been undermined by a calculated leak to Tiny Rowland about the opposition to the purchase within the Independent's own camp.

For everyone else it looked like the best possible news. The sale had 'saved' the Observer. It had given the Guardian the Sunday title that it had wanted for years. And it had perpetuated competition for the Independent on Sunday, which was now perceived as weakening the daily title by diverting resources from it.

By acquiring the Observer, the Guardian had avoided its only other option: to launch its own Sunday newspaper, an idea that had been briefly entertained. Fenby recalled, 'We had done a successful Saturday paper at the Guardian and so had some weekend experience ... The idea was for a

Guardian on Sunday with low staffing that might break even on sales of 300,000. I recall a meeting in the Guardian canteen with Alan Rusbridger (who I thought should be editor), David Brook [the marketing director], and some others to kick the idea around.' It had gone no farther when Harry Roche and Jim Markwick went out and bought the Observer.

In the week after the purchase, Preston met the Observer's independent directors, originally appointed in 1981 to act as guarantors of the paper's editorial independence under Lonrho ownership. Their effectiveness in the role had been questioned from the start. John Cole, who it will be remembered had left the Guardian when Preston was preferred for the editorship, moved from the Observer to the BBC as soon as Lonrho took over. 'I jumped before I was pushed,' he commented. The main issue for him had been the 'clear conflict of interest between Lonrho's extensive commercial interests in Africa and the reputation for independence which the Observer had established by its stance when the new black states were emerging'.[15] He had no faith at all in the ability of the independent directors to monitor such a conflict. The same directors, whose role would be taken over by the Scott Trust, now came out unanimously in favour of the Guardian deal.

Towards the end of May the final obstacle was cleared away when Michael Heseltine, the trade and industry secretary, gave his consent for the sale 'as a matter of urgency', saying that the Observer in its present condition was not economic as a separate concern. His decision did away with the need to refer the matter to the monopolies and mergers commission, avoiding the delay that would have involved. (He was right about the Observer's financial performance: in the year to September 1992, the paper had lost £8.7 million.)

Fenby's appointment as editor had been announced on the front page of the Guardian on Saturday 15 May and in the Observer the following day. Hugo Young, as chairman of the Scott Trust, in a statement quoted in both papers, said, 'The trust safeguards will be fully extended to the Observer, which will be edited independently of the Guardian and retain its separate character.' The words 'to be edited independently' had been shrewdly insisted upon by Fenby.[16]

Before the public announcement of his appointment, Fenby had asked Rusbridger out for Sunday lunch in Islington. Many had regarded the innovative features editor as favourite for the job, and Fenby wanted to sound out Rusbridger's position. Fenby (correctly) assumed that Rusbridger had been considered for it - though in fact it was unlikely Preston would risk putting him into the Observer when he was already grooming him to take over the top job at the Guardian. Stephen Glover in the Independent summarised it nicely: 'It was felt that this would have been a bit like sending Caesar to govern Gaul when there was a big vacancy in Rome.'

Rusbridger told Fenby over their lunch - in Fenby's account - that he had not wanted the job, and made it clear that he did not envy Fenby facing what he called the absolutely impossible task of being the Observer's first Guardian-appointed editor. Fenby set aside whatever misgivings he had. He knew he was unlikely to rise further at the Guardian: he had been told as much, in a roundabout way. There had been a dinner for an anniversary of Preston's editorship and David McKie had asked Fenby whether he would stand in as night editor so that Phil Osborne could attend. 'You won't mind, you'll understand, won't you?' Then McKie, not an unkind man, added, 'After all, you're not family.'

Fenby's appointment as editor of the Observer now opened the path for Rusbridger's ascent at the Guardian, through the vacated deputy editorship to the throne itself. Unlike Fenby, Rusbridger was family.

When the moment came for the Guardian to make its first visit to Battersea, an element of high farce entered the proceedings. It was decided that, since the austerity-focused message they were carrying was not one of unalloyed joy, they would avoid anything that might be taken for triumphalism on their part. Their company BMWs were left in Farringdon Road and they made the journey, four quite large men - Hugo Young, Peter Preston, Ian Wright and Jonathan Fenby - to Marco Polo House in a Renault Clio belonging to Preston's wife, Jean. As they arrived at the Observer the car park attendant stepped forward and said, 'I'm afraid you can't park there, sir, that's Mr Trelford's place.' Preston, the driver, replied, 'I think we can, we've bought it.'

Preston's 20-minute 'rivers of money' speech to the Observer staff, as it came to be known, made an indelible impression on all who heard it.[17] The political sketch writer Simon Hoggart, who had annoyed Preston 11 years earlier by leaving the Guardian to go to the Observer, recalled how the euphoria with which the Guardian ownership had been greeted had been instantly dispelled when, as he put it, 'Peter Preston arrived on a morale-lowering visit.'[18] It was the first time that Preston had set foot in the building. In retrospect Preston conceded that he might have been slightly overwound on that Tuesday morning, the start of the working week for the Sunday newspaper. 'The Guardian had had a very good run, in terms of things we'd done which had worked or seemed to work ... [Looking back] we were hugely overconfident. Anyway we went down there and gave a speech, which intrinsically said, "You're among friends. Of course it won't be easy. You've got to live the way the Guardian lives."' And there was the rub.

'If we can make a success of this deal then, at last, after decades of uncertainty, we may be able to offer a great paper a home that will last it for another 202 years,' Preston declared, with a reference to the Observer's birth in 1791, 30 years before the Guardian. But this prize came with a dire warning, prefaced by a sentence that seemed to echo CP Scott's famous essay: 'It is well to be frank; it is even better to be fair.' Preston's version had a harder edge to it. 'It is well to be frank, even stark, about the difficulties we face. A couple of weeks ago the Observer was saved, at the very last gasp, from extinction as a separate title. It was sliding, like the News Chronicle, into the maw of another paper – and within a few months, like the News Chronicle, it would have been only a memory invoked over champagne cocktails at the Garrick Club bar.' An involuntary shudder may have run through older members of his audience at this point: the liberal News Chronicle had been absorbed into the Daily Mail in 1960. Preston often demonstrated that he had a long memory.

'Why were you, and why are you, in such a deep plight? You are losing rivers of money, a haemorrhage that has got to be staunched. And in every other way you have been losing ground too swiftly.' He reminded his audience of the 25% decline in readership over the past three years. 'The situation in every respect is deadly serious, whoever owns you. This has got to be tackled; and that is bound to be painful.'

The Guardian group, he told them, had the great advantage of being owned by the Scott Trust, which meant that the money it earned went back into the group and not in dividends to external shareholders. 'But that also means we only have what we earn. We cannot go to the markets and raise cash by share offers for Spaniards or Italians [as the Independent had done] ... We cannot and will not be able to afford to maintain the Observer unless your mountain of loss is reduced at the double, to at least break even.'

Costs would have to be slashed by amalgamating every possible commercial operation. 'Deep savings' would be made in editorial. There would be many job losses. The Marco Polo building would be vacated by autumn and the Observer transferred to Farringdon Road.

The chilling effect of this on the newly rescued Observer journalists was palpable. Trelford, who was present pending his imminent departure, recalled Alan Watkins, the Observer's brilliant political columnist, muttering to him, 'They're like a conquering army. Who do they think they are?'[19] Watkins defected to the Independent on Sunday shortly afterwards. Simon Hoggart summed up: 'Basically what he was saying was the days of spending are over; you now work for the Guardian, it's bread and cheese from now on.'

The Observer journalists had a lot to lose: they were better paid than their Guardian colleagues and enjoyed first-class rail travel and often business-class flights: all that would have to go. When negotiations on the issue commenced in earnest two or three weeks later, the Observer union representative challenged Markwick: 'I bet you don't go economy.' 'Well, fortunately I had my economy ticket to New York in my desk. Although,' Markwick added, 'I didn't tell them that I often got upgraded.'

The disparity had not ended there. In 1981, when Simon Hoggart moved to the Observer after more than a decade on the Guardian, he was dispatched to Washington to write about Reagan's first months as president. 'I remember saying to the foreign editor, "I'll book a room at the Holiday Inn" - $50 a night or whatever. And he said, "Oh no, no, no. You're representing the Observer. You must stay at the Jefferson" - about $150 or $200 a night. "We can't have the Observer man staying in the Holiday Inn."'

Preston in his speech made several unfortunate references to Jonathan Mirsky, the Observer's China correspondent, as an example of profligacy. He and Preston had once been on the same flight out from London to Hong Kong and on arrival had shared a cab, 'Me,' Preston said, 'to my very simple downmarket hotel and Mirsky to the [five-star] Mandarin.' This is where, according to Hoggart, Preston really did 'get up people's nostrils'. Mirsky was something of a hero both to colleagues and to the people of Hong Kong for his courageous reporting from Beijing of the massacre in Tiananmen Square, where he had been badly beaten by the troops. Hoggart believed he received a preferential room rate at the Mandarin in recognition of this, although there was a subversive suggestion that he probably received a special price as a long-time regular guest of the hotel.

Either way, Preston's remarks about Mandarin Mirsky did not go down well. One Observer journalist remarked, 'It's as though Fortnum has been bought by Tesco.' Michael White said there were some situations for which Preston had a 'bad proboscis': this, he suggested, was one of them.

Fenby had listened to Preston's speech with growing dismay. 'However right and proper the message was, it was appallingly misjudged, tin-ear stuff, and, inevitably, it cast me as the grim reaper. I knew I had to make significant cuts in editorial spending, and would have wished to do so with minimal disruption. But this was now impossible. After that meeting, the resentment in the air was enormous - though Donald Trelford sailed over it in typical fashion: he took me to lunch at Bibendum to "mark my card" on the journalists' - an exercise of very limited use, Fenby decided. On the way to the restaurant in Fulham Road, perhaps with Preston's austerity speech in mind, 'Trelford went into a long riff about how the man at the wheel of his company car [a Jaguar] was not a chauffeur but his "driver" - there was an important difference, it seemed, which I fear escaped me.'

The completion of the sale on 1 June at the offices of the Guardian's lawyers in Holborn was a calculatedly restrained affair. Jim Markwick, for the Guardian, handed over a cheque for £13,500,000 - the first of the two equal instalments - and Harry Roche, the group chairman, raised his glass of buck's fizz with the words, 'It's all down to us now.'[20] It was to turn out that he had been far too optimistic in his estimates of the speed with which Observer losses could be reduced. 'Break-even' was a light only intermittently visible at the end of a very long tunnel.

Chapter 22
Teething Troubles – And a Painful Extraction

'You will wish to resign.'

Hugo Young's words to Jonathan Fenby

As soon as the ink had dried on the deal for the Observer, the promised changes began to take shape. It was the commercial staff who bore the initial brunt of the cutbacks. In the first few months of Guardian ownership 186 people out of a total Observer staff of 305 were made redundant, the great majority in non-editorial departments.[1] Those who survived to make the journey from Battersea to Clerkenwell were greeted by a giant poster on the hoarding across the road saying, 'The Guardian welcomes the Observer'. It somehow felt not only like a ready embrace for the new arrivals but also an admonition to their hosts. Greeters were on hand to guide incoming Observer employees to the recently opened staff restaurant for breakfast, where they had a friendly briefing from senior executives before being escorted to their desks on the fifth floor.

Each new arrival was given a copy of a 52-page glossy booklet, the nicely named Clerkenwell Observer, produced by the PDU. It provided a map of the district and a floor-by-floor guide to the Farringdon Road building. It also carried an introduction by Hugo Young, which pointed out that the purchase of the Observer had necessitated a change in the structure of the company, indicated by a change in the name from Guardian and Manchester Evening News plc [GMEN] to Guardian Media Group plc.

The Scott Trust, Young told his readers, 'has provided for the Guardian a unique form of newspaper ownership, with benefits which it should not be difficult to transmit to the Observer'. During the cyclical crises that were to dog the Scott Trust ownership, Young's statements were examined again and again. Did they or did they not incorporate a commitment to ensure publication of the Observer 'in perpetuity'? It was well understood that before the purchase the Trust's core purpose was to guarantee the continuation of the Guardian 'in perpetuity'. So what else could Young have meant when he said, 'The Trust safeguards will be fully extended to the Observer,' or when he referred to the benefits of a form of ownership 'which it should not be difficult to transmit to the Observer'?

In fact, Young's statements, which were intended to guarantee to the Observer the same editorial independence that the Guardian enjoyed, had carefully stopped short of extending to it the promise of everlasting life. It was a question he had anticipated when negotiations over the Observer were discussed by the Trust in February. The trustees agreed that, while the Observer would have the benefits that were conferred on any company owned by the Scott Trust, it could not be viewed in the same light as the Guardian. (Not even the Manchester Evening News had ever been allowed to drink the elixir that the Trust reserved for the Guardian.) Furthermore, the trustees agreed that while every effort should be made to bring the Observer into profit this should not be to the detriment of the Guardian.[2]

The next paragraph of Young's welcoming statement in the Clerkenwell Observer was also to resonate: 'No editor of the Guardian has ever been fired and most have had lengthy terms in the job. The Trust appoints the editors of the Guardian, the Manchester Evening News, and now the Observer ... It keeps out of executive decision-making as rigorously as it avoids any discussion of editorial content, let alone voicing an opinion about the line any editor ought to take ... It will also defend the editors against improper pressure from any quarter.' Given that within five years three editors of the Observer had been fired, the first two discharged by Young himself in the best autocratic fashion of Fleet Street, these assurances in retrospect have a somewhat hollow ring.

Bill Quirke, the management consultant who had been hired to help the smooth transfer of staff from Battersea to Farringdon Road, reflecting on the experience a couple of years later, explained that the planning team had looked at the operation very much from the arriving Observer employees' point of view.[3] 'How would they feel walking up the road to the building on their first morning? How separate from their Guardian colleagues would they feel?'

Quirke had no doubt that at the time he was writing the operation in the commercial departments had been a success. 'The relative smoothness of the integration meant that after a month or two the deputy managing director felt it impossible to tell who had come from which title ... This is a good result when judged against the background of many mergers and acquisitions. Issues of identity, wounded pride and different values rage for years afterwards, in some cases bringing about the failure of the acquisition.'

Issues of wounded pride, if not of different values, did rage on the editorial side and to some extent were never to be entirely resolved. There was certainly an identity crisis. One element of it was a feeling that conflicts of interest during the Lonrho period had masked the achievements of Trelford's editorship. When Carolyn McCall claimed that after the first few years of Guardian ownership the Observer had become a much better paper,[4] Trelford was stung to reply, 'Really? Better than the Observer of Kenneth Tynan, Michael Frayn, Philip Toynbee, Gavin Young, Patrick O'Donovan, Clive James, Julian Barnes, Hugh McIlvanney, to mention only a few of the writers I had the good fortune to publish?'[5]

Trelford's career had run in parallel with Preston's. They came from similar backgrounds in the north Midlands. They were only six months apart in age. Their grammar schools used to compete with each other on the sports field. Preston went to Oxford, Trelford to Cambridge: both were involved in student journalism. Preston joined Hetherington's Guardian in 1963; Trelford went to David Astor's Observer in 1966. They both became editors in 1975. They had considerable respect for each other.

Much has been made of Telford's talent to survive. '[Trelford] has a remarkable facility for staying upright in a shipwreck,' was how the lawyer Arnold Goodman put it.[6] Preston was more generous, describing Trelford's 18-year helming of the Observer as 'extremely heroic ... I think he did as well as anybody could have done through the instability of the Observer ownership after David Astor, in many ways keeping it afloat.'[7]

Trelford himself recalled that during his time on the paper, prospective purchasers had included the King of Saudi Arabia, President Gaddafi of Libya, the Aga Khan, Sir James Goldsmith, Robert Maxwell, the Shell heiress Olga Deterding, and Sally Aw Sian, the Chinese 'Tiger Balm' businesswoman. A bid for the Observer from Rupert Murdoch was foiled by Trelford in a manner so adroit that he drew from the Australian tycoon a grudging admiration. 'The biggest mistake I made was underestimating

Donald Trelford.'[8] Associated Newspapers were also keen candidates, and that is not to mention the eventual owners, the American oil company Atlantic Richfield, who bought it from the Astors for £1 in 1976, virtually saving it from closure, and Lonrho, the next in line, who paid Atlantic Richfield £6 million in 1981.[9]

Preston's reference to heroism probably went back to Trelford's role in the Observer's resistance to the Lonrho takeover. It was Rowland's international conglomerate whose business practices the prime minister Edward Heath had described in 1973 as 'the unacceptable face of capitalism'.[10] Heath had initiated a Department of Trade and Industry (DTI) investigation following accusations against Lonrho of breaking sanctions on trade with Rhodesia, and numerous other malpractices. Trelford played a big part in the campaign to get Rowland's bid for the Observer vetoed through a referral to the monopolies commission. 'We opposed Rowland as proprietor for obvious reasons. He had huge interests in Africa. The Observer had a big reputation for its coverage of Africa. We thought there were bound to be conflicts. It wasn't just a question of his commercial interests, he was the personal friend of many African leaders and had political [associations] in Africa. We also had a sense that he would be a bullying proprietor; why else buy the Observer?'[11] The deal was allowed to go through with the proviso that independent directors be appointed. It was during a break in late-night discussions over these that Rowland shook Trelford's hand, and said 'You're not making it very easy for me, Mr Trelford.'

Rowland also had aspirations in another direction. He wanted to gain control of Harrods. The Monopolies Commission had effectively barred Lonrho from bidding for Harrods in 1981, the same year it bought the Observer. The former Labour prime minister James Callaghan told Trelford that he had heard privately from the Thatcher government that Lonrho could have either the Observer or Harrods but not both.[12] Rowland's frustration and anger peaked in 1985 when, despite his efforts to prevent it, House of Fraser with its flagship Harrods was bought by a former director of Lonrho, Mohamed Al-Fayed, for £615 million. The acrimonious battle between Rowland and Fayed was to go on until Rowland's death in 1998 – much of it on Rowland's side conducted through the pages of the Observer.

The feud very quickly became personal. Rowland believed that Fayed had lied to the government about the source and extent of his wealth. In

1985 and 1986, after a number of critical articles had been published about them, Fayed and his brothers sued the Observer, issuing three writs for libel.[13] Towards the end of 1988 Rowland defiantly published the results of his research into his opponent's background in a 200-page paperback, *A Hero from Zero*, circulated free to all who responded to his extensive advertising campaign. Rowland had it translated into French and Arabic and by the end of January he was claiming that 80,000 copies had been circulated.

Rowland's most sensational move came when he acquired a copy of the DTI report of the inquiry into the Harrods takeover by Fayed. The government had declined to publish it ostensibly because of an active investigation by the Serious Fraud Office. Rowland told Trelford he intended to make it public at a meeting of Lonrho shareholders on 30 March 1989. Trelford knew that that would bring immediate injunctions, making it impossible to publish the text in the following Sunday's Observer. Thus the decision was taken to bring out a special edition of the Observer that Thursday morning as the shareholders gathered at the Grosvenor House hotel. That day, 220,000 copies of a broadsheet 16-page edition exclusively devoted to the report were distributed under the front-page banner proclaiming Fayed 'The phoney Pharaoh'. The report vindicated Rowland's accusations, though it stopped short of proving Rowland's claims that he had used the Sultan of Brunei's money to buy Harrods. Fayed's own response to the government report was succinct: 'They have shit on me.' Department of Trade lawyers quickly obtained the expected injunction, and ordered rather hopefully all copies to be withdrawn or pulped.

The Guardian by then had joined in the general condemnation of Mohamed Al-Fayed and his brothers. Yet the leaked report made no difference, even after its official publication the following March. The Harrods sale was not overturned.

The question that hung in the air, years after the Guardian's acquisition, was whether it was right that the Observer should have expended so much time, energy and money on a campaign so clearly in the interests of its proprietor. It was something Donald Trelford considered in a retrospective article, 'Time to set the record straight on the Observer and the Harrods takeover'.[14] Trelford revealed that, 'Between 1985 and 1987 Rowland led an extraordinary worldwide investigation into Fayed and his acquisition of Harrods. He employed several firms of accountants and solicitors, private detectives and freelance journalists in an operation, said to cost many millions of pounds, that was way beyond the scope of any newspaper inquiry.' Illicit bugging devices and bribes were deployed in an attempt to prove the fraudulent dealings that Rowland alleged Fayed had been involved in.

Trelford again: 'There were some editorial doubts about becoming involved in our owner's feud. I consulted [Melvyn] Marckus and assured him of my backing if, as City editor, he didn't want to publish anything. He took the view, which I shared, that if a major British institution had been secured by fraud, and the authorities had been negligent in their regulatory duties, it was a matter of serious public interest. We determined, however, that every line should be double-checked and not accepted simply on Rowland's say-so.'

Anyone who doubted the validity of the Observer's reporting of the affair need only read the DTI report, Trelford declared. He did, however, have afterthoughts about overkill. 'I remember having lunch with David Astor and he said, "You may be right, Donald, but it's out of proportion. This isn't the great Observer cause - it looks as though you are serving the interests of your proprietor."'[15]

But the Observer was in a difficult position. After the Wapping revolution of 1986 it had benefited from massive capital investment from its proprietors. 'If you like it was a kind of Faustian deal. I was very mindful of the Observer's reputation. [But I also] genuinely thought Tiny had been cheated out of Harrods by the British establishment.'

In April 1984 Trelford's demonstration of editorial independence over an African story, which he himself had written, brought him into head-on collision with Rowland. Trelford had gone to Zimbabwe with Rowland, who had facilitated an interview with Robert Mugabe. Trelford did the interview but then on his own initiative went to Matabeleland, heartland of Mugabe's rival, Joshua Nkomo, and wrote a report about the killing and torture carried out by troops of the notorious Fifth Brigade of the Zimbabwe National Army. Rowland had been a supporter of Nkomo but had switched his allegiance to Mugabe. Trelford ordered the Observer to hold his Mugabe interview and run the Matabeleland story instead. His deputy, Anthony Howard, when he read it, told Trelford, 'The shit will hit the fan. This is Lonrho country.'[16]

On the day before publication Rowland telephoned Trelford, now back in London, and, according to Trelford (though later denied by

Rowland), told him, 'If you damage my Zimbabwe interest I may have to sell my newspapers because I won't be able to afford to keep them. You should think about the consequences.' The Observer gave a blow-by-blow account of both sides of the affair the following week. Two days after that appeared, the Observer's five independent directors issued a stinging rebuke to Rowland for 'improper proprietorial interference' with Trelford's editorial freedom.

By the weekend, the dispute between Rowland and Trelford was all over. A prospective deal to sell the Observer to Robert Maxwell was off. Kiss-and-make-up letters were published. Nevertheless, Trelford later said he was 'harassed' by Tiny Rowland to promote his company's interests,[17] suggesting by the use of that word that it was a common occurrence.

David Leigh perhaps also believed that the Observer's soul had been sold to the devil. He had been investigations editor at the Observer since the Lonrho takeover in 1981. Since then he had done his best to insulate himself from what he saw as the 'growing stain' of Lonrho and Tiny Rowland's obsessions. In the summer of 1989 he was involved in a huge internal row over what he and others saw as another attempt to use the Observer to further Lonrho's commercial interests, regarding a story about the alleged payment of bribes by British Aerospace (BAe) to secure contracts. Leigh in the end resigned as a result of complications arising from the dispute.

Georgina Henry, the media editor of the Guardian, offered Leigh the hospitality of her pages to explain, in the words of the headline, 'Why I quit the Observer'.[18] It led to a rare display of fury on the part of Peter Preston, who only learned about it after the piece had been commissioned. He called Henry and Rusbridger, the features editor, into the bunker and emphasised his views by banging the desk: it was not that he had wanted to suppress Leigh's apologia, but he had wanted advance warning of it. There was a hurried and abortive attempt to give Trelford's side of the story alongside Leigh's account. Two weeks later a letter from Trelford was published, in which he pointed out that the independent directors had found no evidence of direct proprietorial influence in the affair. Georgina Henry concluded that an incipient interest in acquiring the Observer had prompted this very rare intervention on Preston's part. 'He intervened [only] when he felt that the interests of the Guardian were at stake.' Shortly afterwards he sent her a note, more or less apologising for blowing up.[19]

The struggle over Harrods plumbed squalid depths, perhaps none deeper than that marked by Donald Trelford's front-page Observer story of 14 July 1991, headlined 'Fayed's war on Lonrho may have doomed efforts to save Bazoft'. The case of Farzad Bazoft has already been mentioned. He was a young Iranian-born freelance journalist, well known for his work for the Lonrho-owned Observer, who had been arrested in Iraq, accused of spying for Israel and hanged in Abu Ghraib prison on 15 March 1990. There was no significant evidence against him and none has subsequently come to light. The thesis of Trelford's story was that in 1989, on the instructions of Mohamed Al-Fayed, letters had been written to Saddam Hussein falsely claiming that Lonrho had supplied arms to Iran, and that this had been a factor in Saddam's decision a year later not to commute the death penalty handed down to Bazoft. In his biography of Tiny Rowland, Tom Bower, noting this story, comments: 'By any measure, both Trelford and Rowland had taken the battle against the Fayeds to a new level.'[20]

There was another event in the early months of Guardian ownership that caused dismay to core Observer staff, not least to Donald Trelford. 'A few months after I left ... I was called by a former colleague who was beside himself with rage. "You'd better get down here," he fumed. So I drove to the glass palace on Battersea Bridge from which the Observer was being shifted, bit by bit, to the Guardian's more spartan offices in Farringdon Road. My friend pointed angrily to a builder's skip in which unwanted Observer items had been dumped. These turned out to be files of letters and other archive material and artefacts that were a priceless part of the history of the oldest Sunday newspaper in the world. Among the dog-eared remains I found a meticulously kept register of advertising, in copperplate handwriting, dating from the 1930s. There were drawings of the paper's post-war staff by Feliks Topolski, a complete set of the Colour Magazine, and letters to the literary editor from reviewers who included some of the century's most famous authors.

'I saved them from the skip and took them to Sheffield University [where Trelford had become professor of journalism] to be sorted and catalogued. I then wrote to the Guardian to ask what they wanted done with them. I am still awaiting a reply.'[21]

All these events formed part of the invisible tail that followed the Observer the four miles across London to Farringdon Road, where it was finally installed by the last week in November 1993. Roy Greenslade, a former Fleet Street editor and media commentator for the Guardian, was not alone in thinking that the Observer during the Lonrho owner-ship had 'completely lost its liberal cachet'.[22] But the disdain was perhaps exaggerated. The paper had continued to be a vehicle for much fine journalism, including photography, and by and large it had continued to reflect an editorial purpose that a writer in the Washington Post had once neatly epitomised as 'to be strong on the side of the weak'.[23] Even when its internecine battles were at a periodic intensity, when in its relationship with Lonrho it appeared to be weak on the side of the strong, the tattered standard of its particular kind of party-free liber-alism had somehow been raised. And it had always been true that the Observer sold more papers than the Guardian, on average an advantage of more than 100,000 through the years immediately before the acqui-sition, even if the difference between the Guardian's Saturday edition and the Observer had dwindled to practically nothing in 1992. When, in the customary manner, the journalists of the Observer were banging out Donald Trelford, they did so with genuine respect. And when they packed their bags for Farringdon Road they did so with a mixture of regret and pride, not shame or inferiority.

There was something symbolic and apt about Jonathan Fenby's returning from his excursion to Battersea at the head of the Observer jour-nalists. The sense of affiliation between the two papers went back much farther than many realised. The Observer's great editor JL Garvin (edited 1908-1942) and the Guardian's CP Scott (edited 1872-1929) were mutually admiring, despite their differing political positions. And in between Garvin and the Observer's greatest modern editor, David Astor, was Ivor Brown, whom even his Observer colleagues referred to as a Guardian man: during the last decade of Scott's editorship he was the paper's drama critic and leader writer. But extraordinarily Astor himself, at least half-seriously, proposed that the papers should combine some of their resources to cover the seven days of the week. 'It would save me the trouble of starting a daily Observer. To facilitate matters a Guardian-Observer confederation could be arranged with a pooling of the sordid side of journalism - printing, adverts, and other such matters could be handled confederally ...'[24]

As Fenby was already discovering, however, bringing a leaner Observer to Farringdon Road was not an untroubled march to the promised land.

He had been charged with cutting editorial costs by 30%. The physical transfer, he acknowledged, had been 'excellently masterminded' by Brian Whitaker, although some functions, the magazine and the Review, for example, had to be accommodated away from the main building, and to begin with there were no proper offices for Fenby or any of his executives. The Observer's incomparable photographer Jane Bown was told there would no longer be facilities for her to print her own work: Fenby provided her with a hideaway where she could continue to do just that.

These were minor irritants compared with some of the difficulties that had arisen in the first months of Guardian ownership - the Observer's last six months in the 'pleasure dome' in Battersea. Fenby had not been received there with open arms; at one point he was refused entry because he did not have a 'certified Observer pass'. One of his main objectives had been to strengthen the news operation. The departure of Alan Watkins as the main political columnist cleared the way for the appointment of Andrew Rawnsley from the Guardian, whom Fenby had wanted in the role. He quickly discovered that this did not meet with the approval of Hugo Young, who mentioned it pretty well every time they bumped into each other. Rawnsley in fact proved to be Fenby's most enduring appointment, playing a key role in the paper's political coverage under five more editors into Katharine Viner's period. But his was by no means the most controversial appointment.

The day after that first visit to Battersea, Fenby announced the appointment of John Price as his deputy, the first of more than a few senior staff he was to recruit from the Independent. Others now followed from Fenby's old paper, among them Mark Rosselli and Paul Dunn, who were brought in to run the news desk, and Lucy Tuck, who became arts editor. As a group they became known as 'the committee'. Fenby also recruited the Independent's admired political editor, Tony Bevins, an appointment that was to ruffle many feathers and play a part in alienating Hoggart, the incumbent. Rawnsley and Bevins were known around the shop as Beauty and the Beast. Altogether, the Independent recruits added to the disorienting effect felt by some of the existing Observer staff who were heard to mutter, 'We thought we had been taken over by the Guardian, not the Indy.'

Amid all the changes, Hoggart and Paul Routledge, his nominal deputy, were jointly bylined on the paper's first real scoop under its new editor, exposing John Major's fight with the 'bastards' in his cabinet. Fenby gave credit to his deputy Price for seeing the implications of that story and ensuring its promotion as the front-page lead. Fenby might later have drawn a parallel with his own problems as the beleaguered Observer editor.

By the time the paper's editorial staff reached Farringdon Road en masse, Hoggart was already happily ensconced at the Guardian again. It turned out that he had also been liaising with Peter Hillmore, a disaffected colleague on the paper he had just left, to plot Fenby's removal as editor, something that was discovered when a dossier of printed-out messages that had passed between the conspirators was covertly deposited on John Price's desk. According to Fenby, Preston's inclination was to regard it all as a kind of Jacobean farce.

Fenby conceded that 'the Independent influx was considerable', but 'I did not particularly want many hirings from the Guardian, and I was certainly not encouraged to take people from there. At one point we wanted to approach Roger Alton but Peter vetoed this.' Fenby was allowed to recruit Melanie Phillips, who became one of the Observer's principal columnists, and Ed Vulliamy who moved over as a US correspondent-at-large with a brief to report from America, 'outside the beltway', which he did brilliantly.

The Observer's financial position continued to be a great concern. Four months before the purchase was completed, Harry Roche had told the Scott Trust that the Observer's losses could be down to £50,000 a month by March 1994, followed swiftly by 'break-even' - the new oft-repeated target - with the possibility of a profit of £1.5 to £2 million within a couple of years. Remarkably - and erroneously - it was later claimed that the Guardian had bought the Observer without seeing any properly audited figures.[25] Jim Markwick explained that the real problem was that the £30 million advertising revenue the Observer had been attracting turned out to have been inflated by some £7 million that had come from Lonrho-associated sources. Reality had quickly dawned. In the circumstances, any reduction in losses would have been regarded as a success. Instead the losses, after an initial drop, were soon rising. In the Guardian's first year of ownership (1993–94), losses amounted to £7.1m, a figure that was reduced slightly in the following year to £6.9 million (the Fenby period), but then rose to £10.2 million and £11.4 million in the next two years. Caroline Marland, in particular, among the Guardian executives - now with special responsibility for the Observer - passionately argued against cutting the price of either the daily or the Sunday title, and was equally passionately committed to investment in the journalism. It was the prevailing view. But by November 1995 - just two years after the Guardian purchase - Roche would be telling the trustees that if costs could not be cut back then 'the only course open to us, it seems to me, is disposal of the Observer'.

There were great efforts, which met with significant success, to sell advertising over the seven days that the two papers now commanded - though even this highlighted tensions between the two papers. Paul Johnson recalled a dinner in the Farringdon Road boardroom for luxury car industry executives and advertisers, attended by commercial and editorial people from both the Guardian and the Observer. John Price, Fenby's deputy, was representing the Observer. Price, Johnson recalled, seemed to have 'an adversarial thing about the Observer and the Guardian in his mind'. They were talking to the advertisers about the differences between the two papers. 'They were quite interested in these differences, then John Price suddenly turned round and said, "Yes but the real difference between the Guardian and the Observer is the relationship over money; getting money out of the Guardian is like getting shit out of a rocking horse."' Johnson left the boardroom that evening with the remark still in mind. 'I thought, a) I don't think that's really true, and b) there's a real antipathy here which is coming out in quite a crude way.'[26]

The overall design of the new Observer when it came was largely the work of Tony Mullins, the art director, who had played a big part in developing the original design for the Independent. One of the main changes was the replacement of the original Observer magazine, founded in 1964, edited at the time of the takeover by Simon Kelner, with something more modest of the same name, edited by Rebecca Nicolson. The main problem with the existing magazine, a glossy, perfectly bound thing of beauty, was that it was losing about £3 million a year. Fenby decided that it had to go. As something of a consolation prize, Fenby asked Kelner to take overall charge of production and design, reporting directly to him. Kelner took this to mean that he would be Fenby's deputy, but John Price was the sitting tenant. A bad-tempered late-night telephone conversation ensued, followed by a terminal lunch in a Marco Pierre White restaurant the following day. Fenby recalled: 'Simon left, qualifying for the big [Lonrho-financed] redundancy terms, and named the extension he built to his house in Crouch End "the Fenby wing".'

The six-section Observer was an ambitious thing despite the strictures. The new deployment now included two tabloid sections, one for sport and the other for arts and books; a stand-alone business section, an expanded main news coverage and two magazines, the redesigned colour magazine and perhaps the star of the redesign, a new Life magazine (the title suggested by Rusbridger), created and edited by Michael Pilgrim. 'Monty Don, Nigel Slater and Kathryn Flett were among its discoveries. Francis Wheen wrote a column while editing Private Eye's Street of Shame (which had regular digs at me),' said Fenby. It became a widely admired success story.

Among editorial coups there was the revelation at the end of November that John Major had opened a back channel of communication with the leadership of the IRA, and a year later a world exclusive with the serialisation of Nelson Mandela's memoirs. Although both appeared in papers that sold above the magic 500,000 mark, it was a figure that was rarely achieved in the intervening year. Generally the range had been between 480,000 and 500,000, dipping to 460,000 in August. Plotted as a graph the figures followed a very similar course to those of the Guardian, but such was the fret around the Observer that no one appeared to take that into account. Fenby could see that only with extra editorial input and a bigger marketing spend could a circulation of half a million be maintained. Nevertheless he was blamed for poor performance.

The paper had become Newspaper of the Year in Granada's What the Papers Say awards for 1993, something in which both Trelford and Fenby staked a claim. In fact the citation, when the award was presented in February 1994, concentrated entirely on the Observer's achievements under its new ownership and editor. The judges said that despite major upheavals the continuity of performance was remarkable, adding: 'By December, the paper had thoroughly re-established itself as one which was likely to be first with the news.'

Despite this outward triumph, there were still internal tensions. There was little general rapport with the Guardian, the occupants of the lower floors in Farringdon Road: their journalists blamed the demands of the Observer for the pegging of their annual salary rise. The Guardian journalists, casting themselves as relentlessly overworked, saw their colleagues on the top floor as the opposite. Perhaps some recalled Hugo Young's remarks in a column when he referred to journalists whose views were reached 'after the days of judicious rumination which are luxuriantly available to a Sunday newspaper'.[27] That was more or less how Simon Hoggart saw it. 'Sunday papers are very different indeed. For one thing you do much less work. Sunday newspaper people will tell you that's not true but it is true and I've worked for both so I know.'[28] All in all the conditions were not conducive to editorial integration, and the lack of progress in that direction was something else for which Fenby was blamed.

By the autumn of 1994, Fenby was feeling overstressed and short of support, sometimes desperately so, not from his small inner circle but from the Guardian and from the Scott Trust. Fenby was described retrospectively by one apparently sympathetic senior management executive as transfixed 'like a rabbit in the headlights'. On a Friday evening with the activity for Sunday's edition peaking, a journalist from the business section put his head round Fenby's open office door, and said, 'So you're going back to Paris' (where Fenby had run the Reuters bureau). 'He explained that he had been told by the Guardian picture desk people that Peter Preston had worked out an arrangement by which I would go to Paris as chief correspondent for both the daily and Sunday so that he could put in Andrew Jaspan [the successful editor of the newly relaunched Scotland on Sunday] to replace me. I went to see Peter and asked him what all this was about. "Rubbish," he said. "I don't know what they were talking about."'

It had been arranged for Fenby to meet the Scott Trust in mid-January, when he would have a chance to outline his plans for the future. But other developments intervened. Preston asked him out for a pre-Christmas drink in a wine bar in Lamb's Conduit Street. As they sipped their beaujolais, Preston said, 'Things are not working out, are they? The Trust is not happy.' Fenby uttered a defence: the circulation figures for October–November, the general editorial performance, his ideas for taking the paper forward. He also made the point that the position of the Observer had been worse than realised at the time of the acquisition and that cuts in expenditure had added to the difficulties. He said no to Preston's next question: 'Wouldn't you be happier in Paris as correspondent for the two papers?' Happiness by then was something outside Fenby's quotidian experience. 'I went to the Auvergne for the Christmas holiday and walked in the cold.'

During the second week in January, a few days before the scheduled meeting of the Scott Trust, Hugo Young asked to see him. 'Hugo told me the Trust had lost confidence in me and had decided to appoint Peter as editor-in-chief of both papers. I would therefore wish to resign. "You mean you are putting me in a position where I have to go," I replied. "No, you will wish to resign," he said. We had a ridiculous semantic wrangle, which ended with Hugo saying, "You must understand, the Scott Trust cannot be seen to sack an editor."'

Ordered to leave the building immediately, Fenby walked home, choosing a route likely to cross the path of his wife, Renée, returning from her job at the BBC. They met in the street.

'You've lost your job, haven't you?' she said.

'Yes, how do you know?'

Renée replied, 'You look happy for the first time for a long time.'

Preston phoned him that evening and memorably said that what had happened had hurt him more than it had hurt Fenby. He had frequently praised Fenby's achievements to the Trust while emphasising the 'triple-headed nightmare' that enveloped his former deputy. Fenby, he reminded the trustees and others, had had to shed a large number of people against a deadline; he had to radically change the configuration of the paper; and he had to prise the Observer out of Marco Polo House and shoehorn it into Farringdon Road.

A statement issued on behalf of the Scott Trust said, 'Jonathan Fenby, editor of the Observer since 1993, has resigned by mutual agreement.' Little more than 18 months had passed since Markwick had breathlessly announced the Observer acquisition. Markwick claimed to be appalled by the manner of Fenby's dismissal. He took him out to dinner and promised to ease the pain with the balm of a generous financial settlement. Within six months Fenby was unexpectedly and happily installed as the new editor of the South China Morning Post in Hong Kong. Twenty years later he reflected, 'Losing the editorship of the Observer was a relief - it was a step that I would not have taken myself but when it was forced on me was absolutely the right course for me, opening up a much more interesting period in my professional and personal life. I guess that, as David McKie said, I was always a mercenary and never part of the family, working for the Guardian but not of it.'

The Guardian ownership of the Observer had not begun well, and there would be no quick improvement. What followed more than justified Preston's apt description as 'a bugger's muddle'. Before that, however, events at the Guardian took what a laconic commentator would call an unexpected turn.

Chapter 23
A Direct Hit on the Guardian's 'Agent Ron'

'If the Russians thought of recruiting you - [then] as one of your colleagues said today - no wonder they lost the cold war.'

Peter Preston, in his letter accepting Gott's resignation

If experience had taught Preston to keep a weather eye out for the sudden squall, it had also taught him that you were unlikely to see it coming. On the wet and windy morning of Thursday 8 December 1994 he was woken by the telephone at 6.30am. He had gone to bed more than usually tired and it was a weary hand that reached for the phone. He was awake very quickly. It was the BBC Radio 4 *Today* programme, coming to a climax towards the end of its night shift. Did he know about the article in the Spectator alleging that Richard Gott had been a paid agent of the KGB? Did he have any comment? The answer was no, and no. Preston ended the call as rapidly as possible.

The blustery weather provided an appropriate accompaniment to the drive from Preston's home in Camberwell in south London to the office in Farringdon Road, and for the day that followed. The Guardian found itself at the centre of the kind of media storm that it had sometimes generated. The Establishment, it seemed, had struck back and scored a damaging hit on the paper that had been running a relentless campaign against sleaze and corruption in the government. In the coming days further shots were to be fired by other papers, particularly the Times, Sunday Times and Sunday Telegraph, alleging that Gott had taken payments amounting to thousands of pounds from the Soviet security service. Among other titbits, they offered the news that Gott had been codenamed by the KGB, rather ludicrously, 'Agent Ron'.

Gott had heard about the Spectator story quite early that morning too. He had been preparing to go into Broadcasting House to record his regular contribution as the Guardian's literary editor to an arts programme on

Radio 2 when Michael White rang. White was also freelancing for the BBC that morning. He was at the Television Centre in west London to review the day's papers for BBC1's *Breakfast* show. They both recalled the conversation. White said, 'Richard, I've been reading the Spectator and either you're a much deeper member of the Fourth International than I remember or you're going to be able to buy a beach hut in Italy from the proceeds of suing the Spectator.' Gott found a copy of the magazine on a newsstand at Euston station and read it on his way to Portland Place. Sheridan Morley, the programme's presenter, was also the Spectator's theatre critic. 'I said to Sheridan, "You know your paper's rather got it in for me this morning." He said, "Oh, is that you? Yes, I vaguely knew they had got some sort of important story up their sleeve."'[1] A benumbed Gott went ahead and did the programme as agreed, and then made his way to Farringdon Road.

'It was getting on towards midday when I arrived. I just walked up the stairs and I knew I'd got to go straight in to see Preston. I was in his office for the next two hours. I said to him, "I just can't see any way out of this," and I offered my resignation immediately. Peter said, "Let's think about it a bit," and he called in the others, Alan [Rusbridger] and Ian [Wright]. They were completely bouleversed.'[2] The significance of the Spectator's attack, coming as it did in the middle of the Guardian's long investigation into the affairs of the Tory minister Jonathan Aitken, was immediately apprehended. The magazine itself had left little room for doubt: the cover had reproduced a front page from the Guardian - of six weeks earlier - leading on the question of a weekend Aitken had spent at the Paris Ritz and who had paid for it (for the full story of the Aitken affair, see Volume 2). Alongside the Guardian masthead, in the Spectator's reproduction the Soviet hammer and sickle had been prominently inserted. In a similar vein, the Sunday Telegraph at the weekend carried a cartoon by Nicholas Garland showing Stalin reading the Guardian.

When Gott had finished explaining the extent of his involvement to the paper's three most senior editorial executives, the editor, deputy editor and managing editor, Preston said, 'What should we do?' Gott did not forget that moment. 'There was a deathly hush. Nobody said anything.' Gott reiterated his offer to resign; as he was at pains to point out later, it was his decision to do so.

He had resigned - as he later tried to make clear - not because he had been 'unmasked' as an 'agent of influence' of the KGB. Nor because in an act of 'culpable stupidity' he had taken, in his own term, 'red gold' - cash payments that he insisted had never been for more than hotel and travel expenses. He had resigned because he had failed to tell his editor what had been going on. He bitterly regretted not going in to see Preston when, more than five years earlier, the security service MI6 had questioned him about his meetings with Soviet intelligence officers. A mutual and warm respect had existed between Preston and Gott, who had worked for the Guardian 'off and on', as he noted, for more than 30 years. His friend Tariq Ali, to whom he spoke that morning, had told him not to do anything hastily. He believed that Gott did not expect his offer of resignation to be accepted, and claimed to know that the view at the Spectator was that if Gott sued he would be likely to win.[3]

When Gott sat down to compose his resignation, he did so with a faint glimmer of hope that Preston might refuse to accept it. 'So when I wrote the letter, instead of saying, "And I resign," I said, "And I offer you my resignation." There was that tiny, tiny thought in my mind.'

But it was to be the last thing he wrote in the Guardian as a member of the staff. There was something more important to a visibly pained Peter Preston than the ultimately provisional friendship between editor and journalist, and that was the reputation of the paper. Had Gott not resigned it seems probable that Preston would have felt it his duty to sack him.

Others shared this view. Ian Wright had a conversation that evening with David Brook, the marketing director. Wright recalled, 'I said, "I'm just distraught by this. Poor Ricky." And David said, "It's not a question of poor Ricky. It's a question of poor Guardian" ... I think that character-ised what people at a senior level thought about it.'[4]

The Spectator article had caused the calculated rumpus. It had carried the sensational headline: 'How the KGB ran the Guardian's features editor', and a strapline promised that the writer, Alasdair Palmer, would reveal 'the true allegiance of one of Britain's most prominent journalists, and how he betrayed the integrity of a great paper'. That the magazine was returning fire in the cause of the Establishment was made clear in the article. 'He did not betray only his readers,' Palmer wrote. 'The editor and staff of the Guardian would have been horrified to discover that one of their most important and trusted journalists was taking money from the KGB. (To gauge how horrified, you need only read the paper's articles on who paid for Jonathan Aitken's stay at the Ritz in Paris.)'

Palmer ended his piece by reiterating a view that made the underlying purpose plain. 'Even though there is no evidence that he has accepted anything from the KGB for 10 years, perhaps he might now think it better to spare us some of his high moral outrage at the corruption of the British Establishment.'

The Russian defector and double agent Oleg Gordievsky - the main source of the Spectator's revelations, both true and false - was known to have dropped hints to Palmer over a number of years about the KGB's connection with an unnamed journalist who worked for the Guardian and specialised in Latin America.[5] Now the allegations were out in the open.

Gordievsky had been deeply dyed KGB. He was born into a KGB family in Moscow in 1938 and he followed his father and elder brother into the state security services. It was in Copenhagen that his career began to flourish, concealing, by his own account, a growing disillusionment with Soviet communism. He later claimed that the brutal suppression of the Prague Spring in 1968 was a personal turning point. The British intelligence services first made contact with him in 1974. For the next 11 years, during which time he rose to the rank of colonel in the KGB, and especially after his return to Moscow in 1978, he supplied MI6 with a valuable 'gold stream' of information. In 1982 he was posted to London, in effect as second in command of KGB operations in the UK. He was in the running to become the head of the KGB in Britain, but came under suspicion after he had told MI6 that an MI5 officer, Michael Bettaney, was spying for Russia. In 1985, Gordievsky was suddenly recalled to Russia, subjected to prolonged interrogation, but then released. Later that year he defected, escaping via Finland to Britain, where he settled in a house in the stockbroker belt of Surrey.[6] He was sentenced to death *in absentia* by the Soviet authorities. It was six years before his wife and children were able to join him. One of his responsibilities as a lieutenant colonel of the KGB in London, it became clear later, would have been debriefing the people that Richard Gott was meeting. The easy identification of Gordievsky behind the Spectator's revelations led to passing speculation as to whether the British secret services were not behind all of them.

The day after the dramatic events of Thursday, Preston, who was described in the Spectator article as 'genuinely incorruptible' - somehow in the context that sounded like a slur too - decided that readers of the

Guardian should be given 'the fullest possible account of events', including the full text of Gott's resignation letter and Preston's reply.

Gott, addressing 'Dear Peter', undertook to give a fairly comprehensive account of his contacts with officials from the former Soviet embassy. 'But first,' he said in reply to allegations in the Spectator of specific payments of up to £600 in used notes, 'I should state quite clearly and unequivocally that I did not receive money from the Russians that I met.' He also said that MI6 had known about such allegations for years and had interviewed him about them in the late 1980s and accepted his word 'that this particular accusation was baseless'.

He added in this open letter to Preston, 'I confess that I now bitterly regret not having come to tell you, my editor, about this encounter with MI6. It would have been sensible for you to have known about this long and essentially harmless saga - since it was bound to leak out eventually.'

Gott revealed that the first approach from someone from the Soviet embassy was made to him while working at the Royal Institute of International Affairs at Chatham House in St James's Square, London, in the 1960s. Several lunches in 'distant suburbs' followed, with Gott rather enjoying 'the cloak and dagger atmosphere'. Contact lapsed for several years while Gott was travelling and working abroad, but the 'irregular lunches' resumed on his return to London in the early 1970s. 'I assumed, through my absolutely transparent presentation of myself as an incorrigible leftist, no harm could come from lunching with these folk.' The lunches with his contact continued into the 1980s - the period with which the Spectator article was mainly concerned - 'But as the Guardian's features editor, essentially bound to my desk, what on earth could I tell him?' (In passing, it was in 1981 that Gott's appointment as editor of the BBC's magazine, the Listener, was vetoed by the security services, apparently because of his political views. An article in the Observer quoted a senior BBC executive: '[Gott's] file went off for "colleging" [BBC jargon for MI5 vetting] and it was blocked. They said he was an ultra-leftist. The phrase was: "He digs with the wrong foot."'[7])

Several invitations to meet KGB officers abroad followed, and Gott took trips to Vienna, Athens and Nicosia, on two of those occasions with a partner. The Spectator's allegation of payment 'verged on the truth'. 'The Russians did pay my fare and my hotel [each time]. So I have to admit that I took red gold, even if it was only in the form of expenses. This, in the circumstances, was culpable stupidity, though at the time it just seemed more like an enjoyable joke.' His close colleagues at the Guardian read this with dismay, and a feeling, now too late, that his resignation had been precipitate, that he should have taken legal advice - and that he certainly should not have offered a hostage to fortune in using a phrase such as 'red gold'.

In an interview, a kind of public interrogation, conducted by the Guardian's former reader's representative or ombudsman Hugh Stephenson, and published the following Monday, Gott confirmed his expenses were paid in cash. But it appeared that nothing remotely interesting, and certainly nothing of any relevance to the security of the nation, was transacted on these trips. Gott explained: 'I thought it was interesting to meet this guy and talk about what was going on in the Soviet Union. They, I think, thought that at some stage I might be useful and helpful to them. But I totally agree that I was supping with the devil ...'

Preston's letter accepting Gott's resignation is an extraordinary document. It recognises that Gott had exposed himself and his paper to injury, but at the same time it is pervaded by a defiance of the forces that had rendered his colleague hors de combat. 'Dear Richard,' he wrote:

> We both agree that the paper should have been told about your trips to Vienna, Athens and Nicosia, and was made vulnerable in ignorance: we both agree that I should have known about your subsequent interview with the man from MI6. Your letter is entirely honourable - as all your colleagues here would expect. The devil is in the detail of principle and not in any broader perception of you as a free and a brilliant journalist who has served the Guardian long and well.
>
> I think I know why the Spectator - three times invoking the case of the Guardian and Jonathan Aitken in its coverage this week - has been able to exhume what you told MI6 long ago. It is slimy stuff to a barely hidden agenda. I don't believe you took packets of used fivers. I know that nothing you wrote or commissioned for the paper was tainted. You were always what you remain to this day: upfront, with your opinions there in print, to be embraced or rejected by your readers. If the Russians thought of recruiting you - [then] as one of your colleagues said today - no wonder they lost the cold war.
>
> I should have known. We should have been told. You have resigned from the staff. That is accepted. But it would be utterly

wrong if this tactical slime from the archives were to prevent you from writing or thinking or speaking out in the future: and I very much hope that your distinctive and eloquent voice will continue to be heard in the Guardian over the coming years.

Many Guardian readers also wrote expressing their support for Gott and his 'quality of writing'.

The row stirred up by the affair went on for several weeks, beyond the last days of Preston's editorship in the New Year. Several days after the original Spectator article had appeared, the Guardian carried a profile of Gordievsky written by Rusbridger and Richard Norton-Taylor, the Guardian's security expert, with some input by Ian Black. It was not flattering, concentrating on demonstrable inconsistencies in Gordievsky's own statements and suggesting a possible link between the revelations attributed to him and a desire to pump up interest in his forthcoming autobiography. 'Should we believe a word that he says?' they asked. Gordievsky had managed to sustain the life of a double agent for a remarkable 11 years. 'Lying and smearing is what he is good at.'[8]

Gordievsky, given space in the Spectator for an extensive reply a month later, called this 'character assassination'.[9] He dismissed any suggestion that he had a grudge against the Guardian as 'simply untrue'. In fact, he said, since as long ago as Malcolm Muggeridge's reports on 'the Stalin-induced famines' of the 1930s, the Guardian had commanded the greatest respect among intellectual Russians, something that he shared.

Intriguingly, he then moved on to a matter that so far had not been raised - the week-long excursion that the Guardian's features department, led by Gott, had made to Moscow in March 1983. Gott, in his resignation letter to Preston, and in his interview with Stephenson, had mentioned one meeting with his KGB contact in Moscow, placing it in a separate category to the other three trips abroad because this had been a 'freebie'. It took place in November 1982 and was paid for by Thomson Holidays, who had flown a party of journalists to Moscow to celebrate the 10th anniversary of their taking tourists to the Soviet Union. (Gott had flown on for a quick round trip to Georgia.) This was the first time that Gott had been to Moscow. 'During the course of the trip, I slipped out to have lunch with my KGB friend ... Since I was going to be in Moscow, it seemed a pity not to say hello.'[10]

It was this 'rather agreeable' trip that gave Gott the idea that it would be possible to organise a mass inflow to Moscow of 15 Guardian journalists, for which he had already set a precedent with a visit en masse to Belfast in 1980. This created a model that has been followed from time to time ever since. Gott said, 'I told Igor Titov [Gott's KGB contact in London][11] of my plan, but the arrangements were all made with the London correspondent of Novosti [the Soviet state news agency].' Among the journalists in the group were Alan Rusbridger, Polly Toynbee, Jonathan Steele, John Carvel, Peter Jenkins and Tim Radford. Gott said he made no effort to contact anyone from the KGB on this trip.

The resulting articles ran in the Guardian daily through the second week of April.[12] Gott also ran during the week the piece he had written as a result of his trip to the Georgian capital Tbilisi the year before. To Gott, Moscow did not 'feel like the capital city of a superpower. It feels - and officials do not thank you for saying so - more like some Third World country, somewhat forgotten and neglected, with a distinctly provincial tone.' Gordievsky in his Spectator article thought it was to the Guardian's 'everlasting credit' that 'the result was a total fiasco'. He claimed that Titov had pressed the international department of the Central Committee to allow the trip, 'after Richard Gott suggested the idea to him'. The Central Committee, he wrote, eagerly awaited their articles. 'They were a terrible disappointment, far worse than expected - mostly very negative, to the effect that the Soviet Union was far more dismal than they had thought possible. The Central Committee was furious. Surprisingly, Gott's reputation hardly suffered at all. It was thought that he couldn't control what his people said - Britain, after all, had a free press. All the blame,' he said, 'fell on Titov.'

Gott commented, 'I can well believe Gordievsky's account of the expedition as "a fiasco" from the Soviet point of view.' Looking back many years later, Gott described these mass excursions to Belfast, Moscow and Tokyo (in 1986) as 'my proudest and most original achievement' as features editor. 'I wanted to try and get people to be motivated in what they were doing and to understand the nature of the era in which we lived and worked ... I felt that people were so inward-looking in the newspaper.'[13]

Gott's resignation from the Guardian over a decade after the Moscow trip was not the end of the affair. New depths were plumbed in February 1995 when the Sunday Times opened its serialisation of Gordievsky's book with a story headlined 'KGB: Michael Foot was our agent'. It claimed that the KGB had regarded him as an 'agent of influence' and given him the code name 'Agent Boot'. Foot sued. The case was still unresolved when Gordievsky's autobiography *Next Stop Execution* was published towards the end of March, with the allegations against Foot now removed. Absent too were any allegations that Gott had been a paid agent. It was to 'another person, who must remain unnamed', that payments were now alleged to have been made. In July Michael Foot was awarded substantial damages and costs against the Sunday Times said together to amount to more than £100,000.

Richard Gott had also indicated that he might not be prepared to continue to take every slur thrown at him. In a letter to the Spectator in March he urged the magazine to come round to his own view, 'that dealings with KGB contacts in the final years of the Cold War should be regarded as a subject for mild satire rather than fierce moral polemic'. Speaking of his own 'well-entrenched reluctance to sue', he warned that it should not be seen as a green light for every minor pen-pusher to defame with impunity. 'One day, the worm might turn.'

Richard Gott began writing for the Guardian again within a few months of his resignation. On 5 June he wrote the cover story from Chile for Guardian Weekend, now edited by Deborah Orr. She had run the idea past both Preston and Rusbridger, who were both 'relaxed' about it. 'I think they both felt that it would be a signal that he hadn't been cast by the Guardian into the outer darkness, which neither of them wanted completely to do,' she recalled.

Gott found that he had to go on issuing rebuttals, for instance in a letter to the Sunday Times in September 2000, after the paper had run a story suggesting that Gott just might be the unidentified Stasi 'Agent Eckart' who had allegedly once worked at Chatham House. 'I am not the "Chatham House mole",' he wrote, '... and I have never been "a Soviet agent" or a "Guardian mole", outed or otherwise ... My resignation was a debt of honour to my paper, not an admission of guilt, although I recognise that not everyone read it as such.'[14]

There was one matter that Richard Gott's sudden resignation in December 1994 had left unattended. That was the vacancy for the coveted job of literary editor. That would be left unfilled for several months. There were two sections, in particular, that had not seemed to be sitting comfortably in the tabloid G2. One was Obituaries; the other was Books. The editor-in-waiting was formulating plans for both of them.

Chapter 24
Heat, Dust and Death on the Books Pages

*'May I commiserate with your literary editors, Richard Gott
and James Wood, whose jobs so plainly make them miserable?'*

Salman Rushdie

Richard Gott would be a hard act to follow, although he was by no means a typical literary editor. His reign of only two years that had ended so sensationally had itself been characteristically sensational. He and his iconoclastic chief literary critic James Wood had been a wonderfully combative duo, producing pages that were never dull, nearly always controversial and occasionally startling.

Gott's Standfirst column of 22 November 1994 - just one month before his dramatic exit - provides one example. The first sentence read, 'The distinguished academic whose book I have just been reading seems to have killed off my tutor.' The academic was Kenneth Dover, 'distinguished authority on homosexuality in Classical Greece' and President of Corpus Christi College, Oxford, Gott's alma mater. His confessional autobiography was called *Marginal Comment*. The deceased tutor was Trevor Aston, a senior research fellow at Corpus Christi, who, wrote Gott, 'taught me all I know about the land tenure systems of medieval England'. Aston's brilliance sometimes caused him to overbalance into 'intolerance, overdrinking, depression and madness'. Dover eventually decided he would have to go for the good of the college, a matter that came down in his mind to the question, 'how to kill him without getting into trouble'. The answer seemed to have been to push him into suicide by dropping a hint that his college fellowship might be terminated. That, or something, seemed to have worked - and in October 1985 the unfortunate Aston was found dead in his rooms.

Claire Armitstead, who combined sub-editing the books pages with her role as theatre critic, recalled what happened when Gott's column appeared. 'The next day, all hell broke loose. The tabloids picked it up and Roger Alton, by then editing G2, was furious with me for letting Richard get away with burying it in his column when it was clearly a news story.'[1] And indeed it made the lead on an inside news page in the Guardian – 'Oxford chief denies killing troubled don' – but almost a week after Gott's column had appeared. 'Richard was delighted by the rumpus.'

Armitstead was right when she said, 'Richard was a rather isolated figure at the time and the books pages were in recession (down to one tabloid spread at their smallest), but Richard and James were actually a rather brilliant team. Richard hired Nick Lezard, from Julie Burchill's Modern Review, as a reviewer-columnist, while calling in an eclectic range of occasional reviewers, from Enoch Powell to Martin Gilbert and Tariq Ali' (he had, as readers who had followed him as features editor would know, rounded up the usual suspects).

The other half of the partnership, James Wood, would have been a natural successor to Gott, but he did not want the job. Not long after Gott's abrupt departure he announced that he wanted to go freelance, and headed for the higher realms of literary criticism in the United States. Armitstead remembered his arrival at the Guardian. 'James had come in with Jocelyn [Targett], both straight from Cambridge, and he was a strangely anachronistic figure – a young man in tweed jackets, mild in person but fearsome (and fearless) on the page. He imported a team of young fiction critics (Philip Hensher, Geoff Dyer, Laura Cumming, Sylvia Brownrigg), but he was always the star turn. He was infuriating to work with on the production side because he would keep us waiting until 10 minutes to deadline – and sometimes rather after it – and would then deliver 1,000 devastating, and perfectly crafted words, usually laying low some giant of the literary world.'

He was well established on the books pages by the time of Gott's arrival on them and already a controversial figure, not least for having upset the only Nobel Prize winner at that time regularly reviewing for the Guardian. William Golding (Sir William, as he now was) had been contributing reviews for three decades, since 1960. Wood went to interview Golding at his home in Cornwall for his 80th birthday and his article appeared on the front of the Review Guardian on 19 September 1991. They had not exactly hit it off. Indeed, according to Golding's biographer, the Nobel laureate broke off his long relationship with the Guardian as a reviewer as a result of the experience.[2] Golding, Wood had asserted, 'is a novelist admired but not much liked'. The interview was an uncomfortable experience for both. 'There are tensions and reverberations in the air. We sit together inside a little chamber of hostility and awkwardness.'

Gott had tried to make the pages less predictable, less self-referential, less conventional. He made that clear enough on his first day in the job with a debut Standfirst column headlined: 'Criticism and culture in a reactionary era',[3] in which he bemoaned the decline of British literary culture. 'The books pages of national newspapers sometimes appear as beleaguered islands in a sea of rock music and cinema, constantly under threat of erosion.'

Then he laid out his manifesto: 'Our chief aim is to reintroduce old-fashioned *criticism* into the books pages. We shall tell you which books are good and which ones are bad, and why. We shall keep an eye on important paperbacks that you can afford, but we shall not be afraid to inform you of the ideas that are floating around within the pages of books that you may never be able to buy. And we shall seek to deliver all this with a polemical punch that will make you yearn for these pages from Thursday to Thursday. Lofty ambitions.' At this time the books pages were still to be found in the broadsheet second section of the paper on Thursdays, Review Guardian, with Mayes (myself) usually editing the front page. This was the case until the advent of G2 in October 1992.

On the day of Gott's manifesto, the Review front was devoted to the plight of Salman Rushdie. Rushdie's own attitude towards the Guardian fluctuated uneasily during his years of enforced internal exile. He went into attack against both Gott and Wood in January the following year when with Bill Buford and AS Byatt he was one of the judges who produced a list of the 20 best young British novelists under the age of 40. It was an exercise carried out under the auspices of Buford's magazine Granta, criticised by Gott in that first manifesto as a journal that delivered culture in slices of 'processed cheese'. Wood had not thought highly of the selection. Of the 20 he found only 10 worth reading at all, and of those just six who had 'the passionate exactitude to call themselves artists in the highest sense'. He concluded, 'To write a great novel demands a ruthless assault on sublimity.'[4]

Salman Rushdie replied from his hideaway a week later. 'May I commiserate with your literary editors, Richard Gott and James Wood, whose jobs so plainly make them miserable? ... Gott is well known for his aversion to all novels, except those which remind this superannuated foreign correspondent of his Latin American glory days; while Wood ... sounds increasingly like one of PG Wodehouse's crustier old dinosaurs.' Gott should be put out to grass and Wood might be released to demonstrate in a novel of his own just what might be achieved by a 'ruthless assault on sublimity'. 'Then perhaps the Guardian's book pages could once again be placed in the hands of someone who, like [Gott's predecessor] the great WL Webb, actually likes reading, and on occasion standing up for, the new voices of our time.' Rushdie returned to his theme in his memoir *Joseph Anton* (2012), calling Wood 'the malevolent Procrustes of literary criticism, who tormented his victims on the narrow bed of his inflexible literary ideologies, pulling them painfully apart or else cutting them off at the knees'.

David Hare, too, made special mention of James Wood in a lecture given at the Royal Society of Literature in April 2010, an edited version of which appeared as the lead in the Guardian Review.[5] 'How can there be a wrong way to make good art? And indeed, what point does criticism serve when it asserts only, "This is not the sort of thing of which I approve"? When a literary critic such as James Wood twists himself into a pretzel explaining exactly why the novel he has under review is the wrong kind of good novel, he sounds like nothing so much as a Railtrack official railing against the wrong kind of snow.'

By that time, James Wood had moved from his first post in the United States on the New Republic to the New Yorker, a move that at the time, 2007, 'caused an extraordinary stir in literary circles', according to a commentator on the Boston Globe.[6] The author declared, 'His hiring is a striking vote for intellectual rigour over magazine breeziness.'

In retrospect, however, the view of Jason Cowley,[7] writing in the New Statesman, seems likely to prevail so far as Wood's Guardian career is concerned. Wood, working alongside Gott, Cowley said, had 'helped absolutely to transform literary culture. For an invigorating period, established reputations - Amis, Barnes, McEwan, Rushdie - were polemically challenged; contemporary British fiction traduced and dismissed as in terminal decline, and politics discussed with ideological engagement. Predictably, publishers hated these *Guardian* pages; advertising revenue collapsed; and Wood and Gott became figures of contempt in literary

London, where the smart career move is always to be nice about other writers in the expectation that, when you eventually publish something yourself, they will be nice about you, too.'

By contrast, Rushdie's mention of 'the great WL Webb' illustrates the literati's veneration of the Guardian's eminent former literary editor. Bill Webb became literary editor in 1959, a post he held for almost three decades. In that time he set up the Guardian Fiction Prize (1965) and chaired the Booker judges (1969), and he established the Guardian books pages, in Gott's words, as a temple of the liberal centre-left, opening the pages to world literature probably to a much larger extent than those of other daily papers. Some of his reviewers were almost equally long-serving, adding to the impression that the pages needed refreshment. Gott said, 'Peter came up to me when I was still features editor and said, "Look, I think I'm going to have to get rid of Bill Webb and I've got the following proposal which is to make him the obituaries editor. And I have to say that I think that this is really suitable because most of his reviewers will soon be coming up for their obits" – which was rather a cruel remark to make.'[8] In fact, it should probably be taken as just one indication among many, that around the time of the Hillman redesign in February 1988, pretty well everything was examined in the light of the bright new day, perhaps sometimes a blinding light.

The chosen successor was the Gott protégé, Waldemar Januszczak, who took over in the summer of 1988. He had already been writing for the Guardian for a little over a decade and was well known to readers as a lively art critic. 'He was terribly good and he just seemed to be a wonderful young thruster,' said Gott. 'And the Guardian had always in the past tried to have a young enthusiastic person writing about art.' Much was to be swept away to make way for change. However, limited progress was made in getting rid of reviewers in whom interest was deemed to be exhausted – several survived through Januszczak and his successor, Tim Radford, before finally falling during the more ruthless Gott regime.

Tim Radford became literary editor after Januszczak left for Channel 4 television. Both would be anonymously criticised in the notorious Casablanca article by Tariq Ali, one of Gott's closest friends. Unfair though that was, neither Januszczak nor Radford was likely to raise the comparative status of the Guardian among the literati, who clung to a kind of Webb nostalgia through this period. Radford in fact belonged to the dwindling and now practically extinct breed of early school leavers who derived their education from or alongside the practice of journalism. He considered it no sort of handicap, rather an advantage 'because I started from a position of complete ignorance and actually have always described journalism as the best university course you can possibly have because you attend a seminar or a tutorial every day and then you actually have to write a paper that day'.[9] He joined the Guardian in time for the last couple of years of Hetherington's editor-ship, becoming arts editor from 1977 to 1980. Through the 1980s he was one of Gott's two deputies, simultaneously writing for and editing the paper's nascent science pages (Futures), and commissioning for them what he claimed was the world's first newspaper mathematics column, by Keith Devlin. It was an unusual background for a literary editor, and indeed throughout his time Radford would be called on to contribute explanatory pieces on the latest volcano, tsunami or earthquake to run alongside reporting on the news pages.

Januszczak, helpfully, had left him an appraisal of all those who ever contributed to or worked on the books pages; and since he left his comments in an open queue on the Atex system they were quickly read by almost everyone in the features department. No one was spared. Radford recalled: 'So I hadn't even started and I walked into trouble because of this set of assassinations and dismissals of everybody asso-ciated with the books pages and what wankers they were - and here was a long list of people who would never deliver their copy, including Peter Preston. And Waldemar said, "If you see Alex Hamilton [the travel editor] approaching, you tell him to fuck off before he opens his mouth" - and all of this. And then off he went ...'

Radford believed that his own appointment signalled a desire to continue clearing away some of the dead wood, a task at which he singu-larly failed. 'But Preston wanted them out and I think Rusbridger wanted them out ... So I wasn't popular but I sat it out for nearly three years.'

What happened then was a seemingly unconnected event that would become the trigger for a series of changes. The science correspondent Nigel Williams resigned and went off to the Wellcome Foundation. Some time earlier, Radford had expressed to Preston his interest in returning to science. The conversation had taken place in a corridor, and Preston, as he sometimes did, paused in passing, poised on one leg, rather like an actor playing the stork in a Noh play. Now, with Williams's departure, there was an opportunity. 'I realised he wanted somewhere to put Richard Gott.' Radford believed Gott would never voluntarily have chosen the job of literary editor for himself, but he may have been mistaken in that; Gott had been the general editor of the Pelican Latin American Library in the 1970s and had published several seminal works. Preston, after his brief pause for thought, went ahead with the changes. Radford became science editor, Richard Gott became literary editor and the revolution on the books pages entered a new phase.

One thing that hardly changed was the amount of space allocated to book reviews. In the February 1992 issue in which Gott's debut Standfirst column appeared, he had two expansive broadsheet pages. Eight months later the books went into the tabloid G2 where they would remain for several years, usually over four pages but occasionally confined to two. In the interim after Gott's departure the pages were run by Claire Armitstead and Jenny Turner, the former literary editor of City Limits. It was Turner who urged Armitstead to apply for the job when Gott left. Stephen Moss also applied – both would get a turn, but not immediately.

Rusbridger was not going to rush into finding a replacement for Gott. The appointment of a new literary editor and the future of the books pages would be an important indicator of the cultural values of the paper under Preston's successor. Perhaps it could be combined with a radical plan to address the widespread dissatisfaction with 'dot dot dot Friday', the tabloid second section in search of an identity. First of all, however, there was a more important matter to be resolved – there was about to be an indicative election before the Scott Trust's appointment of the next editor of the Guardian.

Chapter 25

Changing of the Guard

'Unsurprising, yes; automatic, no.'

**Geoffrey Taylor on the appointment of
Alastair Hetherington as editor in 1956**

To lose one editor may be regarded as a misfortune; to lose two did look a little like carelessness. The end of Peter Preston's era after almost 20 years as editor of the Guardian had been the subject of little more than desultory speculation. The demise of his protégé Jonathan Fenby as the first editor of the Guardian-owned Observer had been, for several months, more confidently predicted. That they should go together, leaving the Scott Trust to enter 1995 with an unprecedented task before it, very few indeed could have imagined. The announcement of the double departure 'stunned everyone', to use Maggie Brown's words in her story for the Independent. Open season was now declared for speculation about the 'real reasons' for Preston's departure, uninhibited by the accompanying announcement that he was not actually leaving but had been appointed editor-in-chief of both titles. That meant he had simply been 'kicked upstairs', said the Sunday Telegraph, an idea that gained currency despite the lack of any real evidence.

In fact, a series of events spanning a year or more contributed to Preston's own decision to quit the editorship of the Guardian. Preston spoke to Hugo Young in the summer of 1994, telling him he was ready for a change, though the seeds had been sown even earlier.[1] Preston blamed himself for the Guardian's mishandling of a story in June 1993 that libelled the Saudi Arabian Prince Bandar and led to a 'grovelling' front-page apology and payout six months later. 'It was at that stage that I told Hugo that I wasn't going to go on forever,' Preston said.[2] In the interim, Preston had initiated the investigations that led to the Hamilton and Greer libel actions over 'cash for questions', and to the still more spectacular action brought by Jonathan Aitken (see Volume 2 for the full account of this story). Amid the commotion that followed, Preston had protested, 'They're out to barbecue somebody and I'm the piece of pork.' Then just before Christmas, the Gott KGB story had run in the Spectator, a seasonal bonus for the media in general but a calculated blow to the Guardian in particular.

Both the Independent and the Sunday Telegraph referred to these recent events as possible contributory factors in ending his editorship. The Sunday Telegraph carried the confident headline, 'Why Preston finally fell at the Guardian'. He was 'moved', according to anonymous Guardian insiders, it said, partly because of question marks about his judgment in the Aitken and Gott affairs. The same report claimed that he was also being held at least partly responsible for the failure of Fenby's Observer to perform to expectation.

The timing of Preston's announcement, when it came, was totally unexpected by his 41-year-old deputy Alan Rusbridger. The general expectation had been that Preston 'would carry on editing for years to come'. As Rusbridger later recalled, 'It was a complete surprise when he took me to the basement of the resolutely unfashionable Italian restaurant in Clerkenwell he favoured, to tell me he had decided to call it a day.'[3] Preston's own account is frank. He remained a member of the Scott Trust. He was still the chairman of the Guardian board. There were plausible reasons for believing that the title editor-in-chief of the Guardian and the Observer described a real and necessary job. Coinciding with his stepping down, or stepping up, he was voted the 'editors' editor' in a Mori poll of national newspaper editors for the second year running. What no one knew at the time was that the ensuing year would be even more tumultuous and stressful than the one just passed.

Nothing quite like the process that preceded the appointment of Alan Rusbridger as editor had occurred in the history of the paper. It was democratic, up to a point - certainly more democratic than anything practised elsewhere in Fleet Street. There were candidates, manifestos, hustings and, if not an election, at least an indicative ballot, initiated by the National Union of Journalists. One of the candidates went so far as to kiss a baby, but then he had spent a long time in the United States. The whole business was, in the end, conducted on the understanding that the result would be advisory and in no way binding upon the Scott Trust, which had the ultimate responsibility for the appointment.

As it happened, the candidate whom the trustees' advisory committee preferred was the runaway winner of the journalists' vote. Preston subsequently pointed out that he had set the process in motion when he chose Rusbridger as his deputy, very much with the succession in mind. What was it exactly that he saw in Rusbridger? 'Witty, calm ... I mean even then that sort of element of reserve he has. You always feel there's a sort of slight ... calmness there. It's like double glazing; the noise penetrates the first area of the window but it doesn't quite get through to the second.' Preston's tone made it clear that he was paying a compliment.

In much the same way that Preston, in his earlier role of production editor, had equipped himself with the knowledge that would enable him to carry forward his ideas for the development of the Guardian during his editorship, so Rusbridger, after visits to the United States, was convinced that he knew which route the Guardian should take into the future. Tony Ageh, the head of the PDU, who accompanied Rusbridger on one of his tours, believes the future editor had a Damascene conversion on this trip. In July 1994, shortly after their return, Rusbridger put down his thoughts in an 18-page paper, 'The Online Future', which became an important marker in the Guardian's digital development. Not surprisingly, the electronic future figured more prominently in Rusbridger's manifesto than it did in that of any of the other three candidates. In retrospect, it provided an extraordinarily clear programme for his editorship.

Until the deaths in quick succession of CP Scott, and then his son and successor as editor, ET (Ted) Scott, the manner in which editors were appointed was hardly a question that had arisen. CP Scott had been in the chair for 57 years when he retired, and he simply appointed, or anointed, his son. When Ted drowned in Windermere in 1932, his elder brother John became the sole proprietor. Among John Scott's many virtues was a genuine belief in the independence of the editor, free from interference from the board. He believed the editor should be free to act as though he were the proprietor: in the manner, in other words, of CP Scott, established during his long occupancy of both roles. The principle of non-interference was therefore easily transferred to the Scott Trust, of which John was the architect, in 1936.

His first appointment after the death of Ted was WP Crozier, only the second editor to come from outside the interrelated Scott–Taylor families since the Guardian began in 1821.[4] When Crozier died in 1944, the responsibility again fell to John Scott and, from a staff depleted by war service, he chose AP Wadsworth. Wadsworth was a popular choice among senior staff, especially with those who, like him, had had to struggle for their education (he had left school at 14). But there was no suggestion of any democratic participation in the appointment on the part of the staff. Neither does it seem likely that the board or the Trust were greatly engaged in the decision.

By the time of Wadsworth's death in the heat of the 1956 Suez crisis, two of Scott's grandchildren were firmly in charge, the cousins Laurence Scott, who was managing director, and Richard Scott, the chairman of the Scott Trust. The more influential of the two cousins at the time was Laurence, who thought that his choice, Alastair Hetherington, would be best able to carry out his plan of printing in London and making the Guardian a truly national newspaper. In effect, Hetherington was appointed by the proprietor in much the same way that an editor might have been appointed elsewhere in Fleet Street.[5] In the event, Hetherington made such a sensational start with his forthright condemnation of Eden's Suez folly that, as a previous historian of the Guardian, Geoffrey Taylor, has mentioned, his appointment came to be wrongly regarded in retrospect as automatic. 'Unsurprising, yes; automatic, no,'[6] Taylor declares.

There were no real moves to democratise the selection process until 1971, when there appears to have been a sudden realisation that with the creation of the group board and a separate operating board for the Guardian after the Times-merger debacle of 1967, which left the authority of Laurence Scott severely reduced, there really was no longer a single proprietor. The appointment process was hastily brought up to date, and then further revised in 1973, shortly before Laurence's final retirement. It entailed much wider consultation than had taken place previously, involving the trustees, the group directors, the Guardian board directors, senior members of the editorial staff and the NUJ chapel.

There were further adjustments to the constitution of the committee when Hetherington finally announced his departure on 13 March 1975. A question mark remained over the will on the part of the trust - and the management - to allow direct union representation. In the end the London and Manchester chapels were each allowed to put forward a list of their preferred candidates. An advisory group of ten members assessed the two dozen applications. Ultimately, it came down to two candidates, Peter Preston and John Cole, and it was Preston's broad range of experience that helped him carry the day.

The appointment exercise was seen as a success but it was 20 years before the apparatus was required again. It was not called into use when the Guardian bought the Observer in May 1993: Peter Preston had simply nominated his deputy Jonathan Fenby and the Scott Trust, with no previous experience of a comparable purchase, endorsed his appointment unanimously.

But only two years later, as we have seen, Fenby was sacked. Almost simultaneously it was announced that Peter Preston was giving up the editorship of the Guardian. And so on 16 January 1995, the Scott Trust, at a special meeting, laid down the selection method for not one but two editors, and the new rules were publicly announced in the following day's Guardian.[7] The Trust, it said, was establishing two advisory committees, chaired by Hugo Young. Preston and Jim Markwick would sit on both. Two additional trustees would be nominated by journalists from the relevant paper to sit on the advisory committee for the Guardian, and two different trustees for the Observer. Each committee would 'make a recommendation to assist the trust in making the appointments, for which it is responsible'.

There were four final internal candidates for the editorship of the Guardian, all male. They all pledged to improve the career prospects for women on the Guardian. In fact at least one woman had thrown her hat in the ring. She later wrote, 'In view of all that had happened to me at the paper, how could I possibly have done that? In view of all that had happened to me at the paper, how could I possibly not have done so?'[8] In any event Melanie Phillips did not go forward to the hustings. And it seems that there were no external candidates either, certainly none who seriously entered the running.

There was in any case an interesting internal field, and a particularly strong candidate in Alan Rusbridger. He was the only one of the four candidates who had had any significant impact on the structure and battle-readiness of the paper. He had launched the Weekend Guardian and G2; he had induced flexibility in the huge features department through wide-ranging staff movements; he had opened the door to the young and ambitious; he had played an important part in opening a gap, although not yet a safe breathing space, between the Guardian and the Independent. Rusbridger had been strongly resistant to entering Murdoch's price war and in favour of responding instead through investment in journalism. He had also demonstrated a prescient interest in the electronic future. And as Preston's deputy editor he had begun what was to be a long and tenacious involvement in the Aitken and Hamilton affairs.

However, what many regarded as recommendations - Weekend, G2 and so on - others saw differently, finding in the same points the contradiction that he was essentially lightweight, lacking in strong political convictions, a brilliant writer, but still rather suspect as an editor, and not someone in whose hands the destiny of the Guardian should be placed. It was partly to address some of these misgivings that at least one of the other candidates had been persuaded by colleagues to put himself forward. He protested later that he did so not with any real notion of winning but with the thought that in coming second he might be appointed deputy editor, and thus be in a position to make up for what some of his supporters saw as weaknesses in the probable winner. It did not turn out like that.

There is just a hint of the complexity of the editor's job and of the relationship that had developed between Rusbridger and Preston in a memo sent by the former to the latter at the beginning of the second week of January 1995 on Preston's return from a short break, just before the succession decision. It demonstrates the obvious point that there is no let-up in the 'commotion of human affairs' to allow for such small matters as a change of editor. It contained 13 items; top of the list was the continuing saga of Mohamed Al-Fayed and his allegations of political corruption that the Guardian had been busy following up. 'Mohamed rang for you on Friday,' Rusbridger told the returning editor. Rusbridger also told Preston that he had responded to yet another Spectator column by Paul Johnson (never to be confused with the paper's own Paul Johnson) attacking the Guardian and its editor. Rusbridger's letter had occupied the equivalent of two columns in the Spectator, where a carefully controlled storm had been raging since the magazine's exposure in December of Richard Gott's KGB connections.

The sudden departure of Gott was another item on the agenda, especially as James Wood was also giving up his staff post on the books pages.

This had caused something of an upheaval in this relatively sheltered literary enclave. '[Wood] came in with Claire Armitstead with a proposal that she edit the pages, with Jenny T[urner] as deputy and Jas Wood as *éminence grise*. I can think of worse solutions, and think highly of Claire.'

In addition, and finally, there was 'Much grumbling about "... Friday".' This, it may be remembered, was the replacement for the weekday G2 on Fridays, introduced in September 1994 in an effort to perk up flagging circulation on the last day of the working week. The unenviable task of producing something fresh to enliven its performance had been put in the hands of Louise Chunn, with the extremely competent John Mulholland as her deputy. Rusbridger's handback note to Preston was fairly damning of the whole production: 'I thought this week was particularly dire. Not so much dire as just *wrong* ... I think the whole thing should go back into the melting pot.' There was no mistaking a certain bouncy anticipation in this list of matters awaiting the editor's attention, compiled as it was by the potential editor-in-waiting.

The problematic Friday section was clearly something that had been preying on many minds. In aiming to be light, bright, young, entertainment- and consumer-oriented – dot dot dot Friday had shamelessly called one section 'Retail' – it had offended 'Guardian' sensibilities. Sitting most uncomfortably in the section were the daily obituaries, often among the best-written pieces in the paper, which Bill Smithies had been editing, where, on Fridays at least, it appeared as a kind of party pooper, a wet blanket dampening the frivolities.

Rusbridger was not the only candidate to have mentioned the problem in his manifesto. The leader writer and duty editor Victor Keegan thought 'The new Friday section appears to be reaching down to a market which may not exist, while turning off traditional readers ...' Alex Brummer, the finance editor and former Washington correspondent, said the paper should aim to avoid the jolt that sometimes occurred 'between the generally serious news values of the front section of the paper and the tabloid culture of G2', describing the Friday section as 'too thin in Guardian terms'. Martin Walker – the Washington correspondent and former head of the Moscow bureau – made the point more generally. 'There are too many days when the Guardian feels a bit like a Chinese meal, leaving me hungry for some more bulk ... We do popular culture very well, but I want more high culture.'

The manifestos provide a fascinating insight into the state of the Guardian and the way it viewed itself at the beginning of 1995. Keegan set the global context: 'We still [as in CP Scott's time] believe in wealth creation without which no reforms are possible and without which our other values - community, compassion, pluralism, equality of opportunity, individual freedom and intellectual inquiry - would be empty words. These values will now be tested in a rapidly changing and paradoxical world context ... Globalisation is bound to breed insecurity. People naturally feel less and less in control of the forces shaping their economic and cultural destiny ... The central moral problem for the world and the Guardian will be what to do about those not empowered, the have-nots of the information revolution.'

Martin Walker also painted a picture of the world which the Guardian and its new editor would have to address: 'The relatively stable British class and social system of the welfare state years threaten to give way to a pattern already emerging in the USA. It is a neo-Victorian social system topped by a large, affluent and adaptable class with good credit, email addresses, and two homes. At the bottom is a swelling and demoralised underclass. And in the middle is a large layer of insecure people, ranging through the working poor, the intermittently working skilled, the underpaid public employees, and the socially mobile who are heading up. Our reporting has to embrace all these groups.'

Rusbridger's manifesto came in retrospect to seem remarkably close to the agenda he followed through the early years of his editorship. He began by squeezing some good news from the circulation figures, which had actually risen slightly in the last six months, despite the surrounding price war. 'This is to put it bluntly a fantastic achievement,' he declared.

The paper had been very fortunate to have Peter Preston as its editor over almost 20 years, Rusbridger continued. 'It is emphatically not a paper in need of a revolution.' But it was a good time to take stock, especially as uncertainties in the job market had meant that stagnation was a danger. 'If no one leaves and no one joins and no one moves jobs internally, then we face the prospect of growing serenely old together ... I don't suffer any illusions about young journalists being better than old journalists. But there are obvious dangers here.'

He emphasized the commitment to investigative reporting, which he saw as one of the paper's strengths, and expressed his hope that the comment pages should be 'the main forum for the debate that will rage on the left and centre-left between now and the next election'. And on the electronic Guardian: 'The old ink and paper Guardian isn't about to disappear. But we should, in cooperation with the rest of the group, give serious attention to the need to develop electronically distributed versions of the paper.'

He became most eloquent when he attempted to express what it was in his view that defined the Guardian. 'I cherish the paper's lack of awe for the establishment. I like its lack of pomposity, its periodic acts of defiance; but also its delicacy of tone and its deftness of touch. I like it when it is in full-throated pursuit of those it genuinely believes to be in the wrong. I like it when it is quietly, stubbornly and naggingly persistent. I am proud of the Guardian's honesty. It is not a paper that boasts that it is inevitably in full possession of the definitive truth ... There is an unspoken contract with the reader: this is our best and candid stab at the truth as far as we could ascertain it at the time we went to press ...'

'I admire the Guardian's diversity. I like its willingness to publish opinions with which it disagrees ... I treasure the freedom the Guardian reporters, feature writers and editors enjoy.'

He went on to emphasise something that he repeatedly stated and continuously developed throughout his editorship. 'I am glad that the paper's main relationship is with its readers rather than with its proprietor.' He emphasised that the paper's independence from proprietorial influence should be mirrored in independence from any political party.

Similar independence would be required for the journalists' vote. The Electoral Reform Society - hired by the chapel to conduct the ballot - provided voting papers and sealed ballot boxes that were strategically placed on the two editorial floors of Farringdon Road. The manifestos were all available to read via the Atex system several days before the vote took place, and telephone voting arrangements were made for those absent. Campaigning by and on behalf of the candidates went on for about a week - it was Martin Walker, the Washington correspondent, who kissed the baby, an opportunity provided by a proud mother who brought the child in to show to her colleagues. The campaign culminated in a crowded midday hustings in an upstairs room at the Horseshoe pub in Clerkenwell. Written questions had been invited and were put directly to the four candidates, who had been given advance sight of them. All the questions, perhaps taking their cue from the general tone of the manifestos, were of a serious nature to do with the future of the Guardian. Well, most of them. David Rowan asked: 'How do you feel about smoking in the office?' and was booed down by the general assembly, clearly on the grounds that it was too trite. (Smoking was increasingly an issue and within a couple of years had been banned throughout the Guardian, demonstrating that Rowan was ahead of his time.)

There was an extremely high turnout: the vast majority of the 250 or so journalists managed to register their preference. There was no need for the second round that the system would have allowed. Rusbridger won on the first round with 138 votes, more than the required 50%, or in other words more than the other three candidates taken together. The nearest contender was Victor Keegan with 57 votes.

Brian Williams, the father of the chapel, insisted that the candidates should be told of the results of the journalists' ballot before they were generally published. He then put out a message on Atex telling everyone in Farringdon Road he was about to announce the results and exactly where they were to be found. Consequently everyone hit the appropriate button at the same time, causing smoke to come out of the server in the computer room. It took two hours to fix, during which time little or no work was possible. Williams said, 'We had accidentally discovered a much more effective tool for industrial action than any we had so far used.'[10]

Happily, Rusbridger's appointment was also recommended unanimously by the Scott Trust's seven-person advisory committee. That included the two journalist representatives, chosen from the editorial floors of Farringdon Road, Michael White from the first floor (news) and Georgina Henry from the second floor (features). It had been their job to gather questions from their colleagues to put to the candidates when they came before the panel for the final interviews. Henry remembered feeling mildly embarrassed at voicing some that expressed anxieties about Rusbridger's seriousness - 'Was he too lightweight?', 'Did he understand politics enough?' One question that she and White put to him was: 'If the prime minister of the day rings you up and says I want to see you to discuss the Guardian's coverage of politics, what would your answer be?' Henry recalled, 'He took one look at Mike and said, "Well, I'd say, as long as I can bring Mike White with me."'[11] Very much later, White, summing up the difference between Preston and Rusbridger in this respect, would say, 'Peter is genuinely interested [in politics] and Alan genuinely isn't. He doesn't have much time for politicians.'[12]

A couple of days after the announcement of his victory, Rusbridger circulated a note to all staff. 'Those of you who were around on Tuesday night when the white puff of smoke emerged (the one from the Boardroom rather than the systems room) will have heard me thank everyone who took part - which means just about all of you. I especially thanked - and would like to thank again - Vic, Alex and Martin for the spirit in which they advanced their candidatures. All of their manifestos had much that was very interesting, thoughtful and right, and I hope to draw on many of their ideas about the paper and the way in which it is run.'

The 'puff of smoke' had gone up from the boardroom in Farringdon Road, at 8.30pm on 24 January, just an hour and a half after the Scott Trust had gathered for their final session. For Preston, in particular, it had been a breathless day. David McKie, writing in Wednesday's paper, recorded it as a formidable foretaste of the 'pleasures and pressures' Rusbridger had let himself in for. Preston had missed the morning conference that he usually chaired because he was meeting the Scott Trust on the editorship of the Observer. Then at noon he was ready to greet an 'immensely distinguished national figure' (unidentified) who had come in for an off-the-record session open to all editorial staff in Preston's office. Immediately after his guest's departure Preston presided over the daily meeting of a gathering of section editors, competing for the allocation of space in the following day's paper. From that he went to a decisive meeting on the Guardian's editorship, now in possession of the result of the journalists' ballot. He left that to take a cab to the Commons, where he appeared before the select committee on members' interests to answer questions arising from the Guardian investigation that had brought down Neil Hamilton and Tim Smith (to be dealt with in the second volume of this book). Throughout the day the Guardian had also been in the High Court defending a libel action brought against Preston and two of his journalists by Paul Judge, the director general of the Conservative Party: he had accused them of 'malice' over a report into donations to the party by the businessman Asil Nadir. As Preston was waiting to be called by the Commons committee, Michael White joined him to say he had had a phone call from Paul Brown at the High Court: the libel action had failed and Judge was ordered to pay costs thought to amount to some £300,000. Buoyed up by this victory, Preston answered questions from the Commons committee before – feeling 'unexpectedly cheery', as McKie noted – dashing back to the Guardian for the confirmation and announcement of Rusbridger as his successor. That evening there was a celebratory party at the Rusbridger home in Highbury.

There was a final paragraph to Rusbridger's message to staff, quoted above. In his first act as editor, a couple of weeks before the handover, he placed a woman in the highest editorial position any had occupied at the Guardian since its foundation in 1821. 'Georgina Henry will be Deputy Editor, responsible for all aspects of the paper.'[13] And he also pre-empted any jostling for his chair of the kind that had taken place when Peter Cole first became deputy to Preston a little over a decade earlier. 'She will edit the paper in my absence. Paul Johnson will be Deputy Editor (News) and will edit the paper when both Georgina and I are away.' Georgina Henry recorded her own reaction. 'I was so flabbergasted. I was 34 and I was inexperienced really. I'd had two years as deputy features editor and before that three years as media editor. I hadn't done much in the way of news, some reporting in previous jobs but on nothing like a national paper. I said I'd have to think about it ... I was so excited, and worried.' She had no doubt that Rusbridger wanted to send the strongest possible signal to the Guardian's female staff. 'Crucially, he wanted a woman in the job,' said Henry. 'I absolutely concede that if I hadn't been a woman I wouldn't have got the job.'[14] In that she was underestimating both her own abilities and the degree to which they were widely recognised by her colleagues, male and female.

It was 1995. A couple of miles down the road from the Guardian offices, a young Tony Blair and Gordon Brown were testing out their 'New Labour' rebranding. In the music charts, the focus of a younger generation, Oasis and Blur were poised to battle it out for Britpop supremacy. From a garage of Jeff Bezos's rented home in Washington, a new company called Amazon was about to sell its first book.

A new era was beginning.

Notes

Introduction

1 *The History Boys*, Faber, 2004.
2 David Ayerst, *Guardian: Biography of a Newspaper*, Collins, 1971; Geoffrey Taylor, *Changing Faces: A History of the Guardian 1956-1988*, Fourth Estate, 1993; William Haslam Mills, *The Manchester Guardian: A Century of History*, Chatto & Windus, 1921.
3 Giles Foden, introduction to *The Guardian Year 2005* (Atlantic Books, 2005), which Foden edited.

Chapter 1 - Sedimentary: The Making of the Modern Guardian

1 Centenary essay 1921.
2 The Gay Hussar sadly closed in 2018.
3 He was not unique in this. It was one of the ways in which hot metal was rendered flexible, although it had become excessively rare long before hot metal was finally phased out in 1987.
4 Cooke in his introduction to *The Bedside Guardian 17*, edited by WL Webb, 1968.
5 I use the word 'paper' throughout to refer to the Guardian in its totality, except where some more specific definition is required.
6 Alan Rusbridger, 'Pilot digital journalism scheme', global email to staff, 22 July 2013.
7 William Haslam Mills in *The Manchester Guardian, A Century of History*, Chatto & Windus, 1921, used this phrase to describe the world into which the Guardian was born in 1821.
8 Jean Stead, news editor, 1970-1979. She gave up motorcycling shortly after coming off her Kawasaki 250 on an oil slick on Blackfriars Bridge, probably, she was told, spilled by the newspaper lorries going in and out of Fleet Street, a curious kind of industrial injury.
9 David Ayerst, 'Our owners: the Scott Trust', Guardian, 1 January 1973.
10 Ayerst, 'The Guardian at 150', Guardian supplement, 5 May 1971.
11 John Russell Scott, obituary, Manchester Guardian, 6 April 1949.
12 David Ayerst, 'Our owners: the Scott Trust', Guardian, 1 January 1973.
13 TS Matthews, *The Sugar Pill: An Essay on Newspapers*, Gollancz, 1957.
14 RCK Ensor recalled in the CP Scott centenary issue, 26 October 1946, 'He once said to me a thing I have never forgotten, "I want you always to feel that the purpose of the paper is to be an organ of civilisation."'
15 Taylor, *Changing Faces*.
16 CP Scott at the presentation of his bust by Epstein to the city of Manchester, MG, 22 October 1926.
17 John Douglas Pringle, 'On the record', Guardian, 30 July 1973, a review of WP Crozier's *Off the Record, Political Interviews 1933-1943*, Hutchinson, 1973.
18 John Douglas Pringle, *Have Pen: Will Travel*, Chatto & Windus, 1973.
19 *The Bedside Guardian 8*, 1959.

20 In his introduction to Crozier's *Off the Record*, 1973.

21 'Andrew Sharf, *The British Press and Jews Under Nazi Rule*, Oxford University Press, 1964.

22 'Haley, the great informer', obituary by AP Ryan, historian of the Times, revised David Ayerst, Guardian, 8 September 1987.

23 AP Wadsworth and Julia de Lacy Mann: *The Cotton Trade and Industrial Lancashire 1600–1780*, Manchester University Press, 1931; reprinted 1965.

24 Matthews, *The Sugar Pill*.

25 Matthew Engel, 'Still the one and only', Guardian, 4 May 1996.

26 Alan Rusbridger, 'The Snowden Leaks and the Public', *New York Review of Books*, vol LX, no 18, 21 November–4 December 2013.

27 The leader appeared on 1 November 1956. See Alan Rusbridger: 'Courage under fire, the Guardian and Observer stand on Suez', Guardian, 10 July 2006.

28 Taylor in *Changing Faces* says that the heavy losses as a result of Suez sometimes alleged did not occur, and the circulation figures he provides actually show an increase for the month of November.

29 Alastair Hetherington, *Guardian Years*, Chatto & Windus, 1981.

30 See his obituary by Brian Jones, Guardian, 23 November 1995. Also by Brian Jones, 'A new beginning', a piece to mark the 25th anniversary of printing in London, Guardian, 11 September 1986.

31 Hetherington, *Guardian Years*.

32 Guardian, 18 May 1987.

33 Haslam Mills, *The Manchester Guardian*.

34 Malcolm Muggeridge, *Chronicles of Wasted Time: The Green Stick,* Collins, 1972.

35 From Hetherington's speech at the Guardian's 150th birthday celebrations in 1971, quoted in Kenneth Roy, ed, *A Man of His Word: Life of Alastair Hetherington*, Carrick Media, 1998.

36 'Alone in a reporters' room that Dickens might just have left', Guardian, 11 February 1988.

37 Ibid.

38 Cole, 'Northern twilight', Guardian, 4 May 1996.

39 Ibid.

40 Harry Whewell, 'A distant sound of paper rustling', Guardian, 11 February 1988.

41 'The Guardian at 150', 5 May 1971.

42 Peter Preston, 'Bricks and mortar don't have much to do with good journalism', Guardian, 8 December 2008.

43 Alan Rusbridger, 'Kings Place, the Guardian's new home', Guardian, 15 December 2008.

44 Alan Rusbridger, the 2010 Andrew Olle media lecture for 702 ABC, Sydney, Australia: http://www.abc.net.au/local/stories/2010/11/19/3071359.htm. The quotation from Scott comes from Scott's introduction to the American edition of Haslam Mills's *The Manchester Guardian: A Century of History*, Henry Holt, 1922.

45 UK newspaper website figures from ABC for July 2015; message to staff from David Pemsel, GMG CEO, 30 July 2015; message to staff from Katharine Viner, 28 August 2015.

Chapter 2 - Preston's Paper: From Insouciance to Mortal Combat

1 Hugh Hebert, 'No need to say it dully', Guardian, 22 March 1975.

2 In Mori polls of national newspaper editors, January 1994 and 1995, Preston was voted most impressive.

3 Taylor, *Changing Faces*.

4 Author interview, 19 August 2008.

5 Author interview, 24 February 2009.

6 Ivor Crewe and Anthony King, *SDP: The Birth, Life and Death of the Social Democratic Party*, OUP, 1995.

7 McKie interviewed on his retirement by Emma Brockes, Guardian, 2 April 2001.

8 Author interview, 12 August 2010.

9 Hebert, 'No need to say it dully', Guardian, 22 March 1975.

10 Milne left the Guardian in October 2015, initially on unpaid leave, to become Jeremy Corbyn's director of communications.

11 Email to the author, 5 December 2011.

12 Author interview, 20 May 2008.

13 Author interview, 16 July 2008.

14 Interviewed by Derek Jameson in BBC Radio 4's *Midweek*, 23 May 1984, quoted in David Caute, *The Espionage of the Saints*, Hamish Hamilton, 1986.

15 Maggie Brown, 'Fleet Street's night of the long knives', Guardian, 28 January 1986.

16 Alan Rusbridger, 'The anguish of swapping to Wapping', Guardian, 28 January 1986.

17 Undated reference to Spectator in Graham Stewart, *The History of the Times, vol VII, 1981-2002: The Murdoch Years*, HarperCollins, 2005.

18 An undated letter marked Personal from Preston to Guardian journalists, June/July 1987.

19 Brian MacArthur, *Eddy Shah: Today and the Newspaper Revolution*, David & Charles, 1988.

20 Stephen Glover, *Paper Dreams: The Story of the Independent and the Independent on Sunday*, Jonathan Cape, 1993; revised edition, Harmondsworth, 1994.

21 Charles Wintour, *The Rise and Fall of Fleet Street*, Hutchinson, 1989.

22 MacArthur, *Eddy Shah*.

23 Stewart, *The History of the Times, vol VII*.

24 This is the amount that Geoffrey Taylor in *Changing Faces*, 1993, estimates that the Guardian had derived from the sale of its shares by the spring of 1990.

25 Hetherington, *Guardian Years*.

26 Archive interview 14 December 2001; see also Marland profiled in Marketing Week, 14 April 1995.

27 Taylor, *Changing Faces*.

28 Harold Jackson, 'Systems on the up', Guardian, 18 February 1988.

29 Ibid.

30 Author interview, 15 May 2008.

Chapter 3 - A Great Editor in His Element

1 http://www.theguardian.com/media-network/media-network-blog/2012/oct/02/european-press-prize-journalism

2 Interview by Jeannette Page, 7 February 2008.

3 Author interview, 6 April 2009.

4 Author interview, 16 July 2008.

5 Peter Preston, 'Survivor's journal of a plague year', Guardian, 5 May 1995.

6 Preston, 'Good news on a bad day for one victim', Guardian, 22 June 2002.

7 Preston, op. cit., 5 May 1995.

8 Author interview, 2 July 2008.

9 Hetherington, 'The Guardian in 1971', in the 150th anniversary supplement, 5 May 1971.

10 Email to the author 28 February 2013. See also Preston in *After Leveson? The Future for British Journalism*, edited by John Mair, Abramis, 2013.

11 Author interview, 14 August 2008.

12 Author interview, 12 August 2010.

13 Christopher Dodd, Guardian, 18 May 1987.

Chapter 4 - Turmoil in the Newsroom and a Shock Departure

1 Martin Harrop contributed the chapter on the press in David Butler and Dennis Kavanagh: *The British General Election of 1987*, Palgrave MacMillan, 1988. I am indebted to this chapter in particular, including the tables it contains, prepared with the help of Deborah Lund.

2 Author interview, undated.

3 Author interview, 1 July 2008.

4 Nikki Knewstub was interviewed by Jeannette Page, 29 April 2008.

5 Melanie Phillips, 'Words I thought I'd never write: I'm a novelist', Times, 26 December 2017).

6 'Traitors', Michael Billington, Guardian, 22 January 1986.

7 Author interview, 20 July 2010.

8 Author correspondence, undated.

9 Email to author, 12 September 2009.

10 Author interview, 11 June 2009.

11 Mandarin, 1990.

Chapter 5 - The Radical Redesign of 1988

1 Letters page, Guardian, 9 January 1988.

2 Author interview, 2 July 2008.

3 Peter Cole, author interview, 1 July 2008.

4 The slogan, devised by Bartle Bogle Hegarty, never quite made it out into the world. See Peter Chippindale and Chris Horrie, *Disaster! The Rise and Fall of News on Sunday*, Penguin, 1988.

5 'Aftermath of disaster', Guardian, 11 November 1988.

6 Song of Solomon 2:8.

7 Michael McNay, 'Liberation from anarchy', Guardian, 7 March 1988.

8 Author interview, 15 May 2008.

9 Author interview, 24 April 2008.

Chapter 6 - The Changing Agenda

1 8 February 1988.

2 Email correspondence with the author, 15 and 19 October 2008.

3 Paul Johnson, 'Quis custodiet?', Spectator, 6 March 1982.

4 Letters to the Editor, Guardian, 4 April 1987.

5 Taylor, *Changing Faces*.

6 Author interview, 8 February 2008.

7 Letter in New Statesman, 6 November 1981.

8 Jonathan Beaty and SC Gwynne, *The Outlaw Bank: A Wild Ride into the Secret Heart of BCCI*, Random House USA, 1993.

9 Ibid.

10 Peter Truell and Larry Gurwin, *BCCI: The Inside Story of the World's Most Corrupt Financial Empire*, Bloomsbury, 1992.

11 Email to author, October 2010.

12 See Martin Wainwright, *The Guardian Book of April Fool's Day*, Aurum Press, 2007.

13 Conversation with Ian Wright, 17 June 2010.

14 The figures are in a letter to the New Statesman, 13 November 1981, from Rory Flanagan, former business/syndication manager, Third World Media.

15 The enterprising literary editor and acting editor of the Third World Quarterly, Maya Jaggi, was to go on to work at the Guardian in the 1990s, developing her advocacy of world literature. Over the next 20 years or so she played an important part in extending the range of literary culture covered in the Guardian.

16 Author interview, 17 June 2010.

17 New Statesman, 6 November 1981.

18 Telephone and email conversation with the author, July 2010.

19 Truell and Gurwin, BCCI.

20 Gauhar to Preston, 23 November 1981, Preston papers, Guardian archive.

21 Victoria Brittain and Michael Simmons (eds), *The Guardian Third World Review: Voices from the South*, Hodder and Stoughton, 1987.

22 'Altaf Gauhar: He devoted his journalistic and business skills to helping the world's poor and founded the Guardian's Third World Review', Guardian, 13 December 2000.

23 Truell and Gurwin, BCCI.

24 David Pallister, Guardian, 17 July 1991.

25 John Willcock, 'BCCI creditors set to act against Bank of England', Guardian, 7 October 1991.

Chapter 7 - The New Look Guardian and the Birth of Weekend

1 Internal message to Rusbridger, 5 January 1996.

2 Author interview, 18 June 2008.

3 Author interview, 13 June 2008.

4 Smithies kindly provided copies of his correspondence with Gott and Preston.

5 Ian Ashcroft, Guardian board minutes, 21 October 1988.

6 http://www.rosasquith.co.uk/cartoons/

7 Stephen Harvey of Chandler's Ford, Hampshire.

Chapter 8 - A Beeline to Beijing

1 Author interview, 15 May 2008.

2 Email to author, 22 June 2012.

3 Anne McHardy, 'By the pricking of my thumbs', Guardian, 27 April 1990; and 'Taking the strain', Guardian, 9 August 1994.

4 Tim Gopsill and Greg Neale, *Journalists: 100 Years of the NUJ*, Profile Books, 2007.

Chapter 9 - The Shock of the New

1 Email to author, 12 March 2011.

2 Author interview, 23 May 2011.

3 Author interview, 17 September 2009.

4 See www.waldemar.tv/biography. He must have changed his mind very quickly; a review by Angela Carter appeared in the Guardian on 23 September 1988, three days before the book's publication date.

5 'Upwardly mobile', Guardian, 22 April 1989.

6 'Middle-brow plumage: Julie Burchill takes a distant view of the sex manual', Guardian, 1 May 1986.

7 Previously called Varsity, a title to which it would later revert.

8 It first appeared on 4 September 1990.

9 Author interview, 19 August 2008.

10 Interview by Jeannette Page, 30 November 2009.

11 Private Eye, 11 May 1990.

12 The source is the unreliable Private Eye again. Scott was 25 when he became editor (Ayerst).

13 Toby Young, *How to Lose Friends and Alienate People*, Little, Brown, 2001.
14 'The town of steel', Guardian, 3 August 1996.
15 Emails to author, December 2010.
16 'Bauwens libel jury split', Guardian, 3 September 1992.
17 'My Modern Review, I miss you so. Well, just a little bit ...', Guardian,
   4 November 2000.
18 Author interview, 10 November 2012.

Chapter 10 - Ethical Issues as the Correspondent Dies
1 Glover, *Paper Dreams*.
2 Media File, Guardian, 21 August 1989.
3 Mick Brown's biography, *Richard Branson: The Inside Story* (Michael Joseph, 1988),
   later came out in several revised editions, but none covered the Correspondent
   episode.
4 Glover, *Paper Dreams*.
5 Cole, 'Son of Corrie', Guardian, 24 September 1990.
6 The victim was James Gatward, chairman of TVS Television; Glover, *Paper Dreams*.
7 Glover, Paper Dreams.
8 The company was known as The Guardian and Manchester Evening News Ltd
   (GMEN) from 1972 until 1993, when it changed its name to Guardian Media Group
   (GMG).
9 Author interview, 1 July 2008.
10 Author interview, 26 June 2008.
11 Author interview, 9 September 2009.
12 Young Guardian was launched under the editorship of Tim Madge on
   1 October 1986. From 1988 it had been edited by Melanie McFadyean, who
   was now away on maternity leave.
13 See John Illman, 'Sleeping with the enemy', British Journalism Review, vol 27, no 1,
   March 2016.
14 Author interview, undated.
15 Author interview, undated.
16 Author interview, undated.
17 Author interview, undated.
18 Author interview, undated.
19 Adrian Addison, *Mail Men: The Unauthorized Story of the Daily Mail*, Atlantic Books,
   2017.
20 Ibid.

Chapter 11 - Europe and Journalism Without Borders
1 Roy Jenkins, *European Diary 1977-1981*, Collins, 1989, cited in Taylor, *Changing
   Faces*.
2 Sun, 1 November 1990.
3 Taylor, *Changing Faces*.
4 Hugo Young, *This Blessed Plot: Britain and Europe from Churchill to Blair*, Macmillan,
   1998.
5 Author interview, 19 August 2008.
6 Roy Greenslade, *Maxwell's Fall: An Insider's Account*, Simon & Schuster, 1992.
7 David McKie's diaries.
8 Martin Gilbert and Richard Gott, *The Appeasers*, Weidenfeld and Nicolson, 1963.
9 Author interview, 4 December 2008.
10 Author interview, 6 May 2009.

11 Mill had the manuscript of Carlyle's *The French Revolution* for comment but a maid thought it was waste paper and threw it on the fire. In fact, a few copies of the dummy European Review survived but it is a rare collector's item.

12 Email to author, 12 May 2009.

13 http://www.magforum.com/european.htm#max is a good source for The European, as is Roy Greenslade's *Maxwell's Fall*. See also Tom Bower, *Maxwell: The Final Verdict*, HarperCollins, 1996, for a postscript.

14 The European was sold to the Barclay brothers in 1992 and lasted until 1998.

15 Email to author, 16 May 2010.

16 Author interview, 21 July 2009.

17 Guardian archive.

Chapter 12 - A Post-prandial Nap and a Rude Awakening

1 Gott, author interview, 4 December 2008.

2 The features sub, Dick Bates, who arrived in September 1987, drew the analogy. He thought it 'a quiet and cosy retreat from the outside world'.

3 Author interview, 26 June 2009.

4 Ed Vulliamy, 'Wagner and the Ring of life', Guardian Weekend, 23 September 1989; and author interview, 26 June 2009.

5 Paul Webster was only three months into the job, having been appointed foreign editor in August 1989 to succeed Alex Brummer.

6 Author interview, 8 May 2008.

7 Ian Mayes, 'Peter Lennon: Obituary', Guardian, 20 March 2011.

8 Jeannette Page interviewed Brenda Polan, 2 April 2009. After she left, Polan went on to become women's editor of the Independent on Sunday.

9 Episode 1, Skin, of *The Singing Detective*. In a later episode during word association with the hospital psychotherapist he responds to the word 'guardian' with 'misprint'.

10 Interview by Jeannette Page, 12 March 2009.

11 Author interview, undated.

12 Author interview, 3 September 2008.

13 Author interview, undated.

14 The author is slightly ashamed to confess that he was the visitor. The sub-editor was the admirable Desmond Christy.

Chapter 13 - Comment, Cartoons and a Touch of Poetry

1 Author interview, 29 May 2009.

2 Michael McNay, 'Papas, beloved Guardian cartoonist, dies aged 72', Guardian, 24 June 2000. See also obituary by Harold Jackson, Guardian, 26 June 2000.

3 Author interview, undated.

4 Heseltine became Tarzan after wielding the mace in the Commons chamber in 1976 in protest at Labour MPs singing 'The Red Flag'; Geoffrey Howe's being depicted as a sheep came from Denis Healey's remark in 1978 that being attacked by Howe was like being mauled by a dead sheep.

5 Guardian, 7 October 1994.

6 Undated notes for an illustrated talk, c. 21-22 October 1994.

7 Peter Preston, 'His nibs', Guardian, 1 May 1999.

8 Email to author, 2009.

9 Kathryn Flett, 'Are you being serious?', Observer, 27 February 2000.

10 Author interview, 6 May 2008.

Chapter 14 - A Tale of Two Exiles in a Time of Turmoil

1 Email to the author, 11 September 2012.
2 See 'How we met: Vitali Vitaliev and Clive James', interviews by Isabel Wolff, Independent, 19 August 1995.
3 Vitaliev's own recollection of these first few days in England may be found in his *Dreams on Hitler's Couch*, Richard Cohen Books, 1997.
4 Vitaliev, op. cit., 1997.
5 Cathy Porter, Korotich interview, Guardian, 27 March 1989.
6 On Martin Walker's advice Vitaliev kept a diary of his last days in the Soviet Union. Large parts of it appear in his book *Dateline Freedom: Revelations of an Unwilling Russian Exile*, Hutchinson, 1991.
7 Salman Rushdie, *Joseph Anton: A Memoir*, Random House Inc., 2012.
8 Her review appeared 23 September 1988.
9 Guardian, 18 January 1989.
10 Guardian, 17 February 1989.
11 Guardian, 2 March 1989.
12 Guardian, 2 March 1989.
13 Michael Foot, 'Historical Rushdie', Guardian, 2 March 1989. It was included in *The Uncollected Michael Foot, Essays Old and New 1953-2003*, Politico's Books, 2003.
14 Guardian, 18 July 1989.
15 Leader, 14 February 1990.
16 Guardian, 14 February 1990.
17 Mark Lawson, 'The row which came in from the cold', Guardian, 22 November 1997. The whole correspondence is worth seeking online. See also Rushdie's reading of it in *Joseph Anton*.
18 Guardian, 20 November 1997.
19 William Shawcross, 'Stinking Satanic self-righteousness', Guardian, 25 November 1997.
20 Rushdie, *Joseph Anton*.
21 Alison Flood, Guardian, 12 November 2012.
22 On 12 August 2022, Rushdie was about to speak at a public event at Chautauqua in New York state when he was attacked on stage by a man with a knife. He was stabbed many times before his assailant was overwhelmed. The attack would deprive Rushdie of his sight in one eye, and the use of a hand. Even during the months of long recovery, it was clear that Rushdie would continue to champion freedom of speech. He wrote directly about his experience in his book *Knife: Meditations After an Attempted Murder* (Jonathan Cape, 2024). He wears an eloquent black patch over the blind eye.

Chapter 15 - War over Kuwait: A Lion Among the Gazelles

1 Hirst's report, 'Iran puts death on show after gas raid', 22 March 1988; the editorial, 'The town where thousands died', Guardian, 24 March 1988.
2 'The horror and the questions it raises', Guardian, 16 March 1990.
3 Stewart, *The History of the Times, vol VII*.
4 Bob Woodward, Rick Atkinson, 'US failed to plan for Iraqi aggression', Guardian, 27 August 1990.
5 Guardian, 3 August 1990.
6 Georgina Henry, 'Rights of access to the action', Guardian, 8 January 1991.
7 John Hooper, 'White House help sought in journalists' feud', Guardian, 25 January 1991.

8   David Beresford, *Truth Is a Strange Fruit: A Personal Journey Through the Apartheid War*, Jacana, 2010.
9   David Sharrock, 'American bomber pilots jostle for their turn over kill zones', Guardian, 13 February 1991.
10 'Techno bloodshed', Guardian, 14 February 1991.
11 Leader, 'Diplomacy is still vital', Guardian, 23 February 1991.
12 See Torie Rose DeGhett, 'The war photo no one would publish', the Atlantic, 8 August 2014.
13 Alan Rusbridger in Sandie Byrne (ed.), *Tony Harrison: Loiner*, Oxford University Press, 1997.
14 Martin Walker, 'World ponders how to end Iraq's nuclear capacity', Guardian, 12 April 1991.

Chapter 16 - Order, Disorder and the Message from Mesopotamia

1   Denis Healey, 'Bloody shambles in the wake of war', Guardian, 22 March 1991.
2   Noam Chomsky, 'The weak shall inherit nothing', Guardian, 25 March 1991.
3   JK Galbraith, 'The call of arms and the poor man', Guardian, 27 March 1991.
4   So described by Salma Khadra Jayyusi (ed.), *Modern Arabic Fiction; An Anthology*, Columbia University Press, 2004.
5   Abdelrahman Munif, 'The war against a civilisation', Guardian, 1 April 1991. Some of the biographical information here is taken from Munif's obituary (as Abdul-Rahman Mounif) in the Guardian by Abdul-Hadi Jiad, 5 February 2004, and some from Jayyusi (see previous note).
6   Eduard Shevardnadze, 'A democratic way with world affairs', Guardian, 3 April 1991.
7   Francis Fukuyama, 'Changed days for Ruritania's dictator', Guardian, 8 April 1991; Theo Sommer, 'A world beyond order and control', Guardian, 13 April 1991.
8   Author interview, 24 February 2009.
9   Undated author interview.
10 'The valleys of death', Guardian, 3 April 1991.
11 The frustration stayed with Steele. Twenty years on (16 August 2011), he contributed to the anniversary a piece that began, 'When is a scoop not a scoop?' and ended, 'There was no website, only the printed paper. I had missed the last edition, and there was nothing to do but run my exclusive account of Gorbachev's liberation some 30 hours after it had happened. No Twitter, no mobile phones, no Internet.' Of course, it was a scoop.
12 There are three main sources for the account of this episode here: the relevant issues of the Guardian; a chapter in Steele's *Eternal Russia: Yeltsin, Gorbachev and the Mirage of Democracy*, Faber & Faber, 1994; and author interview, 2 June 2009.
13 Mikhail Gorbachev, *The New Russia*, Polity Press, 2016 (first published in Russia 2015).
14 James Meek, 'Toilet rolls beyond price', Guardian, 3 January 1992.
15 Author interview, 21 July 2009.
16 James Meek, 'God's disunited kingdoms', Guardian, 12 February 2000.
17 Author interview, 11 October 2013.
18 *Pride of Small Nations: The Caucasus and Post-Soviet Disorder*, Zed Books, 1994.
19 James Meek, 'Chechen hearts belong to Tolstoy', Guardian, 4 August 1994, and author interview.
20 James Meek, 'Hospitals run with blood as bombs fall', Guardian, 4 January 1995.

Chapter 17 - The Guide: A Little Thing That Meant a Lot and Led to More

1 Figures: Audit Bureau of Circulations (ABC).
2 Ageh held this BBC post until 2016, when he became chief digital officer at New York Public Library, a year after he had been awarded an OBE for his services to digital media.
3 Tony Ageh, 'Putting it down in black and white', Guardian, 8 August 1992.
4 For a brief account of Event see Brown, *Richard Branson*.
5 Author interview, 22 September 2009.
6 Ageh, author interview, 15 October 2010.
7 Author interview, 17 August 2010.
8 Email to author, August 2008. Both Ageh and Silverton are to be thanked for making their personal archives of PDU material available to the author.
9 Author interview, 9 July 2010.
10 Stephen Glover, 'Pink and perky', Evening Standard, 3 November 1993.

Chapter 18 - 'Small but Perfectly Informed': The Birth of G2

1 Author interview, 9 January 2009.
2 See Posy Simmonds, 'Meet the Webers', Guardian, 19 October 2012, and Suzie Mackenzie, 'Drawing on life, a profile of Posy Simmonds', Guardian, 10 October 1990.
3 Paul Webster in his speech at Alton's departure from the company in 2008.
4 Author interview, 6 May 2009.
5 Peter Preston, 'Europe is the shared story our papers tell', Observer, 25 June 2017.
6 Email to author from Henry Porter, 6 November 2012.
7 For more on the Guardian coverage of the Bosnian war, see the following chapter.
8 The journalist was from the heroic daily *Oslobodjenje* , which operated from a bomb shelter when the paper's building was destroyed. Five staff members were killed.
9 'It was 20 years ago ...', Guardian, 17 October 2012.
10 Graham Stewart in *The History of the Times, vol VII* is frank about the paper's T2 section introduced on 13 March 2000, 'modelled on the highly successful G2 section of the Guardian'.

Chapter 19 - Witnesses to War in Europe

1 Author interview, 1 May 2013.
2 Ed Vulliamy, 'I must testify: Why one journalist is giving evidence against alleged war criminals in Bosnia', Guardian, 22 April 1998.
3 Vulliamy: 'This war has changed my life,' British Journalism Review, http://bjr.sagepub.com, vol 4, no 2, 1993.
4 Author correspondence.
5 It was while in Afghanistan in 1995, just after the birth of her first child, that she sponsored the emigration of her interpreter, a young woman desperate to get out of Kabul. She lived with O'Kane and her husband, the journalist John Mullin, for the next 10 years, going on to gain a law degree at Glasgow University.
6 22 May 1992.
7 Ed Vulliamy and Davor Huic, 'Food flotilla relieves Dubrovnik', Guardian, 1 November 1991.
8 'Ethnic cleansing denied', Guardian, 30 July 1992.
9 See Vulliamy, *The War is Dead, Long Live the War, Bosnia: The Reckoning*, Bodley Head, 2012.
10 7 August 1992.

11 Haris Nezirovic, 'Inside Srebrenica under siege', Observer, 11 April 1993.

12 Nezirovic, 'The tragic mistakes of Srebrenica', Observer, 18 April 1993.

13 The rescue mission was to prove a temporary reprieve: Irma never recovered from her injuries and died in Great Ormond Street Hospital on 1 April 1995, age seven.

14 Maggie O'Kane, 'Little light at the end of Sarajevo's tunnel', Guardian, 30 August 1993.

15 Martin Wollacott, 'Magic - but making it stick is a new trick', Guardian, 10 February 1994.

16 Julian Borger, 'UN's protective pretence evaporates', Guardian, 20 May 1995.

17 Ian Black started his career at the Guardian in 1980 and was Middle East correspondent based in Jerusalem from 1984 to 1993. He became European editor in Brussels in 2000.

18 Traynor, 'Intended to chasten, each catastrophic airstrike has emboldened its target', Guardian, 30 May 1995.

19 See Frank Westerman for the Dutch newspaper NRC Handelsblad, reproduced in the Guardian as 'Thrown to the wolves in grim gamble', 25 October 1995.

20 John Sweeney, Charlotte Eagar, 'UN conceals massacre by Serbs', Observer, 23 July 1995.

21 Traynor, 'Il Duce of the Balkans', Guardian, 7 August 1995.

22 Srećko Latal, 'Moment of silence, then screams as mortar hits market again', Guardian, 29 August 1995.

23 Guardian, 15 September 1995; included in Tony Harrison, *Collected Poems*, Viking, 2007.

Chapter 20 - The Price of Journalism

1 Observer, 5 September 1993.

2 Figures: Audit Bureau of Circulations (ABC).

3 Hugo Young, 'Rupert, the bare-faced cheek', Guardian, 3 September 1993.

4 Preston, 'Confusion to all the pundits', Guardian, 20 June 1994.

5 Roger Crowe, 'Newspaper price war hits publishing shares', Guardian, 24 June 1994.

6 Author interview, 20 March 2012.

7 ... Friday was launched 16 September 1994.

8 Telephone conversation with author, 11 March 2012.

9 Stephen Glover, 'The price war is over, and it is time to ask who won', Spectator, 13 September 2003.

Chapter 21 - The Observer: A Marriage, but No Honeymoon

1 Anthony Sampson, *The Anatomist: The Autobiography*, Politico's, 2008.

2 Richard Cockett, *David Astor and the Observer*, Andre Deutsch, 1991.

3 Tiny Rowland, 'All's well that ends well', Observer, 23 May 1993.

4 Glover, *Paper Dreams*.

5 Author interview, 20 March 2012.

6 Andrew Culf, 'Observer's name "would survive merger"', Guardian, 29 April 1993.

7 Author interview with Stephen Pritchard, 11 March 2009.

8 Harry Roche, a paper for the Scott Trust, 3 November 1995.

9 Simon Caulkin: 'The inside story: the battle for the world's oldest Sunday newspaper ended in an old-fashioned scoop', Observer, 6 June 1993.

10 Author interview with Markwick, 20 March 2012.

11 David Rose, 'A statement to Observer staff', 25 January 1995, Guardian/Observer archive.

12 Markwick, three-year business plan for Observer presented to Scott Trust and GMG board, March 1997.

13 Glover, *Paper Dreams*.

14 Ibid.

15 John Cole, *As It Seemed to Me: Political Memoirs*, W&N, revised edition 1996.

16 Fenby, email to author, January 2009.

17 The typescript of the speech is in the Guardian/Observer archive: Peter Preston speech to Observer staff, 8 May 1993 (2004/148).

18 Author interview, 26 October 2010.

19 Trelford, 'After 218 years will the Observer fall victim to a historic pledge?', Independent, 10 August 2009.

20 Simon Caulkin, op. cit., 6 June 1993.

Chapter 22 - Teething Troubles - And a Painful Extraction

1 Scott Trust minutes, 24 February 1994.

2 Scott Trust minutes, 17 February 1993.

3 Bill Quirke, *Communicating Corporate Change*, McGraw-Hill, 1996.

4 Quoted in Peter Cole, 'Why the Observer isn't working', Independent, 9 June 1998.

5 Donald Trelford, 'Where is the Observer's guardian angel?', Independent, 16 June 1998.

6 Lord Goodman quoted in Donald Akenson, *Conor: A Biography of Conor Cruise O'Brien*, McGill-Queen's University Press, 1994

7 Preston, author interview, 16 July 2008.

8 Quoted in Henry Porter, *Lies, Damned Lies and Some Exclusives: Fleet Street Exposed*, Chatto & Windus, 1984.

9 Donald Trelford: 'After 218 years, will the Observer fall victim to a historic pledge?', Independent, 10 August 2009; see also Trelford, 'Where is the Observer's guardian angel?', Independent, 16 June 1998; and Tom Bower, *Tiny Rowland: A Rebel Tycoon*, William Heinemann, 1993.

10 Hugo Young, in *One of Us*, his biography of Margaret Thatcher (Macmillan, 1989), says that Heath's notes suggest that he meant to say 'facet', but what he said, so memorably, was 'face'.

11 Trelford, Guardian archive interview by Robert McCrum, 4 July 2001.

12 Donald Trelford, 'Time to set the record straight on the Observer and the Harrods takeover', Observer, 16 May 2010.

13 In August 1990, the libel actions were abandoned and the Fayeds paid the Observer's costs of £500,000.

14 Observer, 16 May 2010.

15 Trelford/McCrum archive interview, 2001.

16 Bower, *Tiny Rowland*.

17 Donald Trelford, 'The top man's job is to take the rap, even if he was out of the office', Independent, 26 May 2008.

18 Guardian, 3 July 1989.

19 Author interview with Georgina Henry, 6 May 2008.

20 Bower, *Tiny Rowland*; see also Bower, *Fayed: The Unauthorized Biography*, Macmillan, 1998.

21 Trelford, 'Where is the Observer's guardian angel?', Independent, 16 June 1998.

22 Greenslade, Guardian, 17 July 1995.

23 Noted in Donald Trelford (ed.), *Sunday Best 3*, Observer Gollancz, 1983.

24 This letter is quoted undated in Pringle, *Have Pen: Will Travel*.

25 Alan Rusbridger, 'The Observer: a paper for the Scott Trust', July 1997.

26 Author interview, 12 August 2009.

27 Guardian, 20 March 1990. Young was actually referring to Sunday Telegraph columnists.

28 Author interview, 25 October 2010.

Chapter 23 - A Direct Hit on the Guardian's 'Agent Ron'

1 Gott, author interview, 4 December 2008.

2 A Gottism, from the French, shattered/horrified.

3 Telephone interview with Tariq Ali, 9 July 2010.

4 Author interview, 15 May 2008. David Brook in an author interview on 17 August 2010 had no recollection of offering a view on the matter, although the paper's 'image' in the world at large was part of his remit.

5 Dominic Lawson, 'The Left disgraces itself', Spectator leader, 17-24 December 1994.

6 Much of the Gordievsky background here comes from an interview with him by the spy writer Michael Hartland: 'Once a spy, twice a spy', Guardian, 19 October 1991; and from Gordievsky's own autobiographical *Next Stop Execution*, Macmillan, 1995.

7 David Leigh and Paul Lashmar, 'The blacklist in Room 105', Observer, 18 August 1985.

8 'So many faces with so many tales', Guardian, 17 December 1994.

9 Oleg Gordievsky, 'The Guardian's KGB tactics', Spectator, 14 January 1995.

10 Email to the author, 10 May 2012.

11 Titov was one of three Soviet 'officials' expelled from Britain in the spring of 1983, just before the arrival of Gott's party of Guardian journalists in Moscow.

12 'In search of a Russia beyond the rhetoric', Guardian, 11 April 1983.

13 Email to the author, 21 May 2012.

14 Sunday Times, 'I was never an Eastern bloc mole, says Gott', 24 September 2000.

Chapter 24 - Heat, Dust and Death on the Books Pages

1 Email to author, April 2010.

2 John Carey, *William Golding: The Man Who Wrote Lord of the Flies*, Faber 2009. Golding did, in fact, contribute one further review for the Guardian on 9 April 1992.

3 Guardian, 6 February 1992.

4 James Wood, 'Writers and wraiths', Guardian, 13 January 1993.

5 David Hare, 'Mere fact, mere fiction', Guardian, 17 April 2010.

6 Christopher Shea, 'The elegant assassin', Boston Globe, 26 August 2007.

7 Jason Cowley, 'Last man', New Statesman, 19 June 2000.

8 Author interview, 4 December 2008.

9 Author interview, 12 August 2008. Journalists whose formal education stopped short of university were not uncommon at the time. Among sub-editors under Hetherington one of the most remarkable was RJ (Reg) Hollingdale who, having left school at 16, became a leading translator of and authority on Nietzsche. He worked in the foreign department from 1968 to 1991.

Chapter 25 - Changing of the Guard

1 Author interview with Preston, 21 May 2012; see also Harding, Leigh and Pallister, *The Liar: The Fall of Jonathan Aitken*, Penguin, 1997.

2 Author interview, 16 July 2008.

3 Alan Rusbridger, *Breaking News: The Remaking of Journalism and Why It Matters Now*, Canongate, 2018.

4   The first was the founder's original partner, Jeremiah Garnett, who was editor from 1848 to 1861.
5   Taylor, *Changing Faces*.
6   Ibid.
7   'Journalists will advise on new Guardian and Observer editors', Guardian, 17 January 1995.
8   Melanie Phillips, *Guardian Angel: My Story, My Britain*, Bombardier Books, 2018.
9   This is a paraphrase of a favourite quotation from the Washington Post journalist, David S Broder. Rusbridger quoted it again (properly attributed) in his valedictory article, 'Farewell, readers', 30 May 2015. It appears too in Rusbridger's *Breaking News*.
10 Author interview, undated.
11 Author interview, 6 May 2008.
12 Author interview, 12 August 2010.
13 Georgina Henry joined the Guardian in 1989, becoming a founding member of the campaigning group Women in Journalism in 1994. She died aged 53 in February 2014. Later that year Women in Journalism announced the addition of an annual Georgina Henry Award for Innovation in her honour, to be presented at the British Press Awards.
14 Author interview, 6 May 2008.

Select Bibliography

Addison, Adrian, *Mail Men: The Unauthorised Story of the Daily Mail*, Atlantic
    Books, 2017

Akenson, Donald Harman, *Conor: A Biography of Conor Cruise O'Brien*,
    McGill-Queen's University Press, 1994

Ayerst, David, *Guardian: Biography of a Newspaper*, Collins, 1971

Beaty, Jonathan and Gwynne, SC, *The Outlaw Bank: A Wild Ride into the Secret
    Heart of BCCI*, Random House USA, 1993

Bower, Tom, *Tiny Rowland, A Rebel Tycoon*, William Heinemann, 1993

Bower, Tom, *Maxwell: The Final Verdict*, HarperCollins, 1996

Bower, Tom, *Fayed: The Unauthorized Biography*, Macmillan, 1998

Brittain, Victoria and Simmons, Michael (eds), *The Guardian Third World
    Review: Voices from the South*, Hodder and Stoughton, 1987

Brown, Mick, *Richard Branson: The Inside Story*, Michael Joseph, 1988

Chippendale, Peter and Horrie, Chris, *Disaster!: The Rise and Fall of News on
    Sunday*, Penguin, 1988

Cockett, Richard, *David Astor and the Observer*, Andre Deutsch, 1991

Cole, John, *As It Seemed to Me: Political Memoirs*, W&N, 1995; revised edition,
    1996

Crozier, WP, *Off the Record: Political Interviews 1933-43*, edited with an
    introduction by AJP Taylor, Hutchinson, 1973

Glover, Stephen, *Paper Dreams: The Story of the Independent and the
    Independent on Sunday*, Jonathan Cape, 1993; revised edition,
    Harmondsworth, 1994

Gopsill, Tim and Neale, Greg, *Journalists: 100 Years of the NUJ*, Profile Books,
    2007

Gordievsky, Oleg, *Next Stop Execution*, Macmillan, 1995

Greenslade, Roy, *Maxwell's Fall: An Insider's Account*, Simon & Schuster 1992

Harding, Luke, Leigh, David and Pallister, David, *The Liar: The Fall of Jonathan
    Aitken*, Penguin, 1997, revised 1999

Hetherington, Alastair, *Guardian Years*, Chatto & Windus, 1981

MacArthur, Brian, *Eddy Shah: Today and the Newspaper Revolution*, David &
    Charles, 1988

Mair, John (ed.), *After Leveson? The Future for British Journalism*, Abramis, 2013

Matthews, TS, *The Sugar Pill: An Essay on Newspapers*, Victor Gollancz, 1957

Mills, William Haslam, *The Manchester Guardian: A Century of History*, Chatto & Windus, 1921 (plus the US edition, Henry Holt, 1922)

Muggeridge, Malcolm, *Chronicles of Wasted Time, Part One: The Green Stick*, Collins, 1972

Phillips, Melanie, *Guardian Angel: My Story, My Britain*, Bombardier Books, 2018

Porter, Henry, *Lies, Damned Lies and Some Exclusives: Fleet Street Exposed*, Chatto & Windus, 1984

Pringle, John Douglas, *Have Pen: Will Travel*, Chatto & Windus, 1973

Quirke, Bill, *Communicating Corporate Change*, McGraw-Hill, 1996

Roy, Kenneth (ed.), *Alastair Hetherington: A Man of his Word*, Carrick Media, 1998

Rusbridger, Alan, *Breaking News: The Remaking of Journalism and Why It Matters Now*, Canongate, 2018

Sampson, Anthony, *The Anatomist: The Autobiography of Anthony Sampson*, Politico's, 2008

Sharf, Andrew, *The British Press and Jews Under Nazi Rule*, Oxford University Press, 1964

Steele, Jonathan, *Eternal Russia: Yeltsin, Gorbachev and the Mirage of Democracy*, Faber & Faber, 1994

Stewart, Graham, *The History of the Times, vol VII, 1981-2002: The Murdoch Years*, HarperCollins, 2005

Taylor, Geoffrey, *Changing Faces, A History of the Guardian 1956-1988*, Fourth Estate, 1993

Truell, Peter and Gurwin, Larry, *BCCI: The Inside Story of the World's Most Corrupt Financial Empire*, Bloomsbury, 1992

Vitaliev, Vitaly, *Dreams on Hitler's Couch*, Richard Cohen Books, 1997

Vulliamy, Ed, *The War is Dead, Long Live the War, Bosnia: The Reckoning*, Bodley Head, 2012

Wadsworth, AP and Mann, Julia de Lacy, *The Cotton Trade and Industrial Lancashire 1600-1780*, Manchester University Press, 1931; reprinted 1965

Wainwright, Martin, *The Guardian Book of April Fool's Day*, Aurum Press, 2007

Wintour, Charles, *The Rise and Fall of Fleet Street*, Hutchinson, 1989

Young, Hugo, *One of Us: A Biography of Margaret Thatcher*, Macmillan, 1989

Young, Hugo, *This Blessed Plot: Britain and Europe from Churchill to Blair*, Macmillan, 1998

Young, Toby, *How to Lose Friends and Alienate People*, Little, Brown, 2001

Acknowledgements

I thank Alan Rusbridger, who commissioned this book on behalf of the Scott Trust, as well as his managing editor, Chris Elliott, long-time friend, support and companion on therapeutic trips 'in and out the Eagle' (and his assistant Wendy Collinson). Katharine Viner, who inherited the book unfinished, is thanked, not least for the appointment of Lindsay Davies as the hands-on editor. Lindsay quickly proved to be assiduous, tireless and unfailingly focused. I can't thank her enough. Did I forget to say ruthless?

Words can't express my thanks to Nick Hopkins whom Katharine Viner put in charge of the project to oversee it to publication. His commitment has been decisive. The text has benefited from the close scrutiny of the copy editor, Jacqui Lewis. Murray Armstrong read the book chapter by chapter as I wrote it and was unnervingly quiet in the process, before finally declaring, 'It leaps off the page!' David McKie, Peter Preston's deputy for a long time, read a passage from it at Peter's memorial service, slipping in a kind word about the source. I asked Richard Norton-Taylor to read a section: we were in a favourite Chinese restaurant, and he indicated approval by a thrust of his chopsticks. Jane Glentworth helped me fathom the Ray Street genesis of the website. Jeannette Page, former letters editor, undertook some historical research and a number of interviews for me, all credited as they occur. We went together to explore CP Scott's West Country homeland and rambled among his familial tombs. Thank you, Jeannette. I want to mention Helen Hodgson as a most valued friend and colleague over many years both in the office of the readers' editor and in helping to restore Hazlitt's grave in Soho and in the creation of the Hazlitt Society.

To all my former colleagues I offer my sincere gratitude for their toleration, and for extending it, one hopes, to include the omissions and mistakes they may find here. A special word for Desmond Christy and Matthew Engel, whom I followed to the Guardian each along a roundabout route from Northampton. Des died alas as this volume neared publication.

Almost all the interviews I recorded for this history were professionally transcribed by Libby Bowles, who lived near me. A stranger on a train from Euston (Eve Watson) told me about her; the result is a large, searchable database of Guardian and Observer journalists and others, talking about themselves (and other things). Thank you again, Libby. The actual recordings will join those already in the Guardian sound archive, which Leslie Plommer did so much to build.

Richard Nelsson, head of the Guardian's information department (library) and Jason Rodrigues his colleague, chased down many elusive quotes etc, and, in the archive, Mariam Yamin, Philippa Mole, Emma Aitken and Susan Gentles were valuable allies.

John ('Dick') Whittington almost single-handedly turned a dilapidated summerhouse at Mentmore into a cocoon-like, all-weather study for me to work in, a short daily 'commute' up the garden path from the house, for which many thanks, Dick. The incomparable London Library must be among the most-thanked literary institutions. During the Covid incarceration, its postal service supplied my requests; books to be both read and inhaled. Dr Williams's Library is an important repository of Unitarian history that I was glad to consult.

The two volumes of this book have taken a long time to complete. I particularly want to thank my partner Ann McGuire, who took up the cause with great spirit and walked the last several miles with me. (I dedicate Volume 2 to her.)

My lifelong friend Nigel Horne joined her in several forays and other attempts to fan the fire when the flames seemed to be burning low. As someone said, you need endurance to write. You also need friends.

I want to thank two much admired friends both born in Kharkiv in Ukraine (then in the Soviet Union), Vitali Vitaliev and Andrei Richter: the former a prolific writer now resident in England, the latter an international expert in media law, whose home is now in Vienna; both long-time friends of the Guardian.

Several supportive friends have chosen the long gestation of this book as a time to die. Desmond Christy I have mentioned. Norman Sherry, the indefatigable biographer of Graham Greene, who called me his 'Guardian Angel'; Eamonn McCabe, photographer, picture editor and friend about whom I write in this volume; and Peter Lennon, who knew how to express affection (for Ireland in particular) while looking askance - and loved to talk, preferably over lunch.

I'm so sad to add to these the name of Gennady Selyutsky, my contemporary in age, revered ballet master at the Mariinsky Theatre in St Petersburg, my daughter's mentor, who always asked after 'the book' whenever we met, whether in Russia or England. I will make sure his family have a copy.

A few words about my great friend Margaret Busby, to whom I have dedicated this volume. Our friendship goes back more than 30 years, to October 1989 when together we edited an entirely Africa-themed issue of the new Weekend Guardian. Ages ago, Margaret gave me an advance of £5 for a book, any book! And now - although not suddenly, Margaret - two come along!

Thank you all.

With love to my children: Hannah Mayes, William Wystan Mayes and my dancing daughter Isabella McGuire Mayes. And my grandson, Harry Mayes.

Picture Credits

Author photo page ii: Linda Nylind/The Guardian

Index

Abedi, Agha Hasan 84
advertising 34, 132, 234, 252
Afghanistan 137, 180, 213
Ageh, Tony 215-19, 219-20, 220-1, 222, 223, 251, 302
Agenda page 79-81, 83
Aitken, Ian 6, 23, 179
Aitken, Jonathan 285, 286, 289, 300-1
Al-Fayed, Mohamed 272-6, 305
Ali, Tariq 87, 224, 285, 294, 297
Alić, Fikret 242
al-Nahyan, Zayed bin Sultan 84
Alton, Roger 95, 108, 113, 120, 156, 160-1, 174-5, 177, 228, 229, 230, 279, 294
Ang, Swee Chai 101-2
Antarctica 61
anti-Semitism 55
Apicella, Enzo 77
The Appeasers (Gott) 146
April Fool's Day hoaxes 85, 114-15
Ardill, John 61
Armitage, Simon 172
Armitstead, Claire 173, 174, 293-4, 299, 305-6
Armstrong, Murray 71, 99, 158
Arnett, Peter 192
Arnold-Forster, Val 118-19
Ashcroft, Ian 148, 218
aspirations 1
Asquith, Ros 100, 217
Associated Press 37
Astor, David 84, 259, 274, 277
Atex 38, 70, 94, 98, 122, 155, 298
Atkins, Ronald 173
Atkinson, Rick 187
Austin, David 189, 194, 198
Auto Trader cluster 27, 261
Ayerst, David 3, 8, 16

Baker, James 189
Bandar, Prince 300
Bandic, Darko 246
Bank of Credit and Commerce International 84-5, 86, 86-9

Banks-Smith, Nancy 118, 227-8
Barker, Paul 53
Bates, Richard, King's Cross station fire 71-2
Bates, Stephen 60, 136, 136-7
Batt, Vera and Roger 78
Baum, Louis 182
Bauwens, Mona 121
Bazoft, Farzad, hanging of 185-6, 276
BBC 134, 214-15, 264, 284-5
Bedside Guardian 116-17
Beldam, Mr Justice 69
Belfast 57-58, 137, 239, 291
Bell, Emily 252
Bell, Steve 169-71, 217
Bellos, Alex 135
Benn, Tony 81, 188, 222, 248
Bennett, Alan 113
Bennett, Catherine 133, 135-6
Beresford, David 194-5
Berlin Wall, fall of 139, 142, 159, 167, 168, 199, 239
Bernard, Jeffrey 113
Bettaney, Michael 287
Bevan, Aneurin 6
Bevins, Tony 278
Bhutto, Benazir 87
Bhutto, Zulfikar Ali 83-4, 87
Biffen, John 81
Billington, Michael 55, 117, 119, 219
Black, Conrad 253-4
Black, Ian 245, 247, 290
Blair, Tony 151, 170, 312
Blake, David 125
Blunkett, David 26
Board of Directors 33, 104
Boer War 13
books pages 293-9
Borger, Julian 236-7, 245, 246, 247
Bosnian war 236-49
    battle for Vukovar 240
    concentration camps 240-1
    Dayton peace agreement 246, 249
    editorial 14 August 243-4
    final phase 248-9

Krajina offensive 247
Nato bombing operations 247-8
Operation Irma 244
rape camps 237
reporting styles 236-7
safe havens 243
Sarajevo marketplace massacre 248-9
sectarian rivalries 239
siege of Goražde 238-9, 245
siege of Sarajevo 233-4, 238, 240, 244-5
Srebrenica massacre 237, 245-6
'The shame of Omarska' 242-3
UN hostages 245
war crimes trials 237-8, 246, 249
Boston, Richard 101, 156
Boston Globe 296
Bown, Jane 92, 278
Branson, Richard 125-6, 216, 217
Breeze, Hector 166
Brexit referendum 140
Bridge, Roderick 248
British Press Awards 86, 205, 208-9
Brittain, Victoria 40-1, 59, 79, 88, 89
broadsheet-tabloid combination 231
Brody, Neville 216
Brook, David 218-19, 221, 234, 251, 257, 264, 285
Brooks, Richard 254
Brown, Gordon 312
Brown, Ivor 277
Brown, Maggie 26, 300
Brown, Mick 125
Brown, Paul 61, 62, 310
Brownrigg, Sylvia 294
Brummer, Alex 37, 306
Bryant, John 130
Buckingham, Lisa 252
Bunting, Madeleine 151
Burchill, Julie 113-14, 122, 294
Bush, George HW 94, 187, 189, 193, 196, 198, 199, 200
bylines 91

Cable News Network 192
Campaign 164, 251
Campbell, Duncan 63, 217
Campbell, Katie 164
Carroll, Rory 137
Carter, Angela 179
cartoons 166, 168-71, 188, 189, 194, 198, 228, 232
Carvel, John 291

Casablanca 224, 297
Caulkin, Simon 261
Cebrián, Juan Luis 141-2
Chance, Michael and Mariella 77-8
Chancellor, Alexander 66, 96
Chapman, Andrea 162-3, 164
Chatham House 146
Chechnya and Chechen wars 212-13
Chernobyl nuclear accident 61
Chicago Tribune 128, 129, 131
Choices 95-6
Chomsky, Noam 200
Christie, Julie 63
Christy, Desmond 71, 95, 151, 156
Chunn, Louise 162-4, 306
CIA 191
circulation 2, 6, 20, 21, 27, 34, 39, 45, 48, 66, 70, 82-3, 90, 102, 126, 127, 130, 132, 219-21, 228, 230, 235, 250-1, 253, 254, 255, 257, 263, 281, 307
City Life 217
City Limits 216-18, 299
City Pride 59, 62
Clapham Junction train crash, 1988 94
Clark, Nobby 92, 101
Clarke, Mary 172, 219
Clarke, Peter 168, 194
Clements, Andrew 172
Clerkenwell Observer booklet 269-70
Cobain, Ian 137-8
Cohen, Roger 59
Cold War 139, 146
Cole, John 6, 16, 47-8, 56, 264, 304
Cole, Peter 25-6, 53, 57, 58, 60, 62, 63-6, 66-7, 69, 96, 124, 125-6, 128, 130, 132, 312
Coleman, Terry 23, 24, 30, 96
Coles, Joanna 118, 227
Comment & Analysis 166-71, 199
Computer Guardian section 37-8
computerisation 2, 31, 36-7, 36-9
Cook, Robin 184
Cook, William 121
Cooke, Alistair 5-6, 23
Cookson, Paul 77
Cooper, Roger 180, 205
Country Diary 166
Cowley, Jason 296
criticism, openness to 3-4
critics' meetings 172-3
Cross Street, Manchester 14-17, 45
Crown, the 62
Crozier, William 11, 11-12, 91, 302

Cuban missile crisis 146
Culf, Andrew 252, 262
Cumming, Laura 294
Cunningham, John 171, 177, 179
cunt decision 164
Cusack, Cyril 112

Dacre, Paul 135, 138
Dahrendorf, Sir Ralf 263
Daily Express 138
Daily Mail 16-17, 135-8, 174
Daily Mirror 51, 215
Daily Telegraph 27, 29, 34, 133, 220, 250, 253-4, 258
Dallman, Nicholas 14
Dalyell, Tam 248
David Holden International Reporter of the Year prize 86, 208-9
Davies, Gavyn 65
de Jongh, Nicholas 116-17
Dean, Malcolm 21
Deansgate, Manchester 14, 15-17
Denselow, Robin 173
Desmond, Richard 216
Devlin, Kevin 297
digital development 2, 6, 302
direct input 31, 39, 50, 70
diversity 308
Docklands, move to 31
Dodd, Christopher 14, 15, 46-7, 50, 156, 226
Dodd, Vikram 135
Don, Monty 281
Doris 100
double standards 54-5
Dover, Kenneth 293
Downing, Mick 103
Driver, Christopher 46, 169
Dunn, Paul 278
Duval Smith, Alex 151, 226
Dyczok, Marta 209
Dyer, Geoff 294

Eagar, Charlotte 246
editorial staff 46
Education Reform Act of 1988 115
eG 115, 130
El Mundo 142, 145, 192, 195
El País 141-2
Electoral Reform Society 308
electronic page make-up 106, 109
Elliott, Chris 133

Ellison, Michael 63, 64
employment laws 28
Engel, Matthew 12, 96
English, Sir David 135
Ensor, Patrick 226
Environment Guardian 61-2
Europe 140-5
European, the 144, 150
European Community 139
European correspondents 153
European Economic Community, British accession 140-1
European Parliament elections, 1989 61
European Press Prize 49
European Review 139, 144-50, 218
Euroscepticism 139
Ezard, John 190

factional tension 23
Fairhall, David 248
Falklands War 54, 169
Farringdon Road 4, 17-18, 34, 36, 38, 39, 48, 50, 63, 69-70, 74, 84, 98, 221, 276-7, 279, 283
features department 110, 116, 155-7, 161-5, 171-5
features section 75
feminism 162
Fenby, Jonathan 23, 66, 130, 134-5, 203, 225-6, 230-2, 237, 260, 268
    dismissal 281-3, 300, 304
    takeover as editor of the *Observer* 263-5, 277-9, 280, 304
Financial Times 84-5
Flanagan, Rory 88
Flett, Kathryn 174, 281
Foden, Giles 3-4
Foisie, Philip 143
Foot, Michael 6, 181, 291-2
Fordham, John 172-3, 216-17, 219
Forgan, Dame Elizabeth 7, 18
Forgan, Liz 128-9, 157-60, 161
Fort, Matthew 99
Fountain, Nigel 217
Frankfurter Allgemeine Zeitung 145
Frankland, Mark 207-8
Freedland, Jonathan 49, 126, 133-4, 135
Freeman, Simon 126
front page layout 91, 93-5
Fukuyama, Francis 168, 201
Fuller, Roy 112
Fussell, Paul 101

G2 145, 153, 167, 175, 230-5, 251, 256, 294, 299

Galbraith, JK 113, 200

Galvin, Martin 58

Gardner, John 53

Garland, Nicholas 285

Garvin, JL 277

Gates, William 84

Gauhar, Altaf 83-5, 86, 87-8

Gay Hussar, Greek Street, Soho 5, 6-7, 10, 12-13, 18

Gazeta Wyborcza 145

general election, 1983 21

general election, 1987 21, 50, 51-2, 53, 70

Germany, reunification of 199

Gibbard, Les 169, 188

Gibbings, Peter 33

Gilbert, Martin 294

Gittings, John 59, 105, 186, 187, 190

Glaister, Dan 152

Glass, Charles 202

global financial crisis, 2008 7

globalisation 307

Glover, Stephen 29, 115, 124-5, 127, 224, 258, 263, 265

Goldenberg, Suzanne 211

Golding, William 294-5

Gorbachev, Mikhail 199, 205-9

Gordievsky, Oleg 287, 290, 291-2

Gordimer, Nadine 182

Gordon, John 37-8

Gott, Richard 21, 22, 59, 79-81, 83, 89, 95-6, 107, 110, 120, 142, 151, 167, 237
    European Review project 144-50
    features sitrep 155-6, 165
    as literary editor 293-7, 299
    manifesto 295
    resignation 284-7, 289-90, 292, 305-6
    Spectator's KGB attack 284-92, 301
    visit to Bolivia 156

Gow, David 51, 153

Gray's Inn Road 14, 29, 32, 34, 35, 45, 48, 69

Greenfield, Edward 219

Greenslade, Roy 144, 277

Guardian alumni lunches 5, 7

Guardian Europe 130, 139-40, 141, 149, 150-4, 171, 173

Guardian Fiction Prize 297

Guardian Media Group 3, 7, 259-68, 269

Guardian New Poetry 172

Guardian North 12

Guardian Unlimited 154

Guardian Weekly 143, 154

The Guide 251
    background 214-18
    impact 219-21
    launch 219
    planning 218-19

Gulf War 134-5, 151, 167, 170, 185-98, 199-200, 223
    coalition force assembled 188
    consequences of 202-5
    hostages 189, 190
    invasion of Kuwait 186-7
    'The real face of war' 197-8
    response to invasion of Kuwait 186-92
    sanctions 187, 191-2
    UN Resolution 687 198
    war coverage 192-8

Gulshan group 59, 224

Gutteridge, Moira 67

Hackett, David 75, 97

Hadzimuratovic, Irma 244

Halabja poison gas attack 185

Haley, William 9, 12

Hamilton, Alex 298

Hamilton, Neil 310

Harding, Luke 135

Hardy, Bert 112

Hare, David 296

Hargreaves, Ian 255

Harpur, Merrily 166

Harrison, Tony 198, 248-9

Harrods takeover 272-6

Harrop, Martin 52

Hastings, Max 253-4

Hattersley, Roy 80, 166

Healey, Denis 199-200

Hearst, David 151, 152-3, 210, 211, 213

Heath, Edward 189, 272

Hebert, Hugh 22

Helsingin Sanomat 145

Helsinki summit 199

Hencke, David 30

Henry, Georgina 125, 137, 174, 190-1, 204-5, 275, 309, 311

Hensher, Philip 294

Herr Schlitter 231

Heseltine, Michael 170, 264

Hetherington, Alastair 6, 10, 13-14, 14, 15, 17, 33, 41, 45, 102, 104, 140, 141, 303

Heysel stadium disaster 59, 92-3

Hildrew, Peter 82, 103

Hillman, David 4, 38, 72-6, 90, 97, 100, 146, 146-7, 148-9, 166, 229, 232
Hillmore, Peter 279
Hilton, Tom 219
Hirst, David 185, 186, 187, 202
Hitchens, Christopher 183-4
Hodgkin, Teddy (EC) 11
Hoffman, Matt 83
Hoggart, Simon 265, 267, 278-9
Holbrooke, Richard 248
Holliman, John 192
Hooper, John 153
Hopkinson, Tom 112
Horwell, Veronica 233-4
hot metal 2, 48, 50
Howe, Geoffrey 170
Huhne, Chris 21
Huntley, Su 91
Hurd, Douglas 170
Hussein of Jordan, King 188-9
Hutton, Will 41

ideological struggles 23-4
Ignatieff, Michael 136
Illman, John 135
Independent 23, 63-5, 115, 142, 251, 263
    circulation 66, 70, 82-3, 90, 220, 230, 235, 253, 255
    and Europe 144
    exodus of readers to 23-4, 68
    Fenby leaves 66
    flagging 224, 260-1
    foreign coverage 185
    general election, 1987 52
    launch 4, 29, 38
    letters 83
    and Preston's departure 301
    price war 252, 253, 254, 255
    recruitment poaching raids 29-30
    Saturday magazine 66, 96, 97
    Sunday market ambitions 66, 124-6
    threat of 2, 38-9, 68-9, 73, 82
Independent on Sunday 115, 127, 128, 132, 182, 252, 260-1, 263, 267
Ingrams, Richard 117
International Criminal Tribunal for the former Yugoslavia (ICTY) 237-8, 246, 249
international edition 154
International Press Institute 49, 142
internet, the 2, 4
intra-Guardian communiqués 80

'Investing in Canada' 36-7
Iran 178, 180, 184
Iraq 134-5, 151, 185-98, 202-5
Irish Times 63
Islamic fundamentalism 180
Isle of Dogs 32, 36, 50, 69
Israel 54

Jack, Ian 263
Jack, Michael 24, 32
Jackson, Dominique 153, 171
Jackson, Harry 35, 36-8, 39, 70, 91
James Cameron award 205
Januszczak, Waldemar 111, 157-60, 297, 298
Jarecke, Kenneth 197-8
Jaspan, Andrew 282-3
Jeffries, Stuart 173, 174
Jenkins, Peter 30, 291
Jenkins, Roy 140
job reductions, 1986 36
Jobs and Careers supplement 220
Johnson, Paul 51, 52-3, 57-8, 62-4, 70, 76-7, 94, 280, 311
Jolly, Bernard 90
journalism 2-3, 6, 142, 211
journalist, definition 6
Judge, Paul 310-11

Karadžić, Radovan 237, 238, 240, 241, 242, 249
Katz, Ian 126, 133-5, 190
Keating, Frank 254
Kee, Robert 113
Keegan, Victor 306-7, 309
Keenan, Brian 180, 230
Kelner, Simon 280
Kennard, Peter 168
Kettle, Martin 23, 59, 64, 80, 139, 149, 150-3, 171
KGB 284-92
King, Philippa 70
King's Cross station fire 71-2
King's Own Fine Writers 96
Kings Place, move to 2, 7, 13, 16, 17-18
Kinnock, Neil 80, 170
Knewstub, Nikki 53, 57
Knight, Andrew 107
Koenig & Bauer presses 31, 69, 70
Krauze, Andrzej 168-9
Kurds 202-5
Kuwait, invasion of 186-92

La Repubblica 142
La Stampa 152
Labour Party 21, 23, 140-1, 170
Landesman, Cosmo 122
Latal, Srećko 248
le Carré, John 182, 183-4
leader conferences 54
leader writers, tortured ramblings 52
Lebanon, Palestinian refugees 101-2
Legge, Stuart 99
Leigh, David 275
Lennon, Peter 101, 161
letterpress printing 31
letters and the letters page 24, 68, 79, 81-3, 164, 166, 167, 224
Lever, Harold 130
Lezard, Nicholas 122, 123, 294
Libbert, Neil 92
libel actions 2, 87, 88, 127, 250, 273, 300, 310-11
Limb, Sue 100
Lindqvist, Sven 145
Lingua Franca 114
Linklater, Magnus 71, 211
Lipsey, David 125, 126
Listener 288
Listings Limited 219
literary editors 293-9
Liverpool Post 45
Lockerbie disaster 94
Locks, Celia 106
London, move to 10, 13, 44-5, 45-6
London Daily News, collapse of 70-1
London Evening Standard 26
London Press Club's Scoop of the Year award 209
Long, Douglas 66, 67
long-form journalism 211
Lonrho 51, 129, 259, 261, 261-2, 264, 271-2, 275, 276, 277
Low, David 169
Lowe, Robert 260-1
Lubov, Ignatsevna 209-10

MacArthur, Brian 28
McCabe, Eamonn 92-5, 101
McCall, Carolyn 29-30, 33, 77, 271
McCarthy, John 180
McCullin, Don 92
McDermott, Quentin 223
Macdonald, Marianne 133, 135
McGuinness, Martin 151

McHardy, Anne 57, 106
Mackenzie, Suzie 163, 228
McKie, David 21, 25-6, 44, 46, 50, 53, 68-9, 82, 132, 188, 227, 265, 283, 310
Mackie, Lindsay 71
Mackrell, Judith 172
Maclean, Christopher 79, 81-2, 83, 99, 158-9
McNay, Michael 47, 72, 72-3, 74, 75-6, 90, 91, 93-5, 169, 223, 226
McPhee, Don 92
Madame Figaro 223, 224
Madge, Tim 163
Mail factor, the 135-8
Mail on Sunday 135-6, 137
Major, John 167, 170, 189, 205, 240, 244, 278-9, 281
Malcolm, Derek 118, 119-20, 219
management reshuffle, 1987 24, 24-5
Manchester 14-17, 45, 71
Manchester Evening News 27, 32-3, 33, 36, 48
Manchester Guardian 9, 10
Mandela, Nelson, release of 167, 199
Marckus, Melvyn 274
Margetson, Clare 152, 173
Markwick, Jim 24, 31, 65-6, 69, 107, 108, 127, 128, 130, 130-2, 141-2, 143, 147, 149-50, 217-18, 254-5, 255-8, 259, 261-2, 264, 267, 268, 279, 283, 304
Marland, Caroline 24, 33, 34, 235, 256-8, 259, 279-80
Marland, Paul 24
Marquand, David 227
Marxism Today 21
masthead 10, 73, 74-5
Maxwell, Robert 70, 71, 129, 144, 149-50, 275
Mayes, Ian 71, 76, 98, 151, 172-3, 173-4, 232, 295
Medium of the Year award 164, 251
Meek, James 202, 209-13
Meikle, James 136
Mellor, David 121
Men and Women supplement 164
Messud, Claire 163
MI6 285, 287
Michnik, Adam 145
MicroGuardian 37
Middle East hostage crisis 167, 180, 182
Midgley, Margaret 234
Milligan, Spike 77, 112

Mills, William Haslam 3
Milne, Seumas 23, 49, 59, 103, 104, 106-8, 108-9
Milošević, Slobodan 248
Minneapolis Star Tribune 38
Mirsky, Jonathan 267-8
Mitford, Diana, Lady Mosley 112
Mitford, Jessica 112
Mladić, Ratko 249
mobile phones 51
Modern Review 113-14, 119, 122-3, 294
Moir, Jan 163
Montague, CE 16
Montgomery, Isobel 152
Moore, Robert 68
Moore, Suzanne 122, 163
Morley, Sheridan 285
Morning Star 21
Morrell, Nicholas 261-2
Morrison, Douglas 146, 147-8, 151
Moscow 145, 153, 176, 178, 196, 201, 205-8, 210-11, 213, 287, 290-1, 306
Moss, Stephen 299
Muggeridge, Malcolm 15, 290
Mulholland, John 215, 218, 219, 306
Mullin, John 193
Mullins, Tony 280
Munif, Abdelrahman 200
Murdoch, Rupert 4, 21, 26-7, 31, 251-8, 271-2
Murrell, Adrian 92
Murtagh, Peter 49, 58, 239

Nadir, Asil 310
National Graphical Association (NGA) 27, 69
National Union of Journalists 36, 39, 82, 94, 103-9, 110, 124, 155, 180, 181, 303
National Union of Students/Guardian Student Journalism awards 111
Nato 243, 243-4, 245
Neil, Andrew 121-2, 132
Neue Zürcher Zeitung 31
New Labour 312
New Society 53, 151, 168
New Statesman 86-8, 168, 296
new technology dispute, 1989 104-9
New World Order 167, 198
'New World Order?' series 199-201
New York Times 182-3, 197
New Yorker 296
News Chronicle 266

News International plant 36
News Layout system 109
News on Sunday 71, 92
Newsnight 76-7, 173
Newspaper of the Year 281
Newspaper Publishers Association 32-3
Newspaper Publishing 126, 128, 129, 252
Nezirovic, Haris 243
Nicolson, Rebecca 280
9/11 terrorist attacks 212
Northern Ireland 57-58, 137, 239, 291
Norton-Taylor, Richard 59, 290
Nott, John 128, 129, 131
Nova 75
Novosti 291
nuclear weapons 101
Nyheter, Dagens 145

obituaries 95, 169, 297
Observer 48, 70, 84, 92, 124, 174, 197-8, 207, 250, 251
    acquisition of 2, 3, 259-68
    archive material 276
    circulation 263, 281
    Fenby's dismissal 281-3, 304
    Fenby's takeover as editor 263-5, 277-9, 280, 304
    financial position 279-80
    global financial crisis, 2008 7
    and Harrods takeover 272-6
    Independent recruits 278, 279
    integration of 269-72, 276-83
    Life magazine 281
    move to Farringdon Road 276-7, 279, 283
    Preston's 'rivers of money' speech 265-7, 267-8
    price war 252, 254, 256, 258
    profligacy 267-8
    redesign 280-1
    relationship with the *Guardian* 3
    sections 281
O'Kane, Maggie 236-7, 237, 238-42, 244-5
Oldfield, Helen 117, 120, 123
'The Online Future' (Rusbridger) 302
online presence 154
op ed page 79-80
Operation Provide Comfort 205
Operation Safe Haven 205
Orr, Deborah 120-1, 173, 217, 292
Osborne, Philip 56-7, 73, 95, 265
Osmanovic, Ferida, suicide of 246

Outlook 225-8
Owen, David 21, 51, 230, 257

Page, Campbell 85
Page, Jeannette 83
page make-up 35
Palestinian refugees, Lebanon 101-2
Pallister, David 59
Palmer, Alasdair 285-6
Palmer, John 153, 247
Papas, William 169
Pass Notes 232-3
Pearce, Edward 50, 167, 189
Pentagram 4, 38, 72, 73
personal journalists 6
Personal page 169
Phillips, Gary 218, 221, 222, 223
Phillips, Melanie 51, 52, 53-7, 64, 70, 181,
    279, 304
    achievements 58-9
    appointed news editor 55-7
    appointed policy editor 52
    background 53-5
    as a columnist 60-1
    education column, 1987 60
    election coverage 51, 53
    Environment Guardian editor
        appointment 62
    Northern Ireland visit 57-8
    plots against 59-60
photographs 91-3, 94, 101
Pick, Hella 190, 193
picture editor 91-3
picture reproduction 28-9
Piggott, Denis 99
Pilgrim, Michael 93-5, 225-6, 228, 281
Pitt, Joyce 77
poetry 172, 198, 248-9
Polan, Brenda 161-2, 163
Poland 168
political independence 22-3
political satire 169-71
poll tax riots 167
popular mass culture 123
Porter, Henry 232-3
Porter, Stanley 130, 131
portrait line drawings 91
Powell, Dilys 112
Powell, Enoch 81, 294
Pratt, Judith 234
Press Association 32-3
Preston, John Whittle 42, 43

Preston, Peter 1, 17, 20, 33, 52, 174, 271
    acquisition of the *Observer* 259, 262,
        264, 265-6
    and Agenda page 79-80
    and Alton 160
    appointed editor 22, 47-8, 304
    appoints Fenby 226
    appoints Phillips news editor 55-6
    and Bell 169, 171
    as chairman of the Guardian board
        24-5, 104
    communication style 26, 49-50
    counter signings 23
    cunt decision 164
    and death of *Sunday Correspondent* 67
    departure 300-1
    direct input negotiations 39
    economic constraints 40
    editorial approach 41
    education 43, 44
    environmental coverage 61-2
    European Review project 144-50
    European tendency 139-40, 141-5
    experience of the press in USA 142
    father 42, 43
    features department innovation 95-102
    as features editor 46-7
    February report, 1993 250-3
    and Fenby's dismissal 282-3
    front page layout redesign 94
    and *G2* 230-2
    and Gauhar 83
    and Gott's resignation 284, 285-6,
        288-90
    on *Guardian Europe* 150
    and Gulf War 186, 190, 191, 192-3, 204,
        205
    illness and rehabilitation 42-4
    J Arthur Composite guise 22
    joins *Guardian* 44-5
    joins IPI 49, 142
    June report, 1995 258
    on launch of the *Independent* 29
    and Leigh's apologia 275
    libel action against 310-11
    liberal toleration 24
    and magic 44
    makes Phillips policy editor 52
    and Meek 210
    memo to Maclean 82
    and Milne 107
    Miscellany column 46

new technology dispute, 1989 107-8
NUJ negotiations 103-5
personal politics 21-2, 24
Peter Cole's departure 65-6
and Polan 161-2
price war 250-8
as production editor 302
qualities 42
recruits picture editor 91-3
redesign, 1988 68-78
'rivers of money' speech 265-7,
  267-8
and Rowan 114-15
and Rumbold 116
on Rusbridger 302
Rusbridger January 1995 memo 305
September report, 1993 251-2
succession 64-5, 301, 304-11
and *Sunday Correspondent* 130-1, 132
and Targett 113, 118
and *Third World Review* 86, 87, 88,
  89
on threat of the *Independent* 39
The Times merger crisis 10, 40, 45-6
Tisdall affair 25-6, 42, 48-9
view of the *Guardian* 22-3
work ethic 40-1
price 47-8, 228
Price, John 278, 279, 280
price war 2, 133, 250-8
Pringle, John Douglas 11
printed newspapers, long-term survival
  called into question 2
printing unions 35
Private Eye 116, 117, 119, 121, 122, 150,
  158, 224, 281
Product Development Unit (PDU)
  221-3, 229, 251, 269
production costs 27, 218
professional neutrality 23
profit 27, 85, 152, 252, 254, 261, 270, 279
Pujol, Jordi 238
Pulitzer Prize 2
Pundik, Herbert 145
Putz, John 14

Quirk, Mick 217
Quirke, Bill 270-1

Radford, Tim 156, 291, 297-9
radical roots 3
Radio Times 214-15

Rainbow Warrior 61
Raven, Charlotte 122
Rawnsley, Andrew 278
Rayner, Jay 110-11, 114, 118
readership 3-4, 7, 19, 68-9, 77-8, 308
Reagan, Ronald 267
'The real face of war' photograph 197-8
recruitment market share 34
redesign, 1988 2, 4, 38, 68-78, 166, 221-3,
  224
  adapting to 90-2
  background 68-72
  brief 73
  casualties 79-89
  creative tension 75-6
  debut 76-7
  dummy pages 72, 74-5
  features section 75
  fee 73
  front page layout 93-5
  front-page heads 91
  headlines 74, 75
  Hillman hired 72-3
  lack of confidence in 97
  masthead 73, 74-5
  news and features 74
  proposals 73-4
  response 77-8
  structure 75
  tabloid proposal 74
  typefaces 74-5
repetitive strain injury 105-6
Rettie, John 145
Reuters news agency, Guardian group
  holdings 32-3
Review Guardian 118
Roberts, Nesta 56
Roche, Harry 24, 35-6, 39, 66, 67, 104-5,
  107, 124, 127, 130, 131, 259, 261-2, 264,
  268, 279
Rojo, Alfonso 192, 195, 196
Rondot, Squadron Leader Mike 194
Rosselli, Mark 278
Routledge, Paul 278-9
Rowan, David 110, 114-15, 228, 309
Rowland, Roland 259, 260, 261-2, 262,
  272-4
Rowson, Martin 122
Royal Institute of International Affairs
  146
Rozenberg, Joshua 55
Rumbold, Judy 116

Rusbridger, Alan 1-2, 2, 12, 17, 18-19, 27, 41, 65, 83, 96, 136, 137, 174, 235, 299
  and acquisition of the *Observer* 264, 264-5
  appointed deputy editor 172
  appointed editor of *Weekend Guardian* 97, 144-5
  appointed features editor 110, 116, 120, 155-7
  appointment as editor 309-11
  appoints deputy editor 312
  appoints Vulliamy *Weekend Guardian* editor 157-8
  axes *Guardian Europe* 153
  and Bell 169-70, 171
  and Comment & Analysis 166-71
  editor application manifesto 307-8
  editor candidacy 304-6
  features department shake-up 157
  and *G2* 153, 230, 231-2, 234
  and Gott's resignation 285, 290
  January 1995 memo 305
  joins *Guardian* 71
  Maxwell job interview 71
  message to staff on appointment as editor 310, 311
  and Milne 107
  Moscow trip, 1982 291
  'The Online Future' 302
  on poems 198
  Preston on 302
  and Preston's departure 301
  price war 255-6, 258
  reinvigorates the features department 161-5
  and Rushdie affair 183
  succeeds Gott 89
  and Targett 111-12, 113, 122
  and Vitaliev 176, 177, 178
  as *Weekend Guardian* editor 101-2
  Weekend Guardian plans 98-100
  and Young 119
Rushdie, Salman 111, 178-84, 295-6, 297
Ryle, Sarah 135

Saddam Hussein 185-6, 187, 190, 199, 202, 204, 276
Said, Edward 113
Sampson, Anthony 3, 259
San Serriffe, April Fool's Day hoax 85
The Satanic Verses (Rushdie) 178-84
satellite printing 69

Saturday magazine 66
Schmidt, Helmut 142-3, 144
Schofield, Jack 37-8
Scott, Catherine 8
Scott, Charles Prestwich 'CP' 5, 8, 9, 10, 13, 15, 16, 17, 18, 19, 91, 266, 277, 302
Scott, Edward 8, 302
Scott, Isabella 8
Scott, John Russell 9, 11-12, 302-3
Scott, Laurence 33, 45, 303
Scott, Richard 8, 10, 11, 45, 303
Scott Trust 7, 9, 40, 45, 49, 104, 124, 260, 264, 266, 269-70, 301
  appoints Rusbridger editor 309-10
  creation of 8-9
  February report, 1993 250-3
  and Fenby's dismissal 282-3
  investment in the *Sunday Correspondent* 127-9, 130
  June report, 1995 258
  September report, 1993 251-2
  succession process 301-11
Second World War 11-12
Self, Will 122
1789 Group 59
Shah, Eddie 28, 38
Sharrock, David 193, 195-6
Shawcross, William 183-4
Shevardnadze, Eduard 201
Shimmon, Ross 234
Shone, Tom 122
Shott, Nick 65, 66-7, 125, 129
Silverton, Peter 221-3, 229-30
Simmonds, Posy 113, 228
Simmons, Michael 85, 86, 88
Slater, Nigel 281
Smallweed 227
Smith, Sean 233-4
Smith, Tim 310
Smithies, Bill 95-6, 97, 156
Smithies, Sandy 215
snapshot journalism 142
Social Democratic Party 20, 82
Socialist Workers Party 23
Society Tomorrow 52
Sommer, Theo 201
sources, protection of 48
South China Morning Post 283
southern Lebanon, Israeli invasion of 54
Soviet Union 176, 177-8, 201, 290-1
  collapse of 167, 199, 209-13
  Gorbachev coup 205-9, 211

special reports 85
Spectator 27, 284-92, 305
Spender, Stephen 112
Sportsweek 92
Stalker, John, and the Stalker Inquiry 58
Stead, Jean 54, 56
Steel, David 51
Steele, Jonathan 153, 178, 202, 206-9,
    209, 223, 237, 291
Stephenson, Hugh 289
stereo workers 28, 35
Stewart, Graham 31
Stothard, Celia 97
succession process 301-11
    journalists' vote 308-9
    manifestos 306-8
    Rusbridger's appointment 309-11
Süddeutsche Zeitung 152
Suez Crisis 13, 303
Sullivan, Caroline 172-3
Sun 139, 188, 215, 252, 254
Sunday Correspondent 65, 66, 66-7, 123,
    133, 134, 135
    circulation 126, 127, 130
    closure 132
    Guardian investment in 127-33
    launch 124-6
    recruitment 126
    relaunch 131-2
    shareholdings 128
Sunday Guardian, April Fool's Day hoax
    114-15
Sunday Telegraph 254, 284, 285, 301
Sunday Times 29, 30, 45, 50, 121-2, 132,
    150, 151, 172-3, 223, 284, 291-2, 292
Sutcliffe, Tom 219
Sweeney, John 246
Sweeting, Adam 172-3, 219
Symonds, Matthew 29, 125
Syria 54

Targett, Jocelyn 110-14, 114, 115-19, 120-2,
    123, 160-1, 172-3, 173, 223, 294
Taylor, AJP 11
Taylor, Annie 163
Taylor, Geoffrey 3, 4, 16, 21, 33, 82, 140,
    166, 303
Taylor, John Edward 8
technological revolution 2, 19, 20, 103-9
That Was Business, This is Personal
    (Campbell) 64
Thatcher, Margaret 20, 22, 25, 28, 50, 60,
    80, 167, 169, 170, 188, 189

Third World Media 83-5, 86, 88
Third World Quarterly 86
Third World Review 79, 83-9
Thornber, Robin 123, 173
Thorpe, Denis 92
Thursday night drink 62-3
Tiananmen Square massacre 105, 268
Time Out 216
The Times 9, 27, 29, 31, 34, 114, 284
    circulation 70, 90, 132, 220, 235, 251,
        254
    merger crisis 10, 40, 45-6, 303
    price war 251-2, 252-5, 258
Tindle, Ray 130, 130-1
Tisdall affair 25-6, 42, 48-9, 103
Tisdall, Sarah 25-6, 48-9
Tisdall, Simon 153, 210
Titov, Igor 290-1
Today 28, 29, 38, 284
Toolis, Kevin 137
Topolski, Feliks 276
Torode, John 21
Tory readers, exclusion of 22
Toynbee, Polly 21, 30, 136, 291
Trader Media Group, share sold 7
Traitors (Phillips) 55, 60
Tran, Mark 246
Travis, Alan 30, 51
Traynor, Ian 153, 236-7, 245, 247, 248,
    249
Trelford, Donald 260, 262, 267, 268, 271-2,
    273-5, 276, 277, 281
Trevor, Trevor 293
Trudeau, Gary 169
Tuck, Lucy 278
Turkey 202-5
Turner, Jenny 299
TV listings, deregulation 214-18
Twitter 7
typesetting 2, 31, 34-5, 48

Ukraine 209-10, 211
unemployment 120
United Nations 243
United Nations Association 86
United Nations Intergovernmental Panel
    on Climate Change 62
United Nations Security Council 187, 198
United States of America
    Bush election victory, 1988 94
    editorial systems fact-finding mission
        38

Guardian Weekly 143
Gulf War 186-7, 188, 189-90, 193, 196
press in 142
Washington office 36-7
web operations 1

values 18
van der Vat, Dan 188
Vasagar, Jeevan 138
Vidal, John 61-2, 194
Vidal-Hall, Judith 84-5, 85
Viner, Katharine 3-4, 19, 163-4, 278
Vitaliev, Vitali 176-8
Voice project 142-3, 144
Vulliamy, Ed 58-9, 74, 113, 157-60, 236, 237-8, 239-40, 241-3, 247, 279

Wadsworth, Alfred Powell 10-12, 303
Waite, Terry 180
Walker, Martin 64, 176-7, 193, 198, 306, 307, 308
Wapping 4, 21, 26-7, 28, 29-30, 31, 34, 35, 41
Wapping refuseniks 41-2
Warrington 28
Warsaw 145
Washington office 36-7
Washington Post 187, 277
Watkins, Alan 267, 278
Watts, David 75
Waugh, Auberon 123
web offset printing 31
Webb, WL (Bill) 5, 7, 169, 177, 179, 296, 297
Webster, Paul 21, 202, 203, 208, 239, 241-2
Webster, Peter 194
Weekend 228-30, 234, 235, 256
Weekend Guardian 95-102, 98, 144-5, 220, 292
　1939 issue 112-13
　under Alton 113, 160-1
　background 95-6
　Booksearch 99
　cover stories 101-2
　the Diary 100
　dummy 97-100
　eighties issue 113-14
　financial constraints 97
　first issue published 63, 102
　Forum 99
　Gallery 99
　Home Front 100

　hostility towards 98
　Image Makers 100
　New Age page 100
　photographs 101
　Rusbridger appointed editor 97
　staff 98-9
　success 102
　Vulliamy as editor 157-60
　witness reportage 101-2
What the Papers Say awards 281
Wheen, Francis 281
Whewell, Harry 12, 15, 16-17
Whitaker, Brian 92, 98-9, 114-15, 157, 173, 221, 235, 278
White, Aidan 103
White, Michael 22, 50, 268, 285, 309-10, 310
Whittam Smith, Andreas 29, 30, 66, 124, 125-6, 129, 130, 254, 255, 260, 263
Wiggins, Marianne 179
Wilby, Peter 66
Williams, Brian 309
Williams, Nigel 298-9
Williams, Richard 133
Williams, Shirley 82
Willis, Pauline 98, 99
Wilson, Charles 114
Wilson, Emily 136
Wimpey 31, 32
Wintour, Patrick 58-9, 189
witness reportage 101-2
women's page 161-4
Wood, James 110, 111, 163, 293-7, 305
Woodward, Bob 187
Woodward, Will 135
Woollacott, Martin 24, 26, 40, 42-3, 85, 187-8, 190, 202-5, 210, 227, 236-7, 245
World Bank 84
Wright, Ian 37, 39, 44, 46, 65-6, 70, 75-6, 85, 86, 104-5, 109, 148, 153, 202, 217, 218, 226, 265, 285

Yeltsin, Boris 206, 207
Yom Kippur war 84
Young, Hugo 30, 127-8, 130, 140, 151, 152, 167, 180-1, 181, 182, 189, 191-2, 252, 254-5, 259, 264, 265, 269-70, 278, 281-2, 282-3, 300, 304
Young, Toby 119-20, 122, 173
Young Guardian 134-5, 163
Young Journalist of the Year award 111, 115